Seniors' Discount

Other *For Better or For Worse*® Collections

Teaching Is a Learning Experience!
She's Turning into One of Them!
Never Wink at a Worried Woman
Striking a Chord
Reality Check
With This Ring
Family Business
Graduation: A Time for Change
The Big 5-0
Sunshine and Shadow
Middle Age Spread
Growing Like a Weed
Love Just Screws Everything Up
Starting from Scratch
"There Goes My Baby!"
Things Are Looking Up . . .
What, Me Pregnant?
If This Is a Lecture, How Long Will It Be?
Pushing 40
It's All Downhill from Here
Keep the Home Fries Burning
The Last Straw
Just One More Hug
"It Must Be Nice to Be Little"
Is This "One of Those Days," Daddy?
I've Got the One-More-Washload Blues . . .

Retrospectives

Suddenly Silver: 25 Years of For Better or For Worse®
All About April
The Lives Behind the Lines: 20 Years of For Better or For Worse®
Remembering Farley: A Tribute to the Life of Our Favorite Cartoon Dog
It's the Thought That Counts . . . Fifteenth Anniversary Collection
A Look Inside . . . For Better or For Worse®: The 10th Anniversary Collection

With Andie Parton

I Love My Grandpa!
So You're Going to Be a Grandma!
Graduation: Just the Beginning!
Leaving Home
Wags and Kisses

Seniors' Discount

A *For Better or For Worse*® Collection by Lynn Johnston

Andrews McMeel
Publishing, LLC

Kansas City

07 08 09 10 11 BAM 10 9 8 7 6 5 4 3 2 1

ISBN-13: 978-0-7407-6841-5
ISBN-10: 0-7407-6841-7

Library of Congress Control Number: 2007924844

www.andrewsmcmeel.com

www.FBorFW.com

———— ATTENTION: SCHOOLS AND BUSINESSES ————

Andrews McMeel books are available at quantity discounts with bulk purchase for educational, business, or sales promotional use. For information, please write to: Special Sales Department, Andrews McMeel Publishing, LLC, 4520 Main Street, Kansas City, Missouri 64111.

This book is dedicated to
my wonderful staff:

Allison, Jackie, Laura,
Liuba, and Stephanie

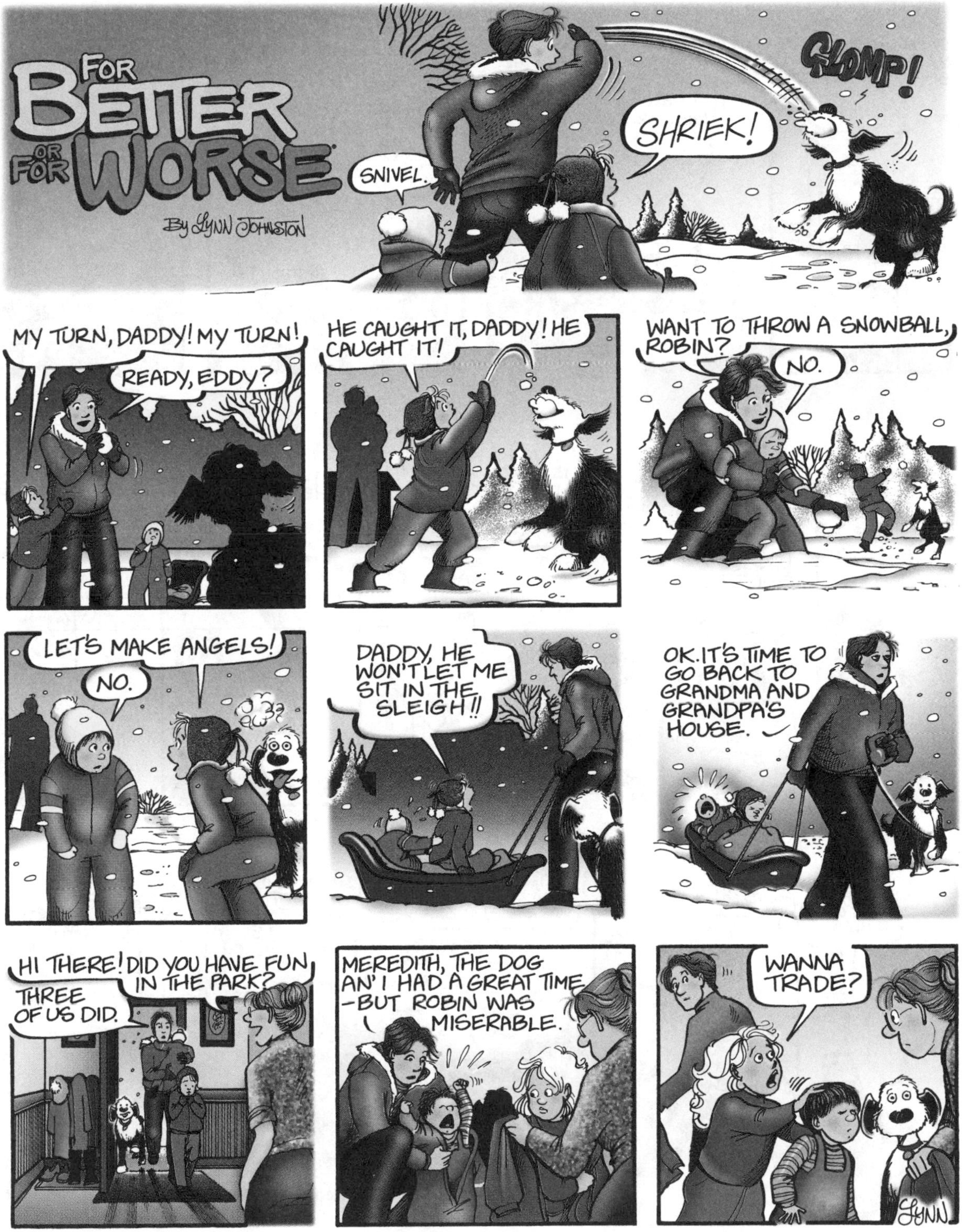
FOR BETTER OR FOR WORSE
By Lynn Johnston
SNIVEL.
SHRIEK!
GLOMP!
MY TURN, DADDY! MY TURN!
READY, EDDY?
HE CAUGHT IT, DADDY! HE CAUGHT IT!
WANT TO THROW A SNOWBALL, ROBIN?
NO.
LET'S MAKE ANGELS!
NO.
DADDY, HE WON'T LET ME SIT IN THE SLEIGH!!
OK. IT'S TIME TO GO BACK TO GRANDMA AND GRANDPA'S HOUSE.
HI THERE! DID YOU HAVE FUN IN THE PARK?
THREE OF US DID.
MEREDITH, THE DOG AN' I HAD A GREAT TIME -BUT ROBIN WAS MISERABLE.
WANNA TRADE?
LYNN

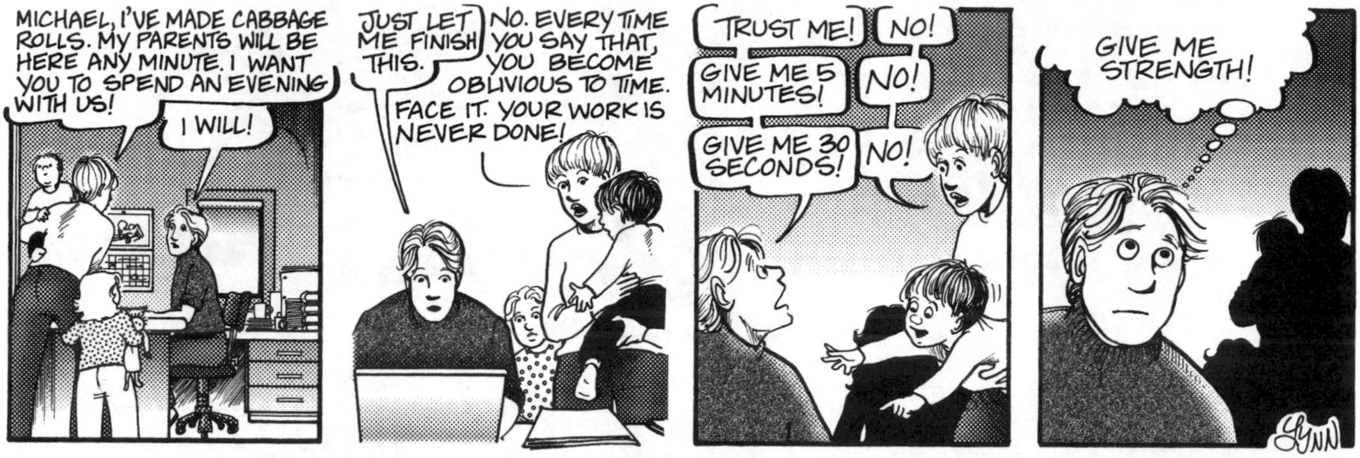
MICHAEL, I'VE MADE CABBAGE ROLLS. MY PARENTS WILL BE HERE ANY MINUTE. I WANT YOU TO SPEND AN EVENING WITH US!
I WILL!
JUST LET ME FINISH THIS.
NO. EVERY TIME YOU SAY THAT, YOU BECOME OBLIVIOUS TO TIME.
FACE IT. YOUR WORK IS NEVER DONE!
TRUST ME!
NO!
GIVE ME 5 MINUTES!
NO!
GIVE ME 30 SECONDS!
NO!
GIVE ME STRENGTH!
LYNN

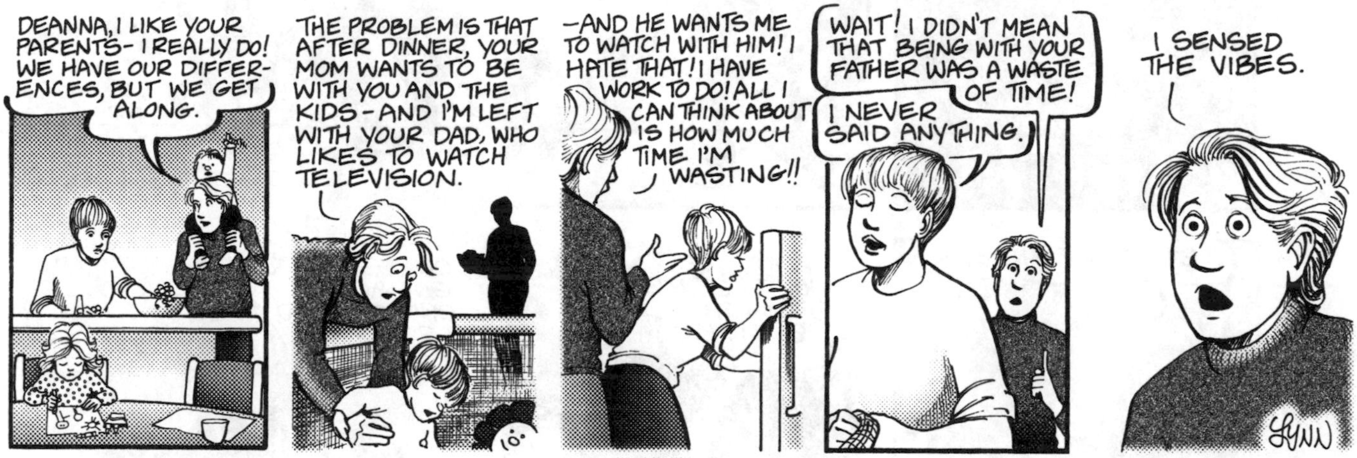
DEANNA, I LIKE YOUR PARENTS- I REALLY DO! WE HAVE OUR DIFFERENCES, BUT WE GET ALONG.
THE PROBLEM IS THAT AFTER DINNER, YOUR MOM WANTS TO BE WITH YOU AND THE KIDS - AND I'M LEFT WITH YOUR DAD, WHO LIKES TO WATCH TELEVISION.
—AND HE WANTS ME TO WATCH WITH HIM! I HATE THAT! I HAVE WORK TO DO! ALL I CAN THINK ABOUT IS HOW MUCH TIME I'M WASTING!!
WAIT! I DIDN'T MEAN THAT BEING WITH YOUR FATHER WAS A WASTE OF TIME!
I NEVER SAID ANYTHING.
I SENSED THE VIBES.
LYNN

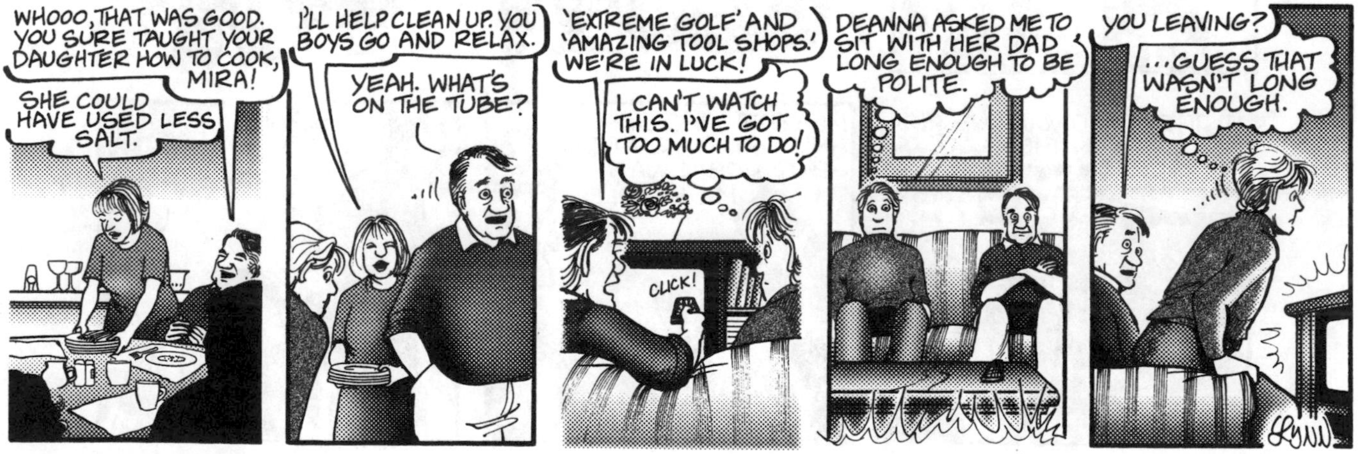
WHOOO, THAT WAS GOOD. YOU SURE TAUGHT YOUR DAUGHTER HOW TO COOK, MIRA!
SHE COULD HAVE USED LESS SALT.
I'LL HELP CLEAN UP. YOU BOYS GO AND RELAX.
YEAH. WHAT'S ON THE TUBE?
'EXTREME GOLF' AND 'AMAZING TOOL SHOPS.' WE'RE IN LUCK!
I CAN'T WATCH THIS. I'VE GOT TOO MUCH TO DO!
CLICK!
DEANNA ASKED ME TO SIT WITH HER DAD LONG ENOUGH TO BE POLITE.
YOU LEAVING?
...GUESS THAT WASN'T LONG ENOUGH.
LYNN

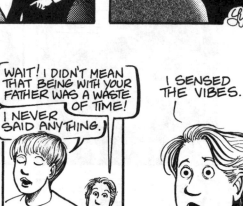

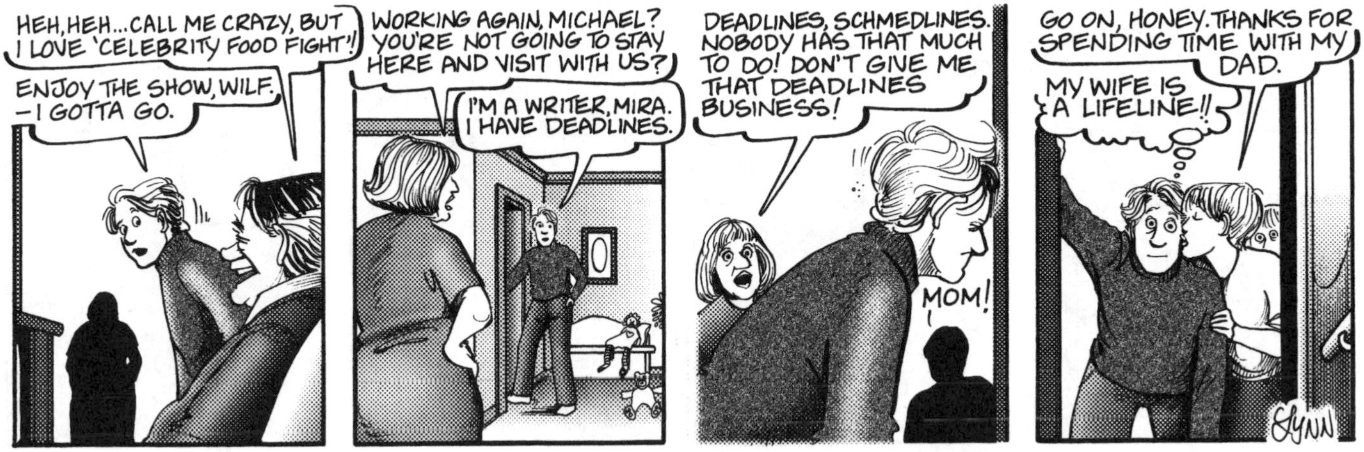
HEH, HEH... CALL ME CRAZY, BUT I LOVE 'CELEBRITY FOOD FIGHT'!
ENJOY THE SHOW, WILF. —I GOTTA GO.
WORKING AGAIN, MICHAEL? YOU'RE NOT GOING TO STAY HERE AND VISIT WITH US?
I'M A WRITER, MIRA. I HAVE DEADLINES.
DEADLINES, SCHMEDLINES. NOBODY HAS THAT MUCH TO DO! DON'T GIVE ME THAT DEADLINES BUSINESS!
MOM!
GO ON, HONEY. THANKS FOR SPENDING TIME WITH MY DAD.
MY WIFE IS A LIFELINE!!

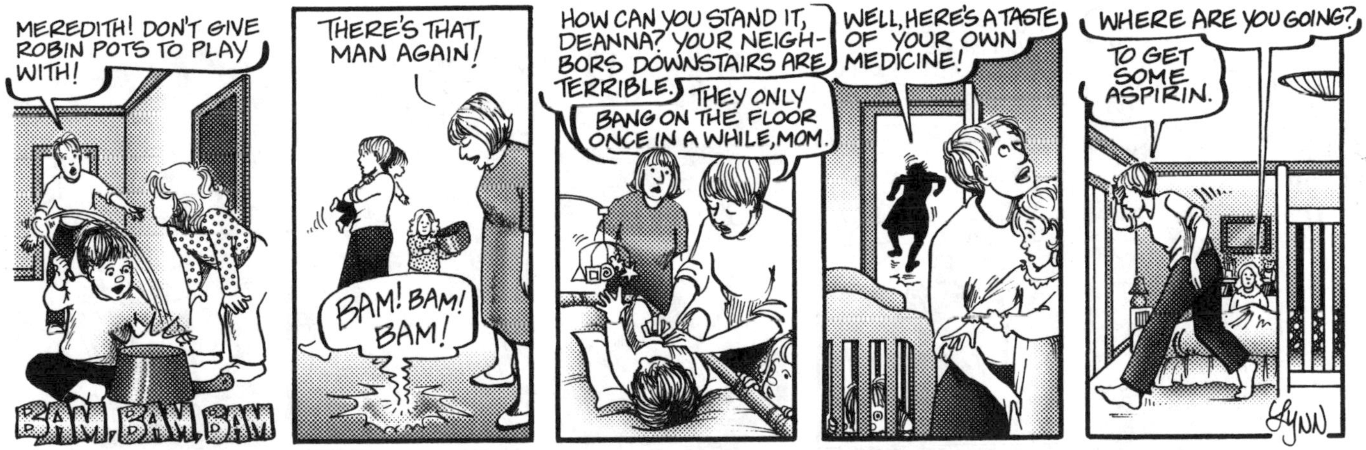
MEREDITH! DON'T GIVE ROBIN POTS TO PLAY WITH!
BAM, BAM, BAM
THERE'S THAT MAN AGAIN!
BAM! BAM! BAM!
HOW CAN YOU STAND IT, DEANNA? YOUR NEIGHBORS DOWNSTAIRS ARE TERRIBLE.
THEY ONLY BANG ON THE FLOOR ONCE IN A WHILE, MOM.
WELL, HERE'S A TASTE OF YOUR OWN MEDICINE!
WHERE ARE YOU GOING?
TO GET SOME ASPIRIN.

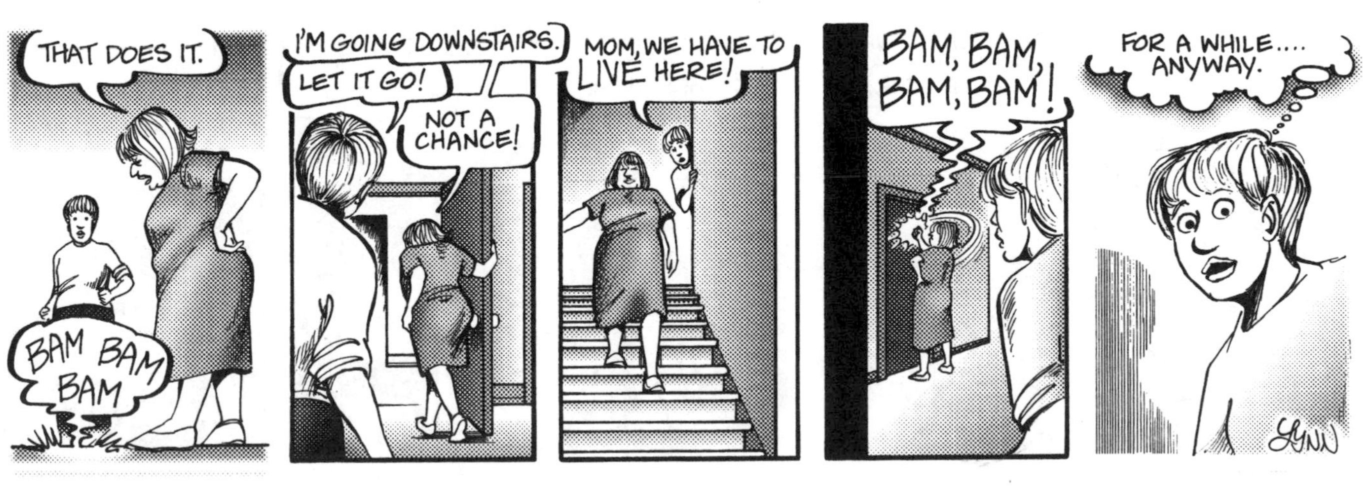
THAT DOES IT.
BAM BAM BAM
I'M GOING DOWNSTAIRS.
LET IT GO!
NOT A CHANCE!
MOM, WE HAVE TO LIVE HERE!
BAM, BAM, BAM, BAM!
FOR A WHILE.... ANYWAY.

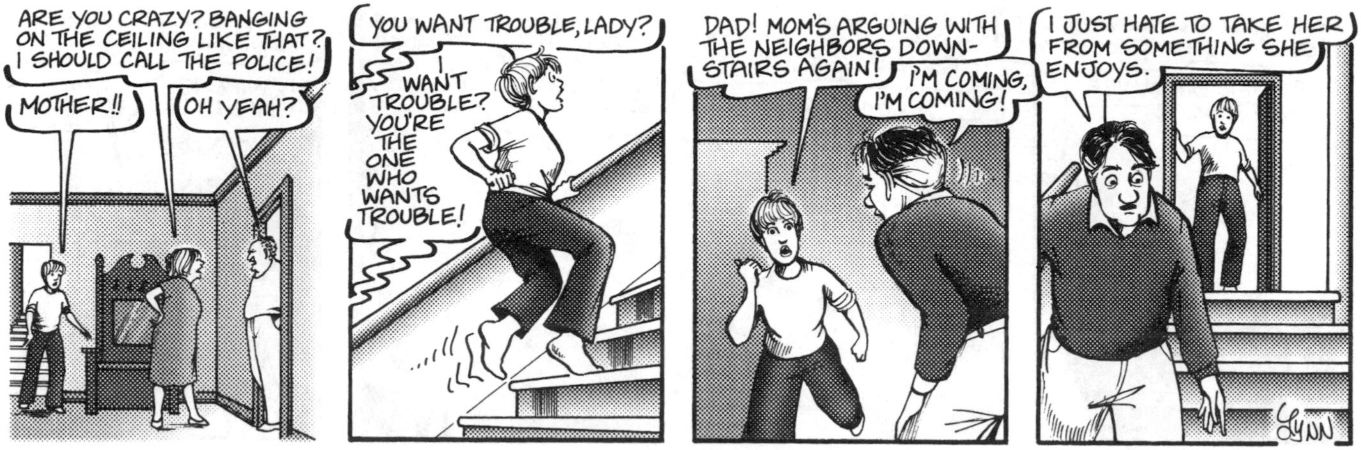
ARE YOU CRAZY? BANGING ON THE CEILING LIKE THAT? I SHOULD CALL THE POLICE!
MOTHER!!
OH YEAH?
YOU WANT TROUBLE, LADY?
I WANT TROUBLE? YOU'RE THE ONE WHO WANTS TROUBLE!
DAD! MOM'S ARGUING WITH THE NEIGHBORS DOWNSTAIRS AGAIN!
I'M COMING, I'M COMING!
I JUST HATE TO TAKE HER FROM SOMETHING SHE ENJOYS.
LYNN

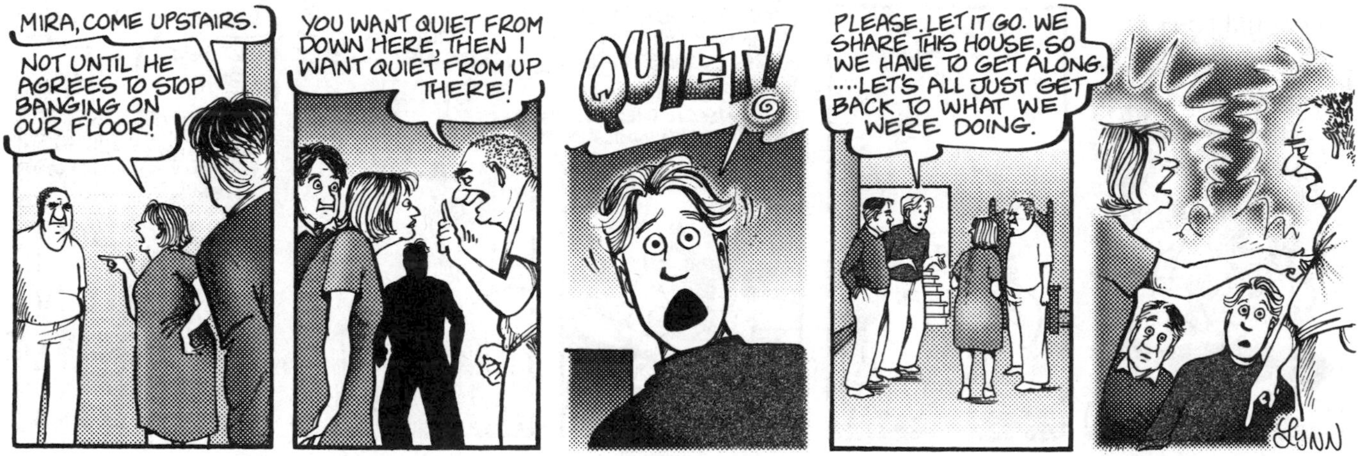
MIRA, COME UPSTAIRS.
NOT UNTIL HE AGREES TO STOP BANGING ON OUR FLOOR!
YOU WANT QUIET FROM DOWN HERE, THEN I WANT QUIET FROM UP THERE!
QUIET!
PLEASE. LET IT GO. WE SHARE THIS HOUSE, SO WE HAVE TO GET ALONG. ....LET'S ALL JUST GET BACK TO WHAT WE WERE DOING.
LYNN

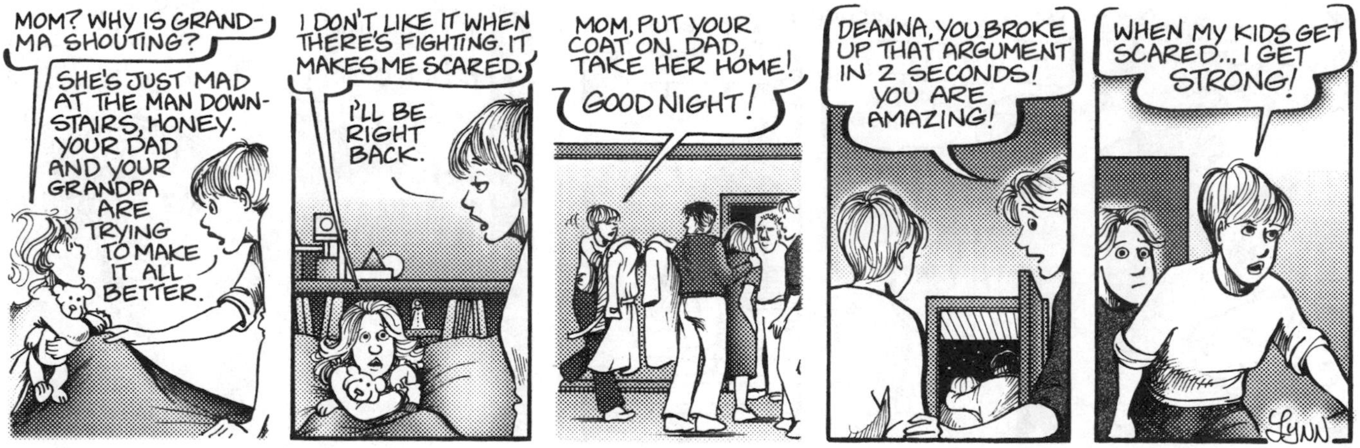
MOM? WHY IS GRANDMA SHOUTING?
SHE'S JUST MAD AT THE MAN DOWNSTAIRS, HONEY. YOUR DAD AND YOUR GRANDPA ARE TRYING TO MAKE IT ALL BETTER.
I DON'T LIKE IT WHEN THERE'S FIGHTING. IT MAKES ME SCARED.
I'LL BE RIGHT BACK.
MOM, PUT YOUR COAT ON. DAD, TAKE HER HOME!
GOOD NIGHT!
DEANNA, YOU BROKE UP THAT ARGUMENT IN 2 SECONDS! YOU ARE AMAZING!
WHEN MY KIDS GET SCARED... I GET STRONG!
LYNN

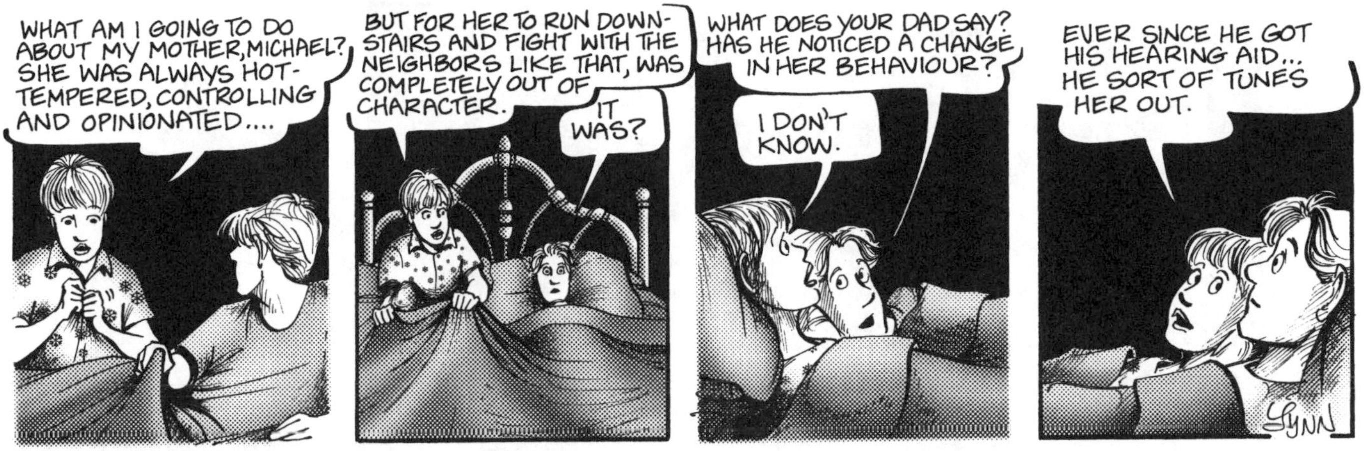

WHAT AM I GOING TO DO ABOUT MY MOTHER, MICHAEL? SHE WAS ALWAYS HOT-TEMPERED, CONTROLLING AND OPINIONATED....
BUT FOR HER TO RUN DOWN-STAIRS AND FIGHT WITH THE NEIGHBORS LIKE THAT, WAS COMPLETELY OUT OF CHARACTER.
IT WAS?
WHAT DOES YOUR DAD SAY? HAS HE NOTICED A CHANGE IN HER BEHAVIOUR?
I DON'T KNOW.
EVER SINCE HE GOT HIS HEARING AID... HE SORT OF TUNES HER OUT.
LYNN

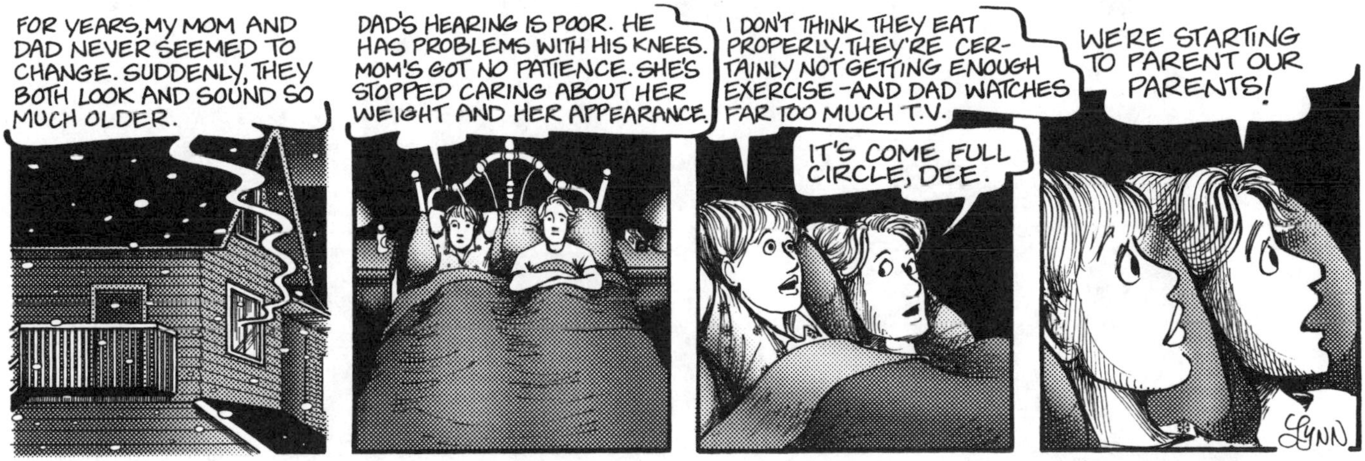

FOR YEARS, MY MOM AND DAD NEVER SEEMED TO CHANGE. SUDDENLY, THEY BOTH LOOK AND SOUND SO MUCH OLDER.
DAD'S HEARING IS POOR. HE HAS PROBLEMS WITH HIS KNEES. MOM'S GOT NO PATIENCE. SHE'S STOPPED CARING ABOUT HER WEIGHT AND HER APPEARANCE.
I DON'T THINK THEY EAT PROPERLY. THEY'RE CER-TAINLY NOT GETTING ENOUGH EXERCISE - AND DAD WATCHES FAR TOO MUCH T.V.
IT'S COME FULL CIRCLE, DEE.
WE'RE STARTING TO PARENT OUR PARENTS!
LYNN

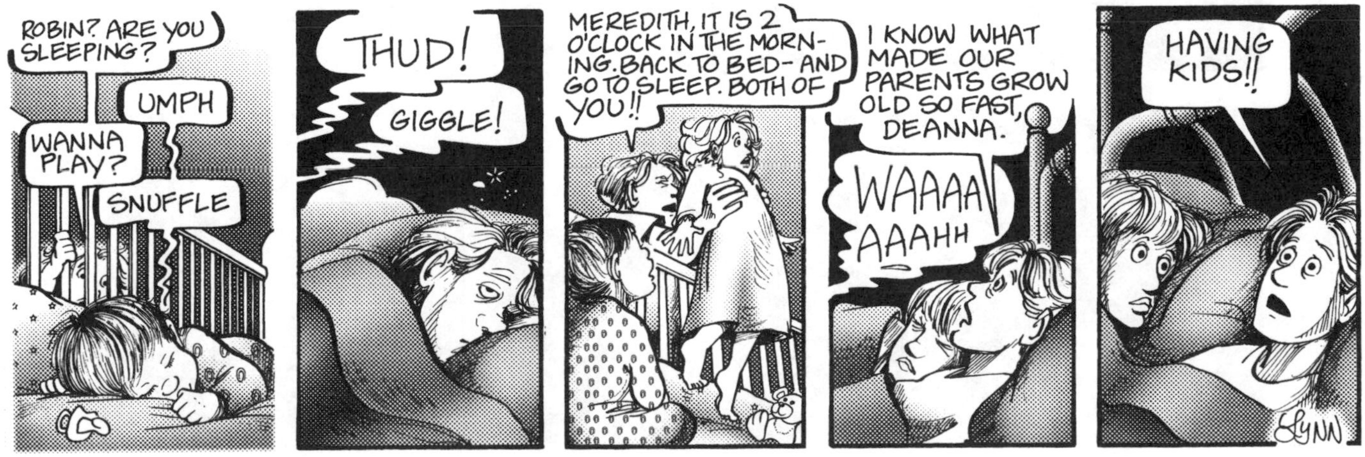

ROBIN? ARE YOU SLEEPING?
UMPH
WANNA PLAY?
SNUFFLE
THUD!
GIGGLE!
MEREDITH, IT IS 2 O'CLOCK IN THE MORN-ING. BACK TO BED - AND GO TO SLEEP. BOTH OF YOU!!
I KNOW WHAT MADE OUR PARENTS GROW OLD SO FAST, DEANNA.
WAAAAA AAAHH
HAVING KIDS!!
LYNN

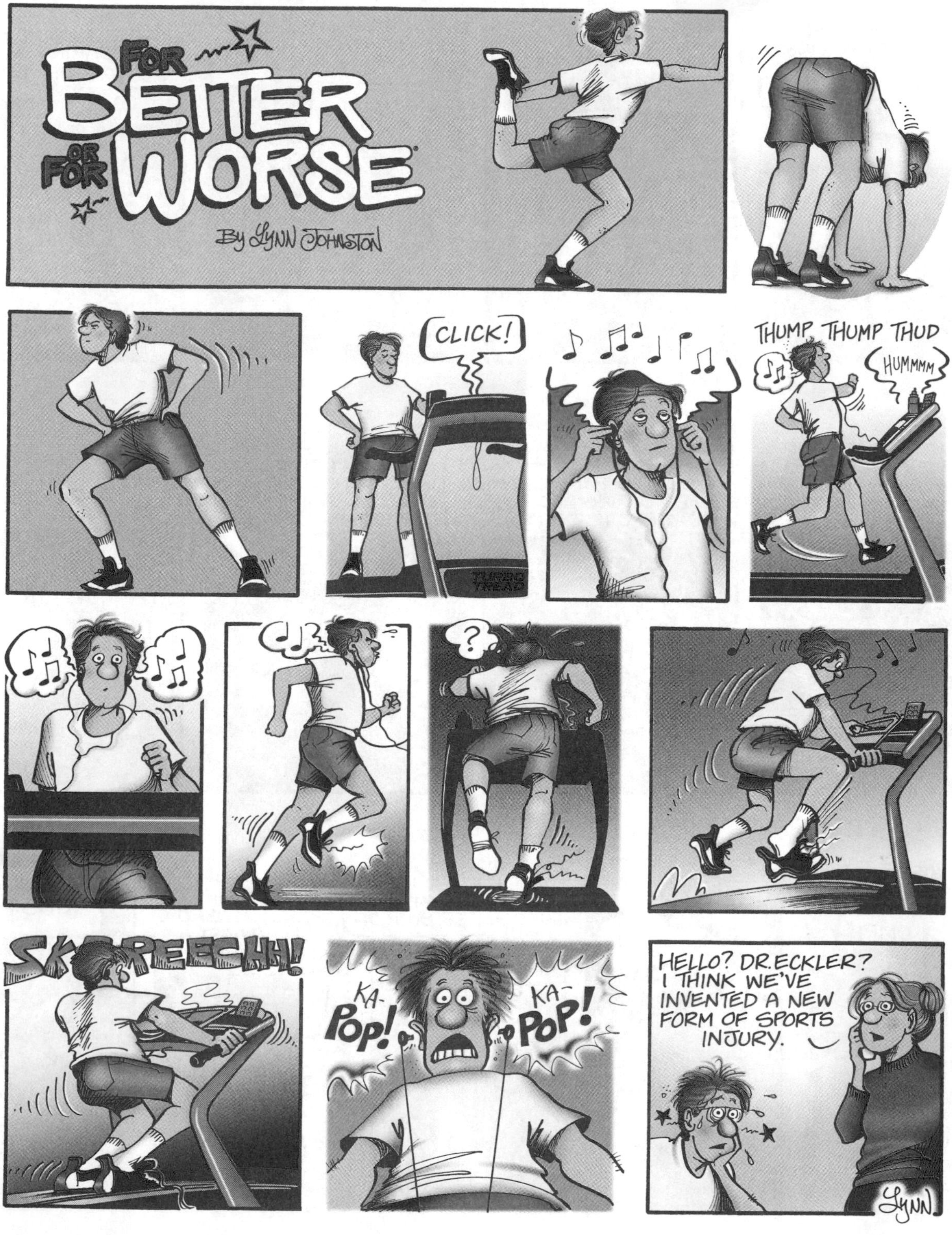
FOR BETTER OR FOR WORSE
By LYNN JOHNSTON
CLICK!
THUMP THUMP THUD
HUMMMM
SKREEECHH!
KA-POP!
KA-POP!
HELLO? DR. ECKLER? I THINK WE'VE INVENTED A NEW FORM OF SPORTS INJURY.
LYNN

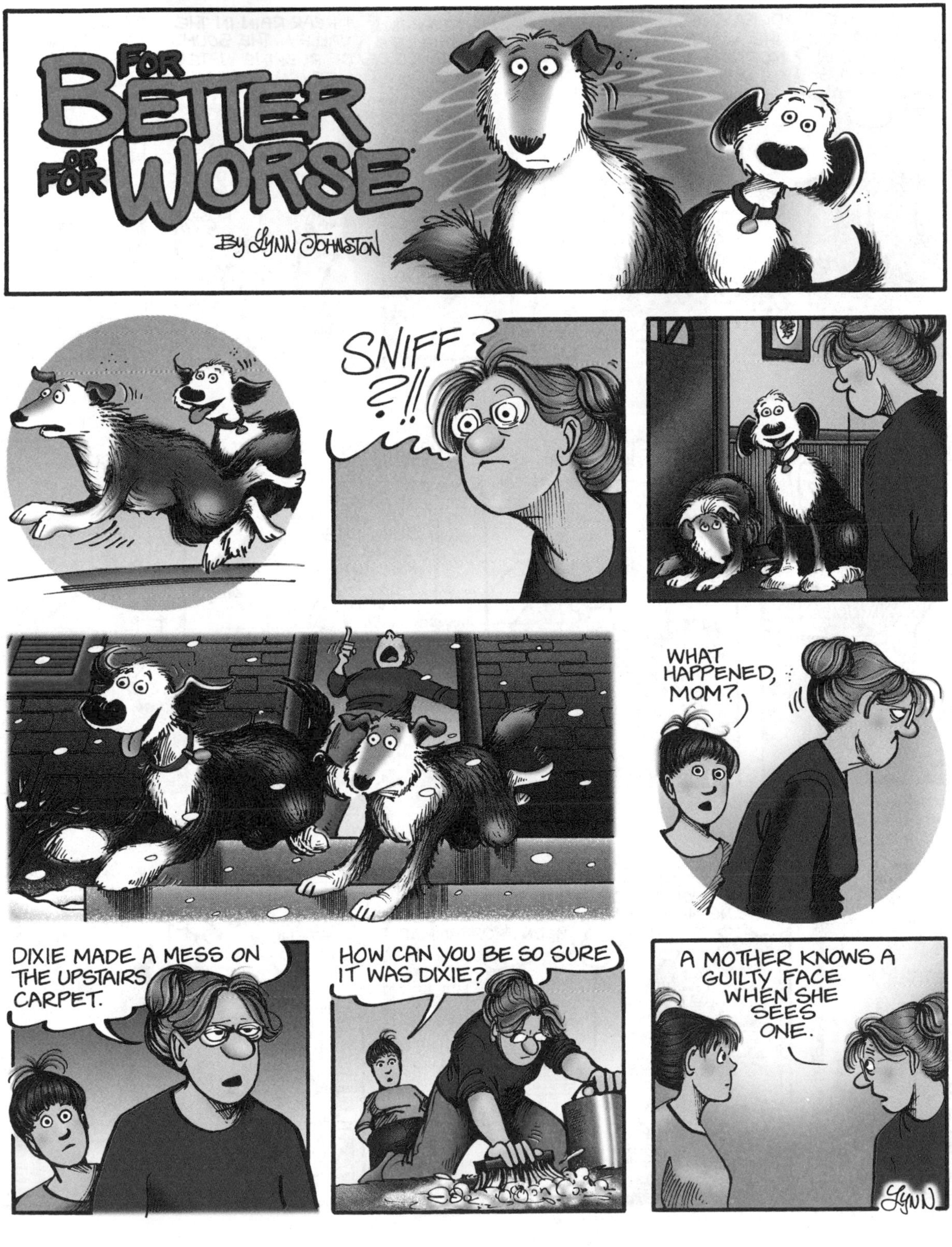
FOR BETTER OR FOR WORSE
BY LYNN JOHNSTON
SNIFF?
?!!
WHAT HAPPENED, MOM?
DIXIE MADE A MESS ON THE UPSTAIRS CARPET.
HOW CAN YOU BE SO SURE IT WAS DIXIE?
A MOTHER KNOWS A GUILTY FACE WHEN SHE SEES ONE.
LYNN

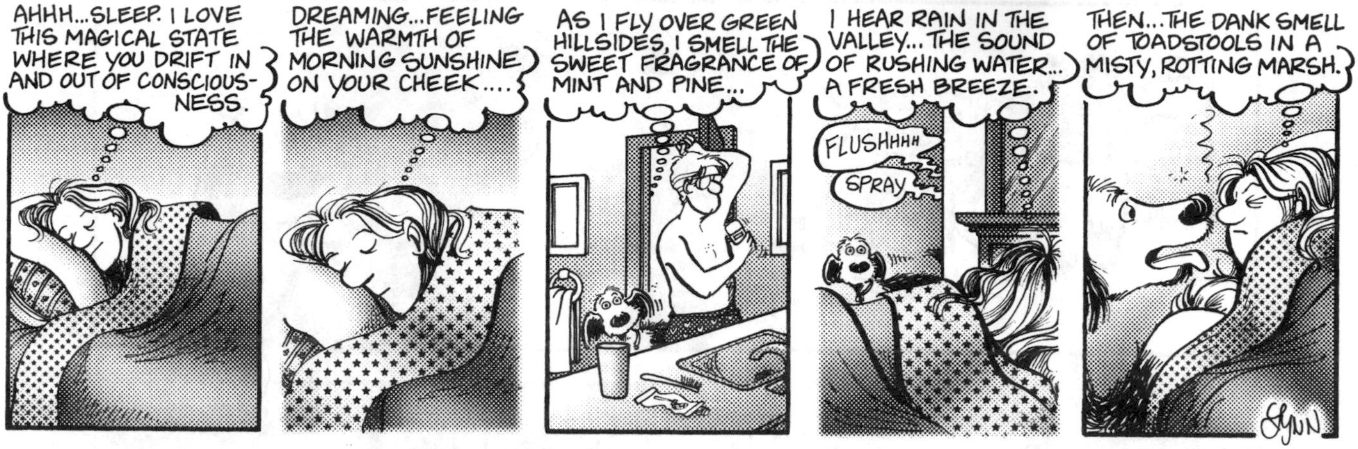
AHHH...SLEEP. I LOVE THIS MAGICAL STATE WHERE YOU DRIFT IN AND OUT OF CONSCIOUSNESS.
DREAMING...FEELING THE WARMTH OF MORNING SUNSHINE ON YOUR CHEEK....
AS I FLY OVER GREEN HILLSIDES, I SMELL THE SWEET FRAGRANCE OF MINT AND PINE...
I HEAR RAIN IN THE VALLEY... THE SOUND OF RUSHING WATER... A FRESH BREEZE.
FLUSHHHH
SPRAY
THEN...THE DANK SMELL OF TOADSTOOLS IN A MISTY, ROTTING MARSH.

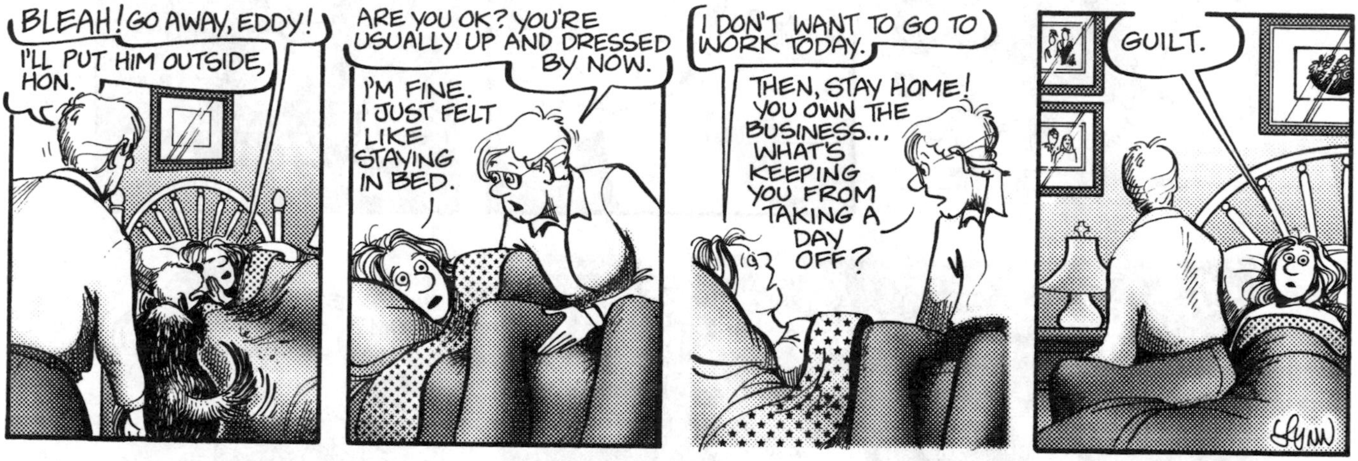
BLEAH! GO AWAY, EDDY!
I'LL PUT HIM OUTSIDE, HON.
ARE YOU OK? YOU'RE USUALLY UP AND DRESSED BY NOW.
I'M FINE. I JUST FELT LIKE STAYING IN BED.
I DON'T WANT TO GO TO WORK TODAY.
THEN, STAY HOME! YOU OWN THE BUSINESS... WHAT'S KEEPING YOU FROM TAKING A DAY OFF?
GUILT.

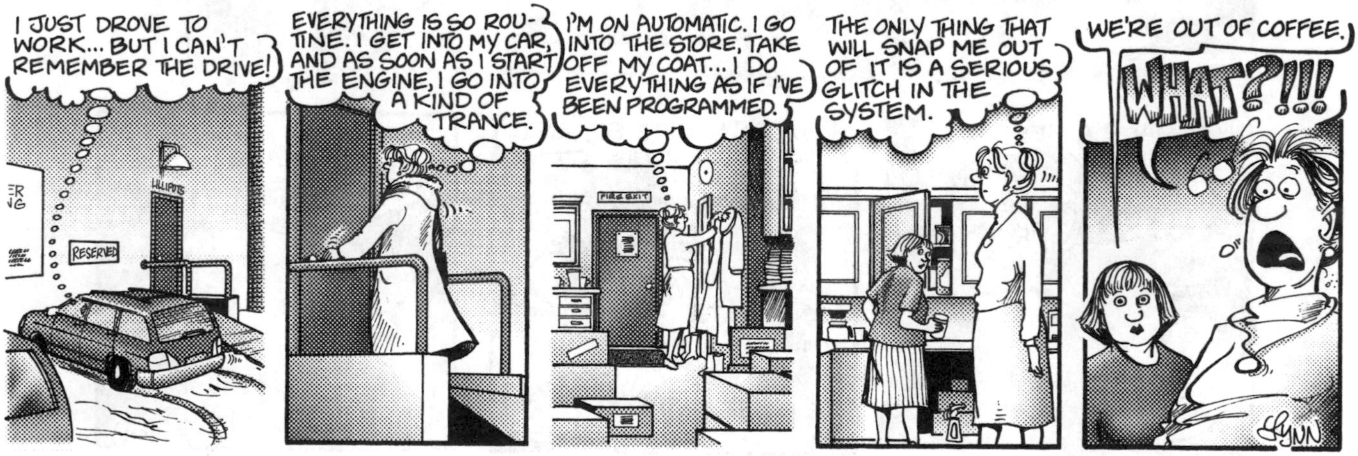
I JUST DROVE TO WORK... BUT I CAN'T REMEMBER THE DRIVE!
RESERVED
EVERYTHING IS SO ROUTINE. I GET INTO MY CAR, AND AS SOON AS I START THE ENGINE, I GO INTO A KIND OF TRANCE.
I'M ON AUTOMATIC. I GO INTO THE STORE, TAKE OFF MY COAT... I DO EVERYTHING AS IF I'VE BEEN PROGRAMMED.
THE ONLY THING THAT WILL SNAP ME OUT OF IT IS A SERIOUS GLITCH IN THE SYSTEM.
WE'RE OUT OF COFFEE.
WHAT?!!!

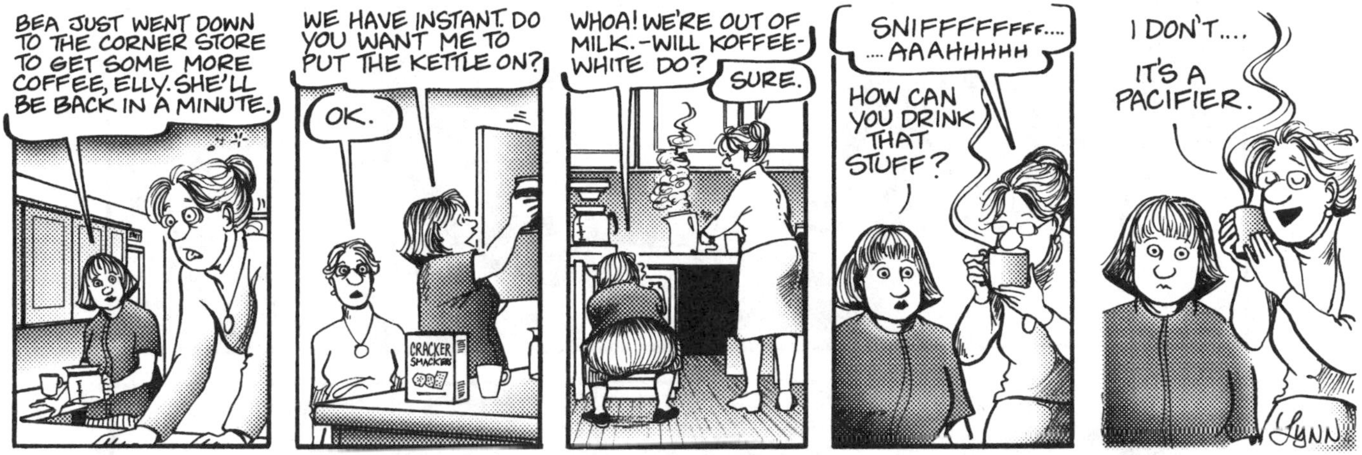
BEA JUST WENT DOWN TO THE CORNER STORE TO GET SOME MORE COFFEE, ELLY. SHE'LL BE BACK IN A MINUTE.
WE HAVE INSTANT. DO YOU WANT ME TO PUT THE KETTLE ON?
OK.
WHOA! WE'RE OUT OF MILK. -WILL KOFFEE-WHITE DO?
SURE.
SNIFFFFFFFFF.... ....AAAHHHHH
HOW CAN YOU DRINK THAT STUFF?
I DON'T....
IT'S A PACIFIER.
Lynn

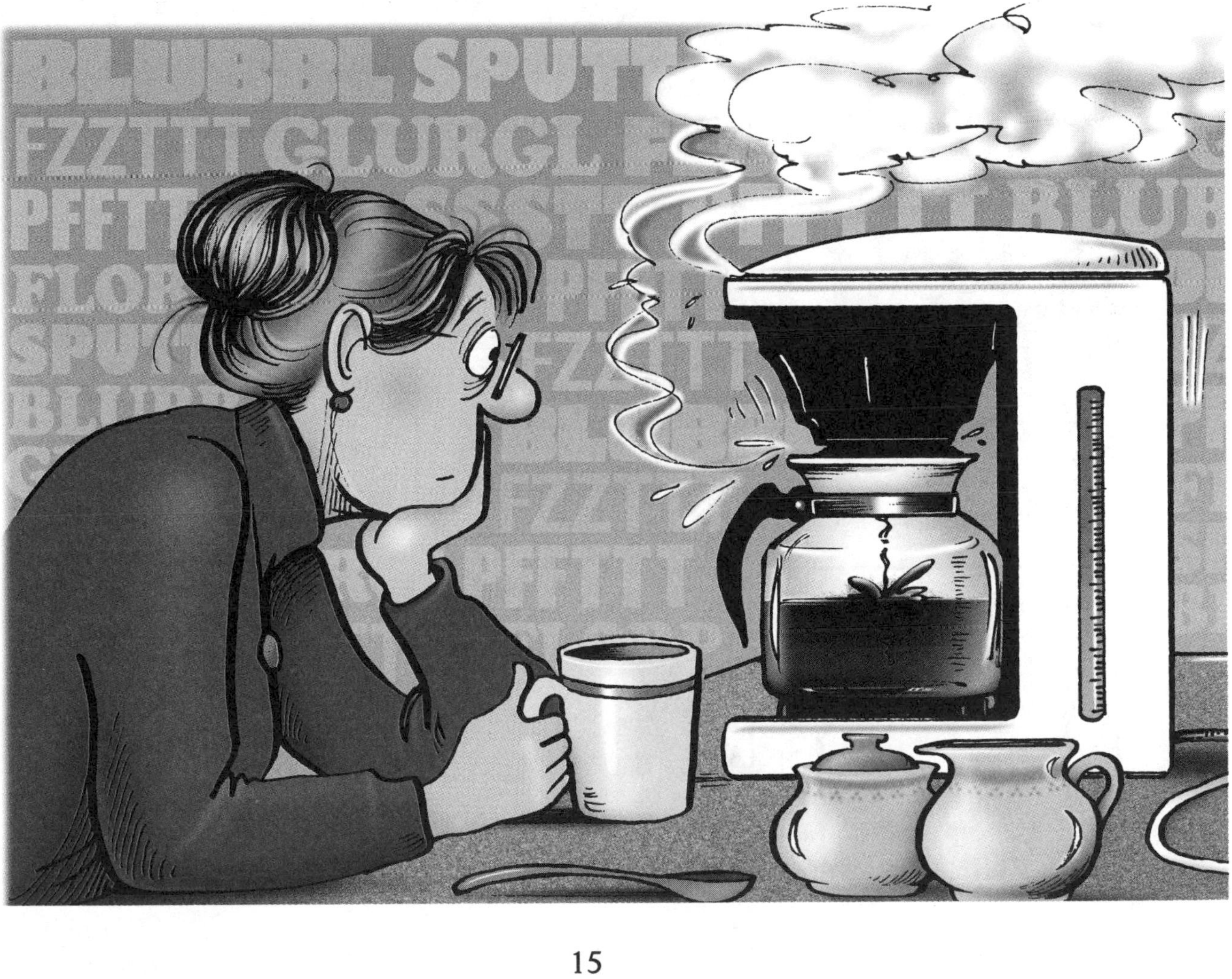
BLUBBBL SPUTT
FZZTTT GLURGL

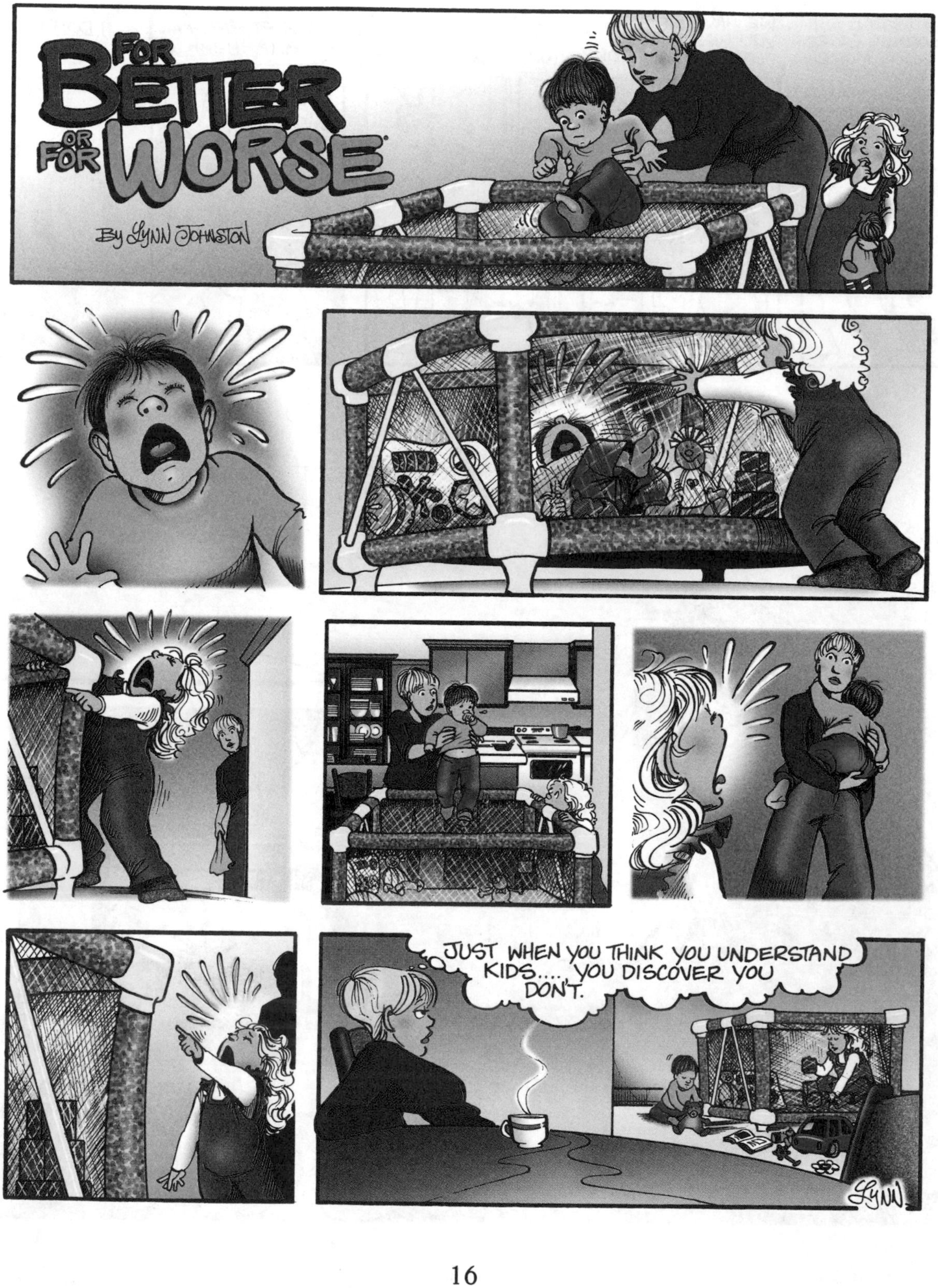
FOR BETTER OR FOR WORSE
By LYNN JOHNSTON
JUST WHEN YOU THINK YOU UNDERSTAND KIDS.... YOU DISCOVER YOU DON'T.
LYNN

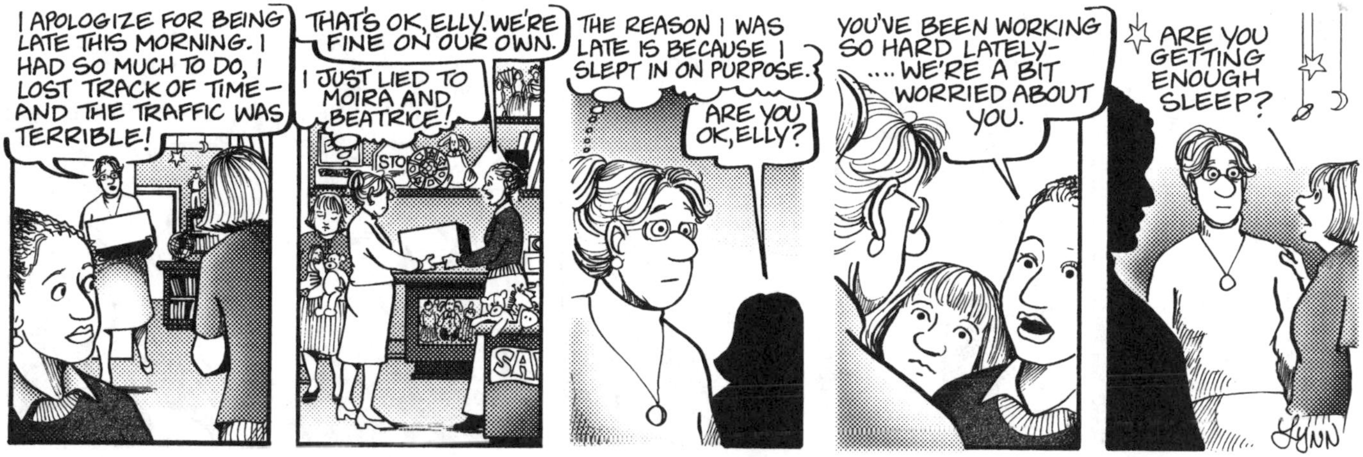
I APOLOGIZE FOR BEING LATE THIS MORNING. I HAD SO MUCH TO DO, I LOST TRACK OF TIME— AND THE TRAFFIC WAS TERRIBLE!
THAT'S OK, ELLY. WE'RE FINE ON OUR OWN.
I JUST LIED TO MOIRA AND BEATRICE!
THE REASON I WAS LATE IS BECAUSE I SLEPT IN ON PURPOSE.
ARE YOU OK, ELLY?
YOU'VE BEEN WORKING SO HARD LATELY- ....WE'RE A BIT WORRIED ABOUT YOU.
ARE YOU GETTING ENOUGH SLEEP?
LYNN

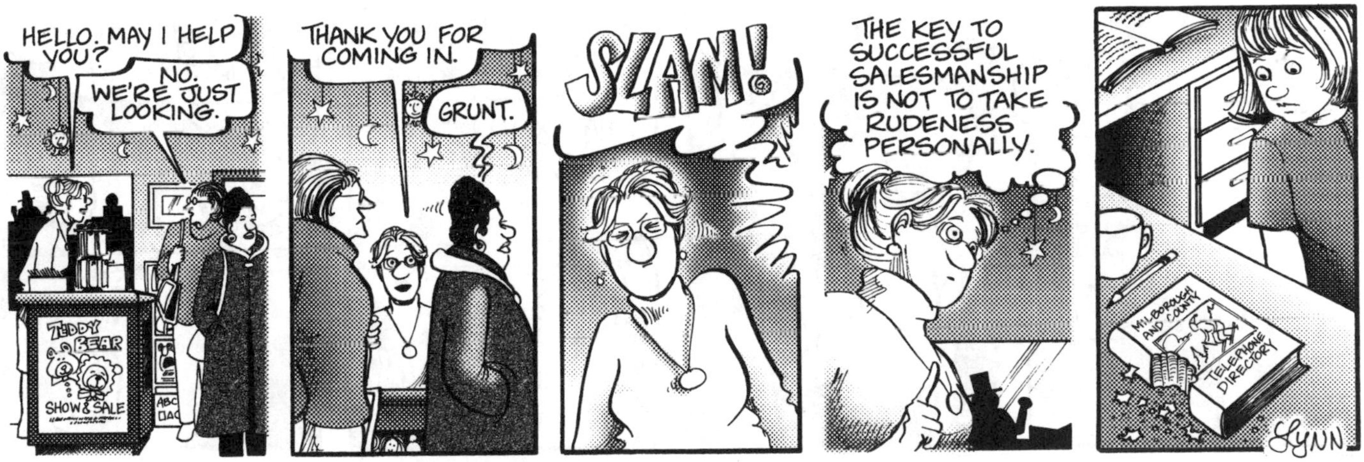
HELLO. MAY I HELP YOU?
NO. WE'RE JUST LOOKING.
TEDDY BEAR SHOW & SALE
THANK YOU FOR COMING IN.
GRUNT.
SLAM!
THE KEY TO SUCCESSFUL SALESMANSHIP IS NOT TO TAKE RUDENESS PERSONALLY.
MILBOROUGH AND COUNTY TELEPHONE DIRECTORY
LYNN

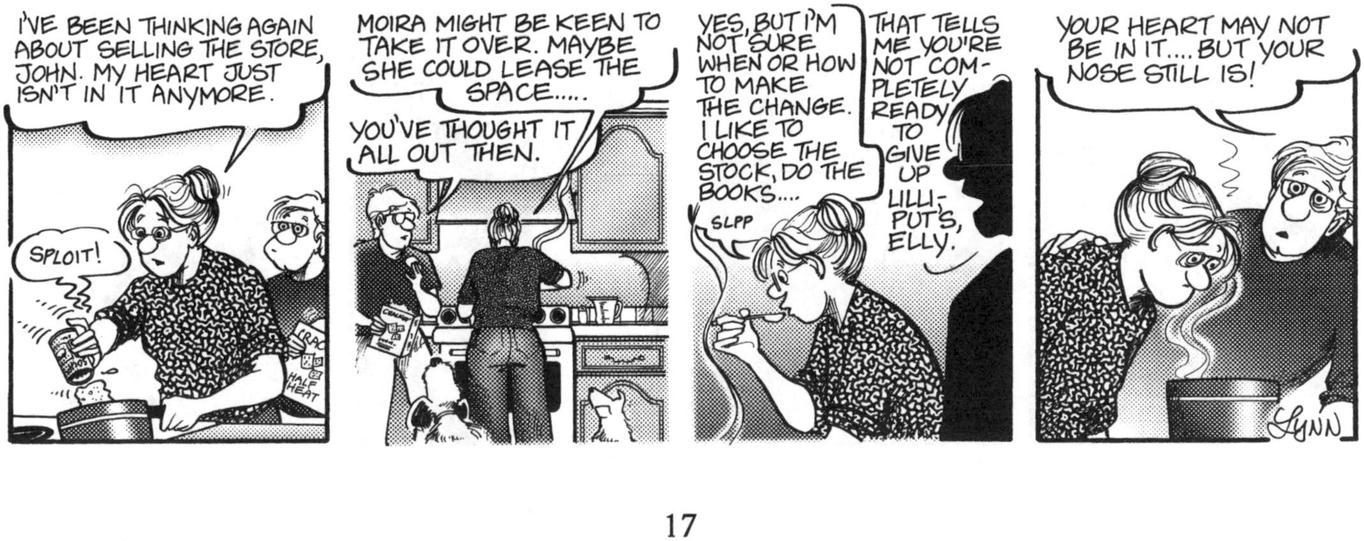
I'VE BEEN THINKING AGAIN ABOUT SELLING THE STORE, JOHN. MY HEART JUST ISN'T IN IT ANYMORE.
SPLOIT!
MOIRA MIGHT BE KEEN TO TAKE IT OVER. MAYBE SHE COULD LEASE THE SPACE.....
YOU'VE THOUGHT IT ALL OUT THEN.
YES, BUT I'M NOT SURE WHEN OR HOW TO MAKE THE CHANGE. I LIKE TO CHOOSE THE STOCK, DO THE BOOKS....
SLPP
THAT TELLS ME YOU'RE NOT COMPLETELY READY TO GIVE UP LILLIPUT'S, ELLY.
YOUR HEART MAY NOT BE IN IT.... BUT YOUR NOSE STILL IS!
LYNN

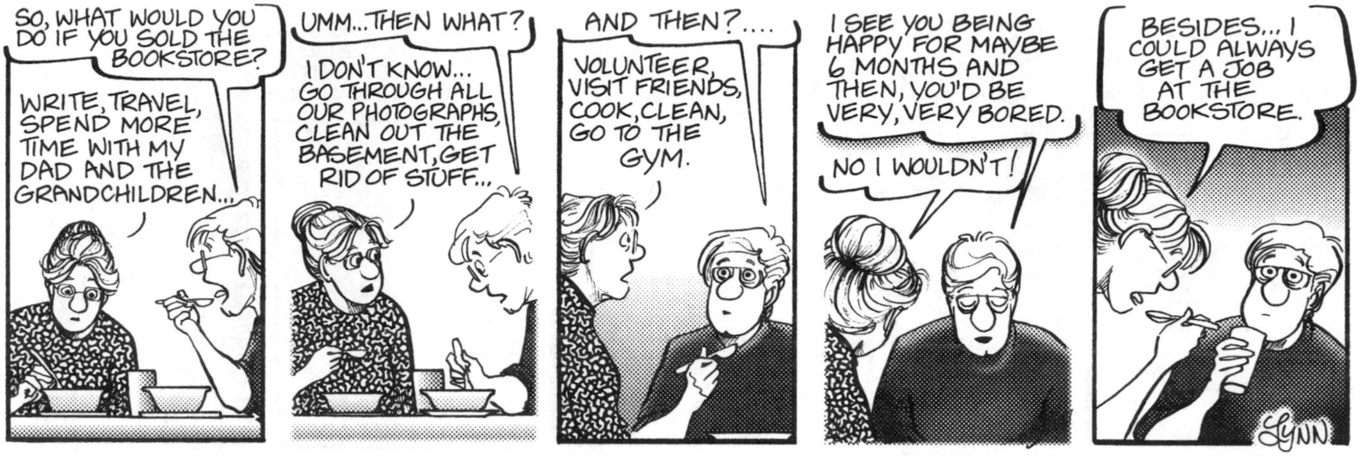
SO, WHAT WOULD YOU DO IF YOU SOLD THE BOOKSTORE?
WRITE, TRAVEL, SPEND MORE TIME WITH MY DAD AND THE GRANDCHILDREN...
UMM...THEN WHAT?
I DON'T KNOW... GO THROUGH ALL OUR PHOTOGRAPHS, CLEAN OUT THE BASEMENT, GET RID OF STUFF...
AND THEN?....
VOLUNTEER, VISIT FRIENDS, COOK, CLEAN, GO TO THE GYM.
I SEE YOU BEING HAPPY FOR MAYBE 6 MONTHS AND THEN, YOU'D BE VERY, VERY BORED.
NO I WOULDN'T!
BESIDES... I COULD ALWAYS GET A JOB AT THE BOOKSTORE.
LYNN

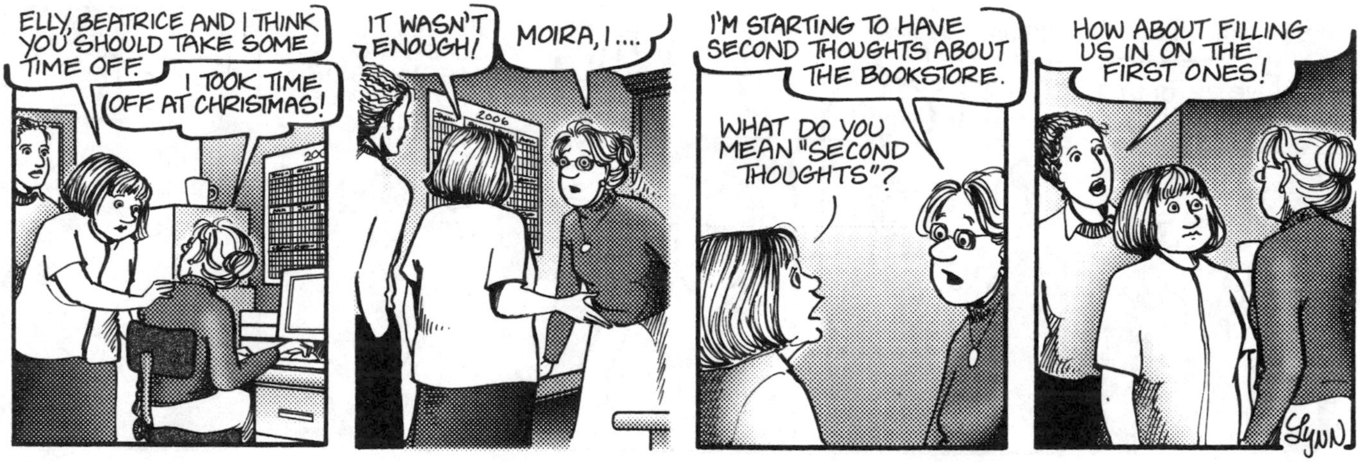
ELLY, BEATRICE AND I THINK YOU SHOULD TAKE SOME TIME OFF.
I TOOK TIME OFF AT CHRISTMAS!
IT WASN'T ENOUGH!
MOIRA, I....
I'M STARTING TO HAVE SECOND THOUGHTS ABOUT THE BOOKSTORE.
WHAT DO YOU MEAN "SECOND THOUGHTS"?
HOW ABOUT FILLING US IN ON THE FIRST ONES!
LYNN

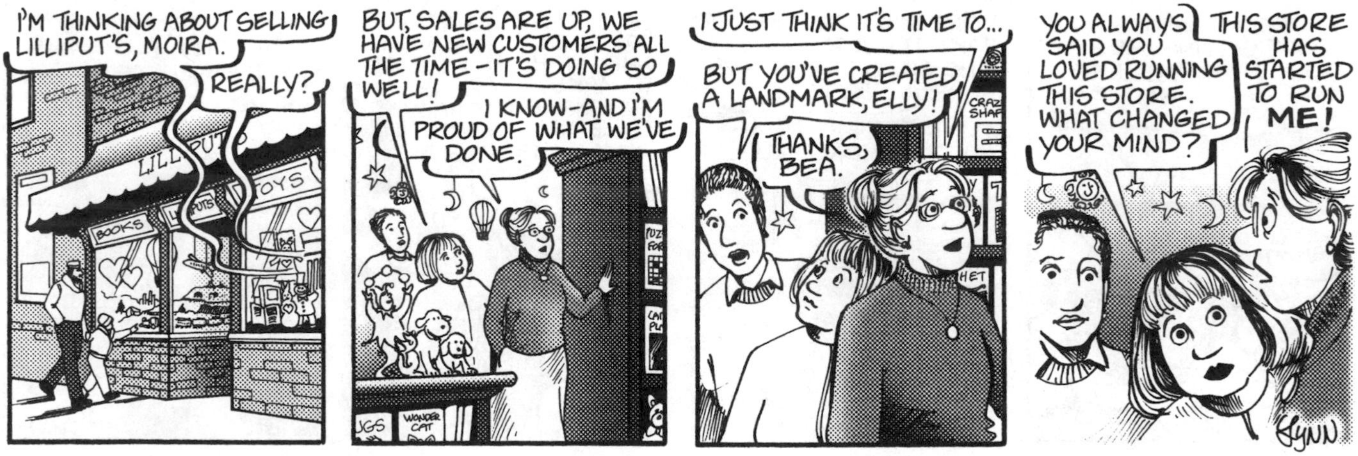
I'M THINKING ABOUT SELLING LILLIPUT'S, MOIRA.
REALLY?
BUT, SALES ARE UP, WE HAVE NEW CUSTOMERS ALL THE TIME - IT'S DOING SO WELL!
I KNOW - AND I'M PROUD OF WHAT WE'VE DONE.
I JUST THINK IT'S TIME TO...
BUT YOU'VE CREATED A LANDMARK, ELLY!
THANKS, BEA.
YOU ALWAYS SAID YOU LOVED RUNNING THIS STORE. WHAT CHANGED YOUR MIND?
THIS STORE HAS STARTED TO RUN **ME!**
LYNN

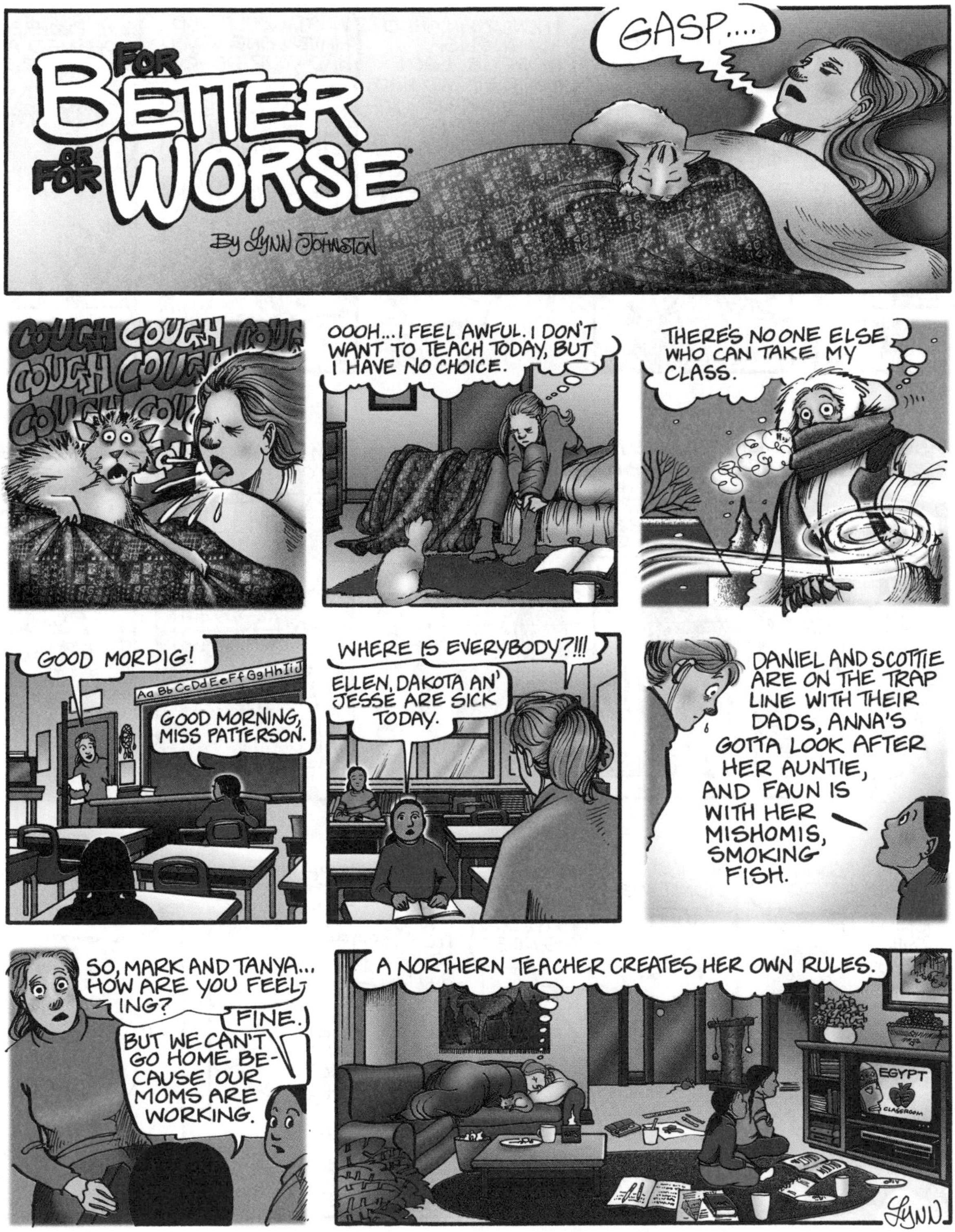
FOR BETTER OR FOR WORSE
BY LYNN JOHNSTON
GASP....
COUGH COUGH COUGH COUGH COUGH
OOOH...I FEEL AWFUL. I DON'T WANT TO TEACH TODAY, BUT I HAVE NO CHOICE.
THERE'S NO ONE ELSE WHO CAN TAKE MY CLASS.
GOOD MORDIG!
Aa Bb Cc Dd Ee Ff Gg Hh Ii Jj
GOOD MORNING, MISS PATTERSON.
WHERE IS EVERYBODY?!!!
ELLEN, DAKOTA AN' JESSE ARE SICK TODAY.
DANIEL AND SCOTTIE ARE ON THE TRAP LINE WITH THEIR DADS, ANNA'S GOTTA LOOK AFTER HER AUNTIE, AND FAUN IS WITH HER MISHOMIS, SMOKING FISH.
SO, MARK AND TANYA... HOW ARE YOU FEELING?
FINE.
BUT WE CAN'T GO HOME BECAUSE OUR MOMS ARE WORKING.
A NORTHERN TEACHER CREATES HER OWN RULES.
EGYPT
CLASSROOM
LYNN

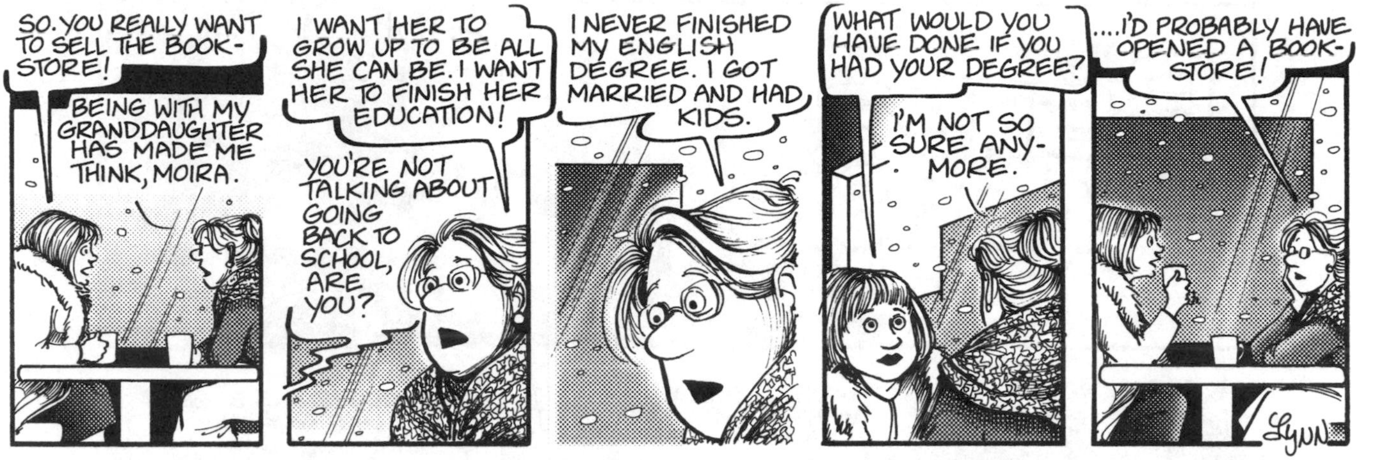
SO. YOU REALLY WANT TO SELL THE BOOKSTORE!
BEING WITH MY GRANDDAUGHTER HAS MADE ME THINK, MOIRA.
I WANT HER TO GROW UP TO BE ALL SHE CAN BE. I WANT HER TO FINISH HER EDUCATION!
YOU'RE NOT TALKING ABOUT GOING BACK TO SCHOOL, ARE YOU?
I NEVER FINISHED MY ENGLISH DEGREE. I GOT MARRIED AND HAD KIDS.
WHAT WOULD YOU HAVE DONE IF YOU HAD YOUR DEGREE?
I'M NOT SO SURE ANYMORE.
....I'D PROBABLY HAVE OPENED A BOOKSTORE!
LYNN

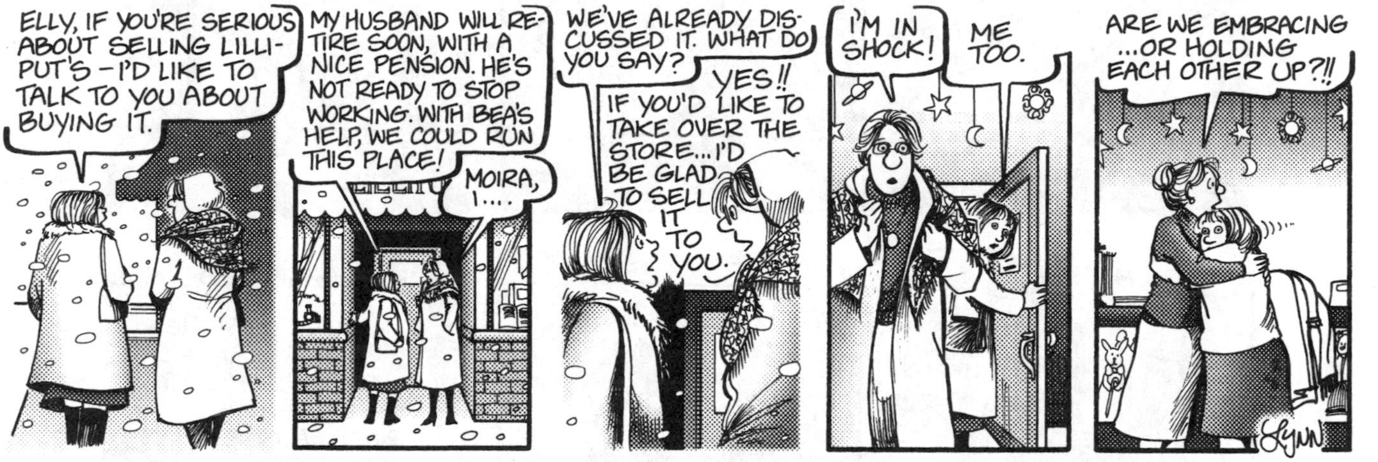
ELLY, IF YOU'RE SERIOUS ABOUT SELLING LILLIPUT'S – I'D LIKE TO TALK TO YOU ABOUT BUYING IT.
MY HUSBAND WILL RETIRE SOON, WITH A NICE PENSION. HE'S NOT READY TO STOP WORKING. WITH BEA'S HELP, WE COULD RUN THIS PLACE!
MOIRA, I....
WE'VE ALREADY DISCUSSED IT. WHAT DO YOU SAY?
YES!! IF YOU'D LIKE TO TAKE OVER THE STORE...I'D BE GLAD TO SELL IT TO YOU.
I'M IN SHOCK!
ME TOO.
ARE WE EMBRACING ...OR HOLDING EACH OTHER UP?!!
LYNN

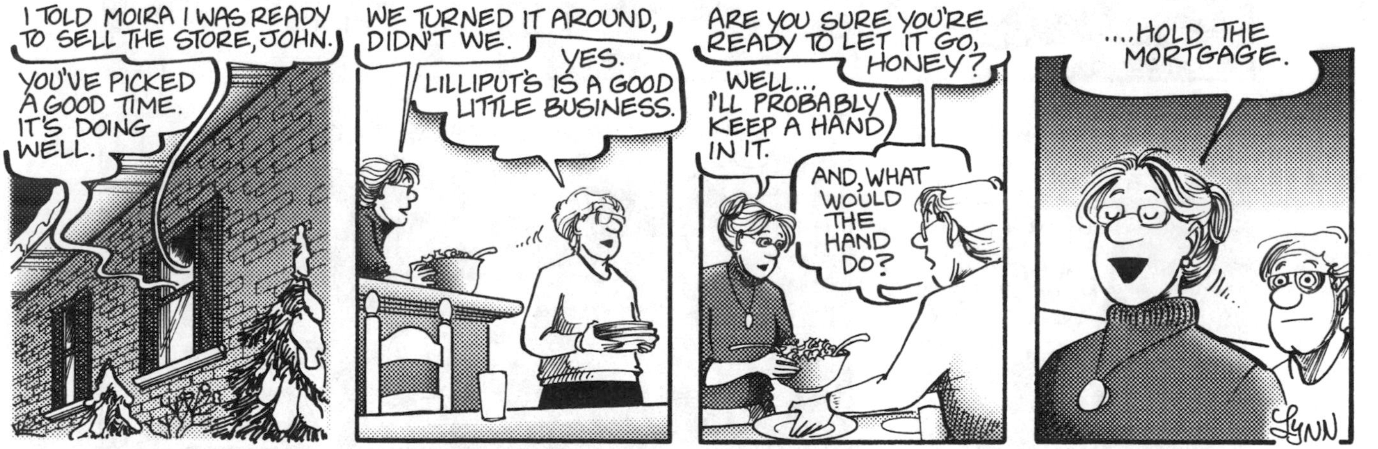
I TOLD MOIRA I WAS READY TO SELL THE STORE, JOHN.
YOU'VE PICKED A GOOD TIME. IT'S DOING WELL.
WE TURNED IT AROUND, DIDN'T WE.
YES. LILLIPUT'S IS A GOOD LITTLE BUSINESS.
ARE YOU SURE YOU'RE READY TO LET IT GO, HONEY?
WELL... I'LL PROBABLY KEEP A HAND IN IT.
AND, WHAT WOULD THE HAND DO?
....HOLD THE MORTGAGE.
LYNN

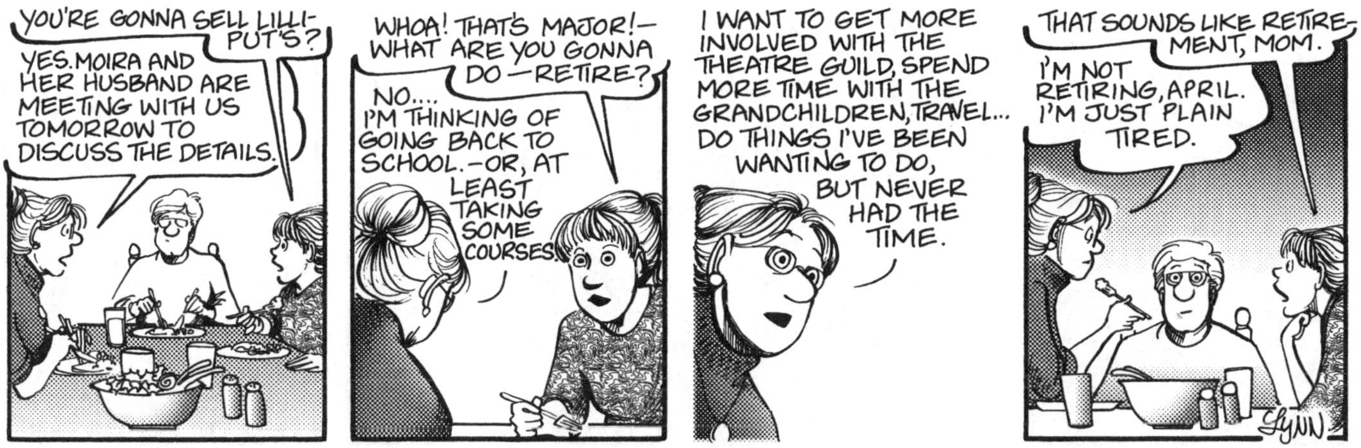
YOU'RE GONNA SELL LILLIPUT'S?
YES. MOIRA AND HER HUSBAND ARE MEETING WITH US TOMORROW TO DISCUSS THE DETAILS.
WHOA! THAT'S MAJOR!— WHAT ARE YOU GONNA DO — RETIRE?
NO.... I'M THINKING OF GOING BACK TO SCHOOL. —OR, AT LEAST TAKING SOME COURSES.
I WANT TO GET MORE INVOLVED WITH THE THEATRE GUILD, SPEND MORE TIME WITH THE GRANDCHILDREN, TRAVEL... DO THINGS I'VE BEEN WANTING TO DO, BUT NEVER HAD THE TIME.
THAT SOUNDS LIKE RETIREMENT, MOM.
I'M NOT RETIRING, APRIL. I'M JUST PLAIN TIRED.
LYNN

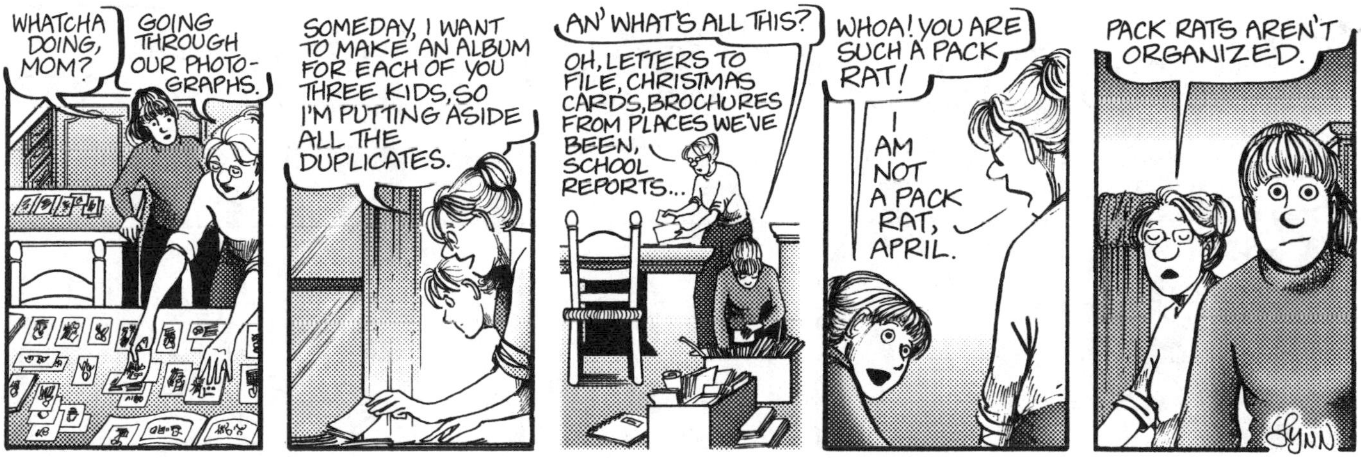
WHATCHA DOING, MOM?
GOING THROUGH OUR PHOTOGRAPHS.
SOMEDAY, I WANT TO MAKE AN ALBUM FOR EACH OF YOU THREE KIDS, SO I'M PUTTING ASIDE ALL THE DUPLICATES.
AN' WHAT'S ALL THIS?
OH, LETTERS TO FILE, CHRISTMAS CARDS, BROCHURES FROM PLACES WE'VE BEEN, SCHOOL REPORTS...
WHOA! YOU ARE SUCH A PACK RAT!
I AM NOT A PACK RAT, APRIL.
PACK RATS AREN'T ORGANIZED.
LYNN

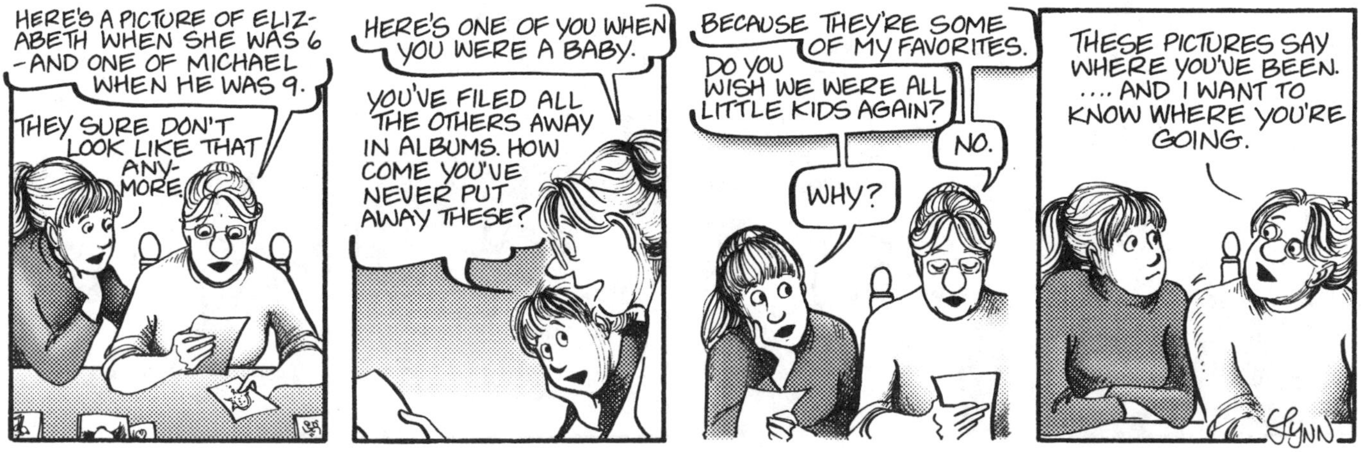
HERE'S A PICTURE OF ELIZABETH WHEN SHE WAS 6 - AND ONE OF MICHAEL WHEN HE WAS 9.
THEY SURE DON'T LOOK LIKE THAT ANYMORE.
HERE'S ONE OF YOU WHEN YOU WERE A BABY.
YOU'VE FILED ALL THE OTHERS AWAY IN ALBUMS. HOW COME YOU'VE NEVER PUT AWAY THESE?
BECAUSE THEY'RE SOME OF MY FAVORITES.
DO YOU WISH WE WERE ALL LITTLE KIDS AGAIN?
NO.
WHY?
THESE PICTURES SAY WHERE YOU'VE BEEN. .... AND I WANT TO KNOW WHERE YOU'RE GOING.
LYNN

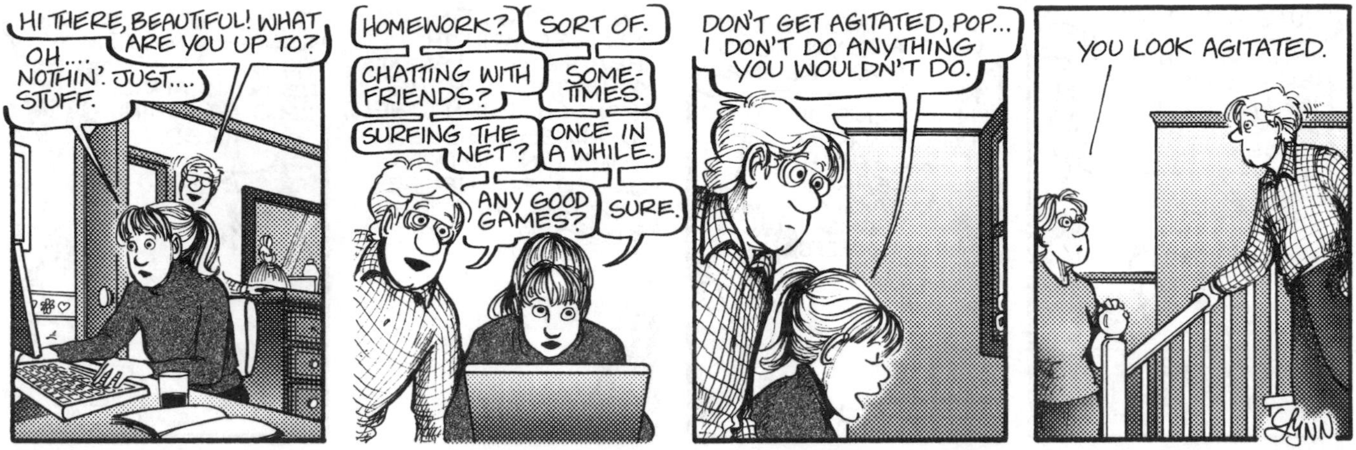
HI THERE, BEAUTIFUL! WHAT ARE YOU UP TO?
OH.... NOTHIN'. JUST.... STUFF.
HOMEWORK?
SORT OF.
CHATTING WITH FRIENDS?
SOMETIMES.
SURFING THE NET?
ONCE IN A WHILE.
ANY GOOD GAMES?
SURE.
DON'T GET AGITATED, POP... I DON'T DO ANYTHING YOU WOULDN'T DO.
YOU LOOK AGITATED.
LYNN

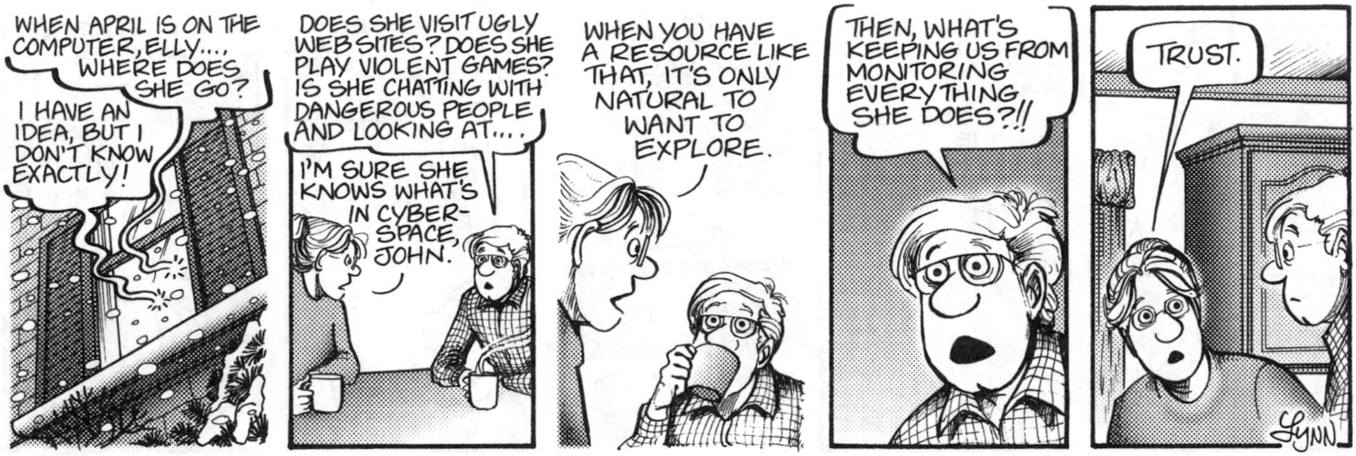
WHEN APRIL IS ON THE COMPUTER, ELLY..., WHERE DOES SHE GO?
I HAVE AN IDEA, BUT I DON'T KNOW EXACTLY!
DOES SHE VISIT UGLY WEB SITES? DOES SHE PLAY VIOLENT GAMES? IS SHE CHATTING WITH DANGEROUS PEOPLE AND LOOKING AT....
I'M SURE SHE KNOWS WHAT'S IN CYBERSPACE, JOHN.
WHEN YOU HAVE A RESOURCE LIKE THAT, IT'S ONLY NATURAL TO WANT TO EXPLORE.
THEN, WHAT'S KEEPING US FROM MONITORING EVERYTHING SHE DOES?!!
TRUST.
LYNN

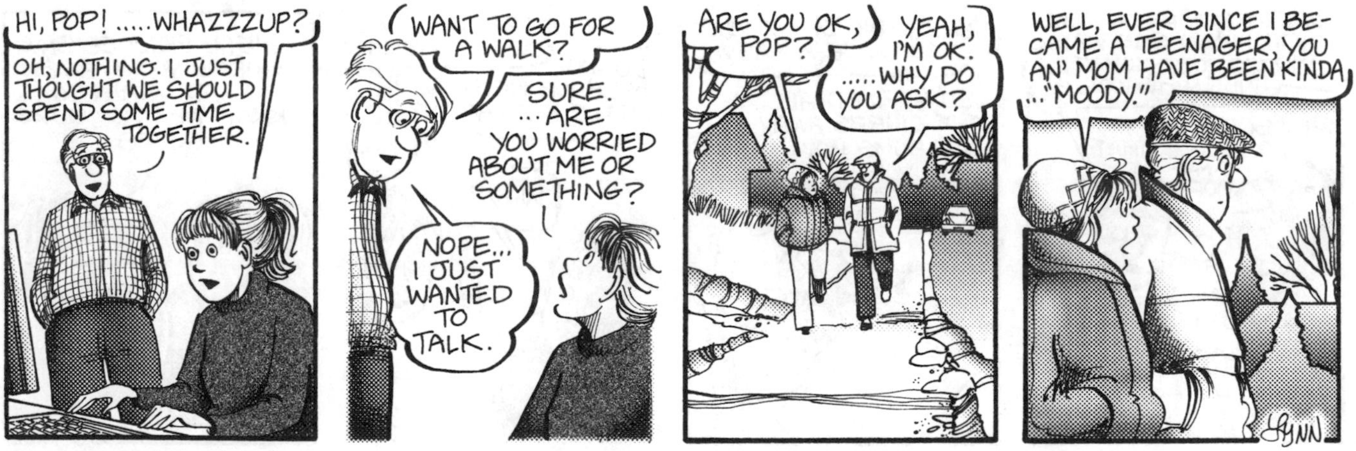
HI, POP! .....WHAZZZUP?
OH, NOTHING. I JUST THOUGHT WE SHOULD SPEND SOME TIME TOGETHER.
WANT TO GO FOR A WALK?
SURE. ...ARE YOU WORRIED ABOUT ME OR SOMETHING?
NOPE... I JUST WANTED TO TALK.
ARE YOU OK, POP?
YEAH, I'M OK. .....WHY DO YOU ASK?
WELL, EVER SINCE I BECAME A TEENAGER, YOU AN' MOM HAVE BEEN KINDA ..."MOODY."
LYNN

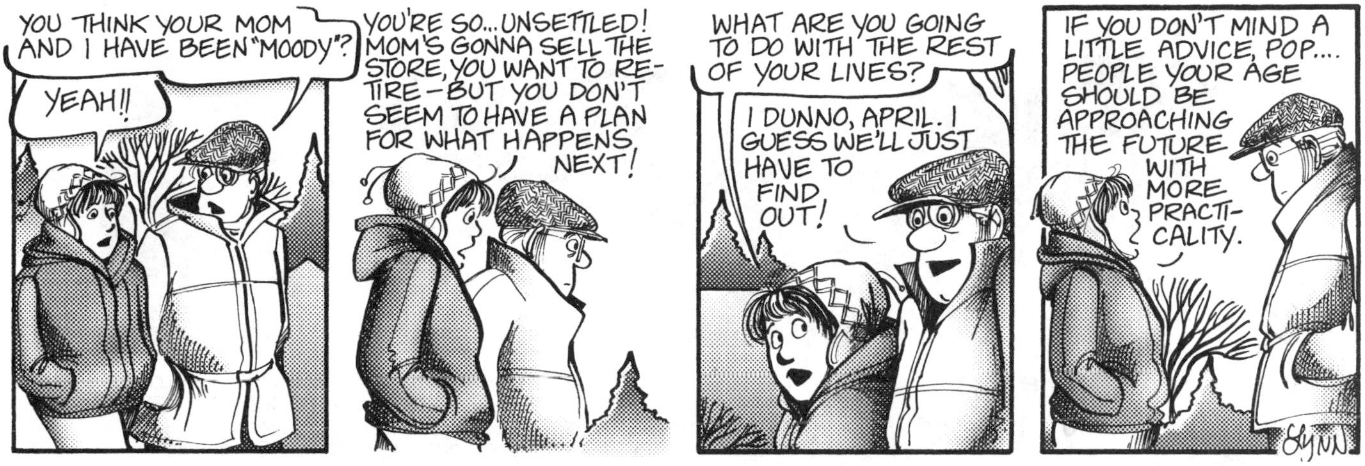
YOU THINK YOUR MOM AND I HAVE BEEN "MOODY"?
YEAH!!
YOU'RE SO...UNSETTLED! MOM'S GONNA SELL THE STORE, YOU WANT TO RE-TIRE—BUT YOU DON'T SEEM TO HAVE A PLAN FOR WHAT HAPPENS NEXT!
WHAT ARE YOU GOING TO DO WITH THE REST OF YOUR LIVES?
I DUNNO, APRIL. I GUESS WE'LL JUST HAVE TO FIND OUT!
IF YOU DON'T MIND A LITTLE ADVICE, POP.... PEOPLE YOUR AGE SHOULD BE APPROACHING THE FUTURE WITH MORE PRACTI-CALITY.
LYNN

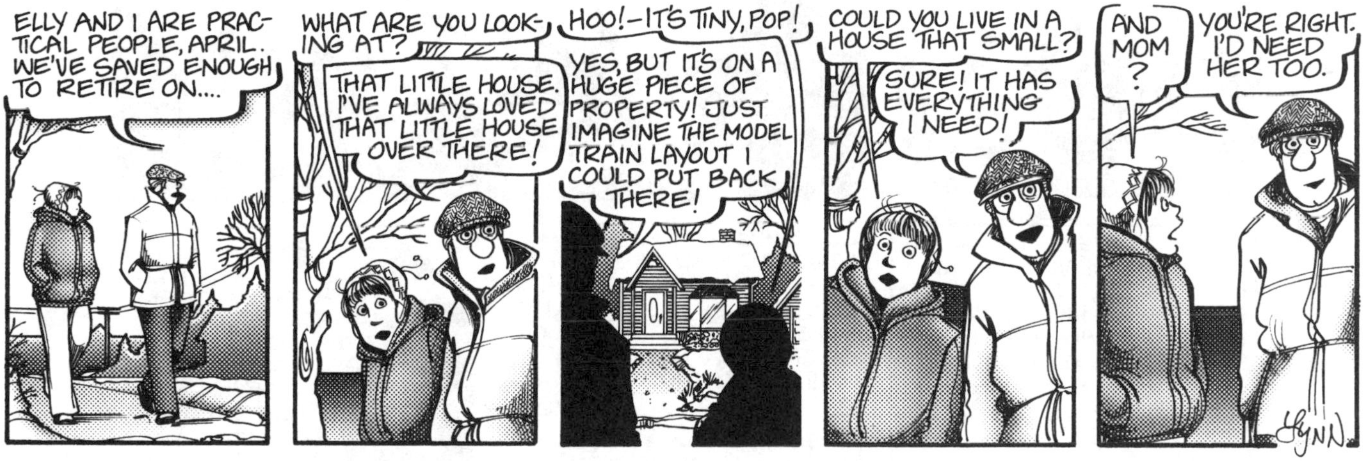
ELLY AND I ARE PRAC-TICAL PEOPLE, APRIL. WE'VE SAVED ENOUGH TO RETIRE ON....
WHAT ARE YOU LOOK-ING AT?
THAT LITTLE HOUSE. I'VE ALWAYS LOVED THAT LITTLE HOUSE OVER THERE!
HOO!—IT'S TINY, POP!
YES, BUT IT'S ON A HUGE PIECE OF PROPERTY! JUST IMAGINE THE MODEL TRAIN LAYOUT I COULD PUT BACK THERE!
COULD YOU LIVE IN A HOUSE THAT SMALL?
SURE! IT HAS EVERYTHING I NEED!
AND MOM ?
YOU'RE RIGHT. I'D NEED HER TOO.
LYNN

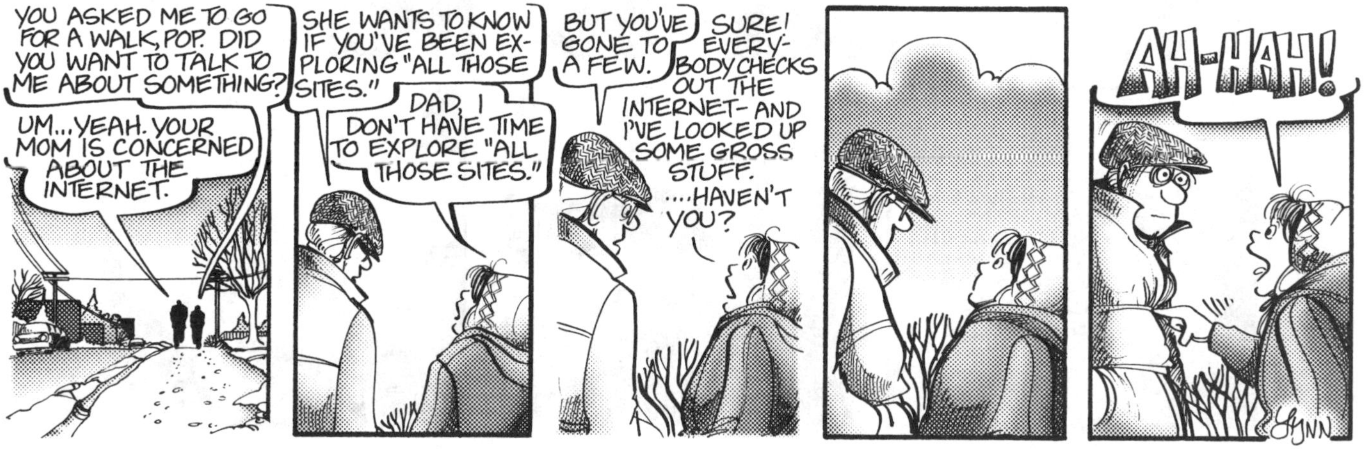
YOU ASKED ME TO GO FOR A WALK, POP. DID YOU WANT TO TALK TO ME ABOUT SOMETHING?
UM...YEAH. YOUR MOM IS CONCERNED ABOUT THE INTERNET.
SHE WANTS TO KNOW IF YOU'VE BEEN EX-PLORING "ALL THOSE SITES."
DAD, I DON'T HAVE TIME TO EXPLORE "ALL THOSE SITES."
BUT YOU'VE GONE TO A FEW.
SURE! EVERY-BODY CHECKS OUT THE INTERNET—AND I'VE LOOKED UP SOME GROSS STUFF.
....HAVEN'T YOU?
AH-HAH!
LYNN

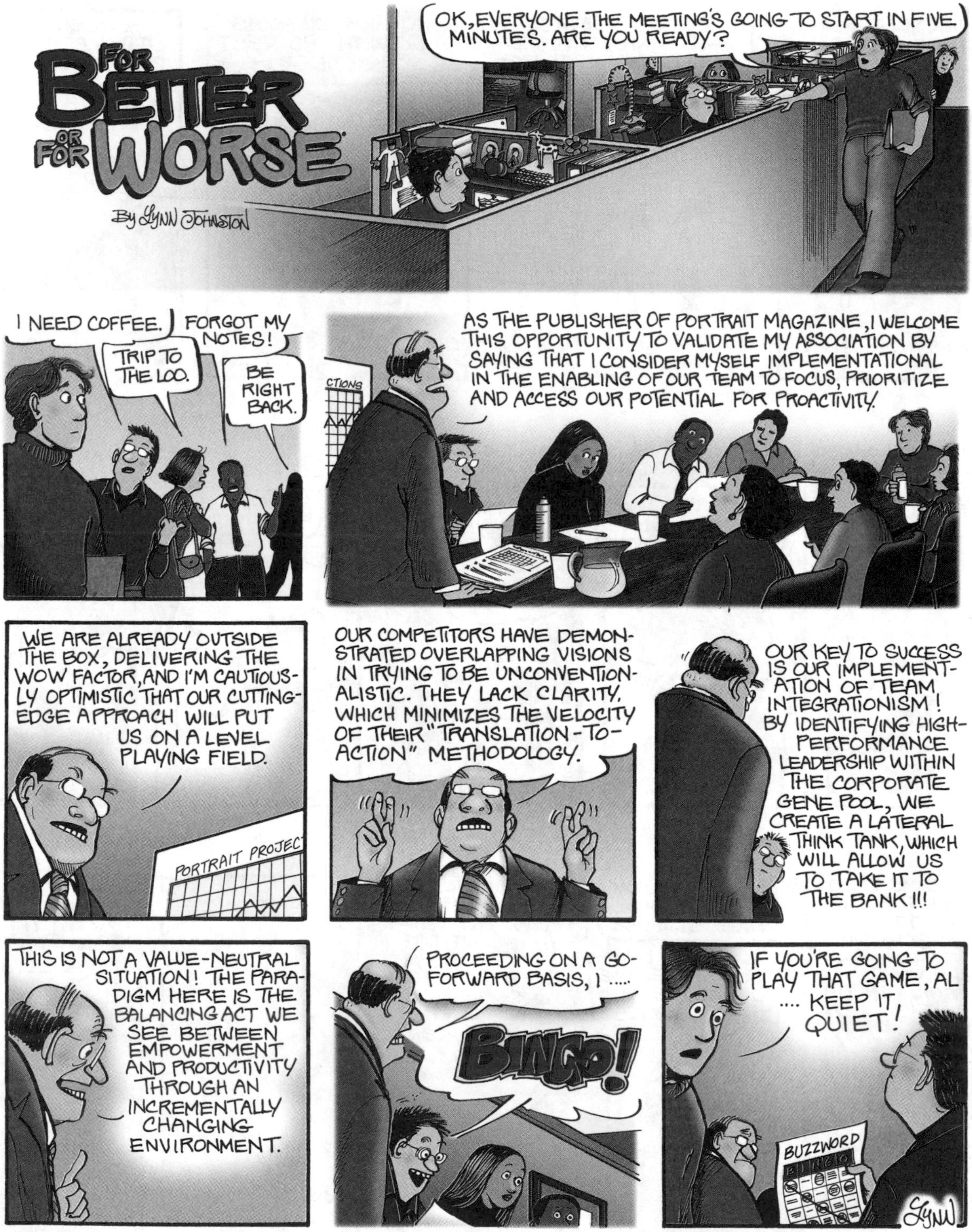
FOR BETTER OR FOR WORSE
BY LYNN JOHNSTON
OK, EVERYONE. THE MEETING'S GOING TO START IN FIVE MINUTES. ARE YOU READY?
I NEED COFFEE.
FORGOT MY NOTES!
TRIP TO THE LOO.
BE RIGHT BACK.
AS THE PUBLISHER OF PORTRAIT MAGAZINE, I WELCOME THIS OPPORTUNITY TO VALIDATE MY ASSOCIATION BY SAYING THAT I CONSIDER MYSELF IMPLEMENTATIONAL IN THE ENABLING OF OUR TEAM TO FOCUS, PRIORITIZE AND ACCESS OUR POTENTIAL FOR PROACTIVITY!
WE ARE ALREADY OUTSIDE THE BOX, DELIVERING THE WOW FACTOR, AND I'M CAUTIOUSLY OPTIMISTIC THAT OUR CUTTING-EDGE APPROACH WILL PUT US ON A LEVEL PLAYING FIELD.
PORTRAIT PROJEC
OUR COMPETITORS HAVE DEMONSTRATED OVERLAPPING VISIONS IN TRYING TO BE UNCONVENTIONALISTIC. THEY LACK CLARITY, WHICH MINIMIZES THE VELOCITY OF THEIR "TRANSLATION-TO-ACTION" METHODOLOGY.
OUR KEY TO SUCCESS IS OUR IMPLEMENTATION OF TEAM INTEGRATIONISM! BY IDENTIFYING HIGH-PERFORMANCE LEADERSHIP WITHIN THE CORPORATE GENE POOL, WE CREATE A LATERAL THINK TANK, WHICH WILL ALLOW US TO TAKE IT TO THE BANK!!!
THIS IS NOT A VALUE-NEUTRAL SITUATION! THE PARADIGM HERE IS THE BALANCING ACT WE SEE BETWEEN EMPOWERMENT AND PRODUCTIVITY THROUGH AN INCREMENTALLY CHANGING ENVIRONMENT.
PROCEEDING ON A GO-FORWARD BASIS, I .....
BINGO!
IF YOU'RE GOING TO PLAY THAT GAME, AL .... KEEP IT QUIET!
BUZZWORD BINGO
LYNN

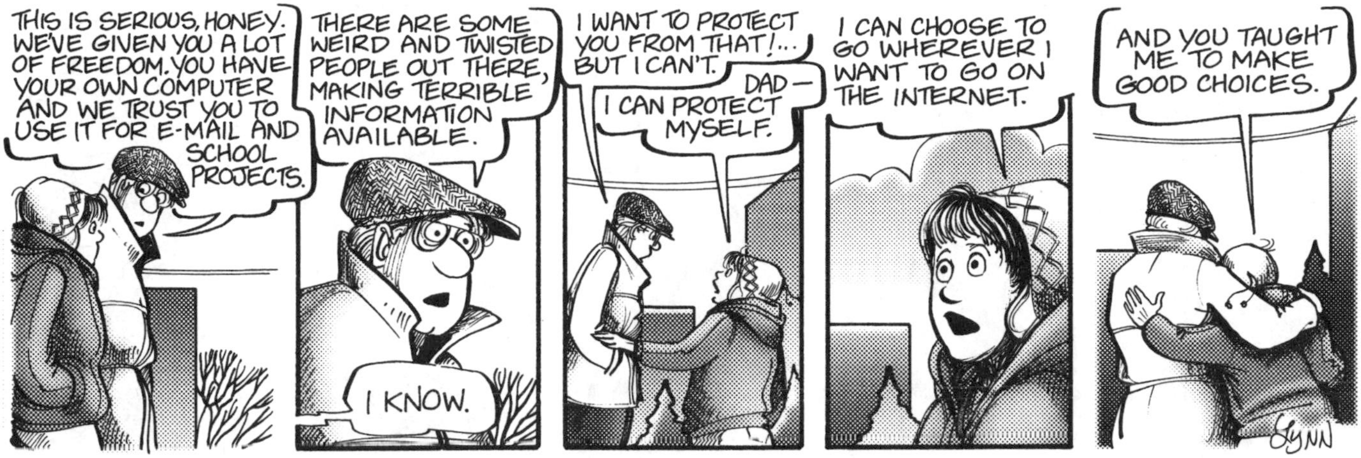
THIS IS SERIOUS, HONEY. WE'VE GIVEN YOU A LOT OF FREEDOM. YOU HAVE YOUR OWN COMPUTER AND WE TRUST YOU TO USE IT FOR E-MAIL AND SCHOOL PROJECTS.
THERE ARE SOME WEIRD AND TWISTED PEOPLE OUT THERE, MAKING TERRIBLE INFORMATION AVAILABLE.
I KNOW.
I WANT TO PROTECT YOU FROM THAT!... BUT I CAN'T.
DAD— I CAN PROTECT MYSELF.
I CAN CHOOSE TO GO WHEREVER I WANT TO GO ON THE INTERNET.
AND YOU TAUGHT ME TO MAKE GOOD CHOICES.

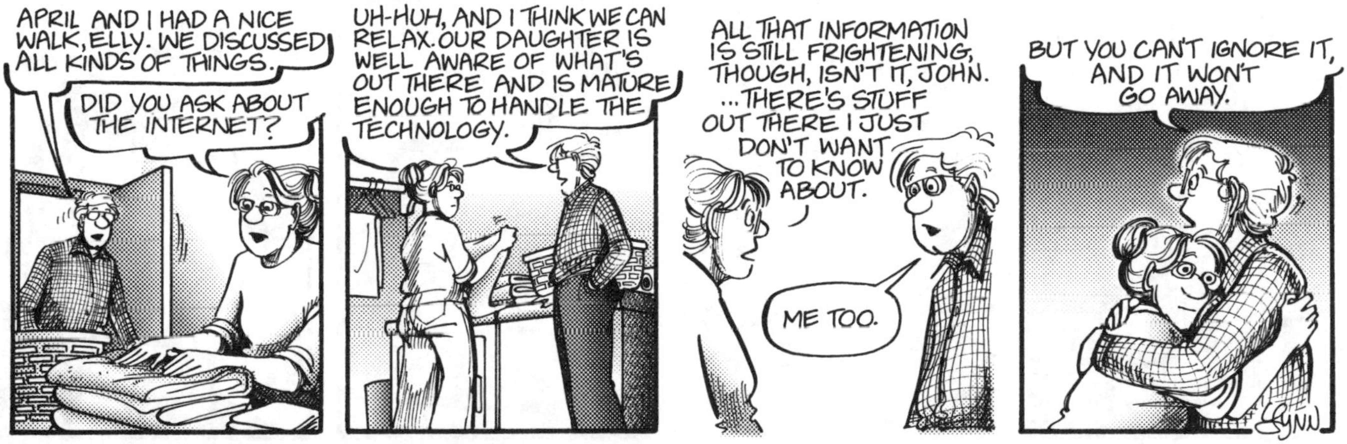
APRIL AND I HAD A NICE WALK, ELLY. WE DISCUSSED ALL KINDS OF THINGS.
DID YOU ASK ABOUT THE INTERNET?
UH-HUH, AND I THINK WE CAN RELAX. OUR DAUGHTER IS WELL AWARE OF WHAT'S OUT THERE AND IS MATURE ENOUGH TO HANDLE THE TECHNOLOGY.
ALL THAT INFORMATION IS STILL FRIGHTENING, THOUGH, ISN'T IT, JOHN. ...THERE'S STUFF OUT THERE I JUST DON'T WANT TO KNOW ABOUT.
ME TOO.
BUT YOU CAN'T IGNORE IT, AND IT WON'T GO AWAY.

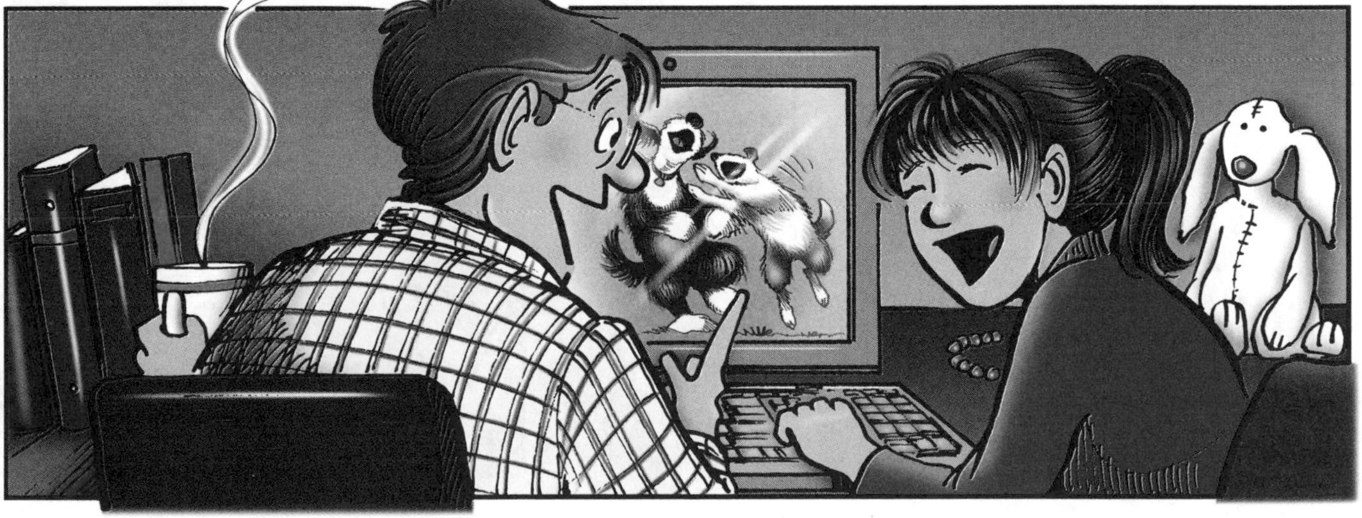

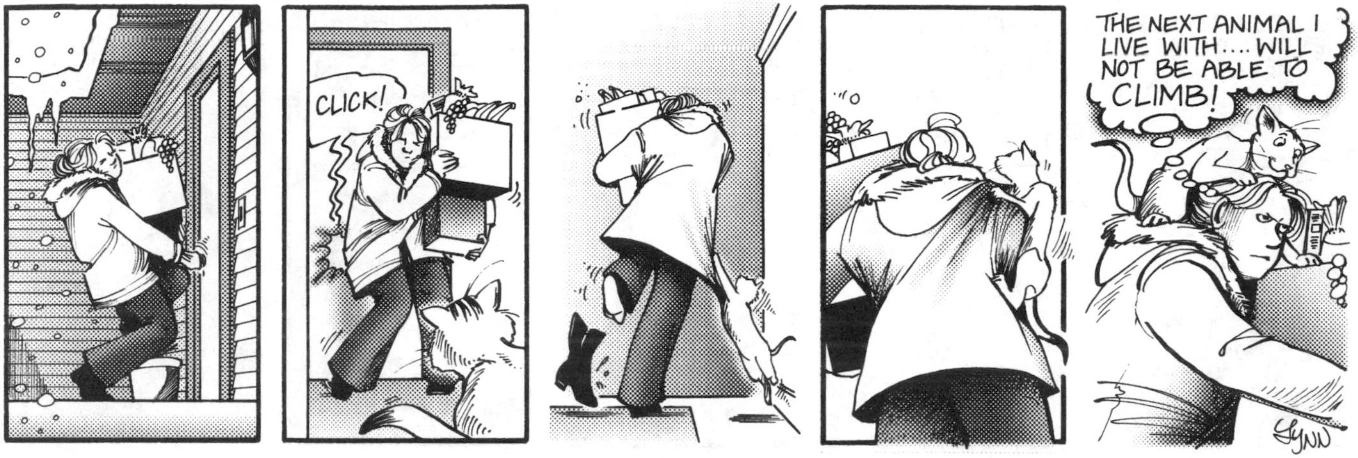
CLICK!
THE NEXT ANIMAL I LIVE WITH.... WILL NOT BE ABLE TO CLIMB!
LYNN

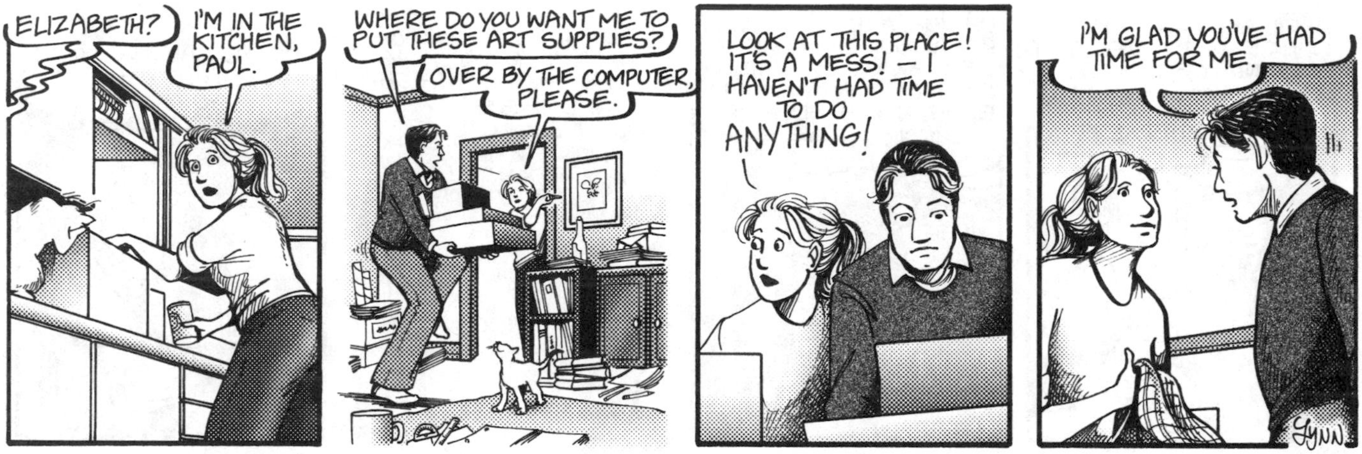
ELIZABETH?
I'M IN THE KITCHEN, PAUL.
WHERE DO YOU WANT ME TO PUT THESE ART SUPPLIES?
OVER BY THE COMPUTER, PLEASE.
LOOK AT THIS PLACE! IT'S A MESS! — I HAVEN'T HAD TIME TO DO ANYTHING!
I'M GLAD YOU'VE HAD TIME FOR ME.
LYNN

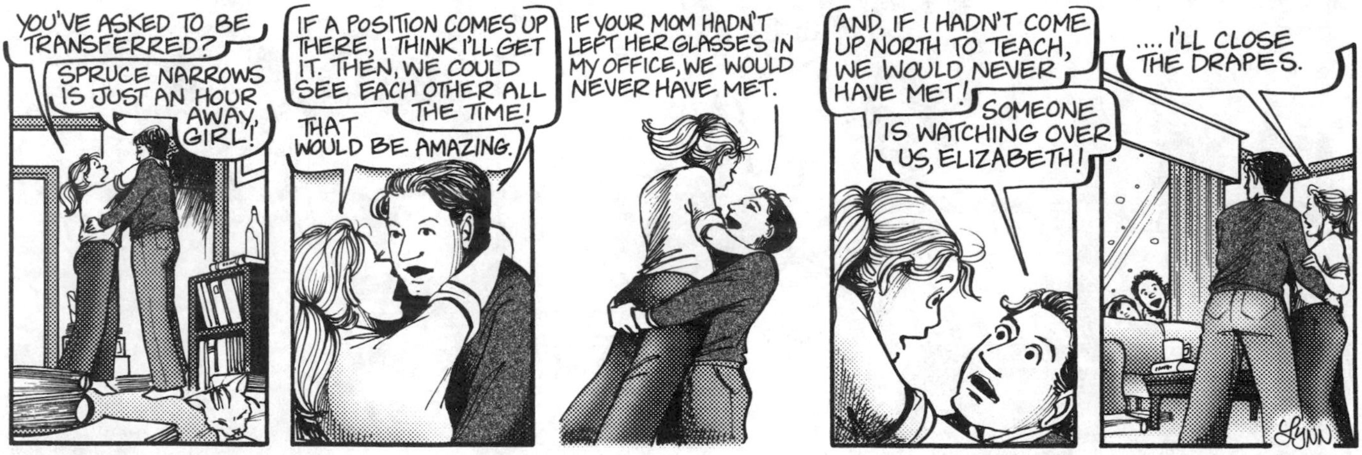
YOU'VE ASKED TO BE TRANSFERRED?
SPRUCE NARROWS IS JUST AN HOUR AWAY, GIRL!
IF A POSITION COMES UP THERE, I THINK I'LL GET IT. THEN, WE COULD SEE EACH OTHER ALL THE TIME!
THAT WOULD BE AMAZING.
IF YOUR MOM HADN'T LEFT HER GLASSES IN MY OFFICE, WE WOULD NEVER HAVE MET.
AND, IF I HADN'T COME UP NORTH TO TEACH, WE WOULD NEVER HAVE MET!
SOMEONE IS WATCHING OVER US, ELIZABETH!
.... I'LL CLOSE THE DRAPES.
LYNN

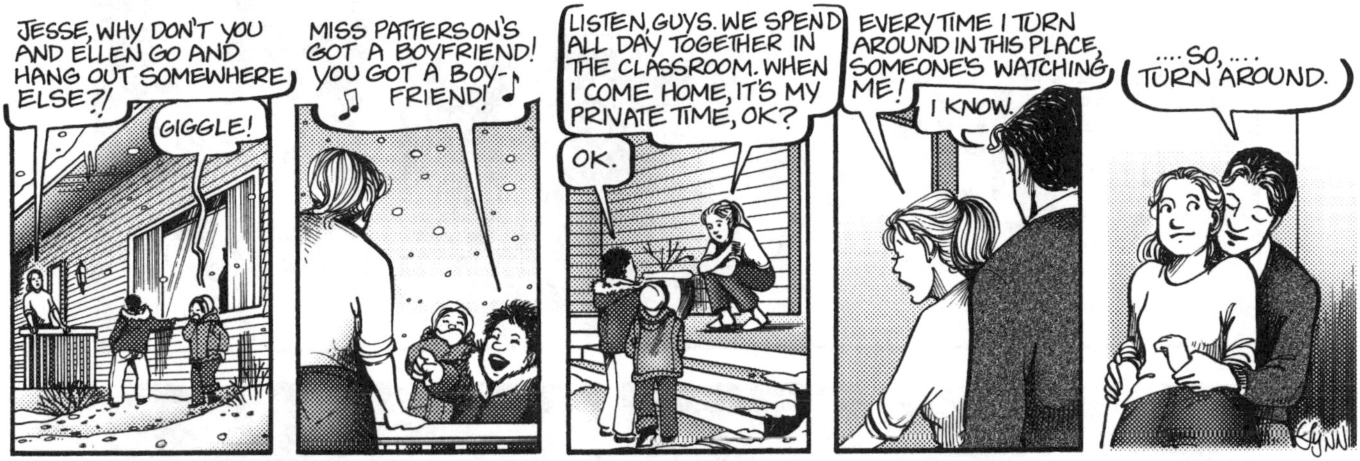
JESSE, WHY DON'T YOU AND ELLEN GO AND HANG OUT SOMEWHERE ELSE?!
GIGGLE!
MISS PATTERSON'S GOT A BOYFRIEND! YOU GOT A BOY-FRIEND!
LISTEN, GUYS. WE SPEND ALL DAY TOGETHER IN THE CLASSROOM. WHEN I COME HOME, IT'S MY PRIVATE TIME, OK?
OK.
EVERY TIME I TURN AROUND IN THIS PLACE, SOMEONE'S WATCHING ME!
I KNOW.
....SO,.... TURN AROUND.

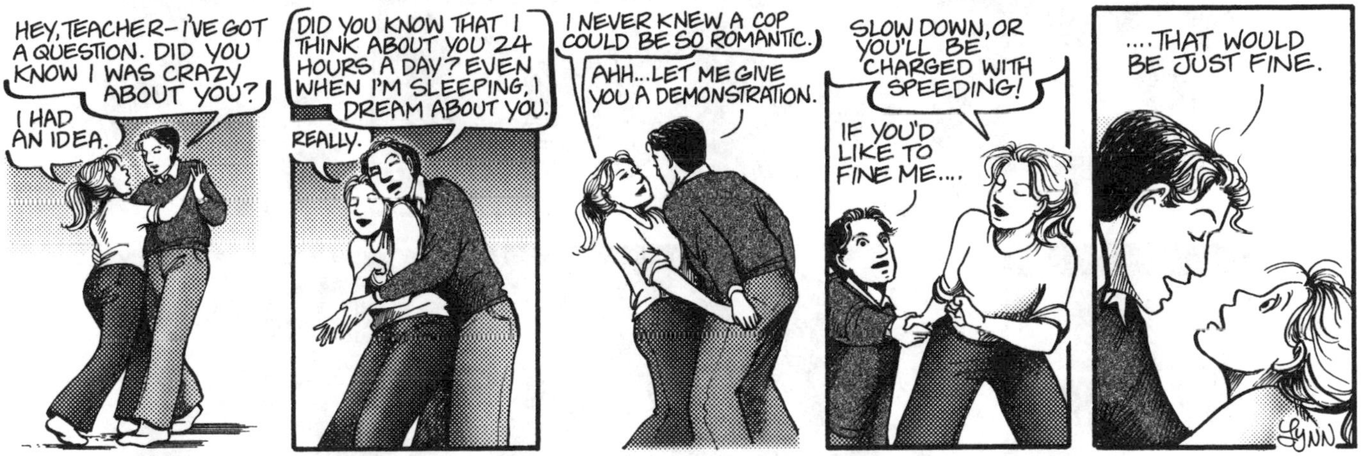
HEY, TEACHER- I'VE GOT A QUESTION. DID YOU KNOW I WAS CRAZY ABOUT YOU?
I HAD AN IDEA.
DID YOU KNOW THAT I THINK ABOUT YOU 24 HOURS A DAY? EVEN WHEN I'M SLEEPING, I DREAM ABOUT YOU.
REALLY.
I NEVER KNEW A COP COULD BE SO ROMANTIC.
AHH...LET ME GIVE YOU A DEMONSTRATION.
SLOW DOWN, OR YOU'LL BE CHARGED WITH SPEEDING!
IF YOU'D LIKE TO FINE ME....
....THAT WOULD BE JUST FINE.

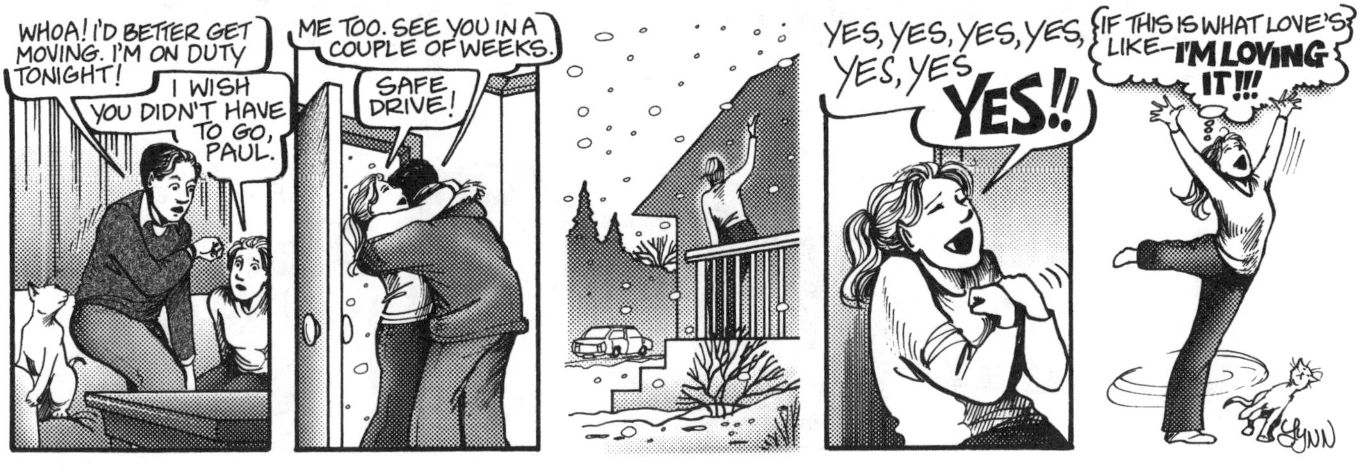
WHOA! I'D BETTER GET MOVING. I'M ON DUTY TONIGHT!
I WISH YOU DIDN'T HAVE TO GO, PAUL.
ME TOO. SEE YOU IN A COUPLE OF WEEKS.
SAFE DRIVE!
YES, YES, YES, YES, YES, YES YES!!
IF THIS IS WHAT LOVE'S LIKE- I'M LOVING IT!!!

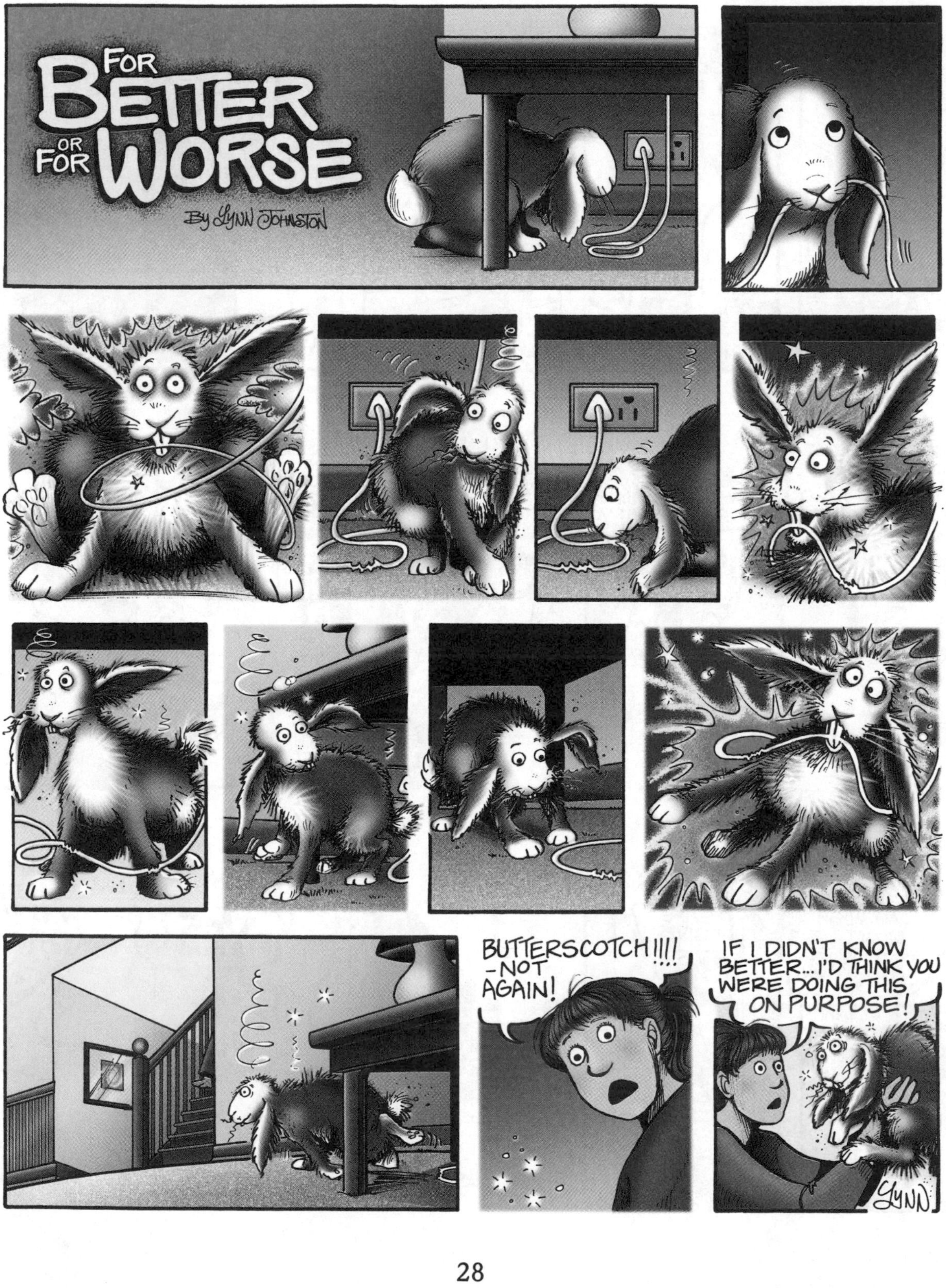
FOR BETTER OR FOR WORSE
By Lynn Johnston
BUTTERSCOTCH!!!! -NOT AGAIN!
IF I DIDN'T KNOW BETTER...I'D THINK YOU WERE DOING THIS ON PURPOSE!
LYNN

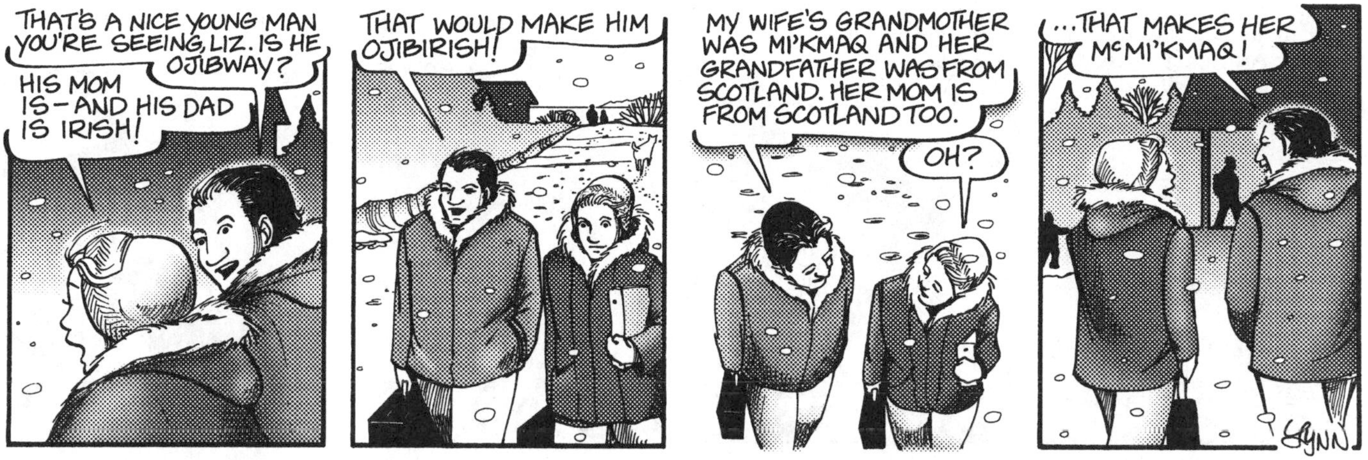
THAT'S A NICE YOUNG MAN YOU'RE SEEING, LIZ. IS HE OJIBWAY?
HIS MOM IS—AND HIS DAD IS IRISH!
THAT WOULD MAKE HIM OJIBIRISH!
MY WIFE'S GRANDMOTHER WAS MI'KMAQ AND HER GRANDFATHER WAS FROM SCOTLAND. HER MOM IS FROM SCOTLAND TOO.
OH?
...THAT MAKES HER McMI'KMAQ!
LYNN

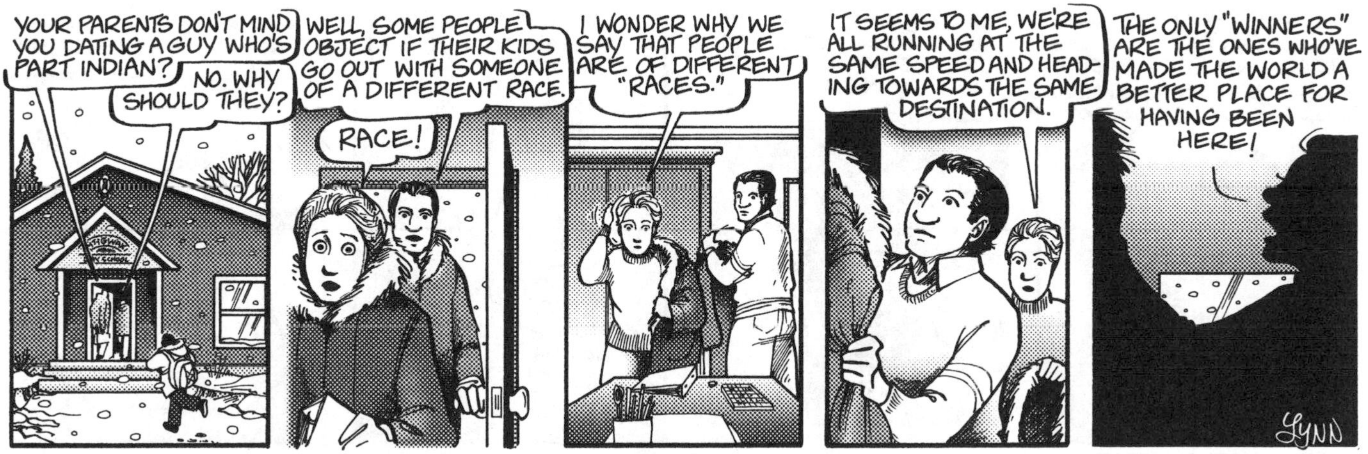
YOUR PARENTS DON'T MIND YOU DATING A GUY WHO'S PART INDIAN?
NO. WHY SHOULD THEY?
WELL, SOME PEOPLE OBJECT IF THEIR KIDS GO OUT WITH SOMEONE OF A DIFFERENT RACE.
RACE!
I WONDER WHY WE SAY THAT PEOPLE ARE OF DIFFERENT "RACES."
IT SEEMS TO ME, WE'RE ALL RUNNING AT THE SAME SPEED AND HEADING TOWARDS THE SAME DESTINATION.
THE ONLY "WINNERS" ARE THE ONES WHO'VE MADE THE WORLD A BETTER PLACE FOR HAVING BEEN HERE!
LYNN

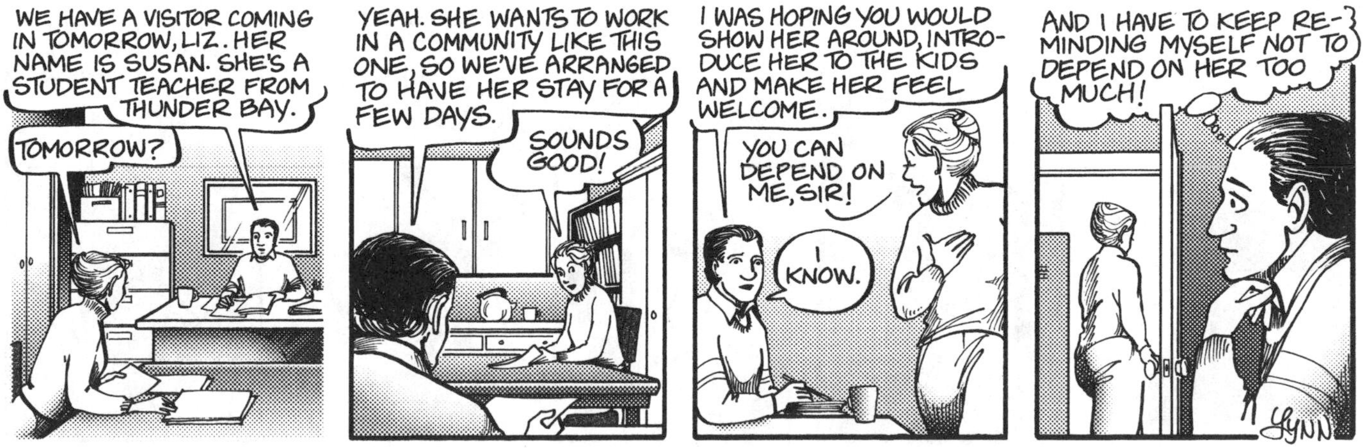
WE HAVE A VISITOR COMING IN TOMORROW, LIZ. HER NAME IS SUSAN. SHE'S A STUDENT TEACHER FROM THUNDER BAY.
TOMORROW?
YEAH. SHE WANTS TO WORK IN A COMMUNITY LIKE THIS ONE, SO WE'VE ARRANGED TO HAVE HER STAY FOR A FEW DAYS.
SOUNDS GOOD!
I WAS HOPING YOU WOULD SHOW HER AROUND, INTRODUCE HER TO THE KIDS AND MAKE HER FEEL WELCOME.
YOU CAN DEPEND ON ME, SIR!
I KNOW.
AND I HAVE TO KEEP REMINDING MYSELF NOT TO DEPEND ON HER TOO MUCH!
LYNN

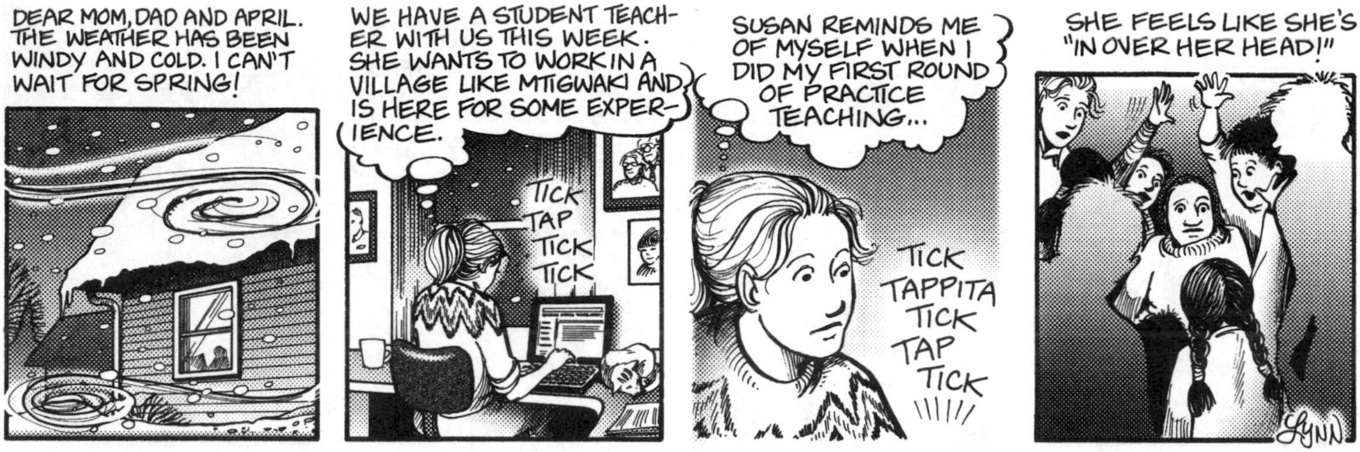
DEAR MOM, DAD AND APRIL. THE WEATHER HAS BEEN WINDY AND COLD. I CAN'T WAIT FOR SPRING!
WE HAVE A STUDENT TEACHER WITH US THIS WEEK. SHE WANTS TO WORK IN A VILLAGE LIKE MTIGWAKI AND IS HERE FOR SOME EXPERIENCE.
TICK TAP TICK TICK
SUSAN REMINDS ME OF MYSELF WHEN I DID MY FIRST ROUND OF PRACTICE TEACHING...
TICK TAPPITA TICK TAP TICK
SHE FEELS LIKE SHE'S "IN OVER HER HEAD!"
LYNN

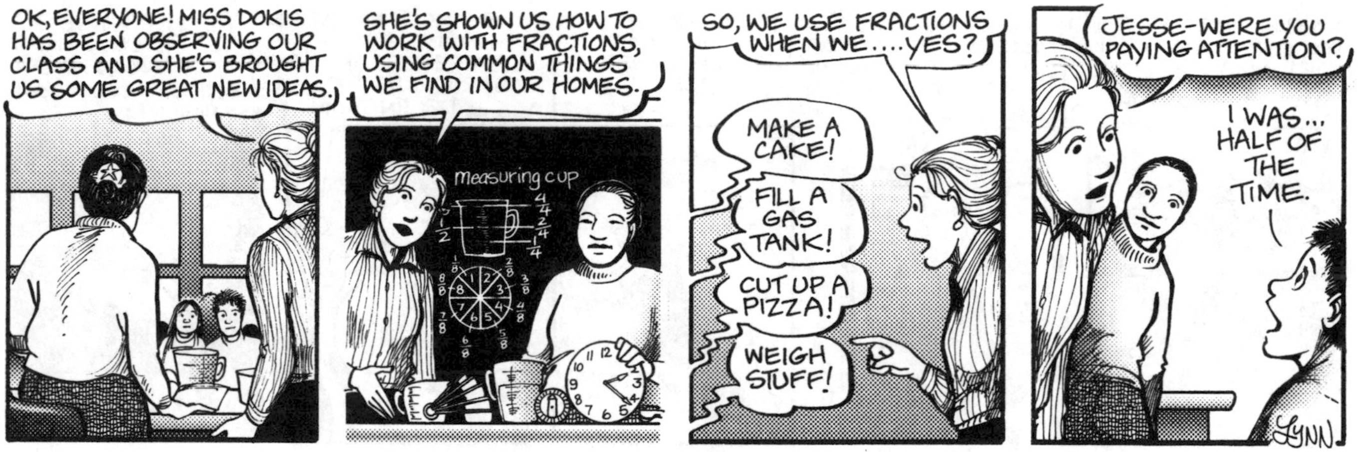
OK, EVERYONE! MISS DOKIS HAS BEEN OBSERVING OUR CLASS AND SHE'S BROUGHT US SOME GREAT NEW IDEAS.
SHE'S SHOWN US HOW TO WORK WITH FRACTIONS, USING COMMON THINGS WE FIND IN OUR HOMES.
measuring cup
SO, WE USE FRACTIONS WHEN WE.... YES?
MAKE A CAKE!
FILL A GAS TANK!
CUT UP A PIZZA!
WEIGH STUFF!
JESSE-WERE YOU PAYING ATTENTION?
I WAS... HALF OF THE TIME.
LYNN

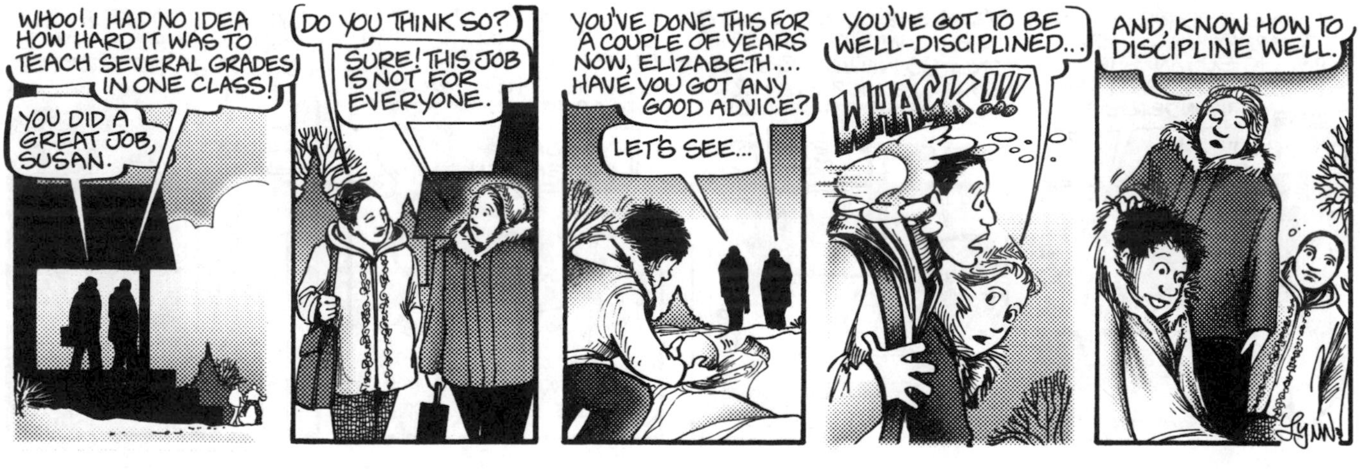
WHOO! I HAD NO IDEA HOW HARD IT WAS TO TEACH SEVERAL GRADES IN ONE CLASS!
YOU DID A GREAT JOB, SUSAN.
DO YOU THINK SO?
SURE! THIS JOB IS NOT FOR EVERYONE.
YOU'VE DONE THIS FOR A COUPLE OF YEARS NOW, ELIZABETH.... HAVE YOU GOT ANY GOOD ADVICE?
LET'S SEE...
YOU'VE GOT TO BE WELL-DISCIPLINED...
WHACK!!!
AND, KNOW HOW TO DISCIPLINE WELL.
LYNN

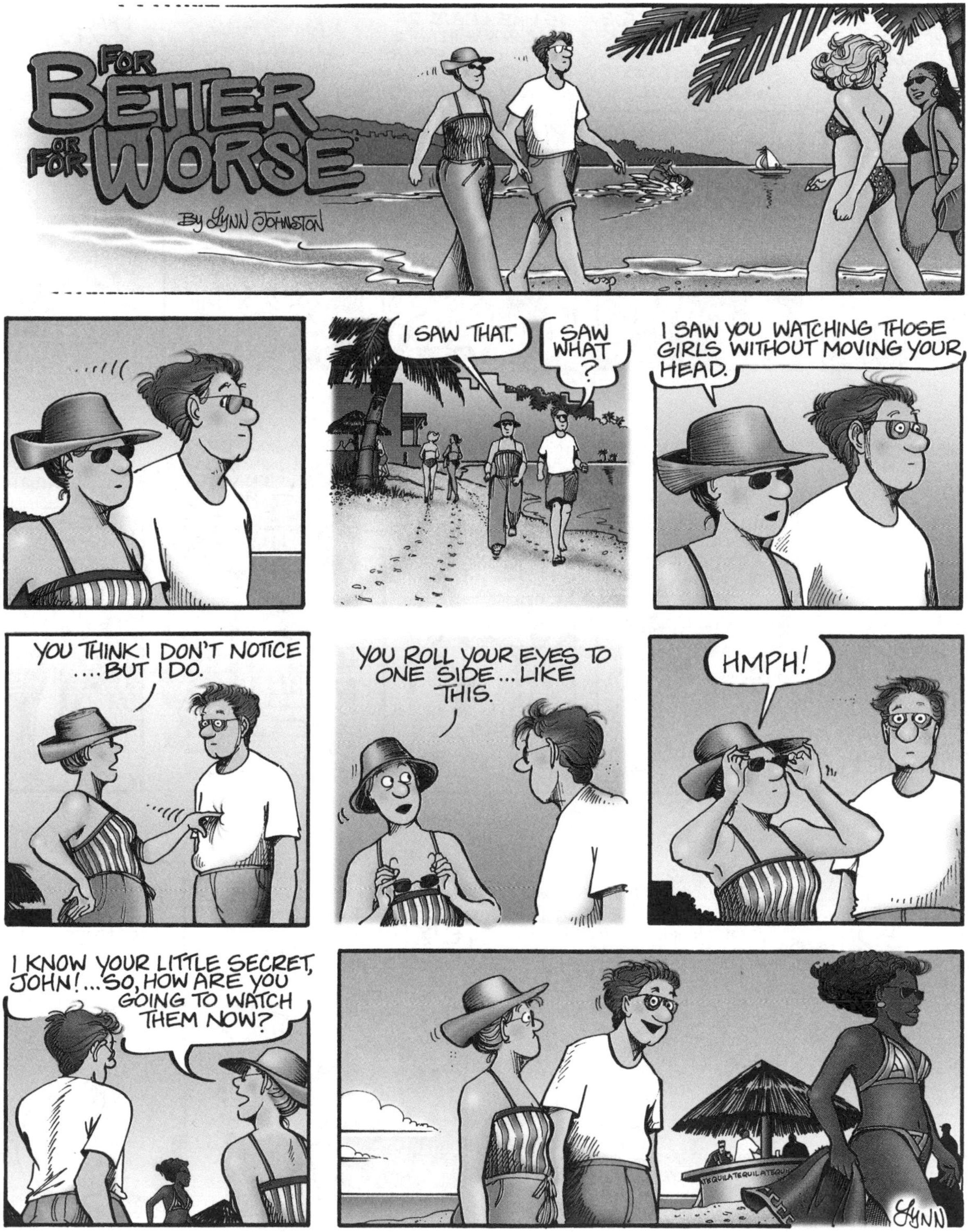
FOR BETTER OR FOR WORSE
BY LYNN JOHNSTON
I SAW THAT.
SAW WHAT?
I SAW YOU WATCHING THOSE GIRLS WITHOUT MOVING YOUR HEAD.
YOU THINK I DON'T NOTICE ....BUT I DO.
YOU ROLL YOUR EYES TO ONE SIDE... LIKE THIS.
HMPH!
I KNOW YOUR LITTLE SECRET, JOHN!...SO, HOW ARE YOU GOING TO WATCH THEM NOW?
TEQUILATEQUILATEQUI
LYNN

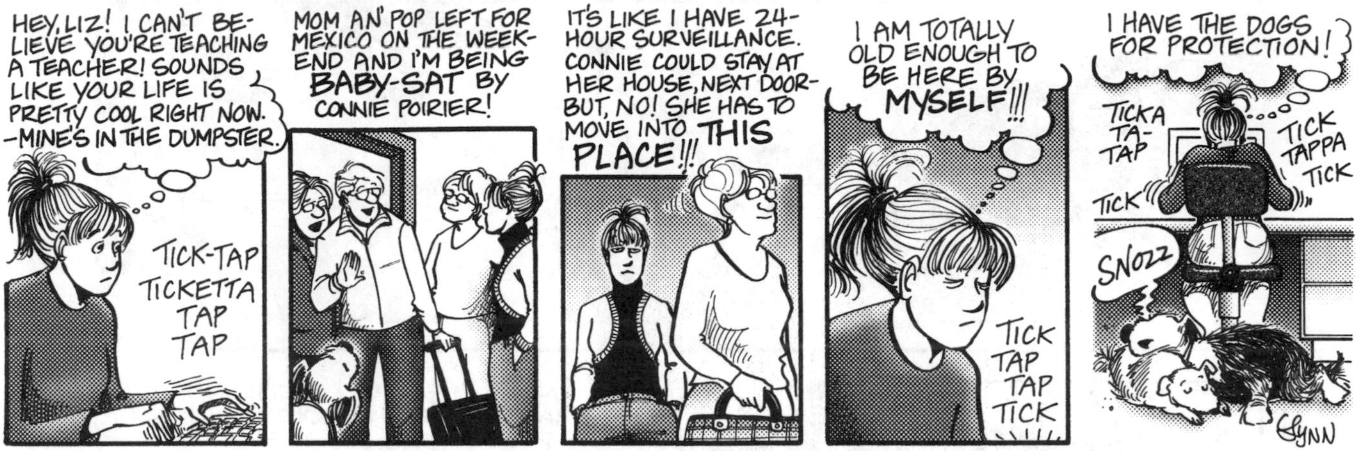
HEY, LIZ! I CAN'T BELIEVE YOU'RE TEACHING A TEACHER! SOUNDS LIKE YOUR LIFE IS PRETTY COOL RIGHT NOW. -MINE'S IN THE DUMPSTER.
TICK-TAP TICKETTA TAP TAP
MOM AN' POP LEFT FOR MEXICO ON THE WEEKEND AND I'M BEING BABY-SAT BY CONNIE POIRIER!
IT'S LIKE I HAVE 24-HOUR SURVEILLANCE. CONNIE COULD STAY AT HER HOUSE, NEXT DOOR - BUT, NO! SHE HAS TO MOVE INTO THIS PLACE!!!
I AM TOTALLY OLD ENOUGH TO BE HERE BY MYSELF!!!
TICK TAP TAP TICK
I HAVE THE DOGS FOR PROTECTION!
TICKA TA-TAP
TICK TAPPA TICK
TICK
SNOZZ
LYNN

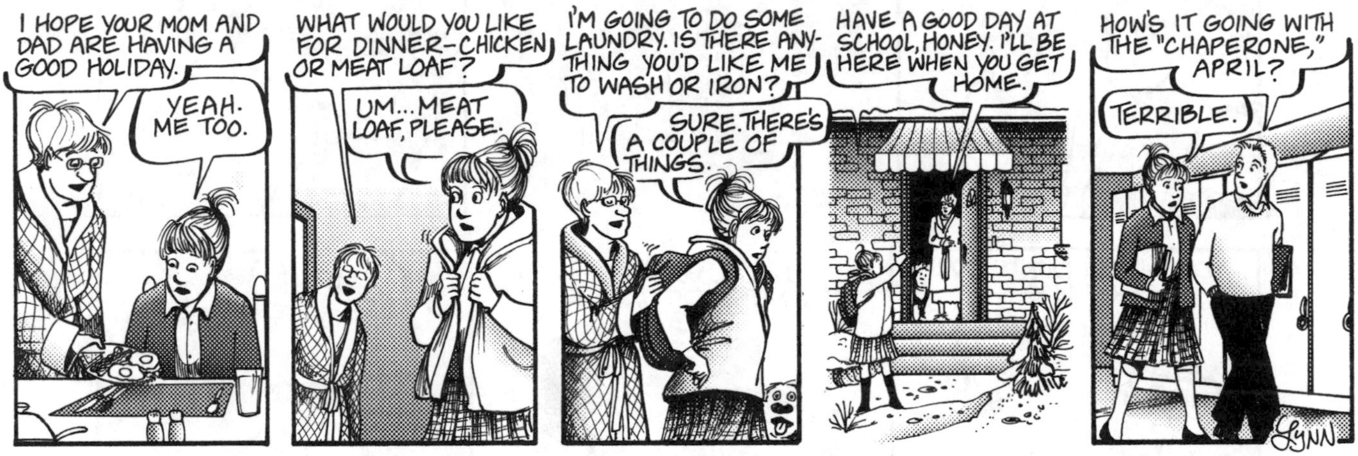
I HOPE YOUR MOM AND DAD ARE HAVING A GOOD HOLIDAY.
YEAH. ME TOO.
WHAT WOULD YOU LIKE FOR DINNER-CHICKEN OR MEAT LOAF?
UM... MEAT LOAF, PLEASE.
I'M GOING TO DO SOME LAUNDRY. IS THERE ANYTHING YOU'D LIKE ME TO WASH OR IRON?
SURE. THERE'S A COUPLE OF THINGS.
HAVE A GOOD DAY AT SCHOOL, HONEY. I'LL BE HERE WHEN YOU GET HOME.
HOW'S IT GOING WITH THE "CHAPERONE," APRIL?
TERRIBLE.
LYNN

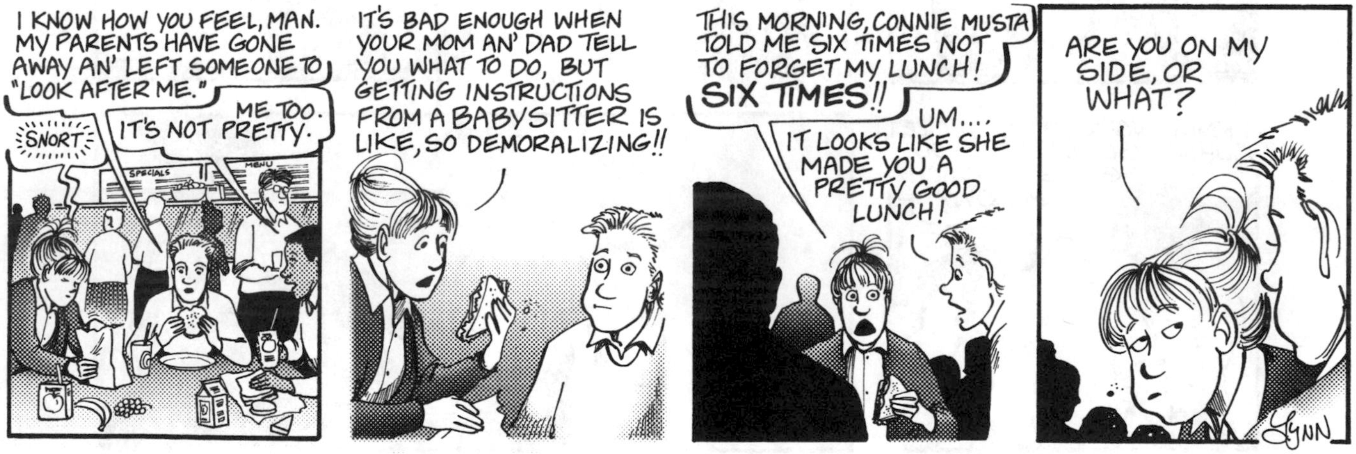
I KNOW HOW YOU FEEL, MAN. MY PARENTS HAVE GONE AWAY AN' LEFT SOMEONE TO "LOOK AFTER ME."
ME TOO.
SNORT
IT'S NOT PRETTY.
SPECIALS
MENU
IT'S BAD ENOUGH WHEN YOUR MOM AN' DAD TELL YOU WHAT TO DO, BUT GETTING INSTRUCTIONS FROM A BABYSITTER IS LIKE, SO DEMORALIZING!!
THIS MORNING, CONNIE MUSTA TOLD ME SIX TIMES NOT TO FORGET MY LUNCH! SIX TIMES!!
UM.... IT LOOKS LIKE SHE MADE YOU A PRETTY GOOD LUNCH!
ARE YOU ON MY SIDE, OR WHAT?
LYNN

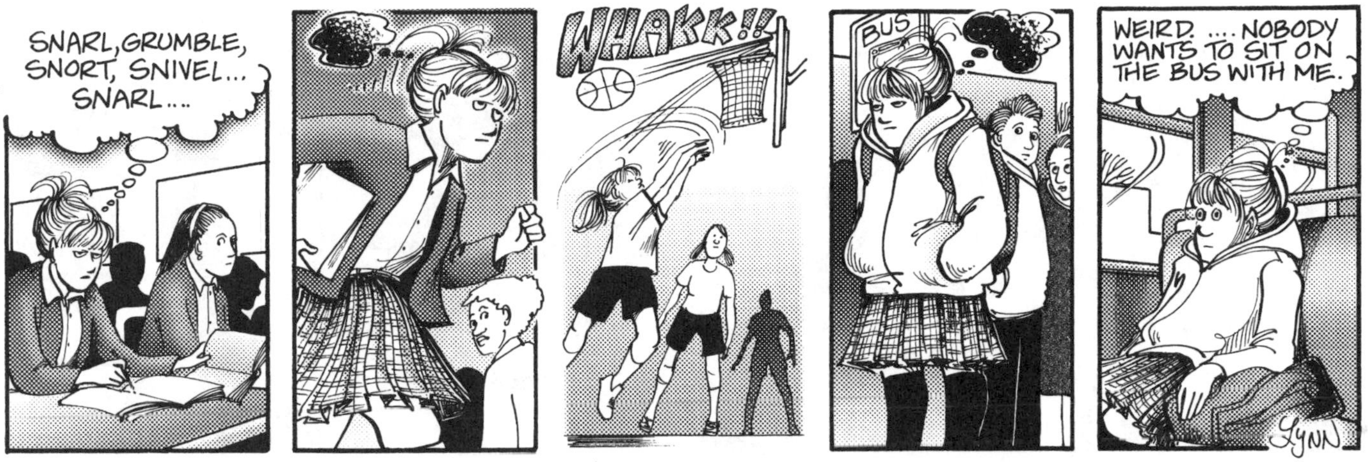
SNARL, GRUMBLE, SNORT, SNIVEL... SNARL....
WHAKK!!
BUS
WEIRD. .... NOBODY WANTS TO SIT ON THE BUS WITH ME.

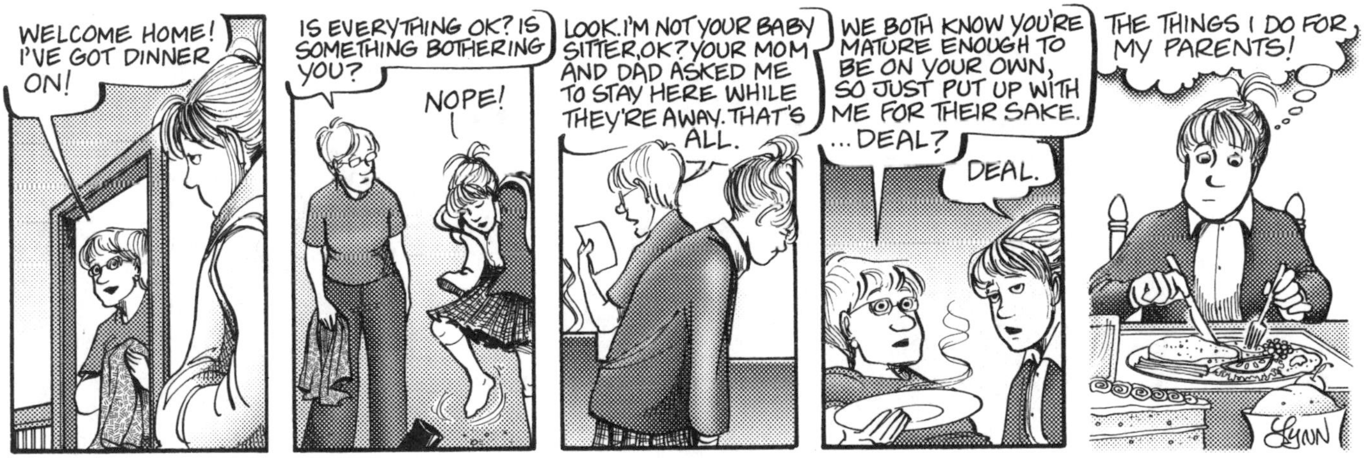
WELCOME HOME! I'VE GOT DINNER ON!
IS EVERYTHING OK? IS SOMETHING BOTHERING YOU?
NOPE!
LOOK. I'M NOT YOUR BABY SITTER, OK? YOUR MOM AND DAD ASKED ME TO STAY HERE WHILE THEY'RE AWAY. THAT'S ALL.
WE BOTH KNOW YOU'RE MATURE ENOUGH TO BE ON YOUR OWN, SO JUST PUT UP WITH ME FOR THEIR SAKE. ...DEAL?
DEAL.
THE THINGS I DO FOR MY PARENTS!

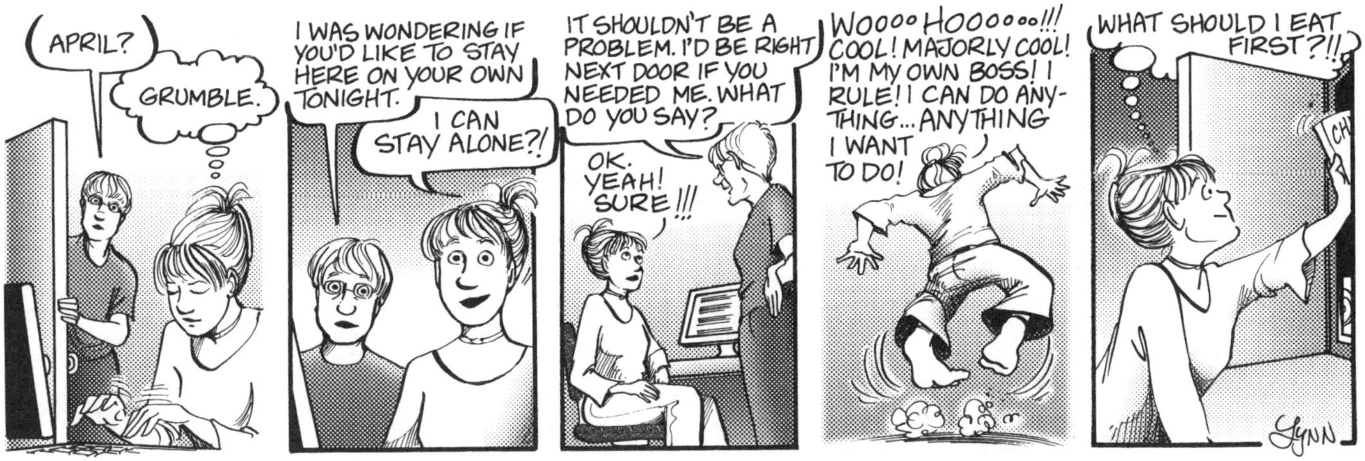
APRIL?
GRUMBLE.
I WAS WONDERING IF YOU'D LIKE TO STAY HERE ON YOUR OWN TONIGHT.
I CAN STAY ALONE?!
IT SHOULDN'T BE A PROBLEM. I'D BE RIGHT NEXT DOOR IF YOU NEEDED ME. WHAT DO YOU SAY?
OK. YEAH! SURE!!!
WOOOO HOOOOOOO!!! COOL! MAJORLY COOL! I'M MY OWN BOSS! I RULE! I CAN DO ANYTHING... ANYTHING I WANT TO DO!
WHAT SHOULD I EAT FIRST?!!

COLA, NIPPY-NUTZ, CHEEZ-O-PUFFS, CHOKO MALLOW BARS, AN' CEREAL! ....A BALANCED DIET!

ALONE, ALONE - I LOVE BEING ALONE! I CAN WATCH T.V., GO ONLINE, TALK ON THE PHONE... I'M **FREE**!

HAH! 12 O'CLOCK! - I'M NEVER ALLOWED TO STAY UP THIS LATE ON A SCHOOL NIGHT!

STUPIDITY ROCKS!

HORROR IN THE HOUSE
THIS FILM IS FO MATURE AUDIENC ONLY

lynn

BIP! IT'S 2 A.M.! I'D BETTER HIT THE SACK.

MAN, THAT WAS THE MOST CREEPY AND DISGUSTING MOVIE I'VE EVER SEEN. ...BUT HEY! I CAN DEAL.

CREAK...CREAK... DRIP......CRAAAKK... MMMMM.....CREAK... WHSHHH ....MMM

I'M ALONE IN THE HOUSE. NO BIGGIE.

CREEAK... DRIP..... WHHSSHHH....CLICK! MMMMMHH....CREAK...

I'M ALONE IN THE HOUSE—AND I'M COOL.

CLICK!...CLICK!...MMM ....CLICK!

I'M ALONE IN THE HOUSE!

lynn

CHILL OUT, APRIL. BE CALM, BE COOL. YOU WANTED TO STAY IN THE HOUSE ALONE.

CREEAK   WHMMM SHHH

YOU WATCHED A MOVIE. IT WAS ONLY A MOVIE. THERE'S NO SUCH THING AS DEMONIC FLESH-EATING ROACH PEOPLE. THERE'S NOBODY DOWNSTAIRS ...NOBODY!

THERE. MY DOOR IS LOCKED. I'M TOTALLY SAFE. NOTHING CAN GET IN.

WHAT DO YOU MEAN, YOU HAFTA GO OUTSIDE ?!!

lynn

34

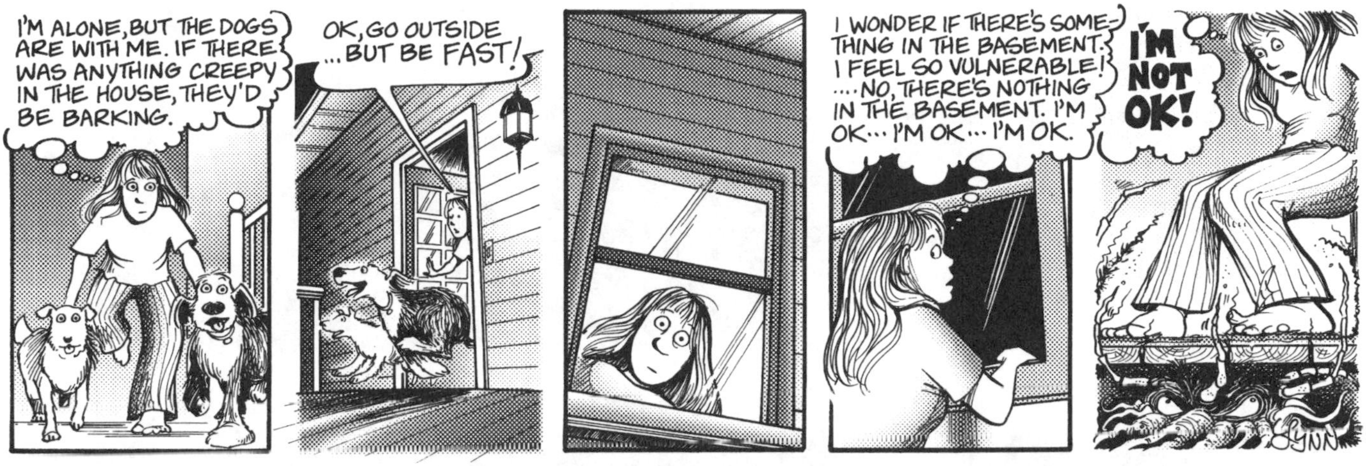
I'M ALONE, BUT THE DOGS ARE WITH ME. IF THERE WAS ANYTHING CREEPY IN THE HOUSE, THEY'D BE BARKING.
OK, GO OUTSIDE ...BUT BE FAST!
I WONDER IF THERE'S SOMETHING IN THE BASEMENT. I FEEL SO VULNERABLE! ....NO, THERE'S NOTHING IN THE BASEMENT. I'M OK... I'M OK... I'M OK.
I'M NOT OK!
LYNN

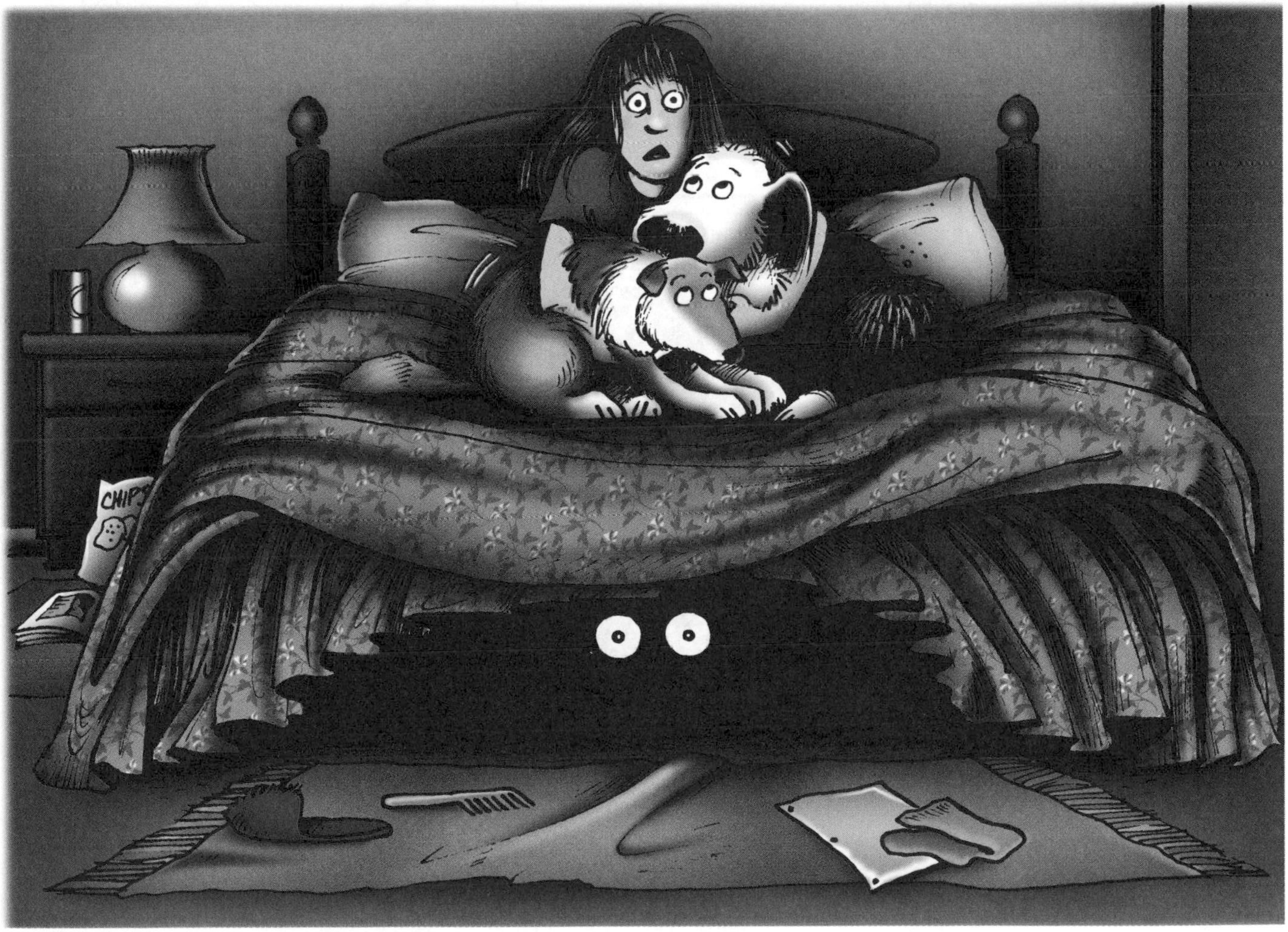
CHIPS

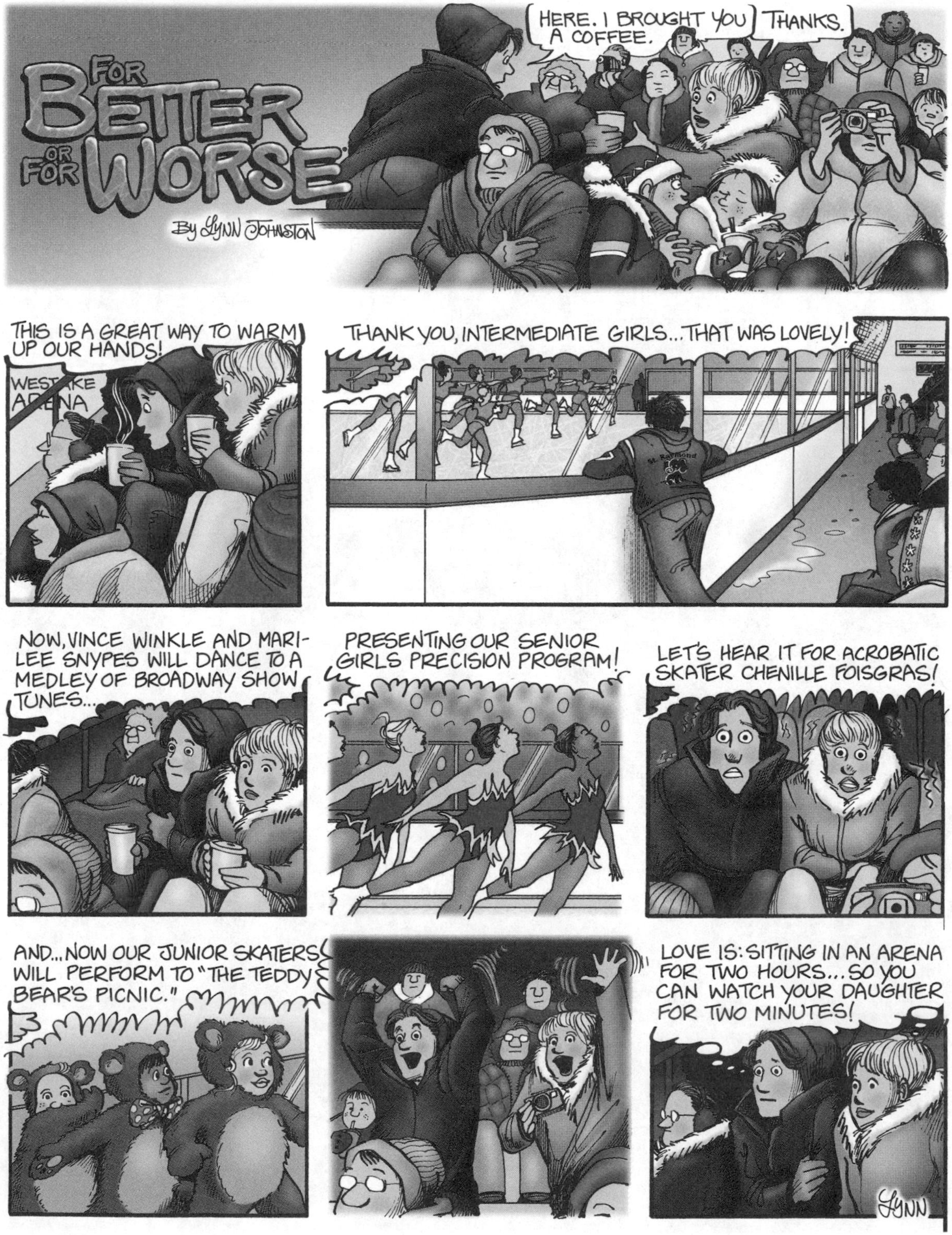
FOR BETTER OR FOR WORSE
BY LYNN JOHNSTON
HERE. I BROUGHT YOU A COFFEE.
THANKS.
THIS IS A GREAT WAY TO WARM UP OUR HANDS!
THANK YOU, INTERMEDIATE GIRLS... THAT WAS LOVELY!
NOW, VINCE WINKLE AND MARI-LEE SNYPES WILL DANCE TO A MEDLEY OF BROADWAY SHOW TUNES...
PRESENTING OUR SENIOR GIRLS PRECISION PROGRAM!
LET'S HEAR IT FOR ACROBATIC SKATER CHENILLE FOISGRAS!
AND... NOW OUR JUNIOR SKATERS WILL PERFORM TO "THE TEDDY BEAR'S PICNIC."
LOVE IS: SITTING IN AN ARENA FOR TWO HOURS... SO YOU CAN WATCH YOUR DAUGHTER FOR TWO MINUTES!
LYNN

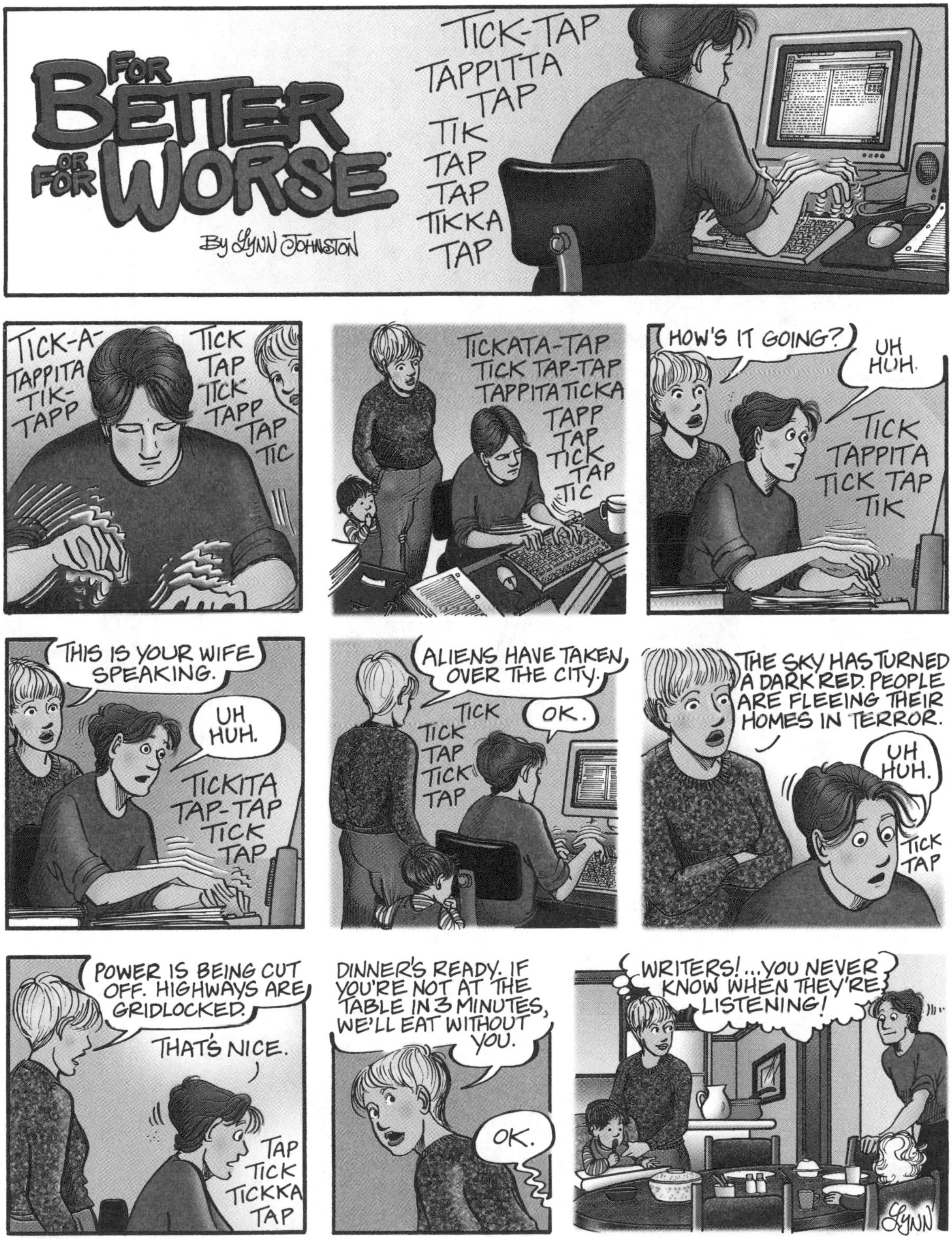
FOR BETTER OR FOR WORSE
By Lynn Johnston
TICK-TAP TAPPITTA TAP TIK TAP TAP TIKKA TAP
TICK-A-TAPPITA TIK-TAPP
TICK TAP TICK TAPP TAP TIC
TICKATA-TAP TICK TAP-TAP TAPPITATICKA TAPP TAP TICK TAP TIC
HOW'S IT GOING?
UH HUH.
TICK TAPPITA TICK TAP TIK
THIS IS YOUR WIFE SPEAKING.
UH HUH.
TICKITA TAP-TAP TICK TAP
ALIENS HAVE TAKEN OVER THE CITY.
TICK TICK TAP TICK TAP
OK.
THE SKY HAS TURNED A DARK RED. PEOPLE ARE FLEEING THEIR HOMES IN TERROR.
UH HUH.
TICK TAP
POWER IS BEING CUT OFF. HIGHWAYS ARE GRIDLOCKED.
THAT'S NICE.
TAP TICK TICKKA TAP
DINNER'S READY. IF YOU'RE NOT AT THE TABLE IN 3 MINUTES, WE'LL EAT WITHOUT YOU.
OK.
WRITERS! ...YOU NEVER KNOW WHEN THEY'RE LISTENING!
LYNN

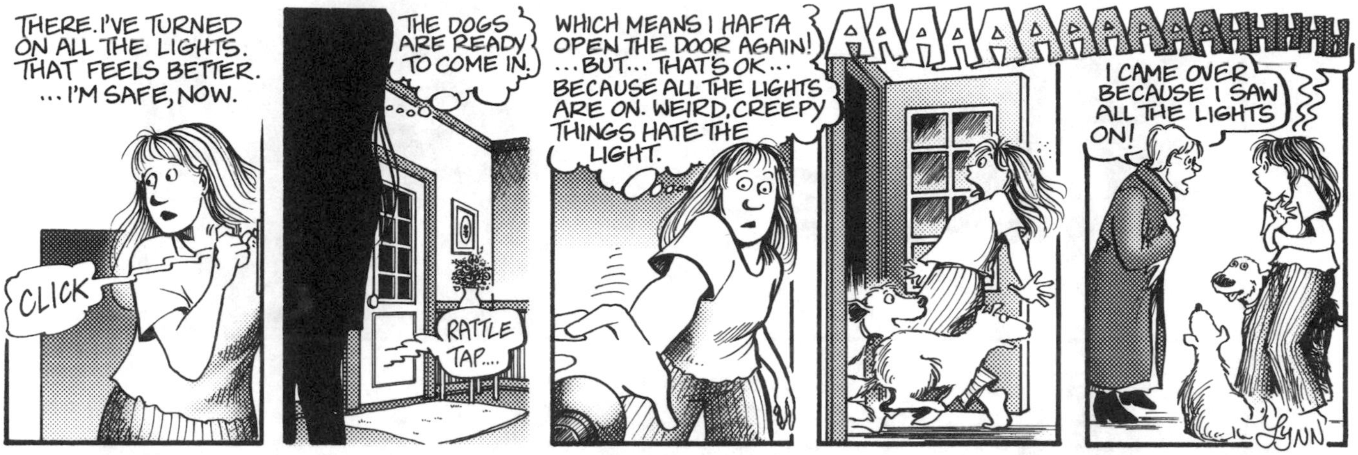
THERE. I'VE TURNED ON ALL THE LIGHTS. THAT FEELS BETTER. ... I'M SAFE, NOW.
CLICK
THE DOGS ARE READY TO COME IN.
RATTLE TAP....
WHICH MEANS I HAFTA OPEN THE DOOR AGAIN! ... BUT... THAT'S OK... BECAUSE ALL THE LIGHTS ARE ON. WEIRD, CREEPY THINGS HATE THE LIGHT.
AAAAAAAAAAAAHHHH
I CAME OVER BECAUSE I SAW ALL THE LIGHTS ON!
LYNN

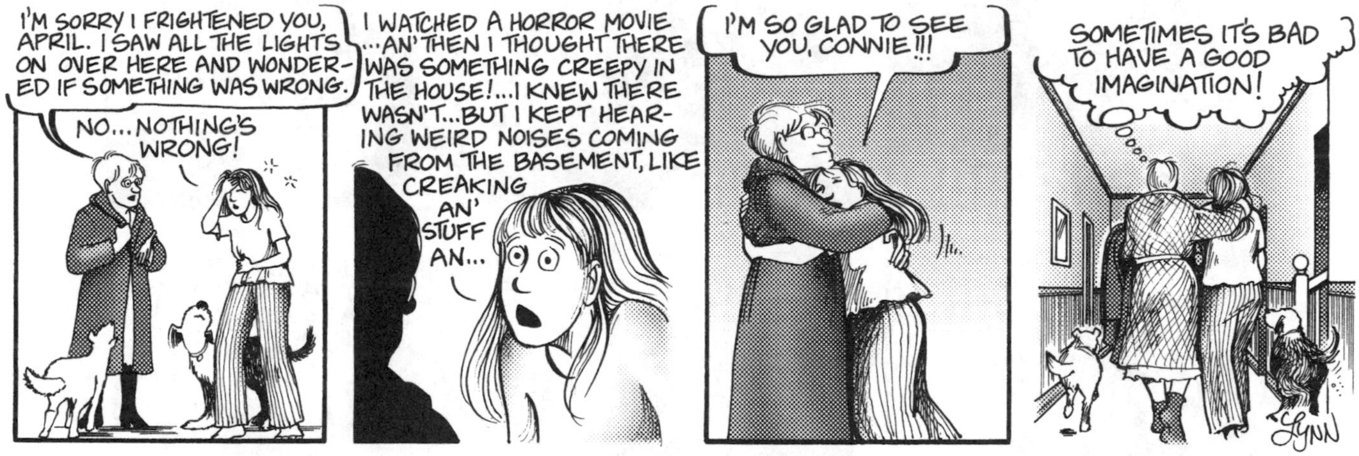
I'M SORRY I FRIGHTENED YOU, APRIL. I SAW ALL THE LIGHTS ON OVER HERE AND WONDERED IF SOMETHING WAS WRONG.
NO... NOTHING'S WRONG!
I WATCHED A HORROR MOVIE ...AN' THEN I THOUGHT THERE WAS SOMETHING CREEPY IN THE HOUSE!...I KNEW THERE WASN'T...BUT I KEPT HEARING WEIRD NOISES COMING FROM THE BASEMENT, LIKE CREAKING AN' STUFF AN...
I'M SO GLAD TO SEE YOU, CONNIE!!!
SOMETIMES IT'S BAD TO HAVE A GOOD IMAGINATION!
LYNN

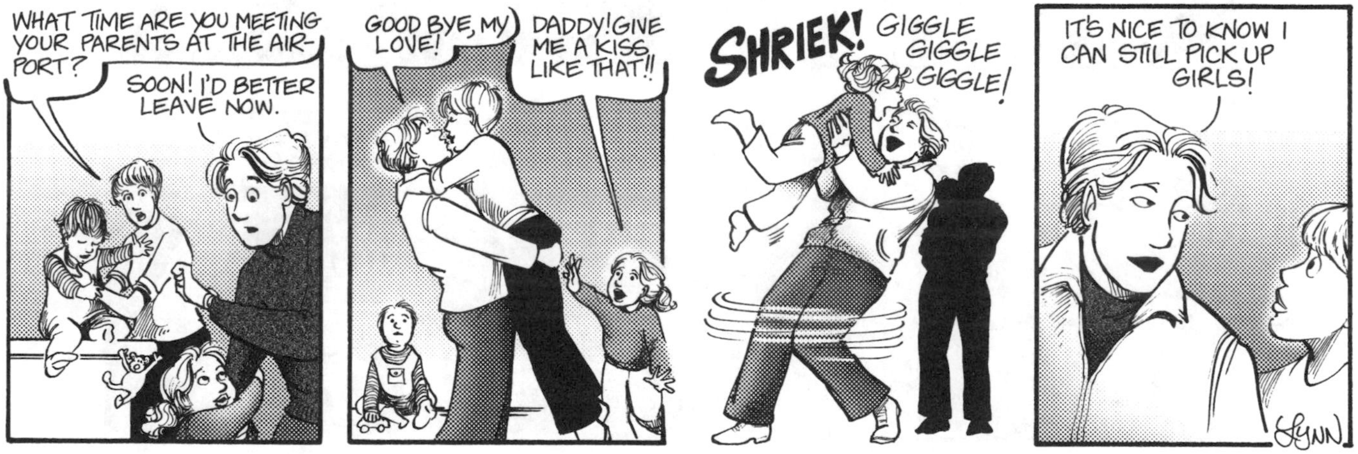
WHAT TIME ARE YOU MEETING YOUR PARENTS AT THE AIRPORT?
SOON! I'D BETTER LEAVE NOW.
GOOD BYE, MY LOVE!
DADDY! GIVE ME A KISS LIKE THAT!!
SHRIEK!
GIGGLE GIGGLE GIGGLE GIGGLE!
IT'S NICE TO KNOW I CAN STILL PICK UP GIRLS!
LYNN

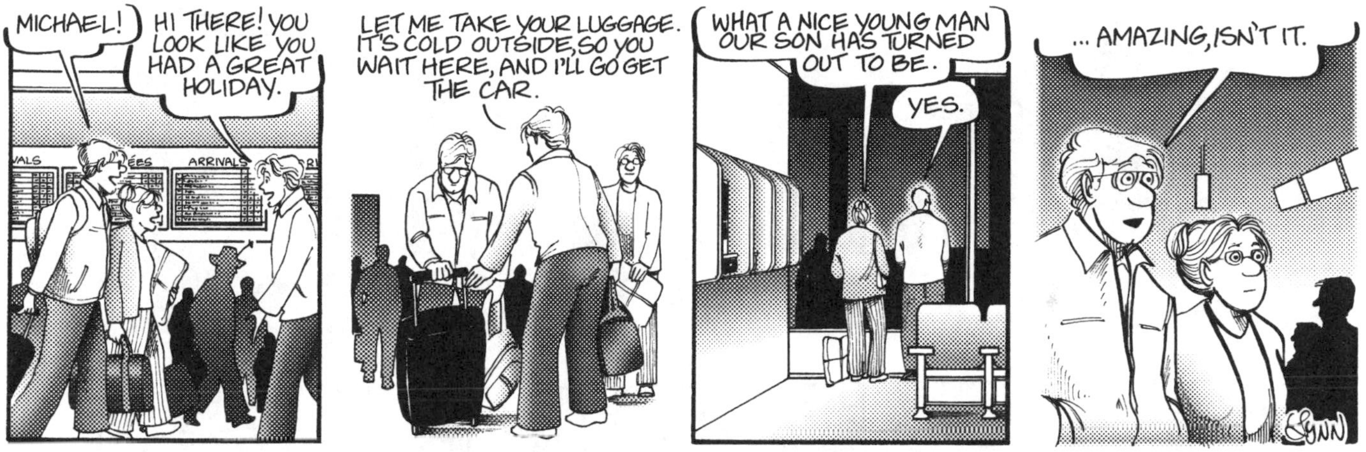
MICHAEL!
HI THERE! YOU LOOK LIKE YOU HAD A GREAT HOLIDAY.
ARRIVALS
LET ME TAKE YOUR LUGGAGE. IT'S COLD OUTSIDE, SO YOU WAIT HERE, AND I'LL GO GET THE CAR.
WHAT A NICE YOUNG MAN OUR SON HAS TURNED OUT TO BE.
YES.
... AMAZING, ISN'T IT.
LYNN

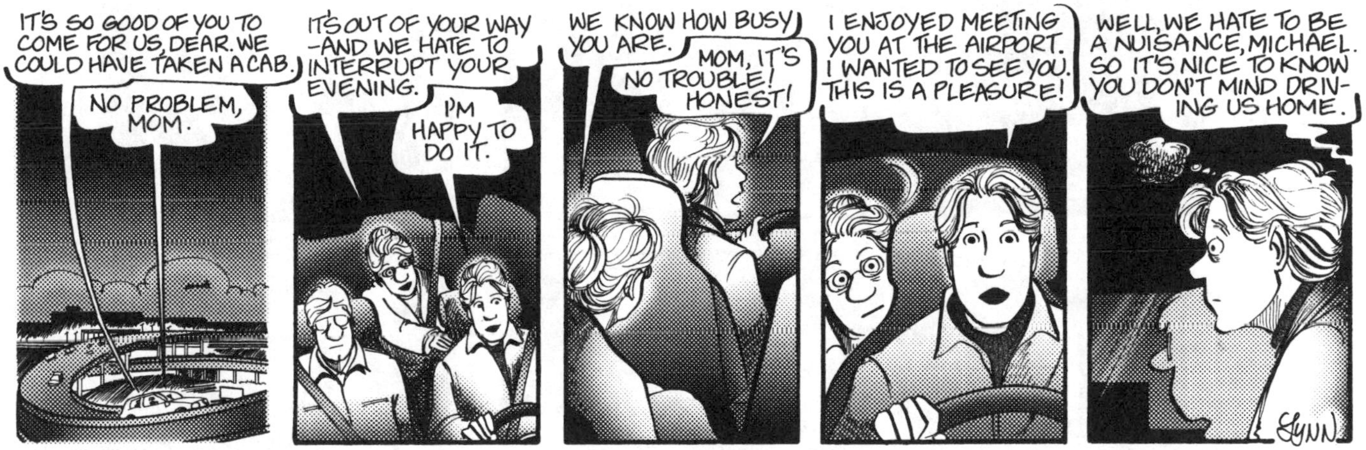
IT'S SO GOOD OF YOU TO COME FOR US, DEAR. WE COULD HAVE TAKEN A CAB.
NO PROBLEM, MOM.
IT'S OUT OF YOUR WAY -AND WE HATE TO INTERRUPT YOUR EVENING.
I'M HAPPY TO DO IT.
WE KNOW HOW BUSY YOU ARE.
MOM, IT'S NO TROUBLE! HONEST!
I ENJOYED MEETING YOU AT THE AIRPORT. I WANTED TO SEE YOU. THIS IS A PLEASURE!
WELL, WE HATE TO BE A NUISANCE, MICHAEL. SO IT'S NICE TO KNOW YOU DON'T MIND DRIVING US HOME.
LYNN

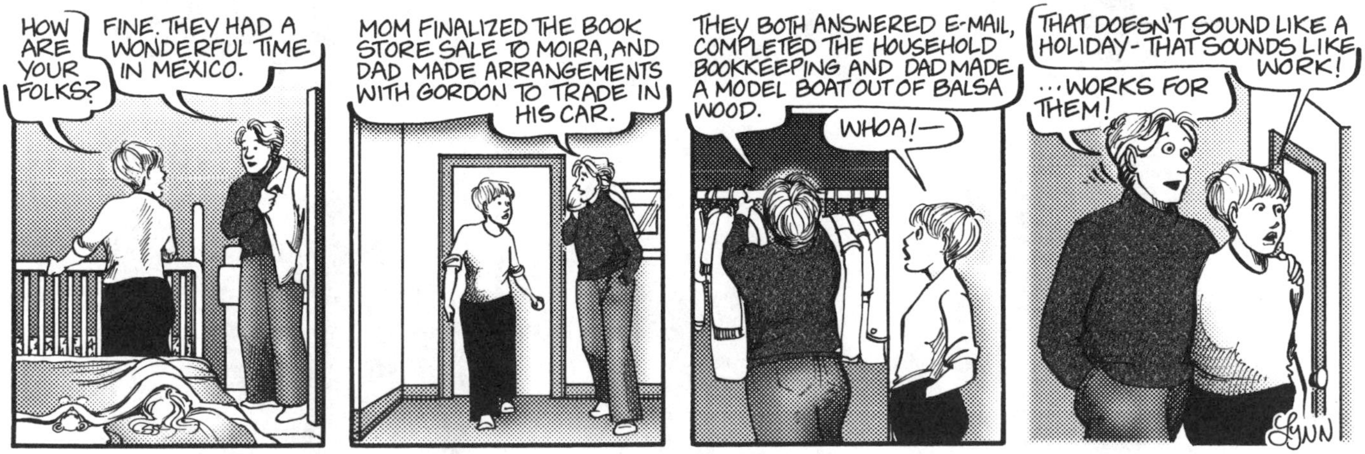
HOW ARE YOUR FOLKS?
FINE. THEY HAD A WONDERFUL TIME IN MEXICO.
MOM FINALIZED THE BOOK STORE SALE TO MOIRA, AND DAD MADE ARRANGEMENTS WITH GORDON TO TRADE IN HIS CAR.
THEY BOTH ANSWERED E-MAIL, COMPLETED THE HOUSEHOLD BOOKKEEPING AND DAD MADE A MODEL BOAT OUT OF BALSA WOOD.
WHOA!—
THAT DOESN'T SOUND LIKE A HOLIDAY- THAT SOUNDS LIKE WORK!
... WORKS FOR THEM!
LYNN

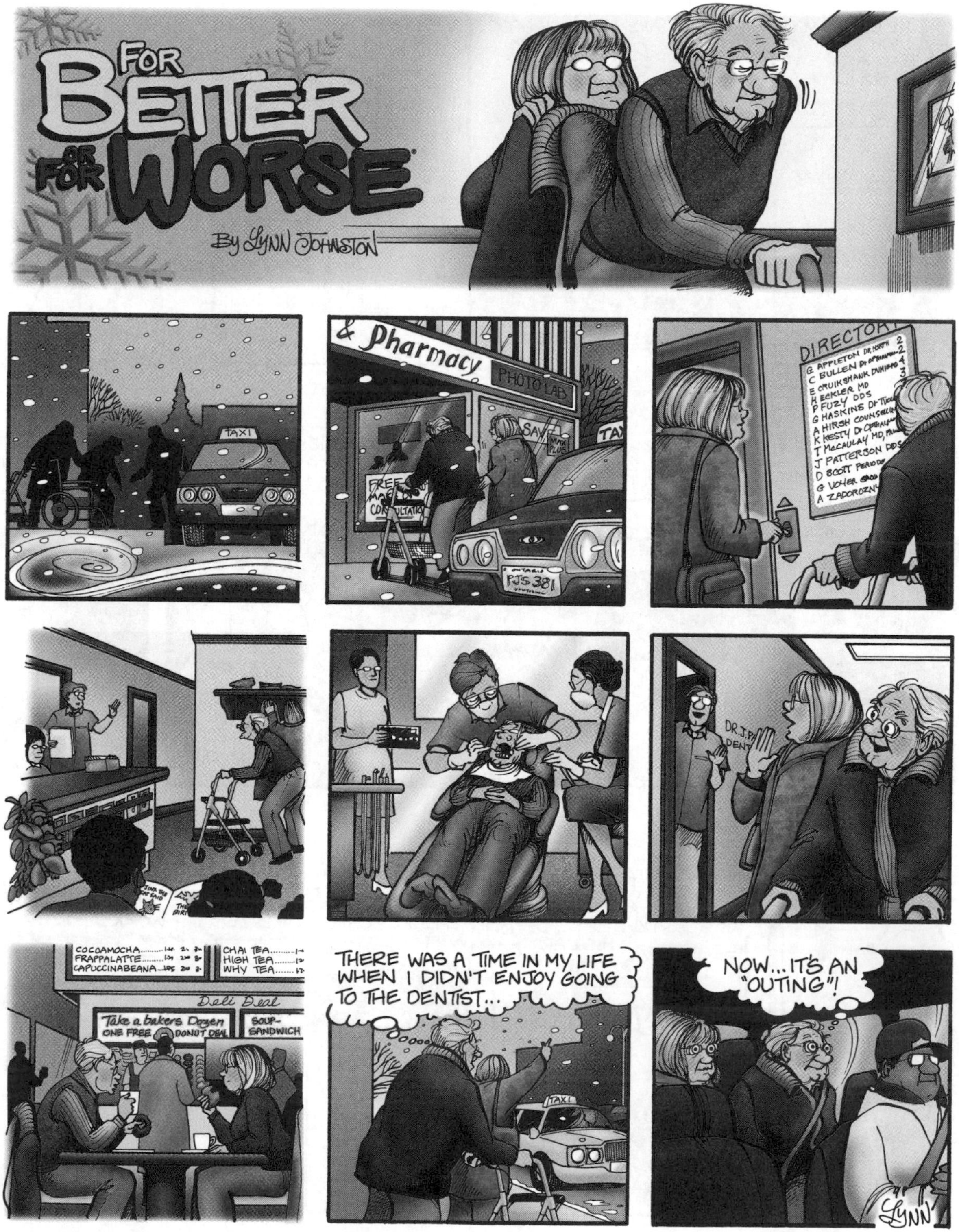
For Better or For Worse
By Lynn Johnston
TAXI
& Pharmacy
PHOTO LAB
COCOAMOCHA
FRAPPALATTE
CAPUCCINABEANA
CHAI TEA
HIGH TEA
WHY TEA
Deli Deal
Take a bakers Dozen
ONE FREE DONUT DEAL
SOUP-SANDWICH
THERE WAS A TIME IN MY LIFE WHEN I DIDN'T ENJOY GOING TO THE DENTIST...
NOW... IT'S AN "OUTING"!
LYNN

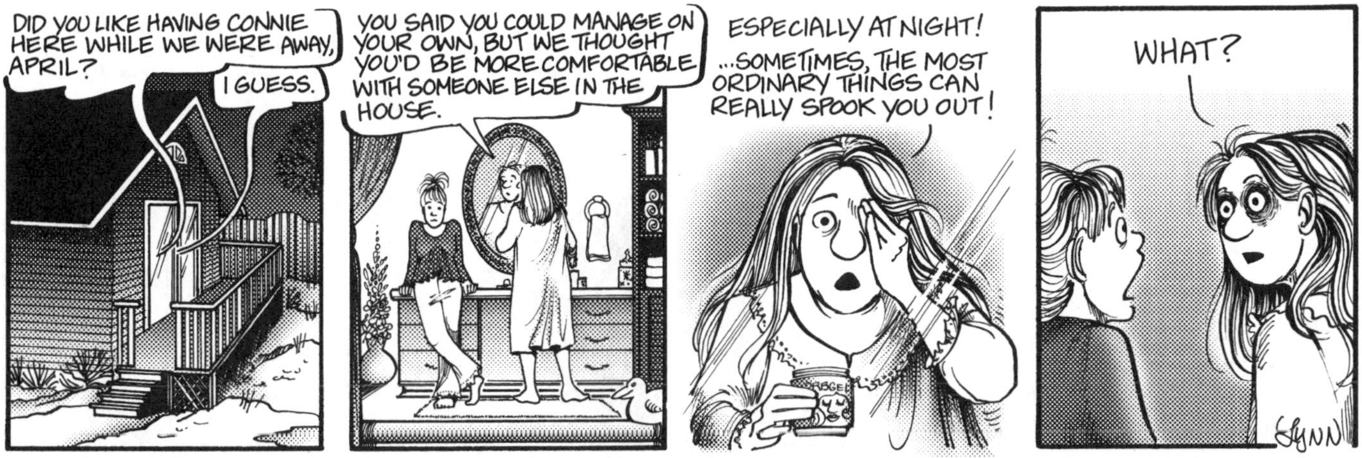
DID YOU LIKE HAVING CONNIE HERE WHILE WE WERE AWAY, APRIL?
I GUESS.
YOU SAID YOU COULD MANAGE ON YOUR OWN, BUT WE THOUGHT YOU'D BE MORE COMFORTABLE WITH SOMEONE ELSE IN THE HOUSE.
ESPECIALLY AT NIGHT!
...SOMETIMES, THE MOST ORDINARY THINGS CAN REALLY SPOOK YOU OUT!
WHAT?

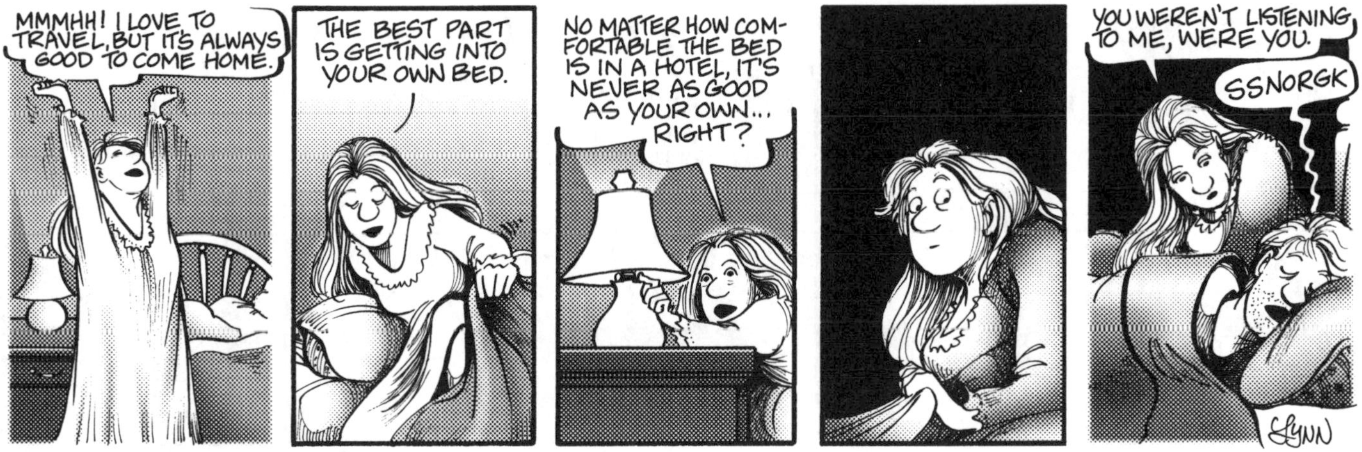
MMMHH! I LOVE TO TRAVEL, BUT IT'S ALWAYS GOOD TO COME HOME.
THE BEST PART IS GETTING INTO YOUR OWN BED.
NO MATTER HOW COMFORTABLE THE BED IS IN A HOTEL, IT'S NEVER AS GOOD AS YOUR OWN... RIGHT?
YOU WEREN'T LISTENING TO ME, WERE YOU.
SSNORGK

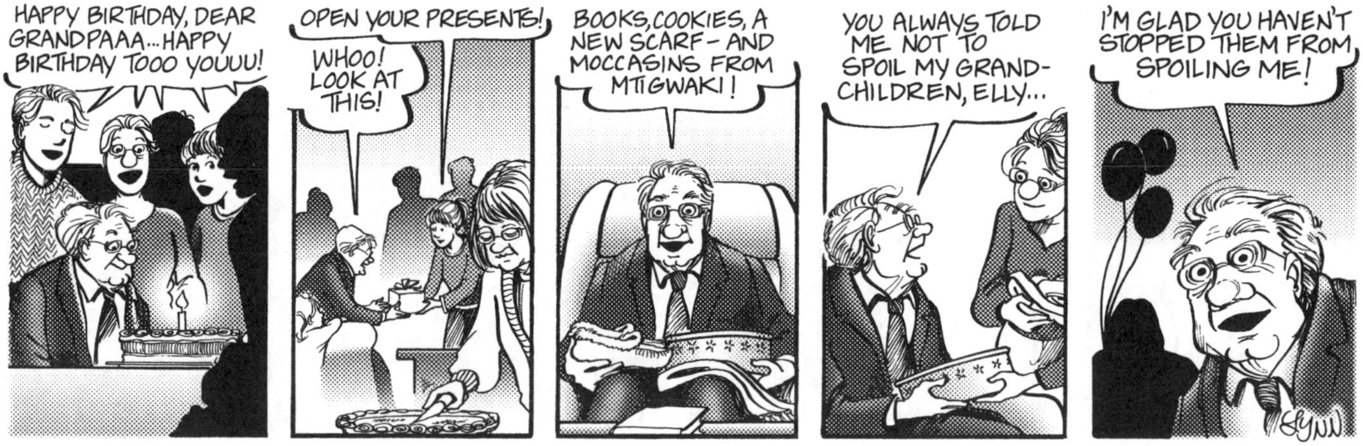
HAPPY BIRTHDAY, DEAR GRANDPAAA... HAPPY BIRTHDAY TOOO YOUUU!
OPEN YOUR PRESENTS!
WHOO! LOOK AT THIS!
BOOKS, COOKIES, A NEW SCARF – AND MOCCASINS FROM MTIGWAKI!
YOU ALWAYS TOLD ME NOT TO SPOIL MY GRANDCHILDREN, ELLY...
I'M GLAD YOU HAVEN'T STOPPED THEM FROM SPOILING ME!

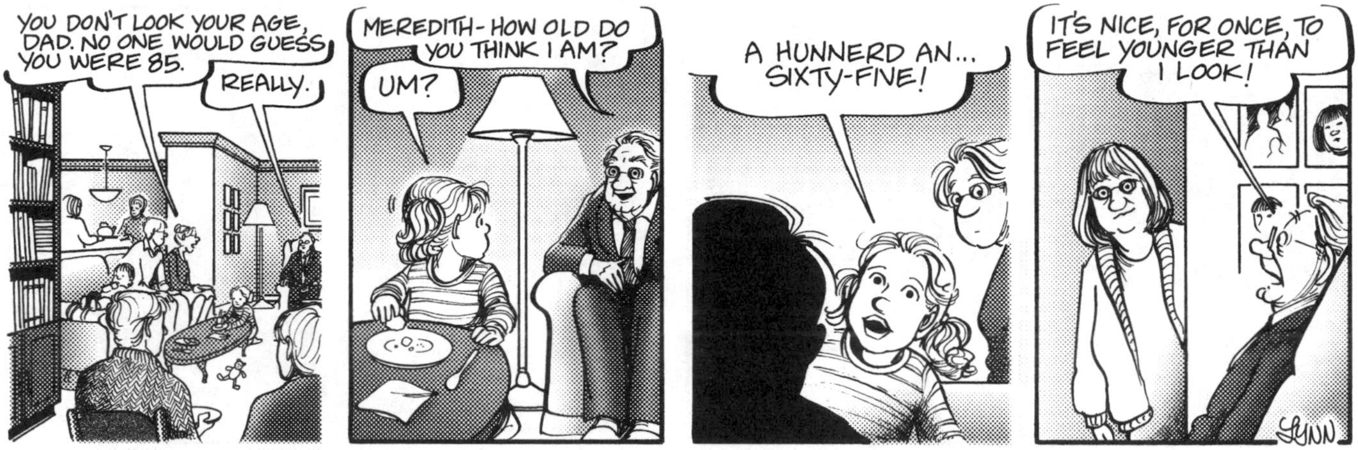
YOU DON'T LOOK YOUR AGE, DAD. NO ONE WOULD GUESS YOU WERE 85.
REALLY.
MEREDITH- HOW OLD DO YOU THINK I AM?
UM?
A HUNNERD AN... SIXTY-FIVE!
IT'S NICE, FOR ONCE, TO FEEL YOUNGER THAN I LOOK!
LYNN

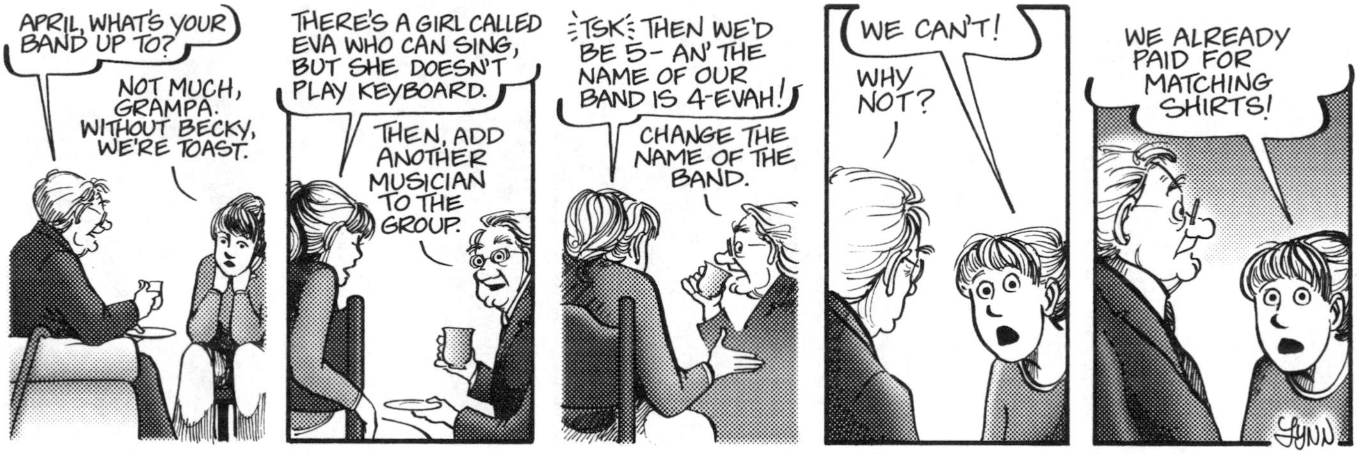
APRIL, WHAT'S YOUR BAND UP TO?
NOT MUCH, GRAMPA. WITHOUT BECKY, WE'RE TOAST.
THERE'S A GIRL CALLED EVA WHO CAN SING, BUT SHE DOESN'T PLAY KEYBOARD.
THEN, ADD ANOTHER MUSICIAN TO THE GROUP.
TSK
THEN WE'D BE 5- AN' THE NAME OF OUR BAND IS 4-EVAH!
CHANGE THE NAME OF THE BAND.
WE CAN'T!
WHY NOT?
WE ALREADY PAID FOR MATCHING SHIRTS!
LYNN

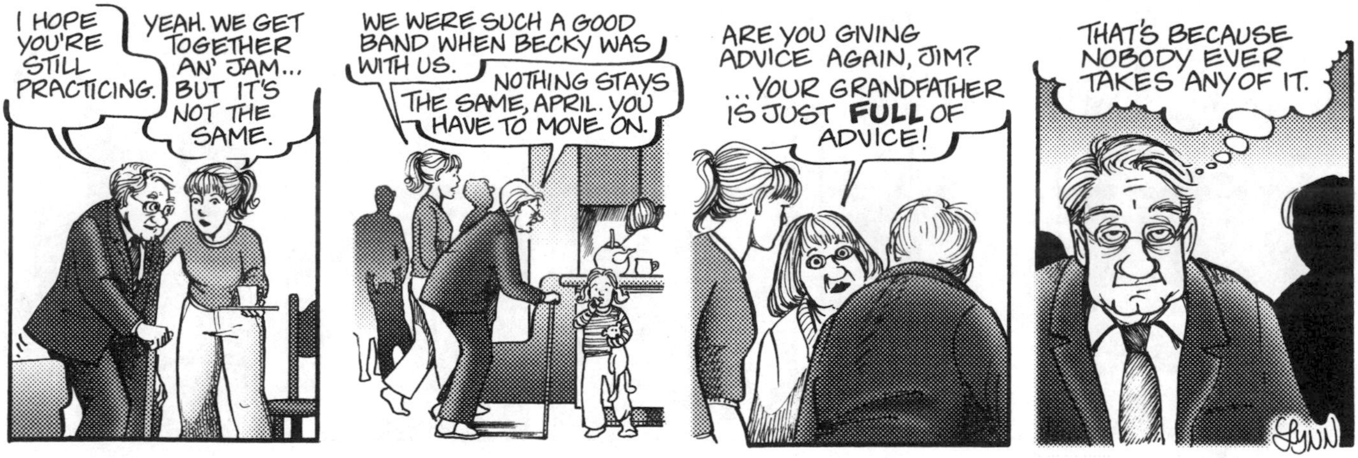
I HOPE YOU'RE STILL PRACTICING.
YEAH. WE GET TOGETHER AN' JAM... BUT IT'S NOT THE SAME.
WE WERE SUCH A GOOD BAND WHEN BECKY WAS WITH US.
NOTHING STAYS THE SAME, APRIL. YOU HAVE TO MOVE ON.
ARE YOU GIVING ADVICE AGAIN, JIM?
...YOUR GRANDFATHER IS JUST FULL OF ADVICE!
THAT'S BECAUSE NOBODY EVER TAKES ANY OF IT.
LYNN

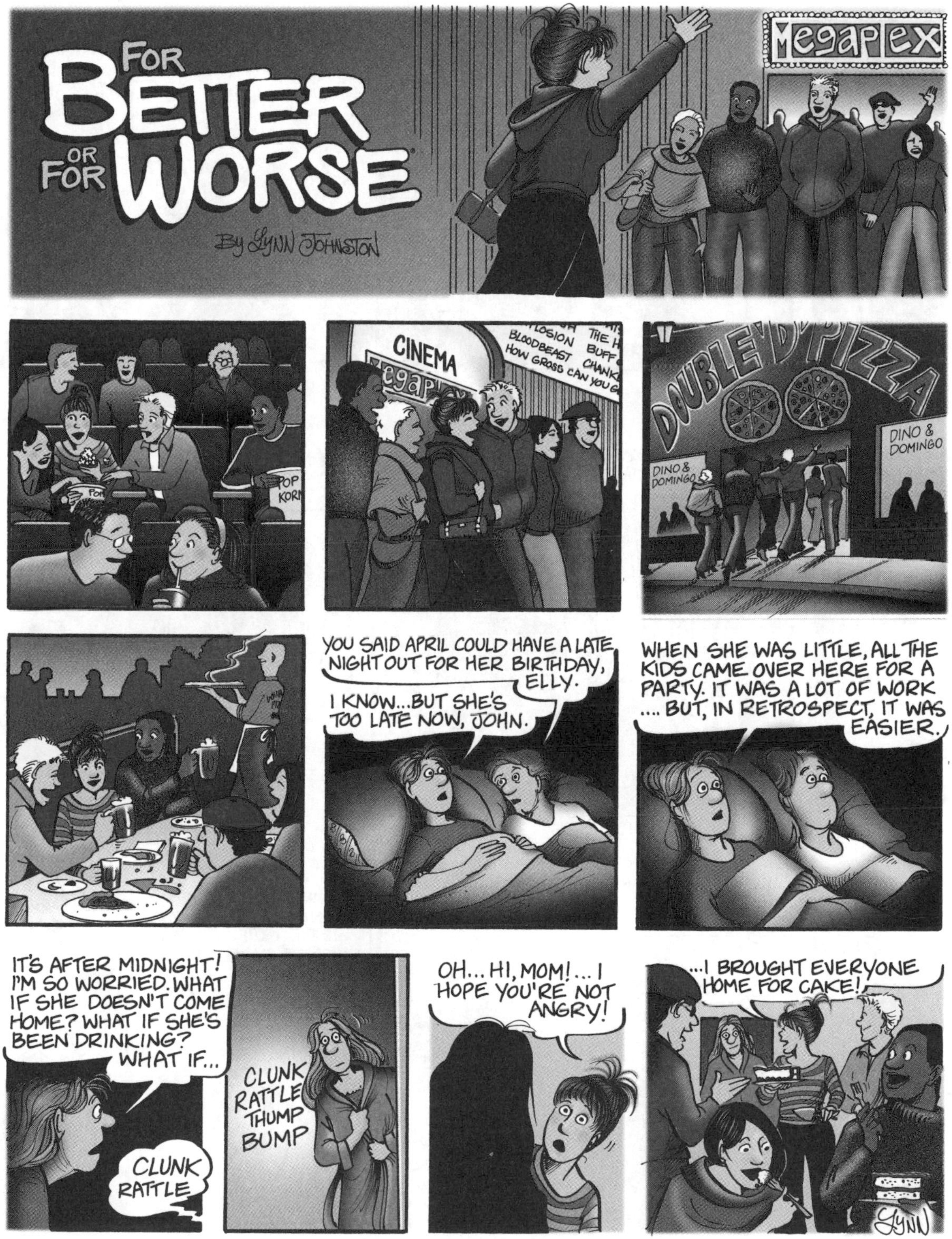
FOR BETTER OR FOR WORSE
BY LYNN JOHNSTON
MEGAPLEX
CINEMA
MEGAPLEX
BLOODBEAST
HOW GROSS CAN YOU
POP KORN
DOUBLE 'D' PIZZA
DINO & DOMINGO
DINO & DOMINGO
YOU SAID APRIL COULD HAVE A LATE NIGHT OUT FOR HER BIRTHDAY, ELLY.
I KNOW...BUT SHE'S TOO LATE NOW, JOHN.
WHEN SHE WAS LITTLE, ALL THE KIDS CAME OVER HERE FOR A PARTY. IT WAS A LOT OF WORK .... BUT, IN RETROSPECT, IT WAS EASIER.
IT'S AFTER MIDNIGHT! I'M SO WORRIED. WHAT IF SHE DOESN'T COME HOME? WHAT IF SHE'S BEEN DRINKING? WHAT IF...
CLUNK RATTLE
CLUNK RATTLE THUMP BUMP
OH... HI, MOM!... I HOPE YOU'RE NOT ANGRY!
...I BROUGHT EVERYONE HOME FOR CAKE!
LYNN

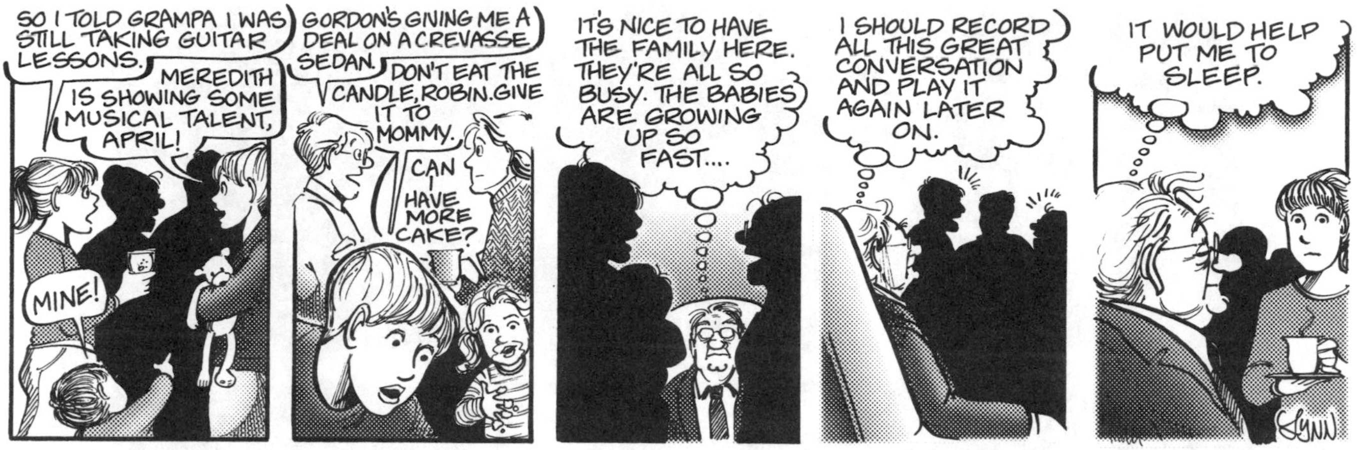
SO I TOLD GRAMPA I WAS STILL TAKING GUITAR LESSONS.
MEREDITH IS SHOWING SOME MUSICAL TALENT, APRIL!
MINE!
GORDON'S GIVING ME A DEAL ON A CREVASSE SEDAN.
DON'T EAT THE CANDLE, ROBIN. GIVE IT TO MOMMY.
CAN I HAVE MORE CAKE?
IT'S NICE TO HAVE THE FAMILY HERE. THEY'RE ALL SO BUSY. THE BABIES ARE GROWING UP SO FAST....
I SHOULD RECORD ALL THIS GREAT CONVERSATION AND PLAY IT AGAIN LATER ON.
IT WOULD HELP PUT ME TO SLEEP.
LYNN

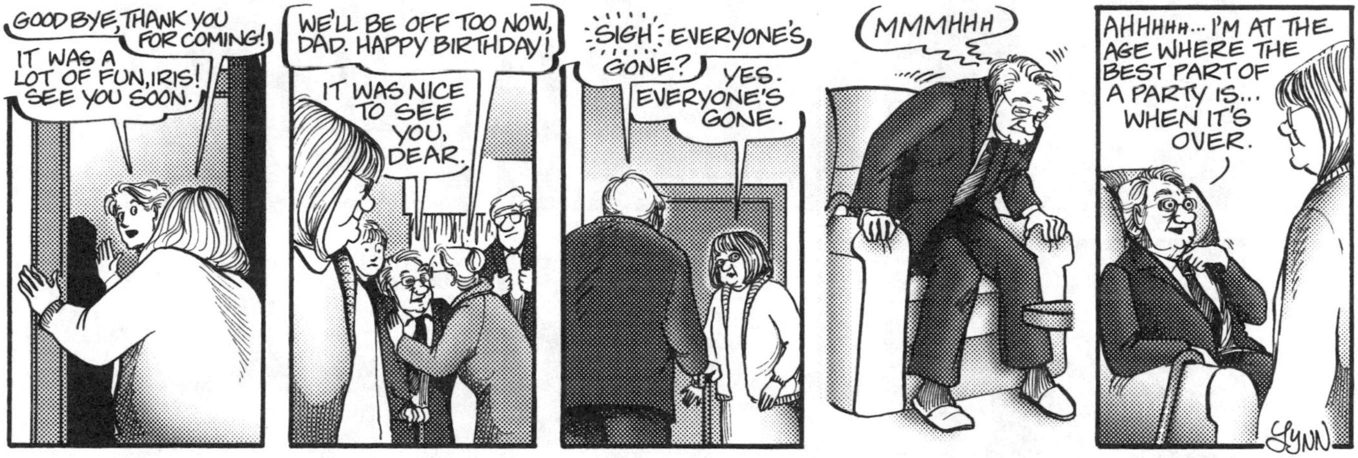
GOOD BYE, THANK YOU FOR COMING!
IT WAS A LOT OF FUN, IRIS! SEE YOU SOON.
WE'LL BE OFF TOO NOW, DAD. HAPPY BIRTHDAY!
IT WAS NICE TO SEE YOU, DEAR.
SIGH EVERYONE'S GONE?
YES. EVERYONE'S GONE.
MMMHHH
AHHHHH... I'M AT THE AGE WHERE THE BEST PART OF A PARTY IS... WHEN IT'S OVER.
LYNN

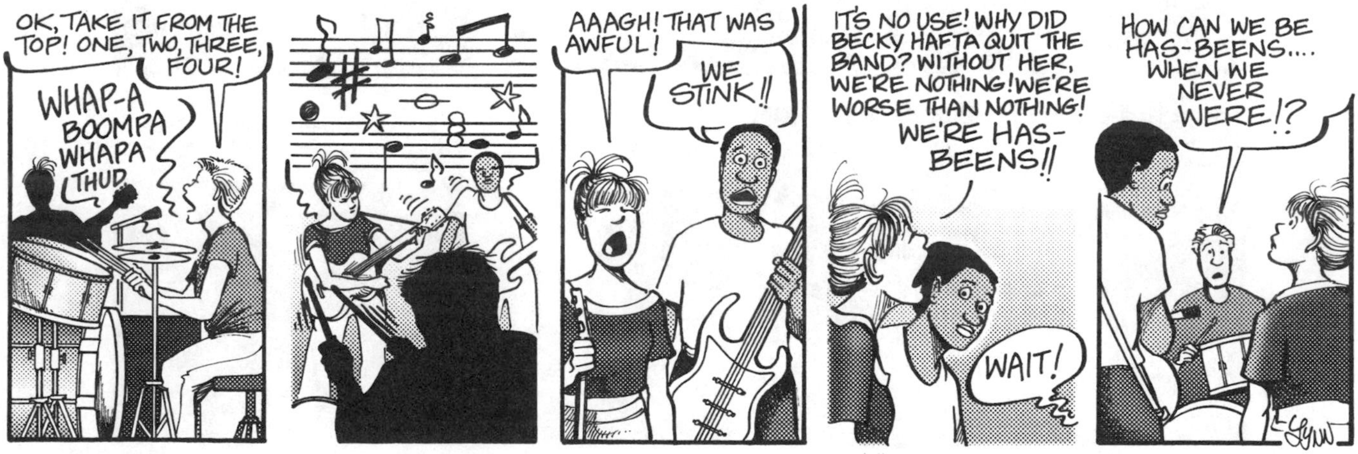
OK, TAKE IT FROM THE TOP! ONE, TWO, THREE, FOUR!
WHAP-A BOOMPA WHAPA THUD
AAAGH! THAT WAS AWFUL!
WE STINK!!
IT'S NO USE! WHY DID BECKY HAFTA QUIT THE BAND? WITHOUT HER, WE'RE NOTHING! WE'RE WORSE THAN NOTHING!
WE'RE HAS-BEENS!!
WAIT!
HOW CAN WE BE HAS-BEENS.... WHEN WE NEVER WERE!?
LYNN

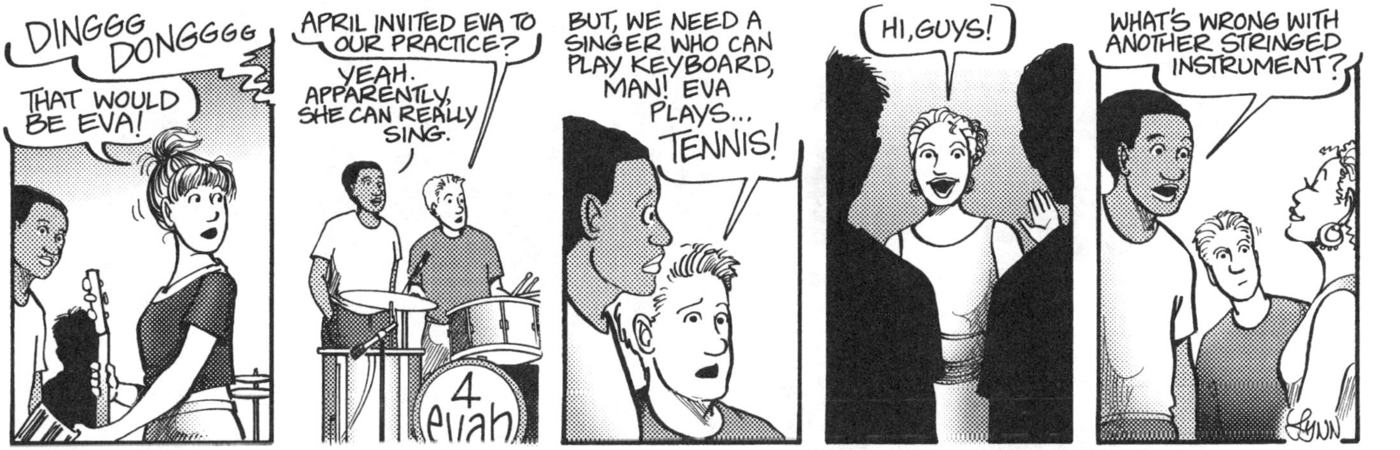

DINGGG DONGGGG
THAT WOULD BE EVA!
APRIL INVITED EVA TO OUR PRACTICE?
YEAH. APPARENTLY, SHE CAN REALLY SING.
4 evah
BUT, WE NEED A SINGER WHO CAN PLAY KEYBOARD, MAN! EVA PLAYS... TENNIS!
HI, GUYS!
WHAT'S WRONG WITH ANOTHER STRINGED INSTRUMENT?
LYNN

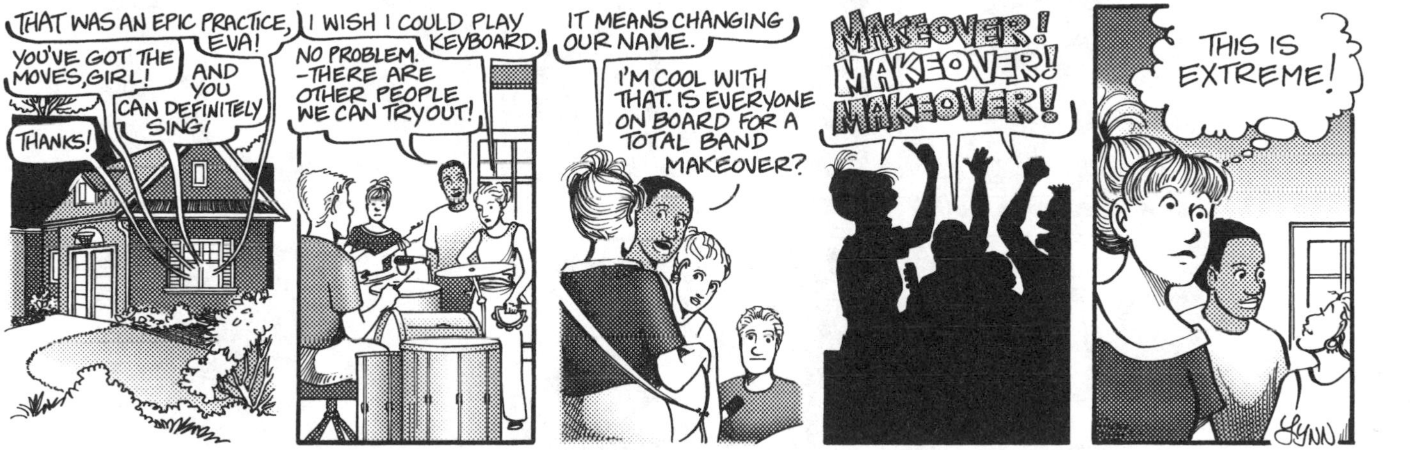

THAT WAS AN EPIC PRACTICE, EVA!
YOU'VE GOT THE MOVES, GIRL!
AND YOU CAN DEFINITELY SING!
THANKS!
I WISH I COULD PLAY KEYBOARD.
NO PROBLEM. –THERE ARE OTHER PEOPLE WE CAN TRY OUT!
IT MEANS CHANGING OUR NAME.
I'M COOL WITH THAT. IS EVERYONE ON BOARD FOR A TOTAL BAND MAKEOVER?
MAKEOVER! MAKEOVER! MAKEOVER!
THIS IS EXTREME!
LYNN

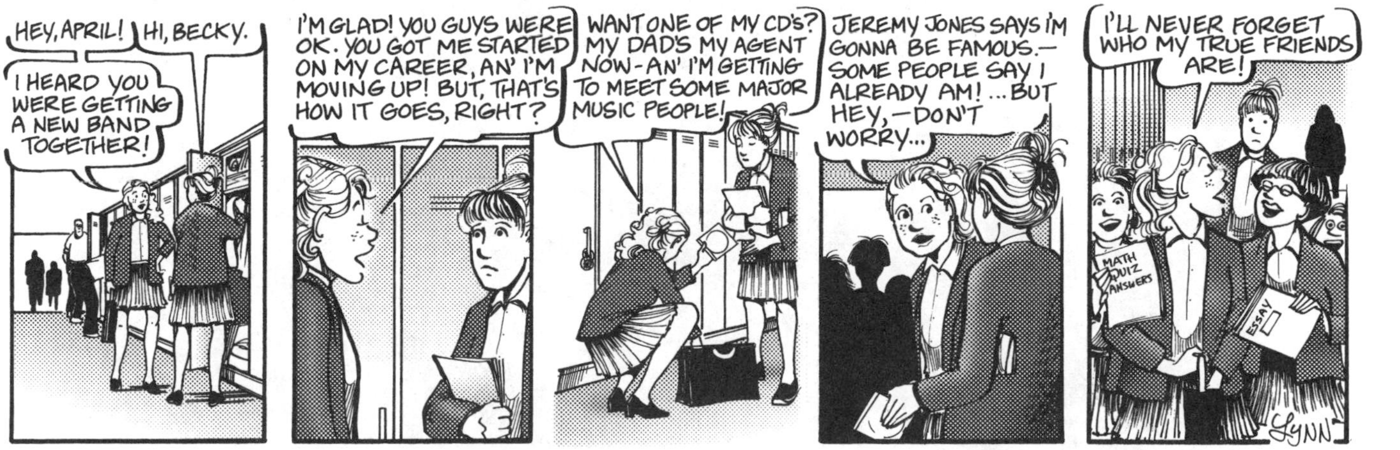

HEY, APRIL!
HI, BECKY.
I HEARD YOU WERE GETTING A NEW BAND TOGETHER!
I'M GLAD! YOU GUYS WERE OK. YOU GOT ME STARTED ON MY CAREER, AN' I'M MOVING UP! BUT, THAT'S HOW IT GOES, RIGHT?
WANT ONE OF MY CD'S? MY DAD'S MY AGENT NOW - AN' I'M GETTING TO MEET SOME MAJOR MUSIC PEOPLE!
JEREMY JONES SAYS I'M GONNA BE FAMOUS.— SOME PEOPLE SAY I ALREADY AM! ... BUT HEY, —DON'T WORRY...
I'LL NEVER FORGET WHO MY TRUE FRIENDS ARE!
MATH QUIZ ANSWERS
ESSAY
LYNN

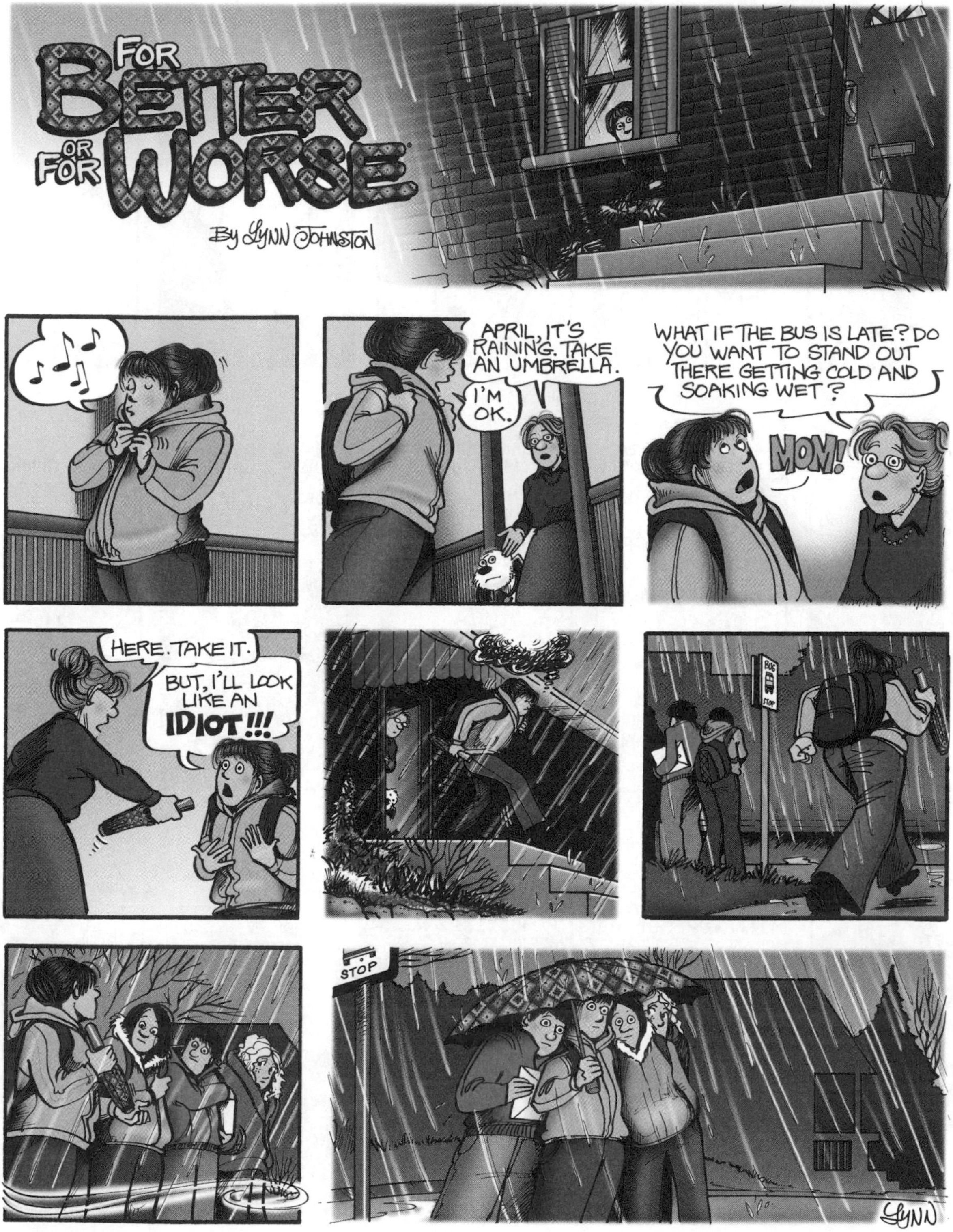

FOR BETTER OR FOR WORSE
By Lynn Johnston
APRIL, IT'S RAINING. TAKE AN UMBRELLA.
I'M OK.
WHAT IF THE BUS IS LATE? DO YOU WANT TO STAND OUT THERE GETTING COLD AND SOAKING WET?
MOM!
HERE. TAKE IT.
BUT, I'LL LOOK LIKE AN IDIOT!!!
BUS STOP
STOP
LYNN

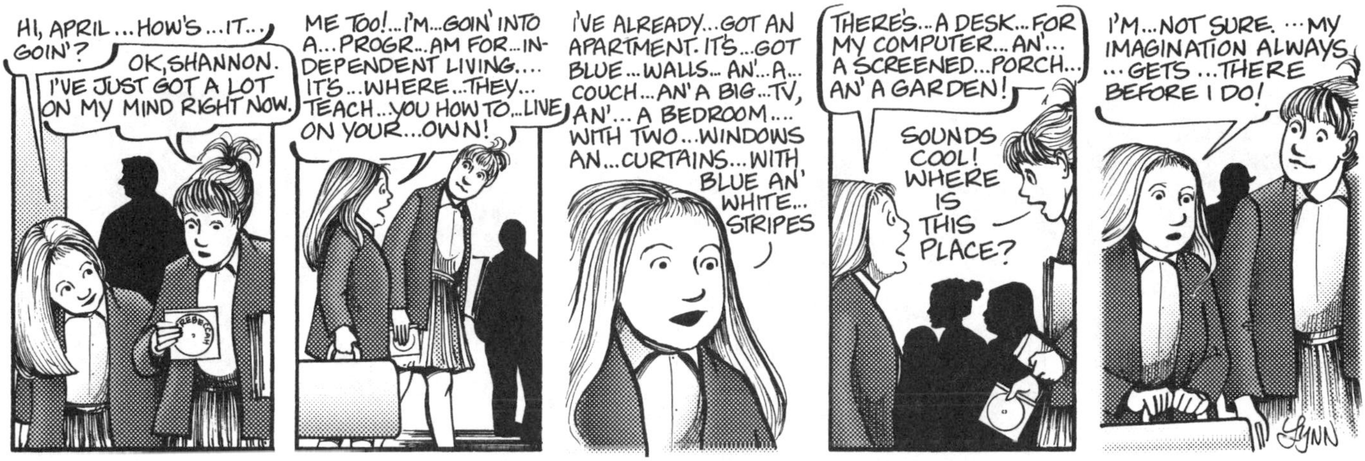
HI, APRIL...HOW'S...IT...GOIN'?
OK, SHANNON. I'VE JUST GOT A LOT ON MY MIND RIGHT NOW.
ME TOO!...I'M...GOIN' INTO A...PROGR...AM FOR...IN-DEPENDENT LIVING.... IT'S...WHERE...THEY... TEACH...YOU HOW TO...LIVE ON YOUR...OWN!
I'VE ALREADY...GOT AN APARTMENT. IT'S...GOT BLUE...WALLS...AN'...A... COUCH...AN' A BIG...TV, AN'...A BEDROOM.... WITH TWO...WINDOWS AN...CURTAINS...WITH BLUE AN' WHITE... STRIPES
THERE'S...A DESK...FOR MY COMPUTER...AN'... A SCREENED...PORCH... AN' A GARDEN!
SOUNDS COOL! WHERE IS THIS PLACE?
I'M...NOT SURE. ...MY IMAGINATION ALWAYS ...GETS...THERE BEFORE I DO!
LYNN

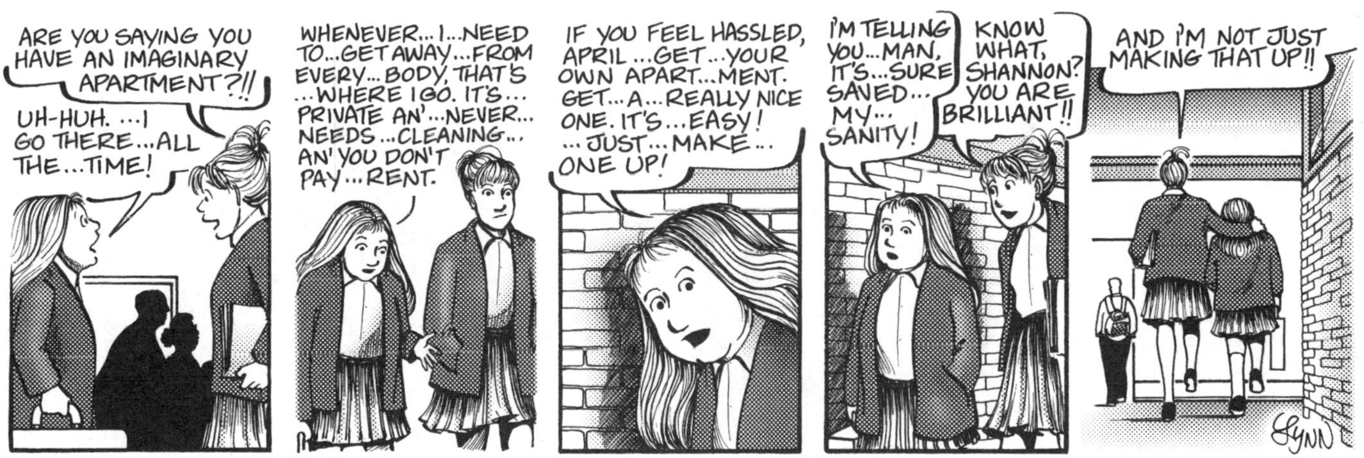
ARE YOU SAYING YOU HAVE AN IMAGINARY APARTMENT?!!
UH-HUH. ...I GO THERE...ALL THE...TIME!
WHENEVER...I...NEED TO...GET AWAY...FROM EVERY...BODY, THAT'S ...WHERE I GO. IT'S... PRIVATE AN'...NEVER... NEEDS...CLEANING... AN' YOU DON'T PAY...RENT.
IF YOU FEEL HASSLED, APRIL...GET...YOUR OWN APART...MENT. GET...A...REALLY NICE ONE. IT'S...EASY! ...JUST...MAKE... ONE UP!
I'M TELLING YOU...MAN, IT'S...SURE SAVED... MY... SANITY!
KNOW WHAT, SHANNON? YOU ARE BRILLIANT!!
AND I'M NOT JUST MAKING THAT UP!!
LYNN

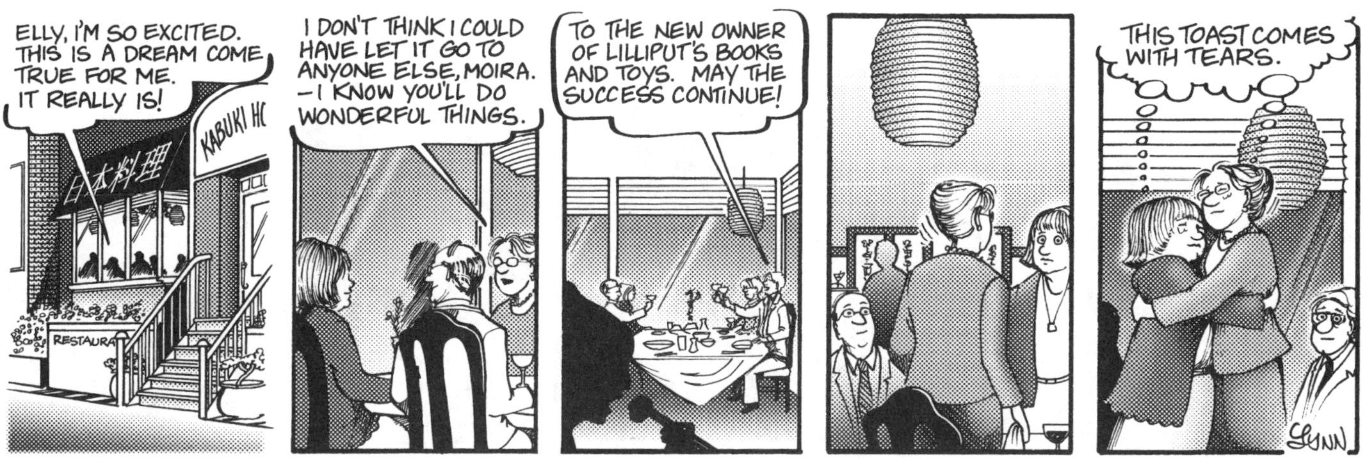
ELLY, I'M SO EXCITED. THIS IS A DREAM COME TRUE FOR ME. IT REALLY IS!
日本料理
I DON'T THINK I COULD HAVE LET IT GO TO ANYONE ELSE, MOIRA. —I KNOW YOU'LL DO WONDERFUL THINGS.
TO THE NEW OWNER OF LILLIPUT'S BOOKS AND TOYS. MAY THE SUCCESS CONTINUE!
THIS TOAST COMES WITH TEARS.
LYNN

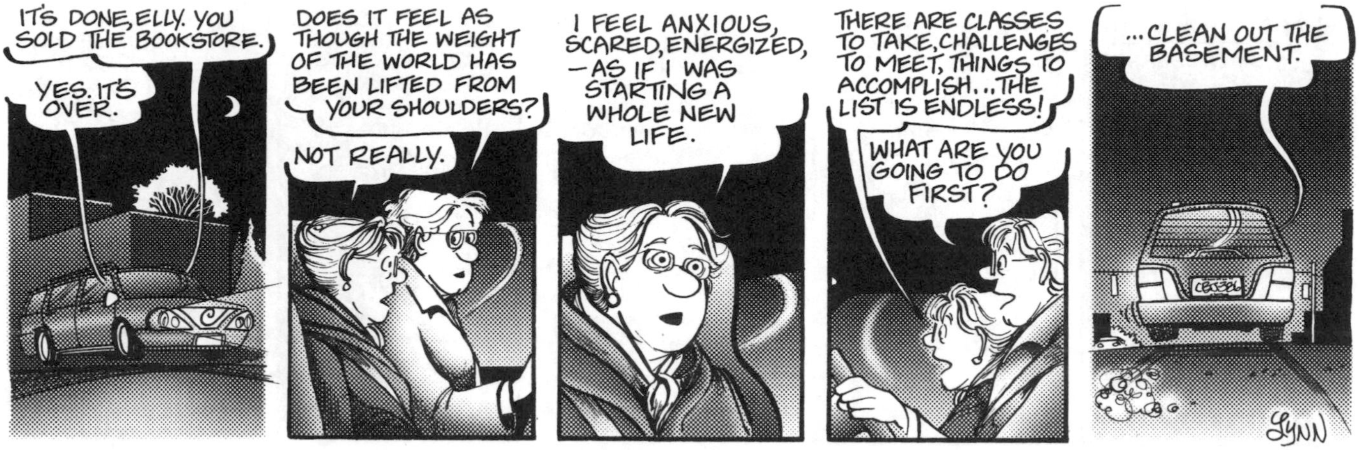
IT'S DONE, ELLY. YOU SOLD THE BOOKSTORE.
YES. IT'S OVER.
DOES IT FEEL AS THOUGH THE WEIGHT OF THE WORLD HAS BEEN LIFTED FROM YOUR SHOULDERS?
NOT REALLY.
I FEEL ANXIOUS, SCARED, ENERGIZED, —AS IF I WAS STARTING A WHOLE NEW LIFE.
THERE ARE CLASSES TO TAKE, CHALLENGES TO MEET, THINGS TO ACCOMPLISH... THE LIST IS ENDLESS!
WHAT ARE YOU GOING TO DO FIRST?
...CLEAN OUT THE BASEMENT.
LYNN

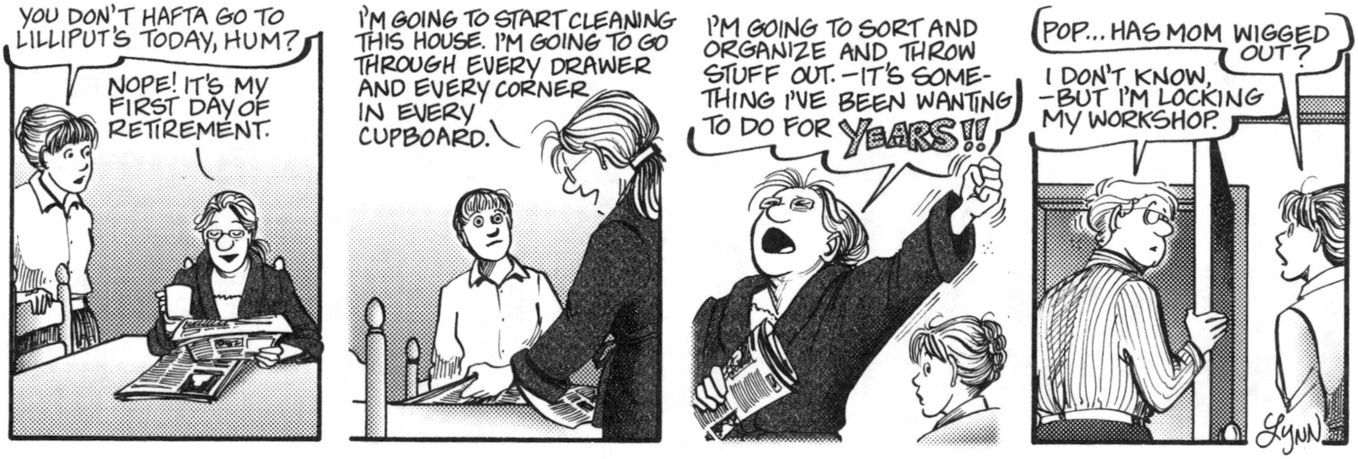
YOU DON'T HAFTA GO TO LILLIPUT'S TODAY, HUM?
NOPE! IT'S MY FIRST DAY OF RETIREMENT.
I'M GOING TO START CLEANING THIS HOUSE. I'M GOING TO GO THROUGH EVERY DRAWER AND EVERY CORNER IN EVERY CUPBOARD.
I'M GOING TO SORT AND ORGANIZE AND THROW STUFF OUT. —IT'S SOMETHING I'VE BEEN WANTING TO DO FOR YEARS!!
POP... HAS MOM WIGGED OUT?
I DON'T KNOW, —BUT I'M LOCKING MY WORKSHOP.
LYNN

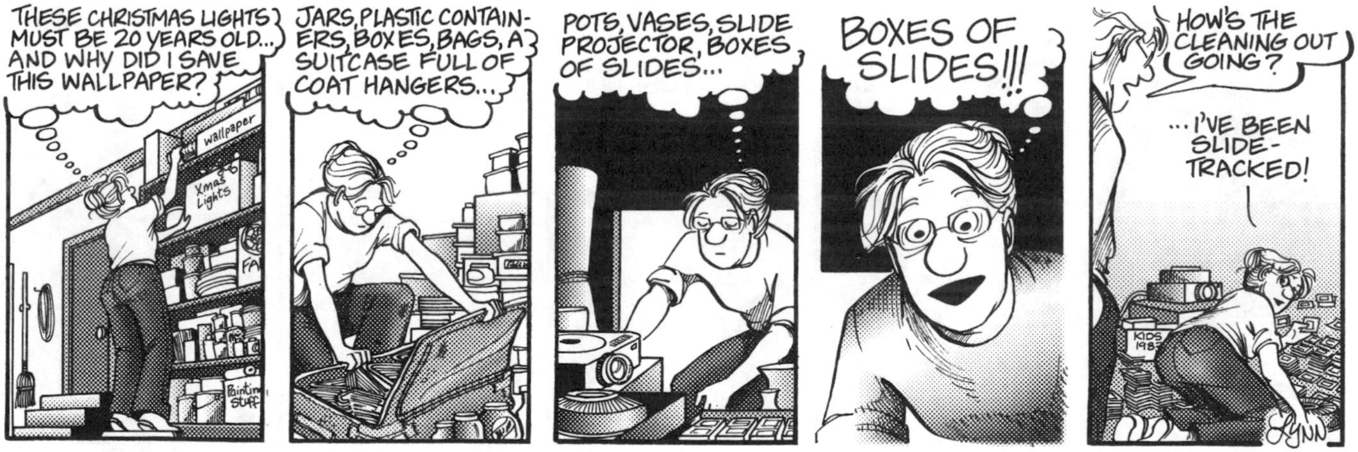
THESE CHRISTMAS LIGHTS MUST BE 20 YEARS OLD... AND WHY DID I SAVE THIS WALLPAPER?
wallpaper
Xmas Lights
JARS, PLASTIC CONTAINERS, BOXES, BAGS, A SUITCASE FULL OF COAT HANGERS...
POTS, VASES, SLIDE PROJECTOR, BOXES OF SLIDES...
BOXES OF SLIDES!!!
HOW'S THE CLEANING OUT GOING?
...I'VE BEEN SLIDE-TRACKED!
LYNN

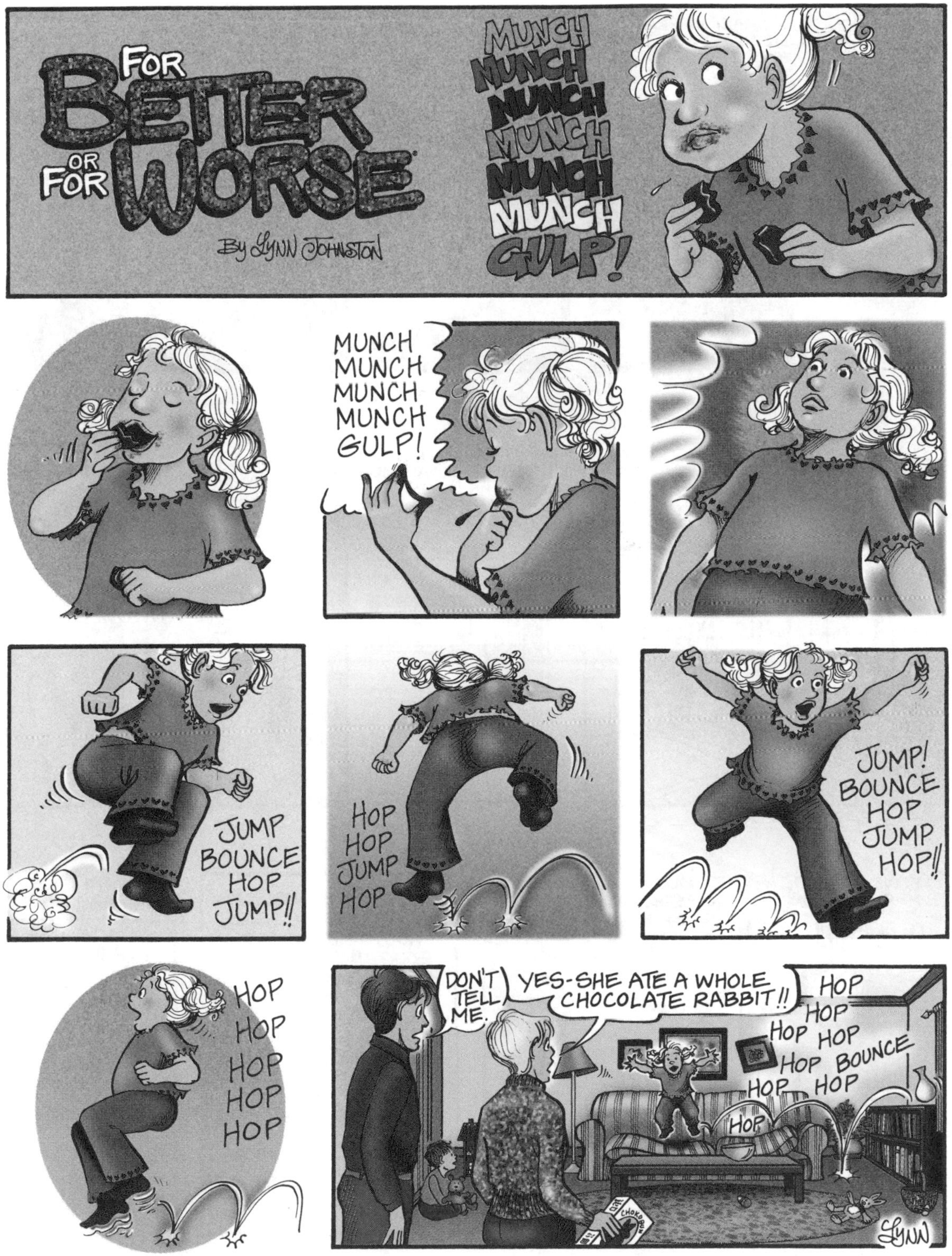
FOR BETTER OR FOR WORSE
BY LYNN JOHNSTON
MUNCH MUNCH MUNCH MUNCH MUNCH MUNCH GULP!
MUNCH MUNCH MUNCH MUNCH GULP!
JUMP BOUNCE HOP JUMP!!
HOP HOP JUMP HOP
JUMP! BOUNCE HOP JUMP HOP!!
HOP HOP HOP HOP HOP
DON'T TELL ME.
YES-SHE ATE A WHOLE CHOCOLATE RABBIT!!
HOP HOP HOP HOP HOP BOUNCE HOP HOP HOP
LYNN

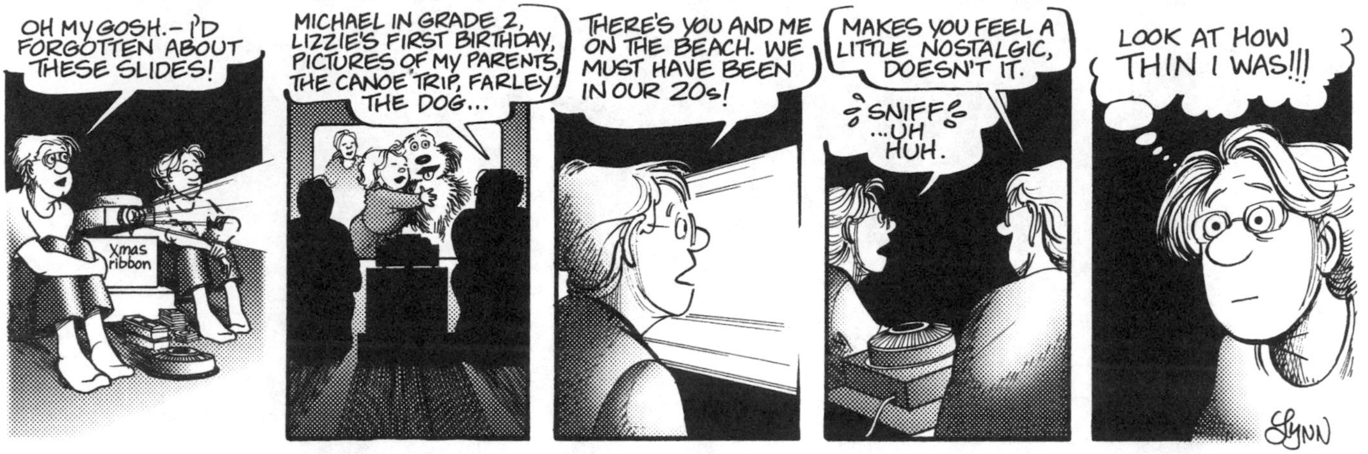
OH MY GOSH.- I'D FORGOTTEN ABOUT THESE SLIDES!
Xmas ribbon
MICHAEL IN GRADE 2, LIZZIE'S FIRST BIRTHDAY, PICTURES OF MY PARENTS, THE CANOE TRIP, FARLEY THE DOG...
THERE'S YOU AND ME ON THE BEACH. WE MUST HAVE BEEN IN OUR 20s!
MAKES YOU FEEL A LITTLE NOSTALGIC, DOESN'T IT.
SNIFF ...UH HUH.
LOOK AT HOW THIN I WAS!!!
LYNN

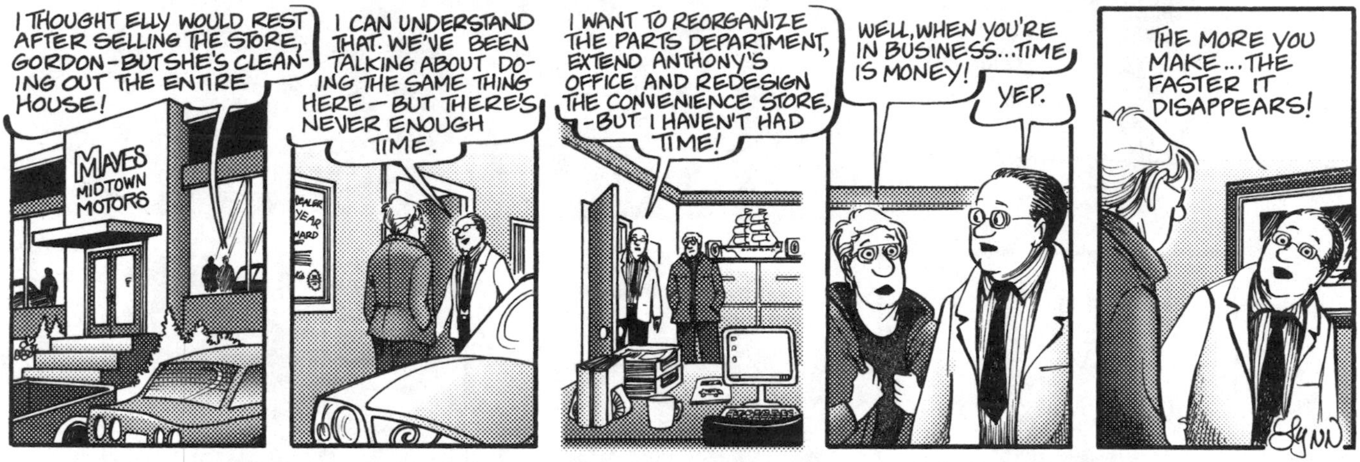
I THOUGHT ELLY WOULD REST AFTER SELLING THE STORE, GORDON-BUT SHE'S CLEANING OUT THE ENTIRE HOUSE!
MAYES MIDTOWN MOTORS
I CAN UNDERSTAND THAT. WE'VE BEEN TALKING ABOUT DOING THE SAME THING HERE-BUT THERE'S NEVER ENOUGH TIME.
I WANT TO REORGANIZE THE PARTS DEPARTMENT, EXTEND ANTHONY'S OFFICE AND REDESIGN THE CONVENIENCE STORE, -BUT I HAVEN'T HAD TIME!
WELL, WHEN YOU'RE IN BUSINESS... TIME IS MONEY!
YEP.
THE MORE YOU MAKE... THE FASTER IT DISAPPEARS!
LYNN

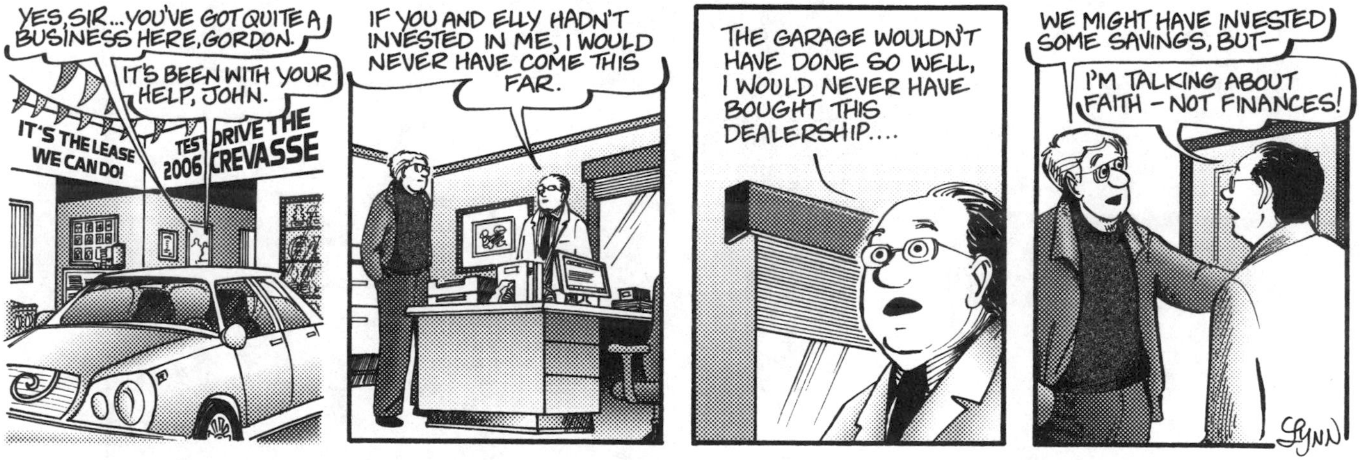
YES, SIR... YOU'VE GOT QUITE A BUSINESS HERE, GORDON.
IT'S BEEN WITH YOUR HELP, JOHN.
IT'S THE LEASE WE CAN DO!
TEST DRIVE THE 2006 CREVASSE
IF YOU AND ELLY HADN'T INVESTED IN ME, I WOULD NEVER HAVE COME THIS FAR.
THE GARAGE WOULDN'T HAVE DONE SO WELL, I WOULD NEVER HAVE BOUGHT THIS DEALERSHIP....
WE MIGHT HAVE INVESTED SOME SAVINGS, BUT-
I'M TALKING ABOUT FAITH - NOT FINANCES!
LYNN

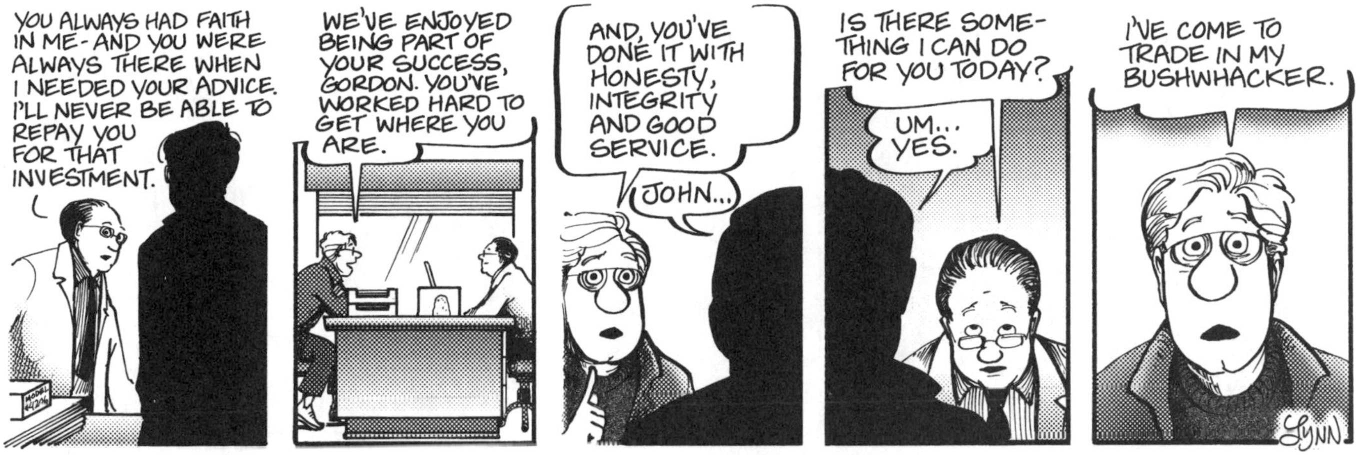
YOU ALWAYS HAD FAITH IN ME - AND YOU WERE ALWAYS THERE WHEN I NEEDED YOUR ADVICE. I'LL NEVER BE ABLE TO REPAY YOU FOR THAT INVESTMENT.
WE'VE ENJOYED BEING PART OF YOUR SUCCESS, GORDON. YOU'VE WORKED HARD TO GET WHERE YOU ARE.
AND, YOU'VE DONE IT WITH HONESTY, INTEGRITY AND GOOD SERVICE.
JOHN...
IS THERE SOMETHING I CAN DO FOR YOU TODAY?
UM... YES.
I'VE COME TO TRADE IN MY BUSHWHACKER.
LYNN

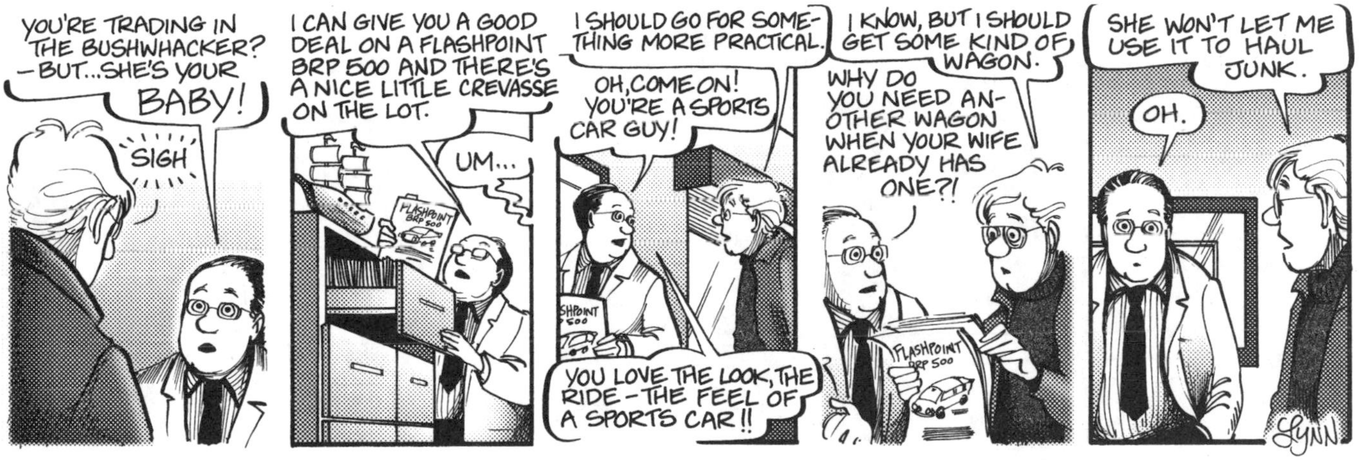
YOU'RE TRADING IN THE BUSHWHACKER? - BUT...SHE'S YOUR BABY!
SIGH
I CAN GIVE YOU A GOOD DEAL ON A FLASHPOINT BRP 500 AND THERE'S A NICE LITTLE CREVASSE ON THE LOT.
UM...
I SHOULD GO FOR SOMETHING MORE PRACTICAL.
OH, COME ON! YOU'RE A SPORTS CAR GUY!
YOU LOVE THE LOOK, THE RIDE - THE FEEL OF A SPORTS CAR!!
I KNOW, BUT I SHOULD GET SOME KIND OF WAGON.
WHY DO YOU NEED ANOTHER WAGON WHEN YOUR WIFE ALREADY HAS ONE?!
FLASHPOINT BRP 500
SHE WON'T LET ME USE IT TO HAUL JUNK.
OH.
LYNN

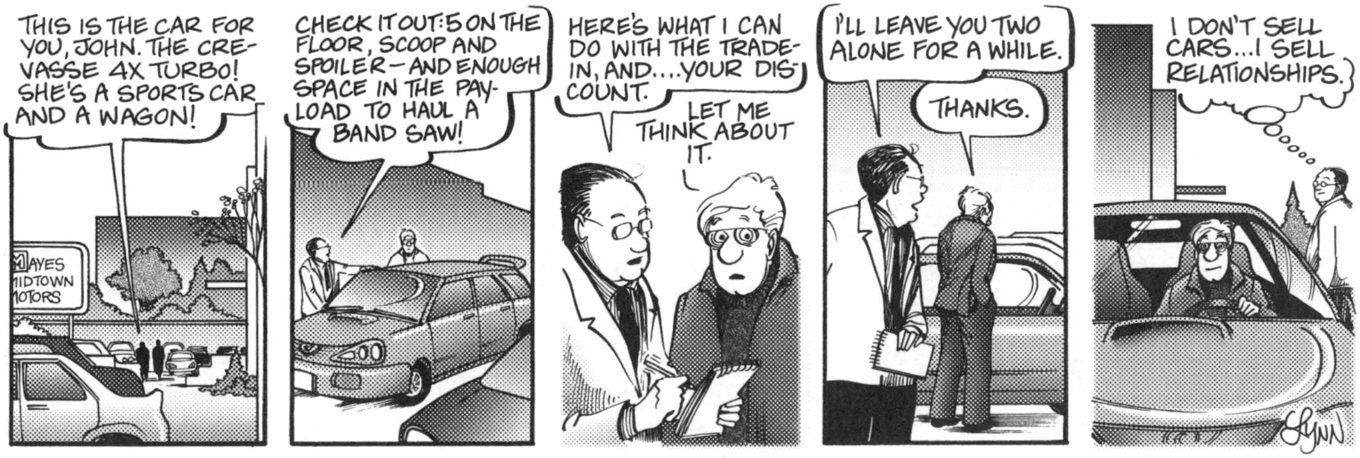
THIS IS THE CAR FOR YOU, JOHN. THE CREVASSE 4X TURBO! SHE'S A SPORTS CAR AND A WAGON!
CHECK IT OUT: 5 ON THE FLOOR, SCOOP AND SPOILER - AND ENOUGH SPACE IN THE PAYLOAD TO HAUL A BAND SAW!
HERE'S WHAT I CAN DO WITH THE TRADE-IN, AND....YOUR DISCOUNT.
LET ME THINK ABOUT IT.
I'LL LEAVE YOU TWO ALONE FOR A WHILE.
THANKS.
I DON'T SELL CARS...I SELL RELATIONSHIPS.
LYNN

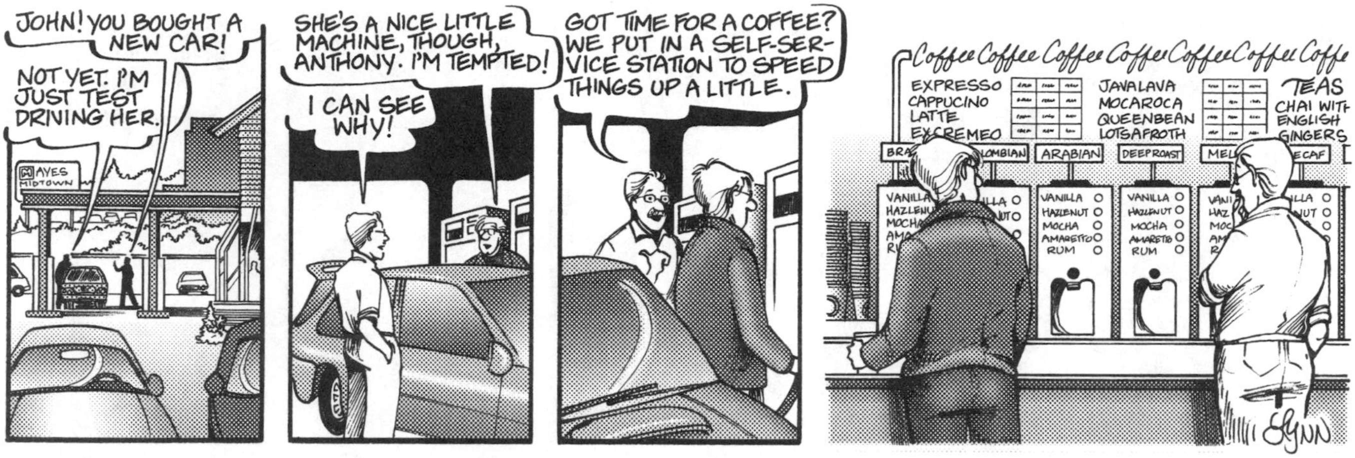
JOHN! YOU BOUGHT A NEW CAR!
NOT YET. I'M JUST TEST DRIVING HER.
SHE'S A NICE LITTLE MACHINE, THOUGH, ANTHONY. I'M TEMPTED!
I CAN SEE WHY!
GOT TIME FOR A COFFEE? WE PUT IN A SELF-SERVICE STATION TO SPEED THINGS UP A LITTLE.
EXPRESSO
CAPPUCINO
LATTE
EXCREMEO
JAVALAVA
MOCAROCA
QUEENBEAN
LOTSAFROTH
TEAS
ARABIAN
DEEPROAST
VANILLA
HAZLENUT
MOCHA
AMARETTO
RUM
LYNN

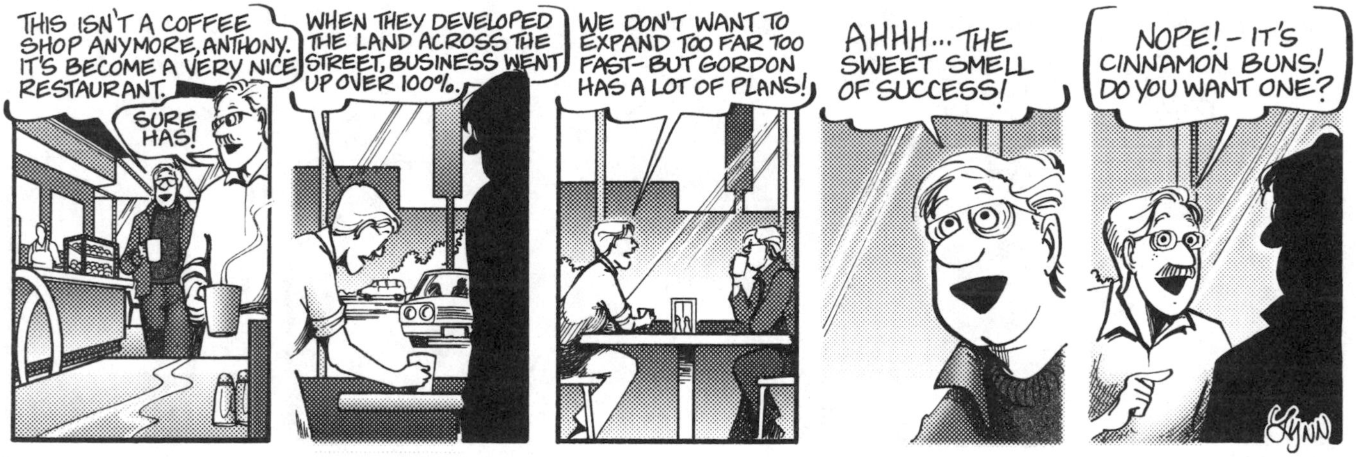
THIS ISN'T A COFFEE SHOP ANYMORE, ANTHONY. IT'S BECOME A VERY NICE RESTAURANT.
SURE HAS!
WHEN THEY DEVELOPED THE LAND ACROSS THE STREET, BUSINESS WENT UP OVER 100%.
WE DON'T WANT TO EXPAND TOO FAR TOO FAST- BUT GORDON HAS A LOT OF PLANS!
AHHH... THE SWEET SMELL OF SUCCESS!
NOPE! - IT'S CINNAMON BUNS! DO YOU WANT ONE?
LYNN

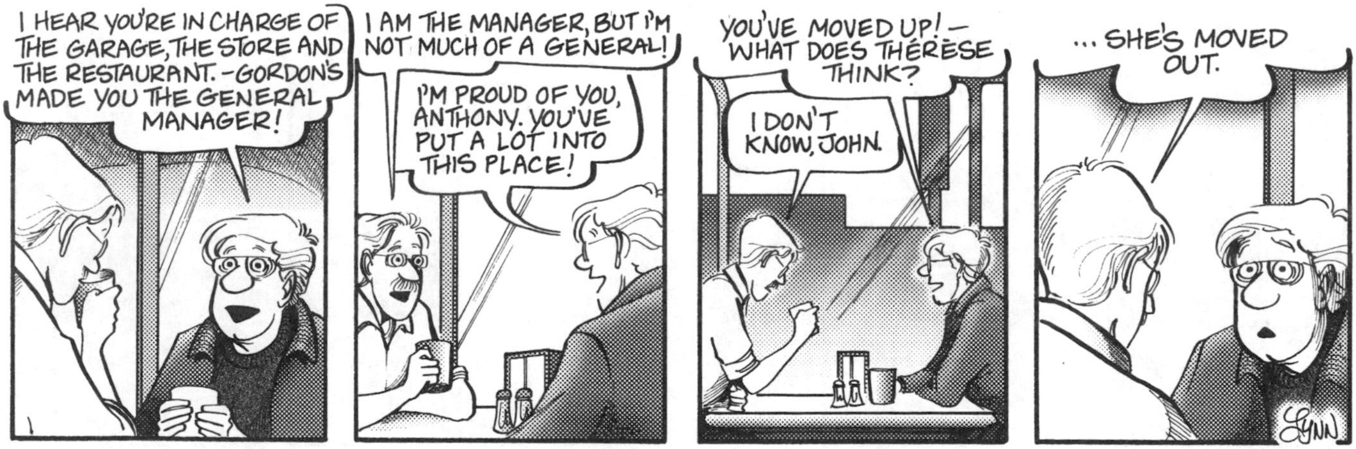
I HEAR YOU'RE IN CHARGE OF THE GARAGE, THE STORE AND THE RESTAURANT. -GORDON'S MADE YOU THE GENERAL MANAGER!
I AM THE MANAGER, BUT I'M NOT MUCH OF A GENERAL!
I'M PROUD OF YOU, ANTHONY. YOU'VE PUT A LOT INTO THIS PLACE!
YOU'VE MOVED UP! - WHAT DOES THÉRÈSE THINK?
I DON'T KNOW, JOHN.
... SHE'S MOVED OUT.
LYNN

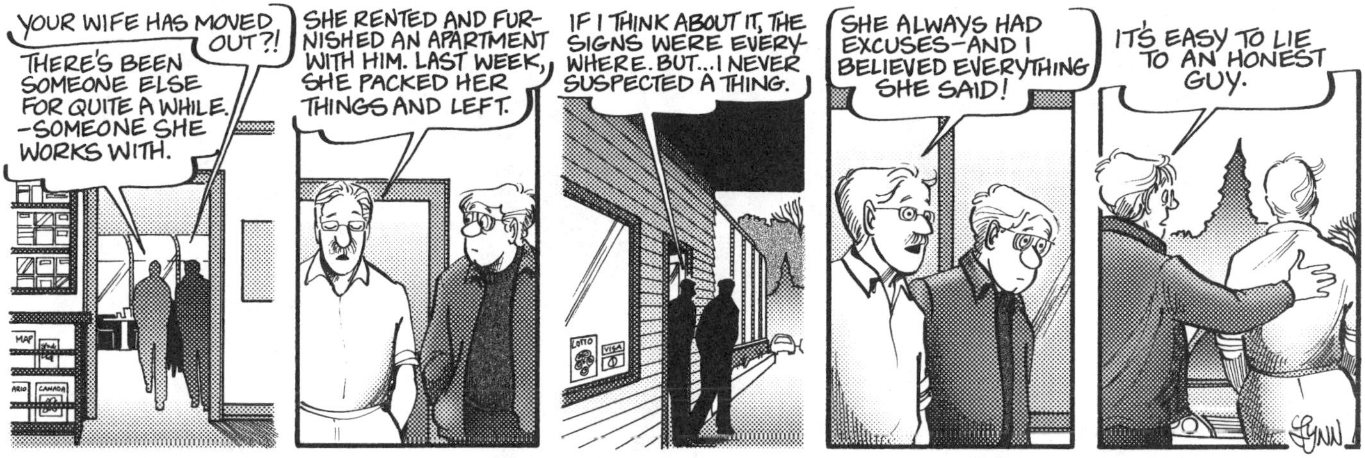
YOUR WIFE HAS MOVED OUT?!
THERE'S BEEN SOMEONE ELSE FOR QUITE A WHILE. -SOMEONE SHE WORKS WITH.
SHE RENTED AND FURNISHED AN APARTMENT WITH HIM. LAST WEEK, SHE PACKED HER THINGS AND LEFT.
IF I THINK ABOUT IT, THE SIGNS WERE EVERYWHERE. BUT...I NEVER SUSPECTED A THING.
SHE ALWAYS HAD EXCUSES—AND I BELIEVED EVERYTHING SHE SAID!
IT'S EASY TO LIE TO AN HONEST GUY.
LYNN

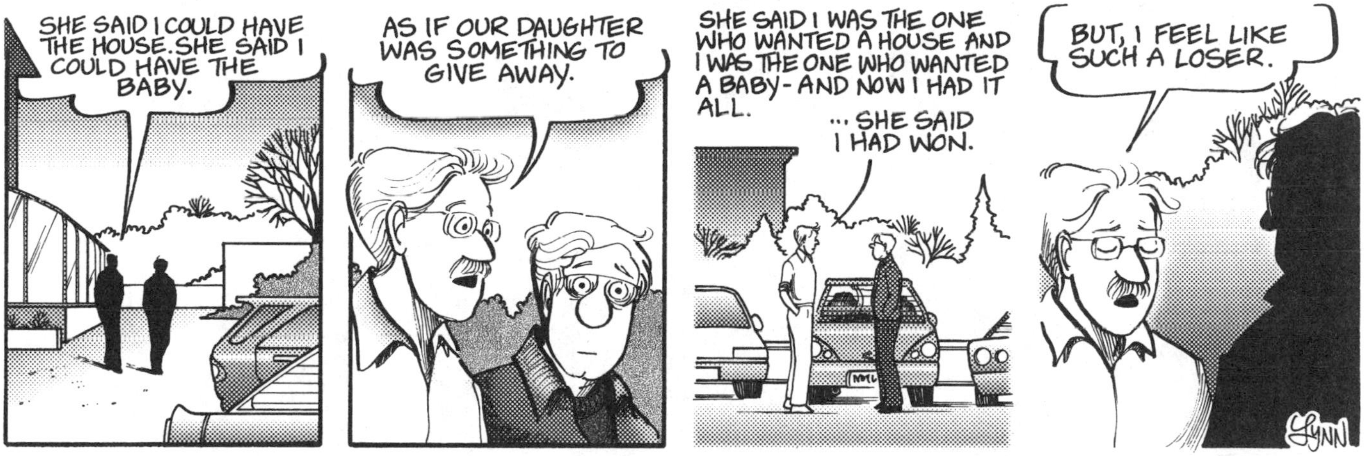
SHE SAID I COULD HAVE THE HOUSE. SHE SAID I COULD HAVE THE BABY.
AS IF OUR DAUGHTER WAS SOMETHING TO GIVE AWAY.
SHE SAID I WAS THE ONE WHO WANTED A HOUSE AND I WAS THE ONE WHO WANTED A BABY- AND NOW I HAD IT ALL.
...SHE SAID I HAD WON.
BUT, I FEEL LIKE SUCH A LOSER.
LYNN

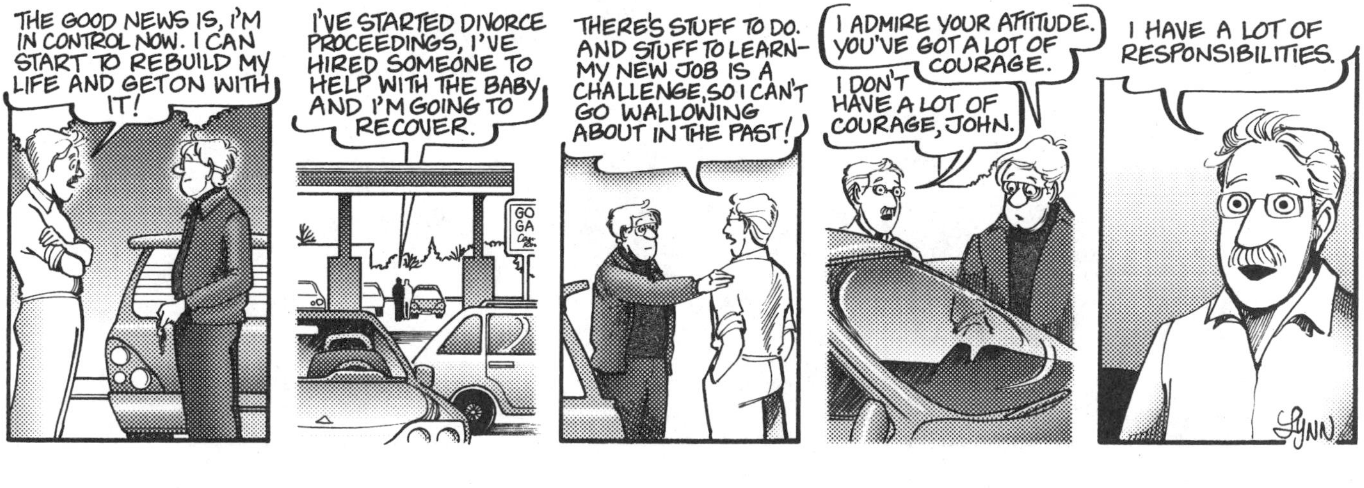
THE GOOD NEWS IS, I'M IN CONTROL NOW. I CAN START TO REBUILD MY LIFE AND GET ON WITH IT!
I'VE STARTED DIVORCE PROCEEDINGS, I'VE HIRED SOMEONE TO HELP WITH THE BABY, AND I'M GOING TO RECOVER.
THERE'S STUFF TO DO. AND STUFF TO LEARN- MY NEW JOB IS A CHALLENGE, SO I CAN'T GO WALLOWING ABOUT IN THE PAST!
I ADMIRE YOUR ATTITUDE. YOU'VE GOT A LOT OF COURAGE.
I DON'T HAVE A LOT OF COURAGE, JOHN.
I HAVE A LOT OF RESPONSIBILITIES.
LYNN

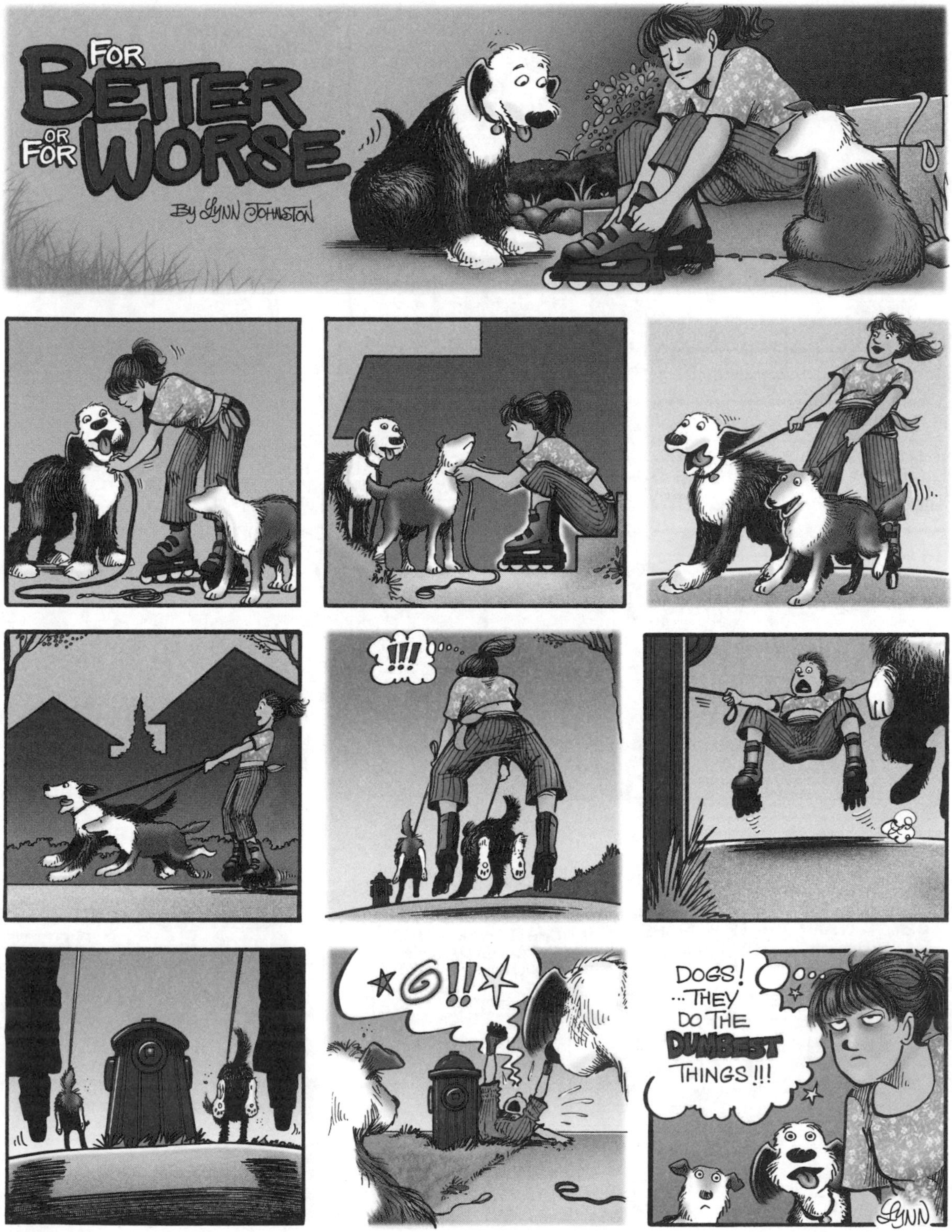
For Better or For Worse
By Lynn Johnston
!!!
★@!!★
DOGS! ...THEY DO THE DUMBEST THINGS!!!
LYNN

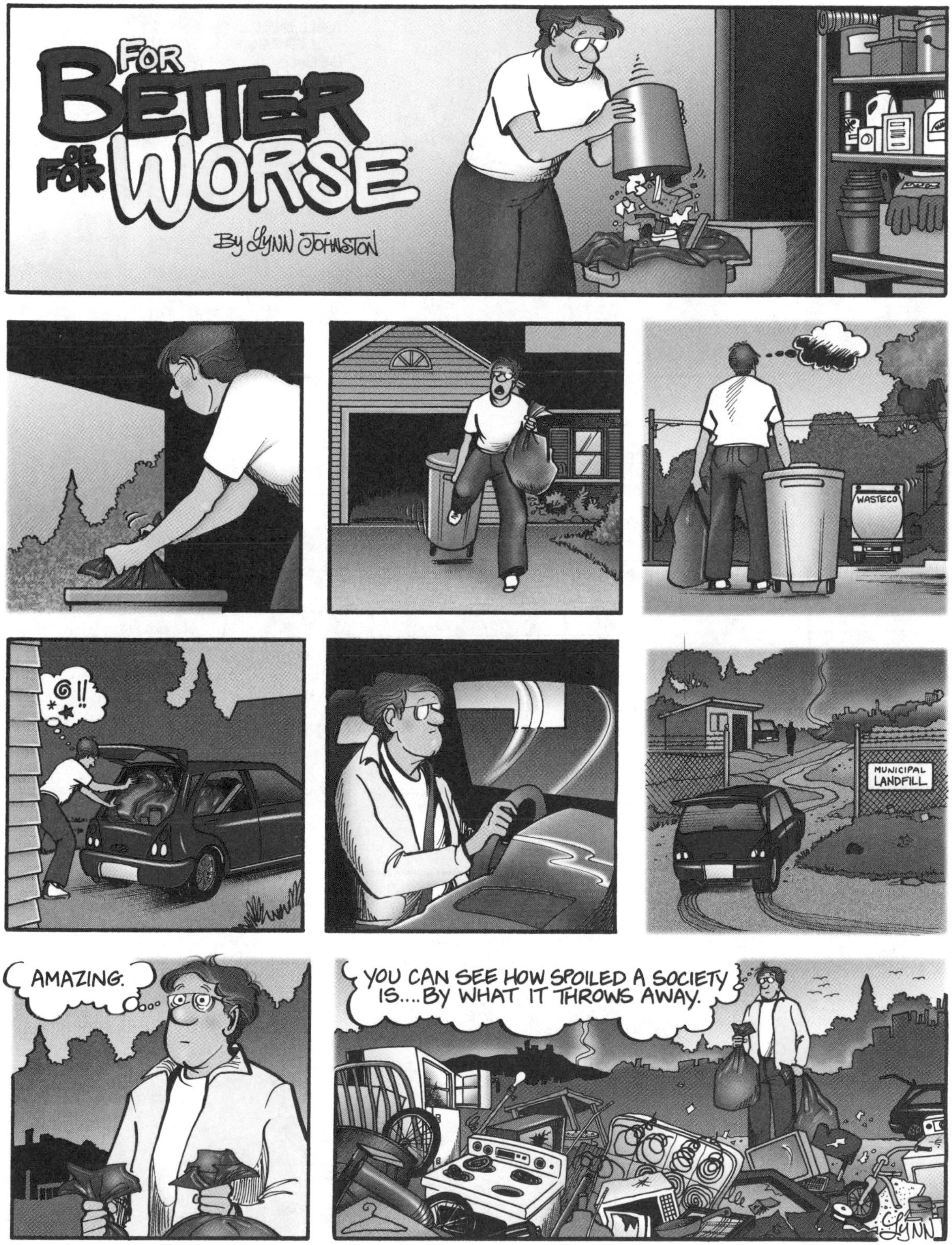
For Better or For Worse
By Lynn Johnston
WASTECO
MUNICIPAL LANDFILL
AMAZING.
YOU CAN SEE HOW SPOILED A SOCIETY IS.... BY WHAT IT THROWS AWAY.
LYNN

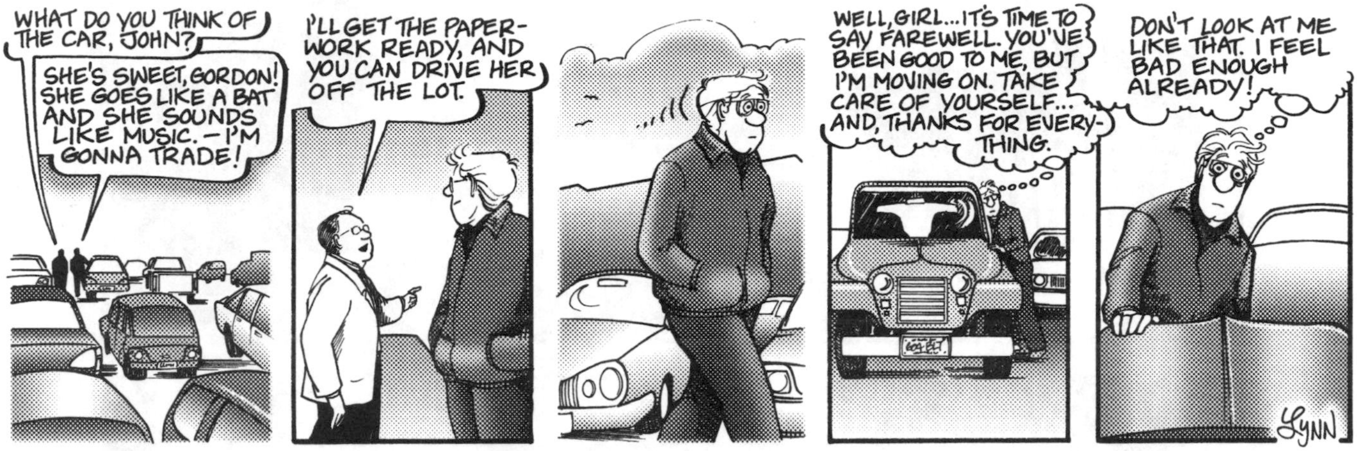

WHAT DO YOU THINK OF THE CAR, JOHN?
SHE'S SWEET, GORDON! SHE GOES LIKE A BAT AND SHE SOUNDS LIKE MUSIC. —I'M GONNA TRADE!
I'LL GET THE PAPER-WORK READY, AND YOU CAN DRIVE HER OFF THE LOT.
WELL, GIRL... IT'S TIME TO SAY FAREWELL. YOU'VE BEEN GOOD TO ME, BUT I'M MOVING ON. TAKE CARE OF YOURSELF... AND, THANKS FOR EVERY-THING.
DON'T LOOK AT ME LIKE THAT. I FEEL BAD ENOUGH ALREADY!
LYNN

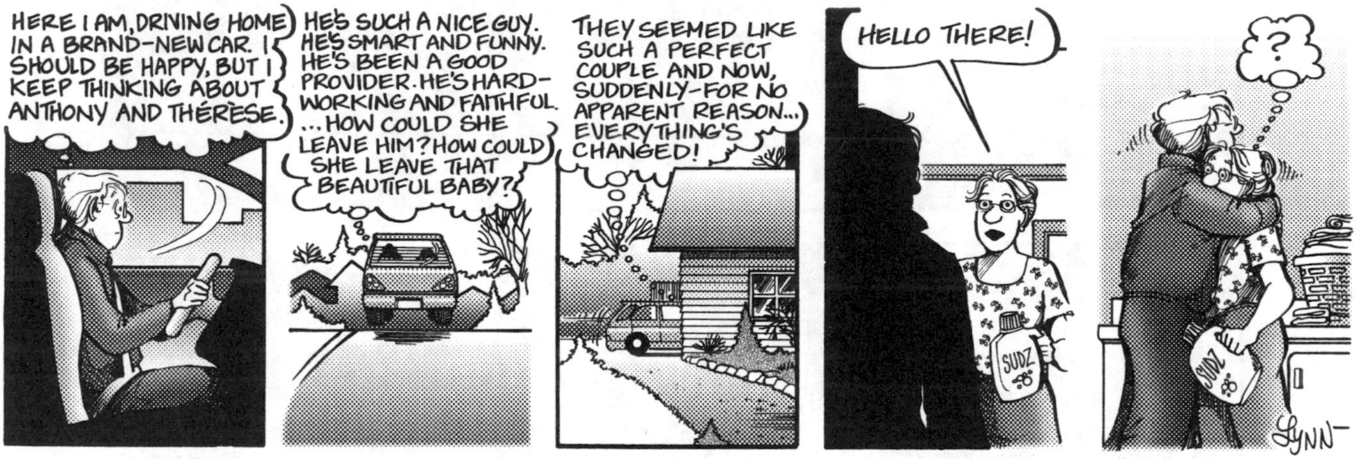

HERE I AM, DRIVING HOME IN A BRAND-NEW CAR. I SHOULD BE HAPPY, BUT I KEEP THINKING ABOUT ANTHONY AND THÉRÈSE.
HE'S SUCH A NICE GUY. HE'S SMART AND FUNNY. HE'S BEEN A GOOD PROVIDER. HE'S HARD-WORKING AND FAITHFUL. ...HOW COULD SHE LEAVE HIM? HOW COULD SHE LEAVE THAT BEAUTIFUL BABY?
THEY SEEMED LIKE SUCH A PERFECT COUPLE AND NOW, SUDDENLY—FOR NO APPARENT REASON... EVERYTHING'S CHANGED!
HELLO THERE!
SUDZ
?
SUDZ
LYNN

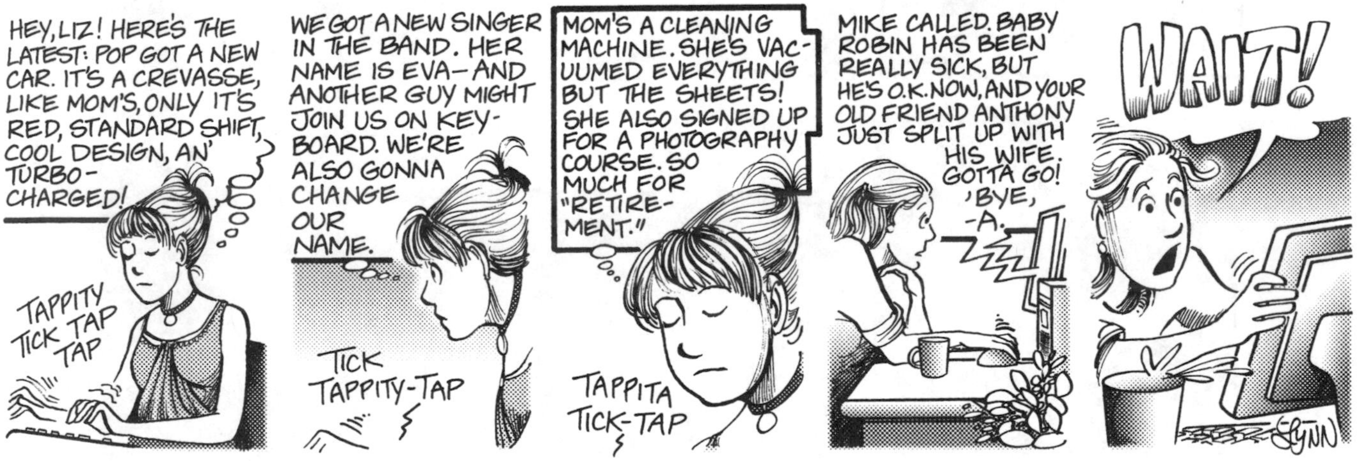

HEY, LIZ! HERE'S THE LATEST: POP GOT A NEW CAR. IT'S A CREVASSE, LIKE MOM'S, ONLY IT'S RED, STANDARD SHIFT, COOL DESIGN, AN' TURBO-CHARGED!
TAPPITY TICK TAP TAP
WE GOT A NEW SINGER IN THE BAND. HER NAME IS EVA—AND ANOTHER GUY MIGHT JOIN US ON KEY-BOARD. WE'RE ALSO GONNA CHANGE OUR NAME.
TICK TAPPITY-TAP
MOM'S A CLEANING MACHINE. SHE'S VAC-UUMED EVERYTHING BUT THE SHEETS! SHE ALSO SIGNED UP FOR A PHOTOGRAPHY COURSE. SO MUCH FOR "RETIRE-MENT."
TAPPITA TICK-TAP
MIKE CALLED. BABY ROBIN HAS BEEN REALLY SICK, BUT HE'S O.K. NOW, AND YOUR OLD FRIEND ANTHONY JUST SPLIT UP WITH HIS WIFE. GOTTA GO! 'BYE, -A.
WAIT!
LYNN

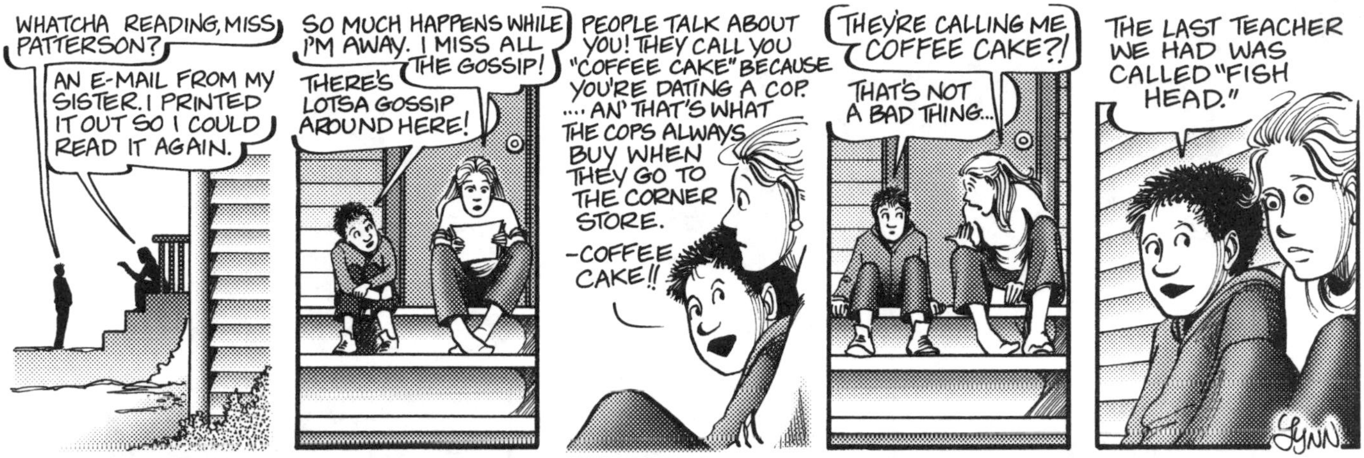
WHATCHA READING, MISS PATTERSON?
AN E-MAIL FROM MY SISTER. I PRINTED IT OUT SO I COULD READ IT AGAIN.
SO MUCH HAPPENS WHILE I'M AWAY. I MISS ALL THE GOSSIP!
THERE'S LOTSA GOSSIP AROUND HERE!
PEOPLE TALK ABOUT YOU! THEY CALL YOU "COFFEE CAKE" BECAUSE YOU'RE DATING A COP. .... AN' THAT'S WHAT THE COPS ALWAYS BUY WHEN THEY GO TO THE CORNER STORE.
-COFFEE CAKE!!
THEY'RE CALLING ME COFFEE CAKE?!
THAT'S NOT A BAD THING...
THE LAST TEACHER WE HAD WAS CALLED "FISH HEAD."
LYNN

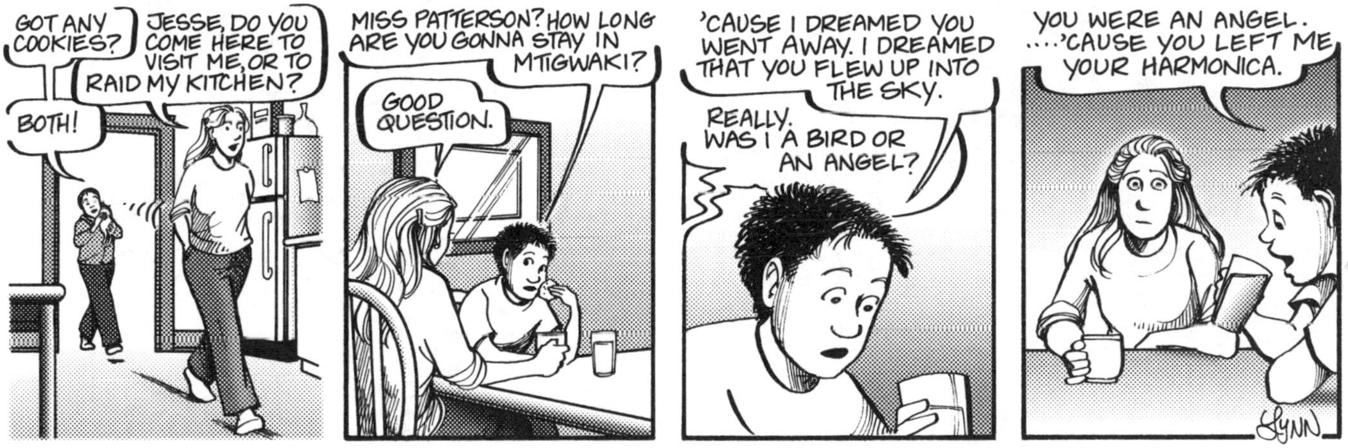
GOT ANY COOKIES?
JESSE, DO YOU COME HERE TO VISIT ME, OR TO RAID MY KITCHEN?
BOTH!
MISS PATTERSON? HOW LONG ARE YOU GONNA STAY IN MTIGWAKI?
GOOD QUESTION.
'CAUSE I DREAMED YOU WENT AWAY. I DREAMED THAT YOU FLEW UP INTO THE SKY.
REALLY. WAS I A BIRD OR AN ANGEL?
YOU WERE AN ANGEL. ....'CAUSE YOU LEFT ME YOUR HARMONICA.
LYNN

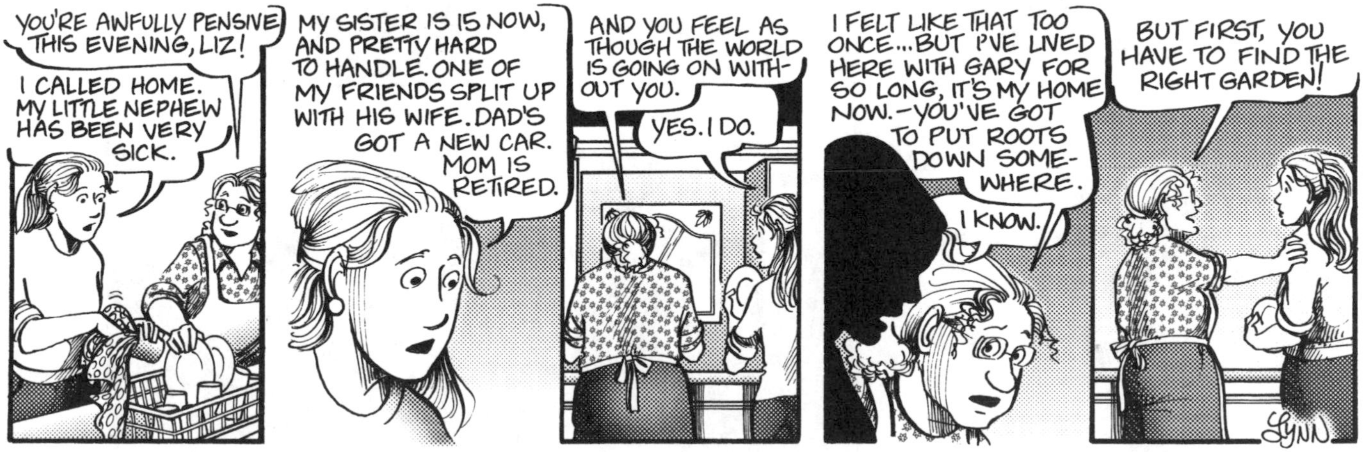
YOU'RE AWFULLY PENSIVE THIS EVENING, LIZ!
I CALLED HOME. MY LITTLE NEPHEW HAS BEEN VERY SICK.
MY SISTER IS 15 NOW, AND PRETTY HARD TO HANDLE. ONE OF MY FRIENDS SPLIT UP WITH HIS WIFE. DAD'S GOT A NEW CAR. MOM IS RETIRED.
AND YOU FEEL AS THOUGH THE WORLD IS GOING ON WITHOUT YOU.
YES. I DO.
I FELT LIKE THAT TOO ONCE... BUT I'VE LIVED HERE WITH GARY FOR SO LONG, IT'S MY HOME NOW. -YOU'VE GOT TO PUT ROOTS DOWN SOMEWHERE.
I KNOW.
BUT FIRST, YOU HAVE TO FIND THE RIGHT GARDEN!
LYNN

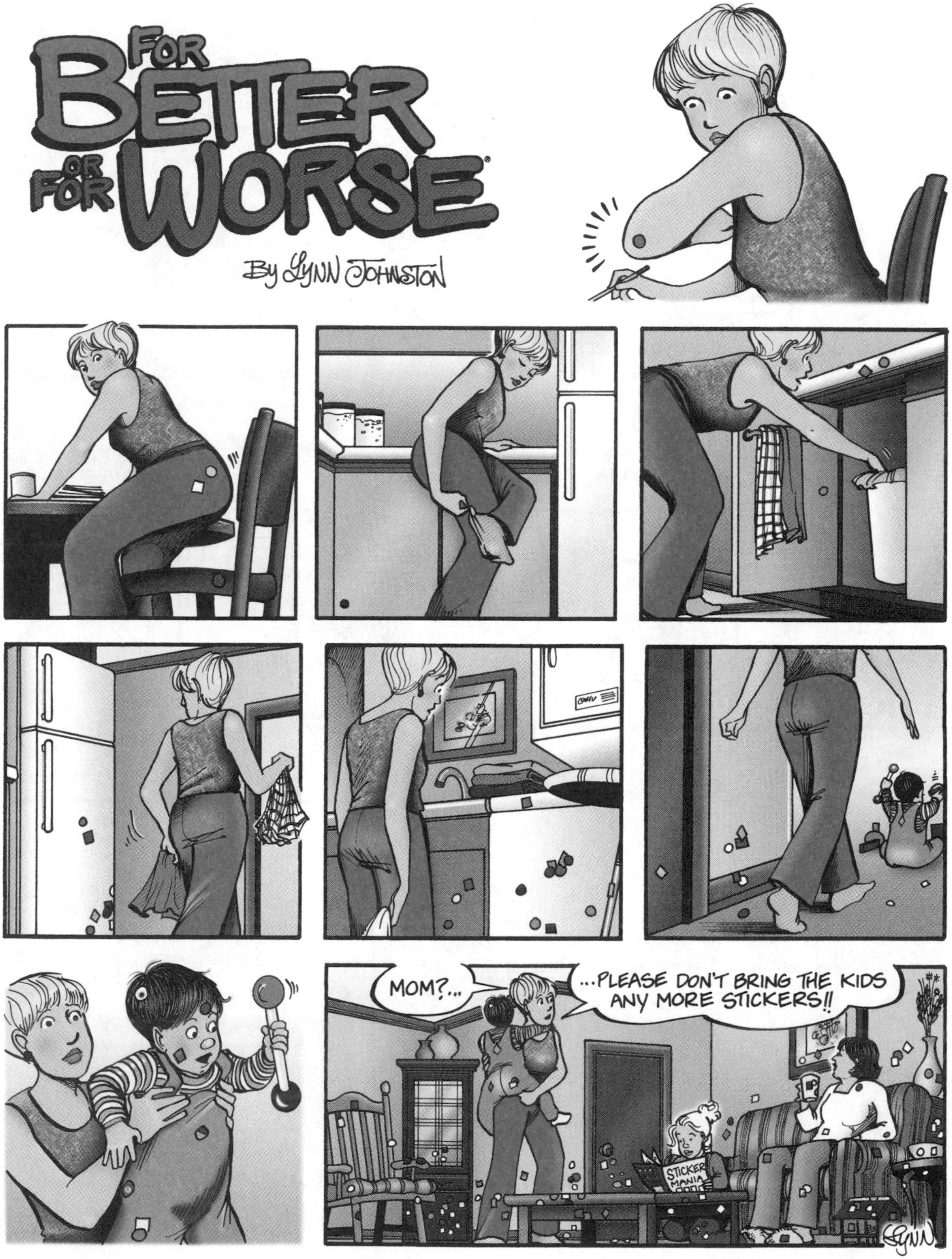
FOR BETTER OR FOR WORSE
BY LYNN JOHNSTON
MOM?...
...PLEASE DON'T BRING THE KIDS ANY MORE STICKERS!!
STICKER MANIA
LYNN

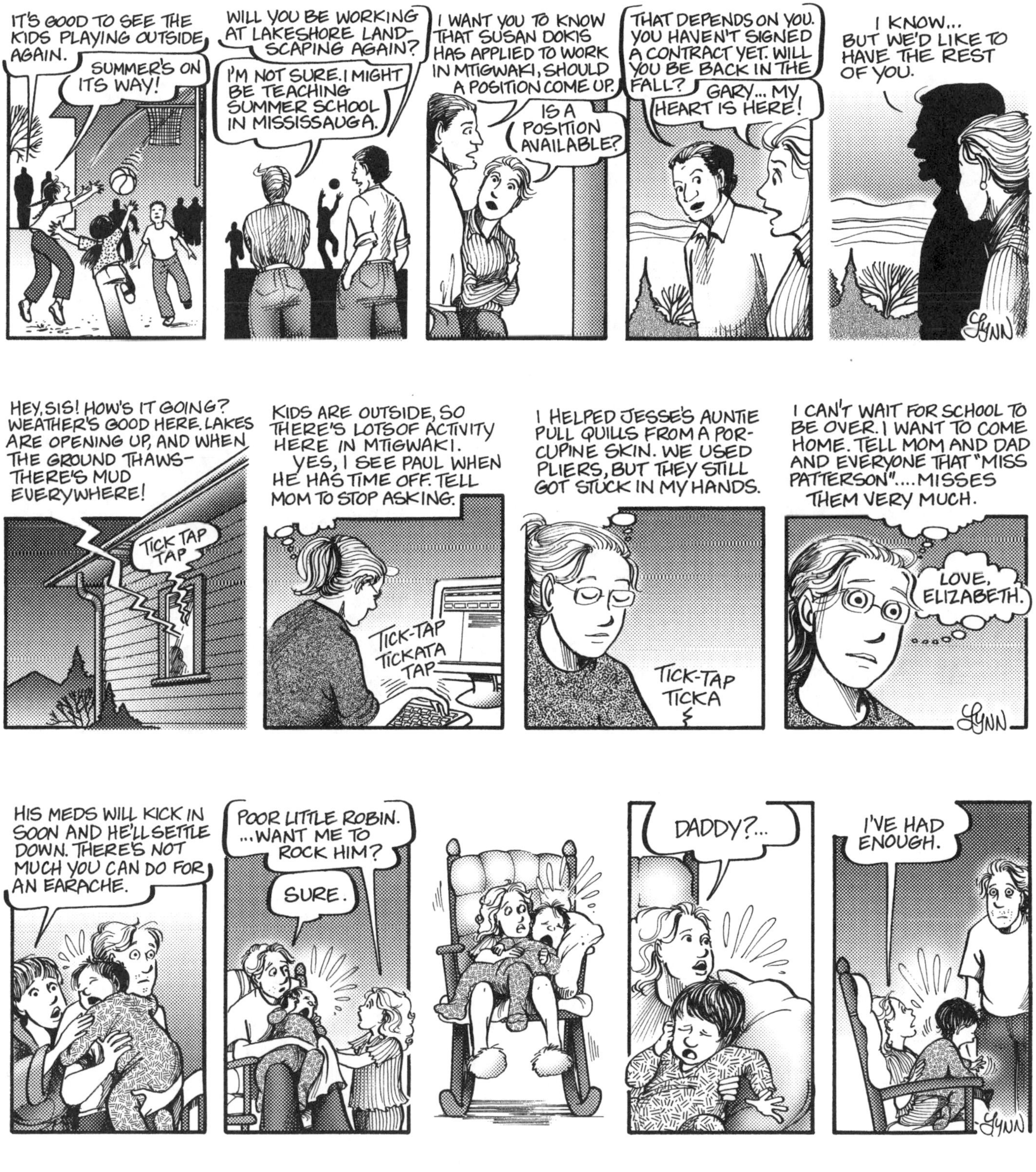
IT'S GOOD TO SEE THE KIDS PLAYING OUTSIDE AGAIN.
SUMMER'S ON ITS WAY!
WILL YOU BE WORKING AT LAKESHORE LANDSCAPING AGAIN?
I'M NOT SURE. I MIGHT BE TEACHING SUMMER SCHOOL IN MISSISSAUGA.
I WANT YOU TO KNOW THAT SUSAN DOKIS HAS APPLIED TO WORK IN MTIGWAKI, SHOULD A POSITION COME UP.
IS A POSITION AVAILABLE?
THAT DEPENDS ON YOU. YOU HAVEN'T SIGNED A CONTRACT YET. WILL YOU BE BACK IN THE FALL?
GARY... MY HEART IS HERE!
I KNOW... BUT WE'D LIKE TO HAVE THE REST OF YOU.
LYNN
HEY, SIS! HOW'S IT GOING? WEATHER'S GOOD HERE. LAKES ARE OPENING UP, AND WHEN THE GROUND THAWS- THERE'S MUD EVERYWHERE!
TICK TAP TAP
KIDS ARE OUTSIDE, SO THERE'S LOTSOF ACTIVITY HERE IN MTIGWAKI. YES, I SEE PAUL WHEN HE HAS TIME OFF. TELL MOM TO STOP ASKING.
TICK-TAP TICKATA TAP
I HELPED JESSE'S AUNTIE PULL QUILLS FROM A PORCUPINE SKIN. WE USED PLIERS, BUT THEY STILL GOT STUCK IN MY HANDS.
TICK-TAP TICKA
I CAN'T WAIT FOR SCHOOL TO BE OVER. I WANT TO COME HOME. TELL MOM AND DAD AND EVERYONE THAT "MISS PATTERSON".... MISSES THEM VERY MUCH.
LOVE, ELIZABETH.
LYNN
HIS MEDS WILL KICK IN SOON AND HE'LL SETTLE DOWN. THERE'S NOT MUCH YOU CAN DO FOR AN EARACHE.
POOR LITTLE ROBIN. ...WANT ME TO ROCK HIM?
SURE.
DADDY?...
I'VE HAD ENOUGH.
LYNN

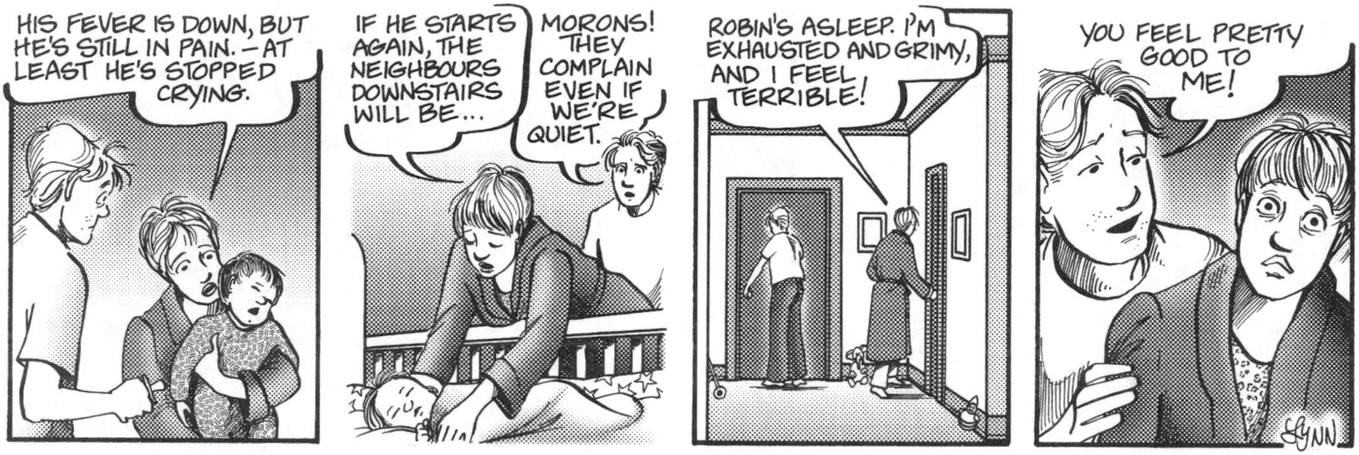
HIS FEVER IS DOWN, BUT HE'S STILL IN PAIN. —AT LEAST HE'S STOPPED CRYING.
IF HE STARTS AGAIN, THE NEIGHBOURS DOWNSTAIRS WILL BE...
MORONS! THEY COMPLAIN EVEN IF WE'RE QUIET.
ROBIN'S ASLEEP. I'M EXHAUSTED AND GRIMY, AND I FEEL TERRIBLE!
YOU FEEL PRETTY GOOD TO ME!
LYNN

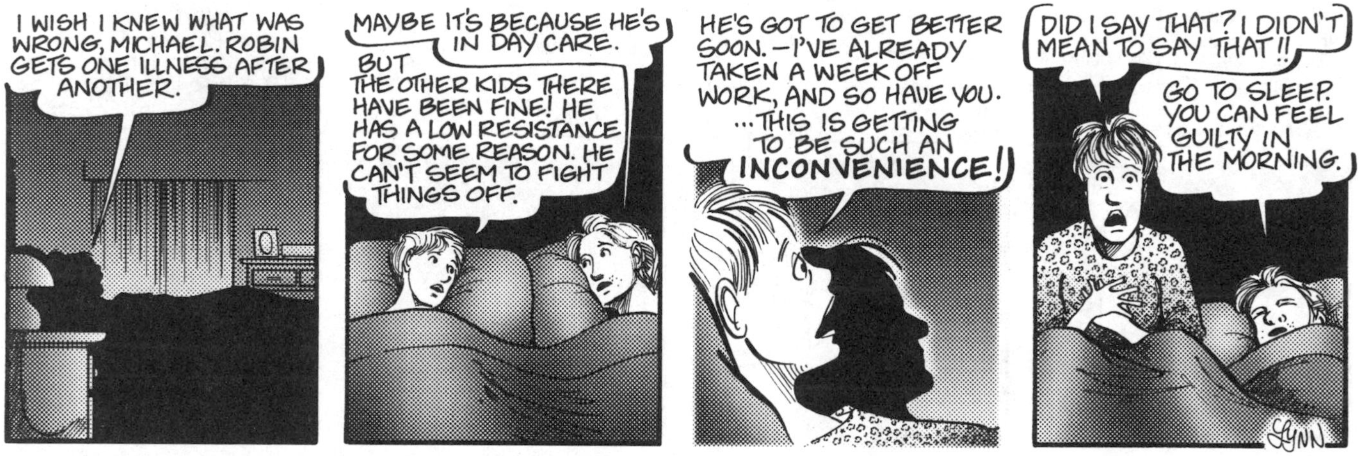
I WISH I KNEW WHAT WAS WRONG, MICHAEL. ROBIN GETS ONE ILLNESS AFTER ANOTHER.
MAYBE IT'S BECAUSE HE'S IN DAY CARE.
BUT THE OTHER KIDS THERE HAVE BEEN FINE! HE HAS A LOW RESISTANCE FOR SOME REASON. HE CAN'T SEEM TO FIGHT THINGS OFF.
HE'S GOT TO GET BETTER SOON. —I'VE ALREADY TAKEN A WEEK OFF WORK, AND SO HAVE YOU. ...THIS IS GETTING TO BE SUCH AN INCONVENIENCE!
DID I SAY THAT? I DIDN'T MEAN TO SAY THAT!!
GO TO SLEEP. YOU CAN FEEL GUILTY IN THE MORNING.
LYNN

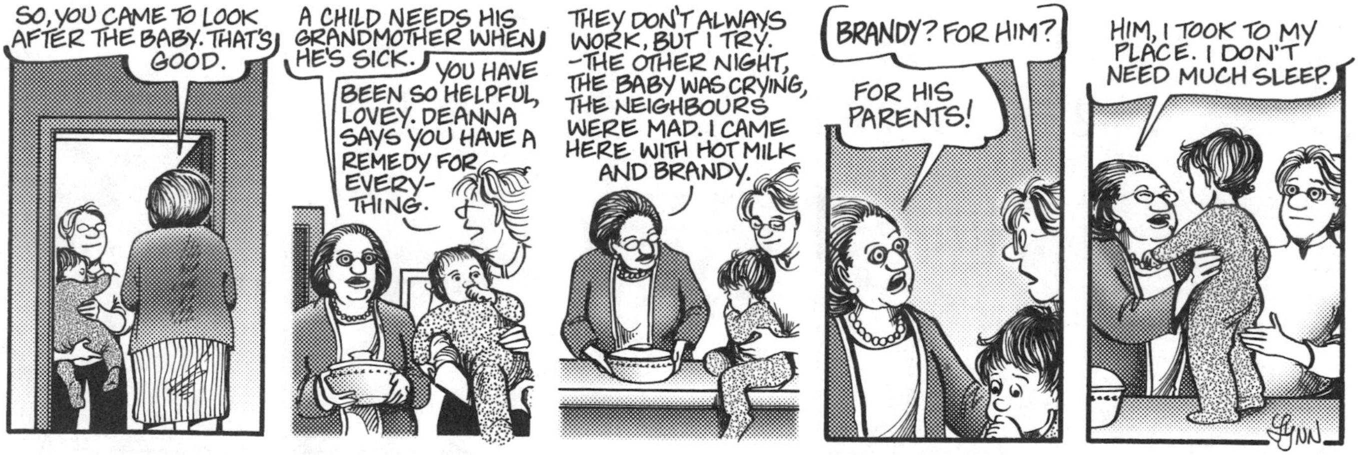
SO, YOU CAME TO LOOK AFTER THE BABY. THAT'S GOOD.
A CHILD NEEDS HIS GRANDMOTHER WHEN HE'S SICK.
YOU HAVE BEEN SO HELPFUL, LOVEY. DEANNA SAYS YOU HAVE A REMEDY FOR EVERY-THING.
THEY DON'T ALWAYS WORK, BUT I TRY. —THE OTHER NIGHT, THE BABY WAS CRYING, THE NEIGHBOURS WERE MAD. I CAME HERE WITH HOT MILK AND BRANDY.
BRANDY? FOR HIM?
FOR HIS PARENTS!
HIM, I TOOK TO MY PLACE. I DON'T NEED MUCH SLEEP.
LYNN

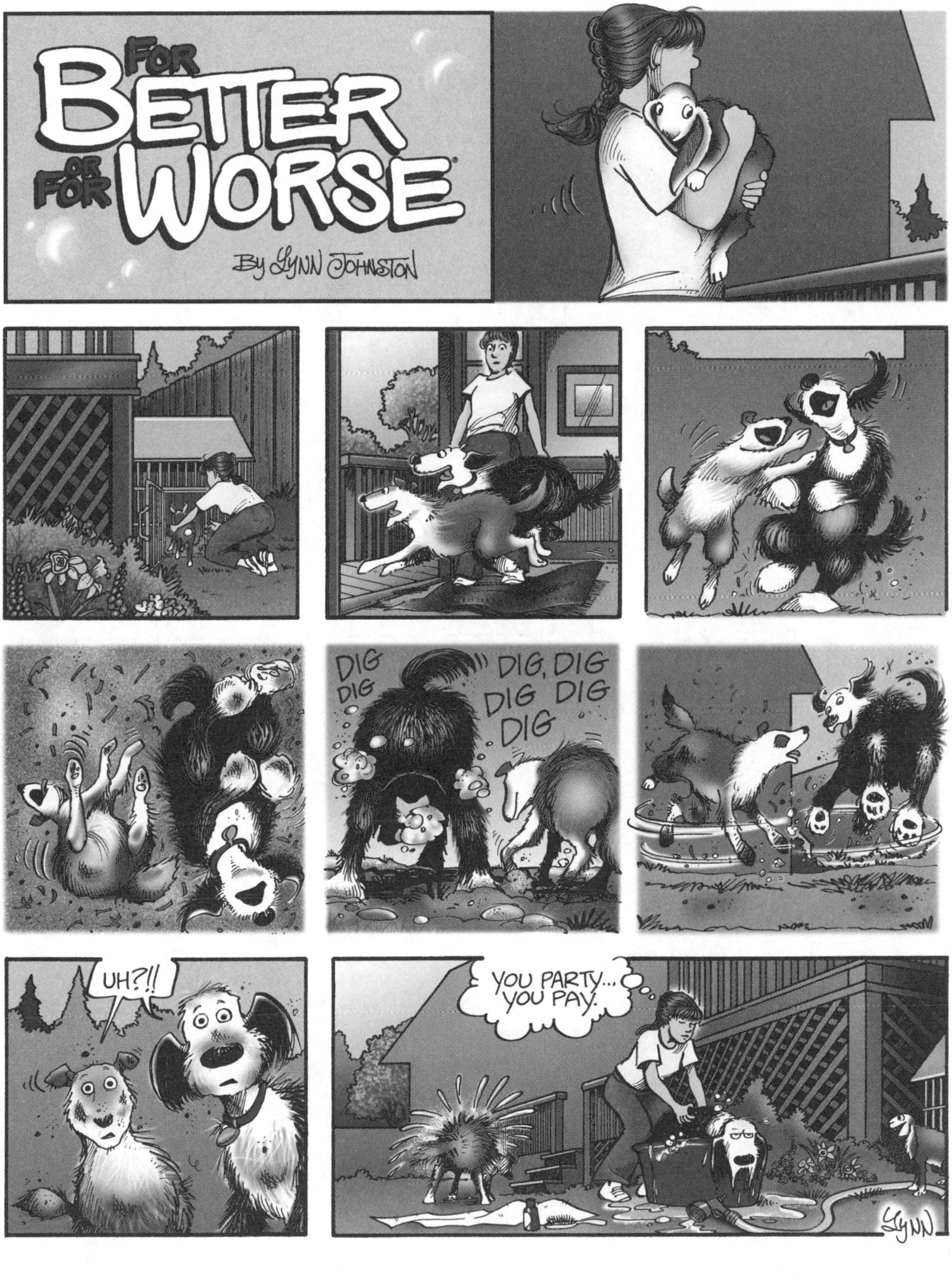
For Better or For Worse
By Lynn Johnston
DIG DIG
DIG, DIG DIG DIG DIG
UH?!!
YOU PARTY... YOU PAY.
LYNN

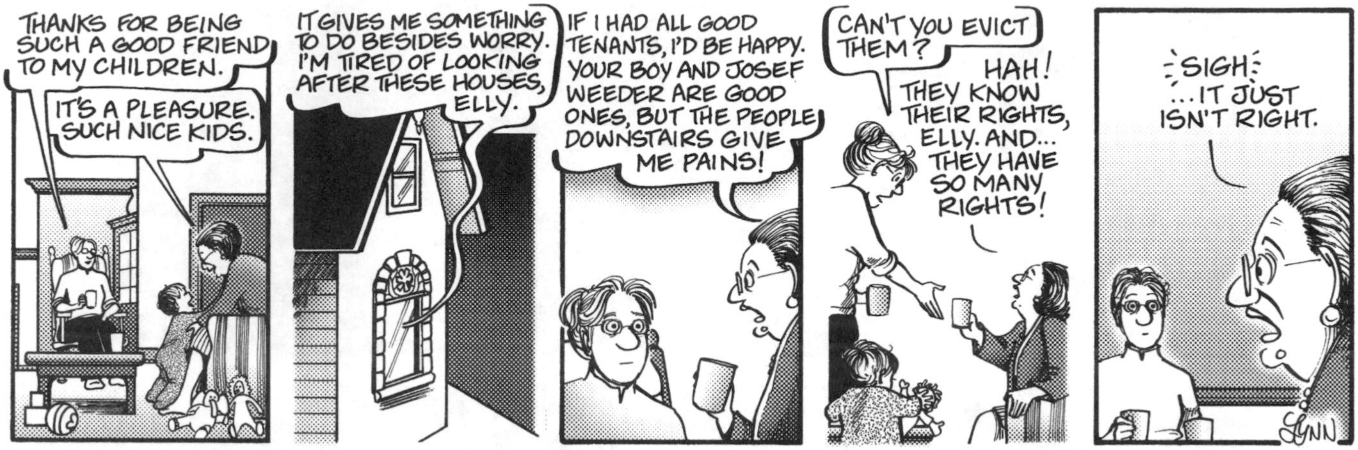
THANKS FOR BEING SUCH A GOOD FRIEND TO MY CHILDREN.
IT'S A PLEASURE. SUCH NICE KIDS.
IT GIVES ME SOMETHING TO DO BESIDES WORRY. I'M TIRED OF LOOKING AFTER THESE HOUSES, ELLY.
IF I HAD ALL GOOD TENANTS, I'D BE HAPPY. YOUR BOY AND JOSEF WEEDER ARE GOOD ONES, BUT THE PEOPLE DOWNSTAIRS GIVE ME PAINS!
CAN'T YOU EVICT THEM?
HAH! THEY KNOW THEIR RIGHTS, ELLY. AND... THEY HAVE SO MANY RIGHTS!
SIGH ...IT JUST ISN'T RIGHT.
LYNN

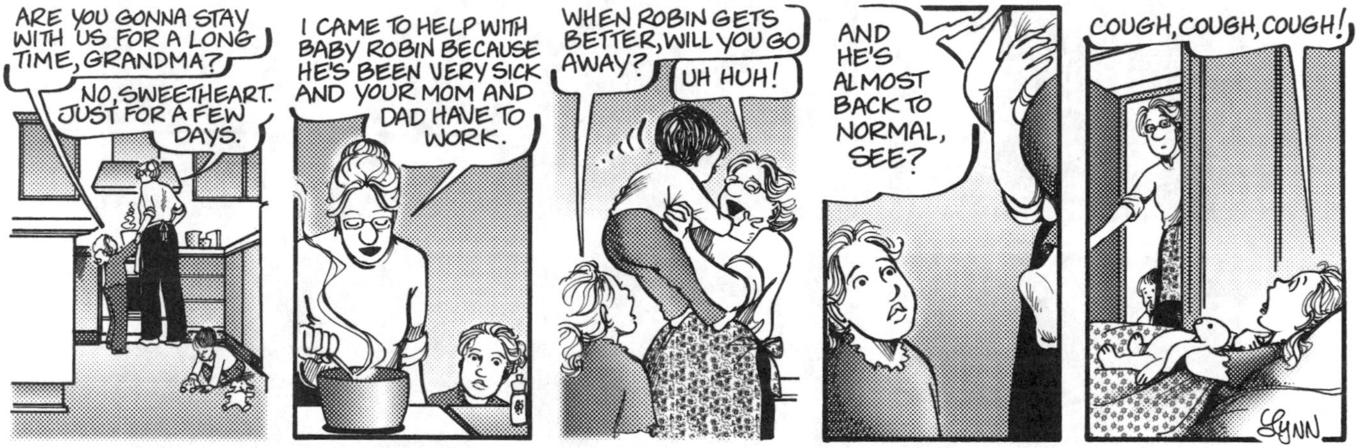
ARE YOU GONNA STAY WITH US FOR A LONG TIME, GRANDMA?
NO, SWEETHEART. JUST FOR A FEW DAYS.
I CAME TO HELP WITH BABY ROBIN BECAUSE HE'S BEEN VERY SICK AND YOUR MOM AND DAD HAVE TO WORK.
WHEN ROBIN GETS BETTER, WILL YOU GO AWAY?
UH HUH!
AND HE'S ALMOST BACK TO NORMAL, SEE?
COUGH, COUGH, COUGH!
LYNN

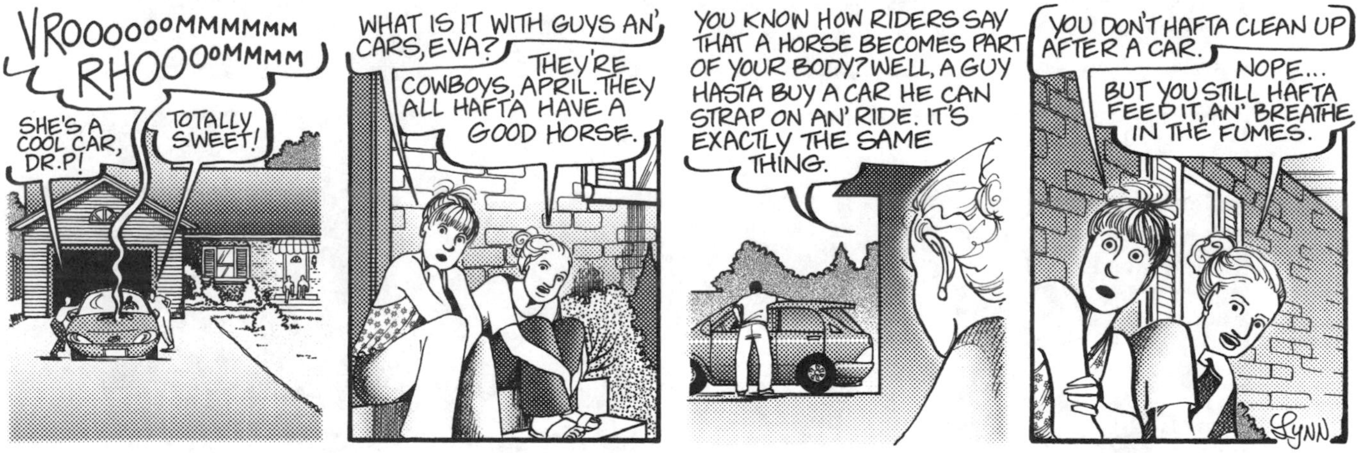
VROOOOOOOMMMMMM RHOOOOMMMMM
SHE'S A COOL CAR, DR. P!
TOTALLY SWEET!
WHAT IS IT WITH GUYS AN' CARS, EVA?
THEY'RE COWBOYS, APRIL. THEY ALL HAFTA HAVE A GOOD HORSE.
YOU KNOW HOW RIDERS SAY THAT A HORSE BECOMES PART OF YOUR BODY? WELL, A GUY HASTA BUY A CAR HE CAN STRAP ON AN' RIDE. IT'S EXACTLY THE SAME THING.
YOU DON'T HAFTA CLEAN UP AFTER A CAR.
NOPE... BUT YOU STILL HAFTA FEED IT, AN' BREATHE IN THE FUMES.
LYNN

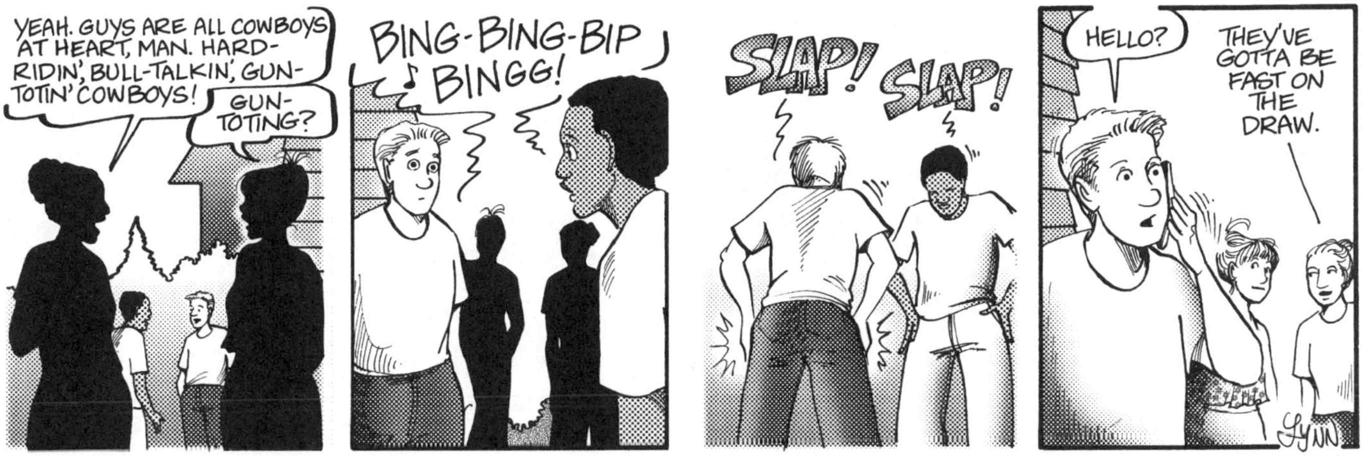
YEAH. GUYS ARE ALL COWBOYS AT HEART, MAN. HARD-RIDIN', BULL-TALKIN', GUN-TOTIN' COWBOYS!
GUN-TOTING?
BING-BING-BIP BINGG!
SLAP! SLAP!
HELLO?
THEY'VE GOTTA BE FAST ON THE DRAW.
LYNN

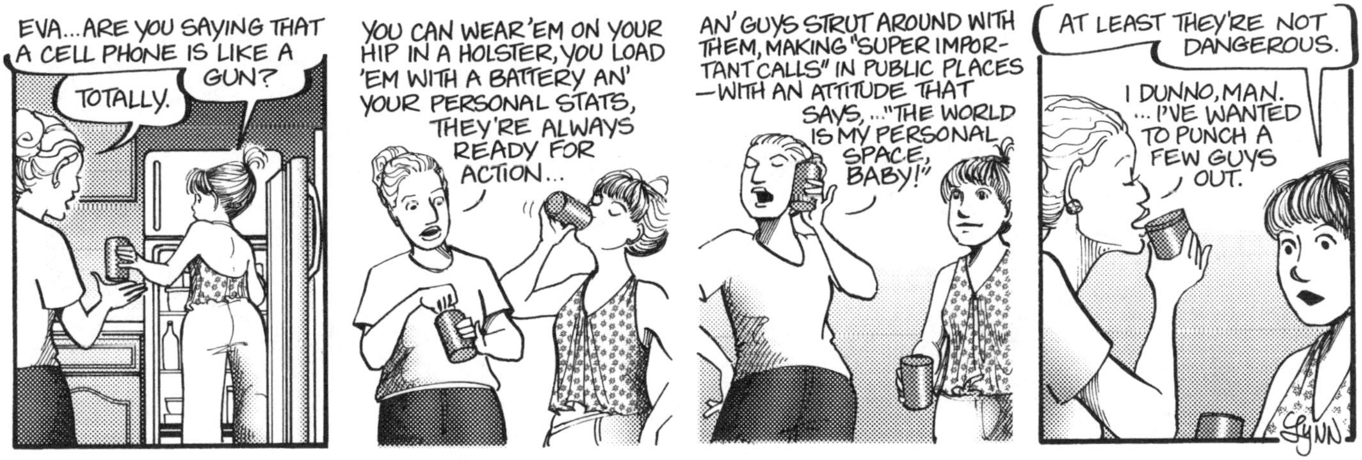
EVA... ARE YOU SAYING THAT A CELL PHONE IS LIKE A GUN?
TOTALLY.
YOU CAN WEAR 'EM ON YOUR HIP IN A HOLSTER, YOU LOAD 'EM WITH A BATTERY AN' YOUR PERSONAL STATS, THEY'RE ALWAYS READY FOR ACTION...
AN' GUYS STRUT AROUND WITH THEM, MAKING "SUPER IMPORTANT CALLS" IN PUBLIC PLACES —WITH AN ATTITUDE THAT SAYS, ..."THE WORLD IS MY PERSONAL SPACE, BABY!"
AT LEAST THEY'RE NOT DANGEROUS.
I DUNNO, MAN. ...I'VE WANTED TO PUNCH A FEW GUYS OUT.
LYNN

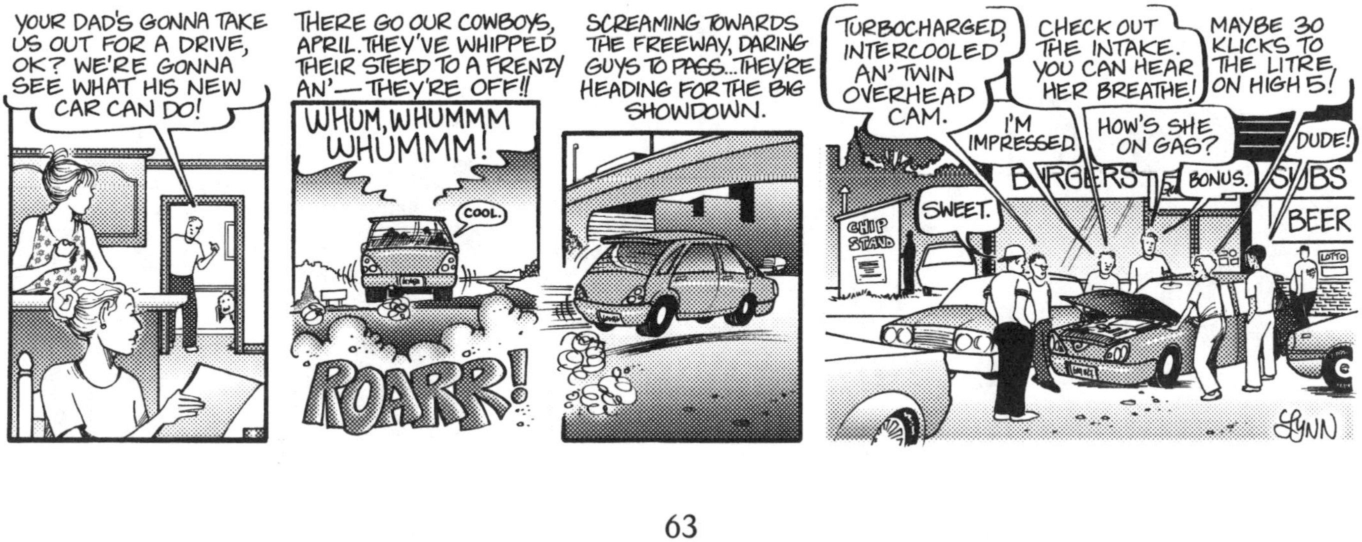
YOUR DAD'S GONNA TAKE US OUT FOR A DRIVE, OK? WE'RE GONNA SEE WHAT HIS NEW CAR CAN DO!
THERE GO OUR COWBOYS, APRIL. THEY'VE WHIPPED THEIR STEED TO A FRENZY AN'— THEY'RE OFF!!
WHUM, WHUMMM WHUMMM!
COOL.
ROARR!
SCREAMING TOWARDS THE FREEWAY, DARING GUYS TO PASS... THEY'RE HEADING FOR THE BIG SHOWDOWN.
TURBOCHARGED, INTERCOOLED AN' TWIN OVERHEAD CAM.
I'M IMPRESSED.
SWEET.
CHECK OUT THE INTAKE. YOU CAN HEAR HER BREATHE!
HOW'S SHE ON GAS?
BONUS.
MAYBE 30 KLICKS TO THE LITRE ON HIGH 5!
DUDE!
BURGERS
SUBS
BEER
CHIP STAND
LOTTO
LYNN

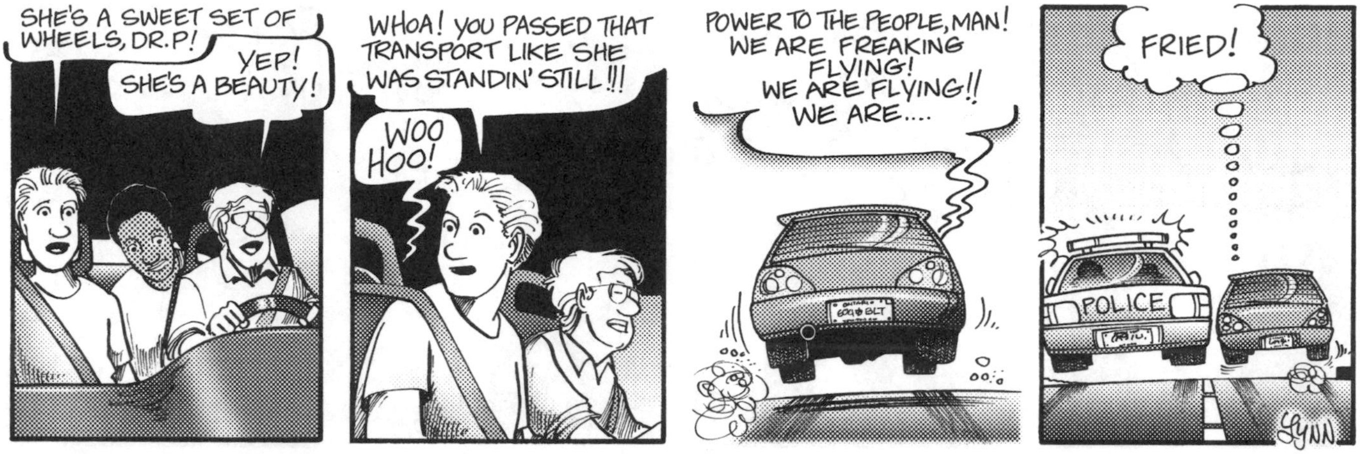
SHE'S A SWEET SET OF WHEELS, DR.P!
YEP! SHE'S A BEAUTY!
WHOA! YOU PASSED THAT TRANSPORT LIKE SHE WAS STANDIN' STILL!!!
WOO HOO!
POWER TO THE PEOPLE, MAN! WE ARE FREAKING FLYING! WE ARE FLYING!! WE ARE....
POLICE
FRIED!
LYNN

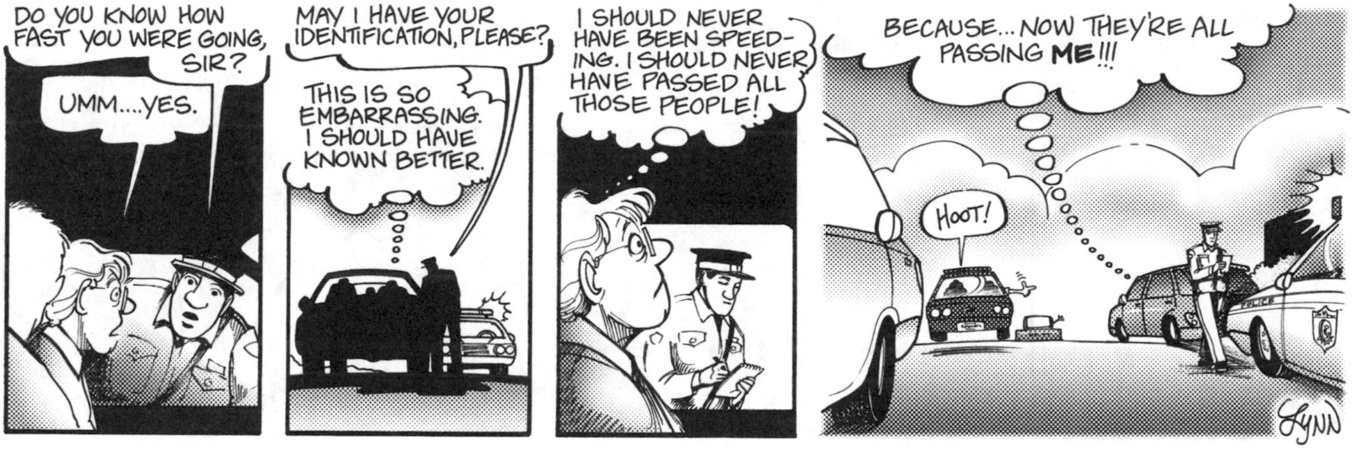
DO YOU KNOW HOW FAST YOU WERE GOING, SIR?
UMM....YES.
MAY I HAVE YOUR IDENTIFICATION, PLEASE?
THIS IS SO EMBARRASSING. I SHOULD HAVE KNOWN BETTER.
I SHOULD NEVER HAVE BEEN SPEEDING. I SHOULD NEVER HAVE PASSED ALL THOSE PEOPLE!
BECAUSE... NOW THEY'RE ALL PASSING **ME**!!!
HOOT!
POLICE
LYNN

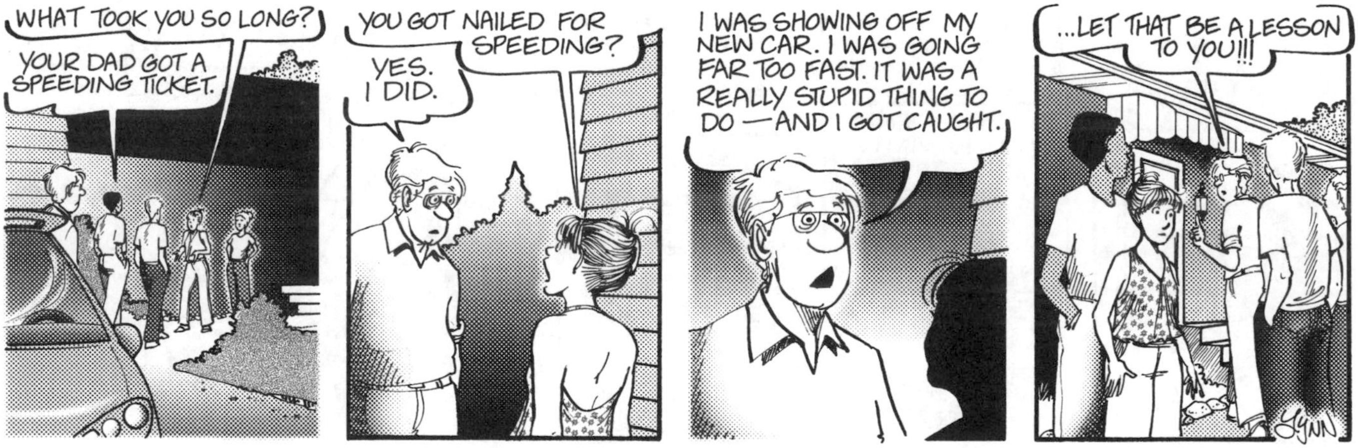
WHAT TOOK YOU SO LONG?
YOUR DAD GOT A SPEEDING TICKET.
YOU GOT NAILED FOR SPEEDING?
YES. I DID.
I WAS SHOWING OFF MY NEW CAR. I WAS GOING FAR TOO FAST. IT WAS A REALLY STUPID THING TO DO — AND I GOT CAUGHT.
...LET THAT BE A LESSON TO YOU!!!
LYNN

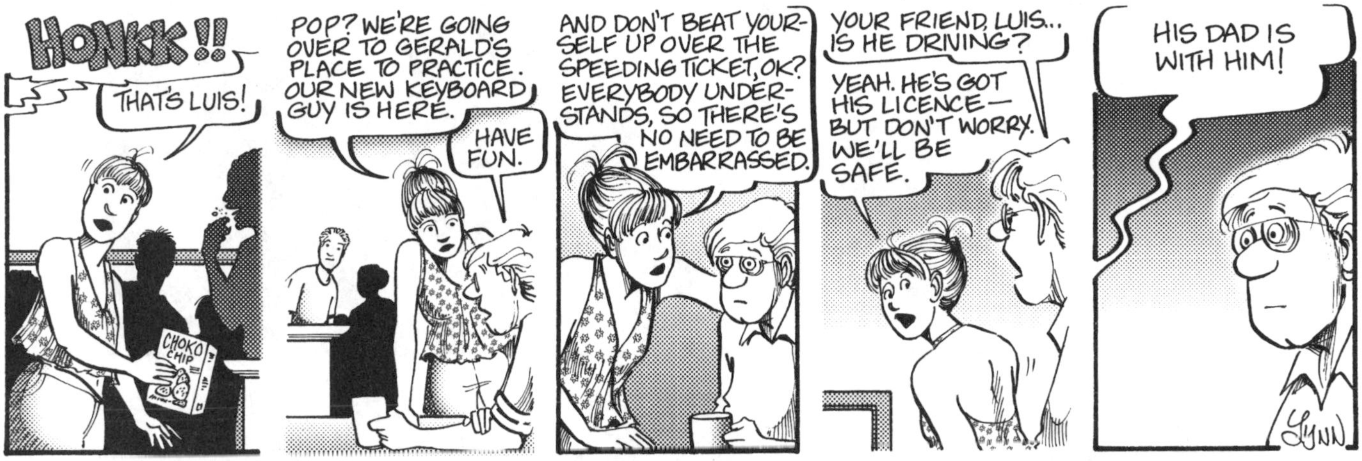
HONKK!!
THAT'S LUIS!
CHOKO CHIP
POP? WE'RE GOING OVER TO GERALD'S PLACE TO PRACTICE. OUR NEW KEYBOARD GUY IS HERE.
HAVE FUN.
AND DON'T BEAT YOURSELF UP OVER THE SPEEDING TICKET, OK? EVERYBODY UNDERSTANDS, SO THERE'S NO NEED TO BE EMBARRASSED.
YOUR FRIEND, LUIS... IS HE DRIVING?
YEAH. HE'S GOT HIS LICENCE— BUT DON'T WORRY. WE'LL BE SAFE.
HIS DAD IS WITH HIM!
LYNN

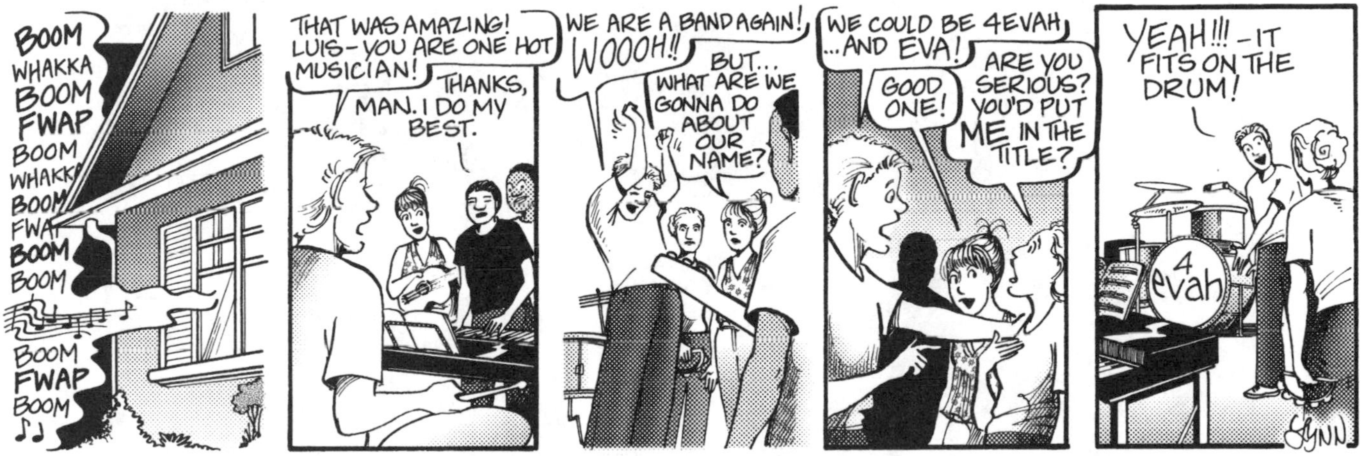
BOOM WHAKKA BOOM FWAP BOOM WHAKKA BOOM FWAP BOOM BOOM
BOOM FWAP BOOM
THAT WAS AMAZING! LUIS—YOU ARE ONE HOT MUSICIAN!
THANKS, MAN. I DO MY BEST.
WE ARE A BAND AGAIN! WOOOH!!
BUT... WHAT ARE WE GONNA DO ABOUT OUR NAME?
WE COULD BE 4EVAH ...AND EVA!
GOOD ONE!
ARE YOU SERIOUS? YOU'D PUT ME IN THE TITLE?
YEAH!!! —IT FITS ON THE DRUM!
4 evah
LYNN

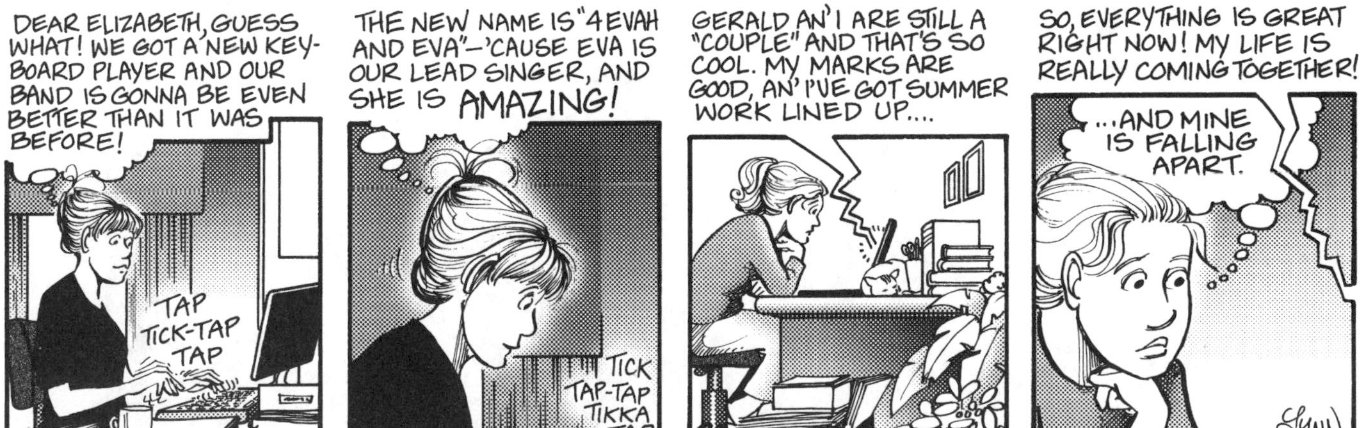
DEAR ELIZABETH, GUESS WHAT! WE GOT A NEW KEYBOARD PLAYER AND OUR BAND IS GONNA BE EVEN BETTER THAN IT WAS BEFORE!
TAP TICK-TAP TAP
THE NEW NAME IS "4 EVAH AND EVA"—'CAUSE EVA IS OUR LEAD SINGER, AND SHE IS AMAZING!
TICK TAP-TAP TIKKA TAP
GERALD AN' I ARE STILL A "COUPLE" AND THAT'S SO COOL. MY MARKS ARE GOOD, AN' I'VE GOT SUMMER WORK LINED UP....
SO, EVERYTHING IS GREAT RIGHT NOW! MY LIFE IS REALLY COMING TOGETHER!
...AND MINE IS FALLING APART.
LYNN

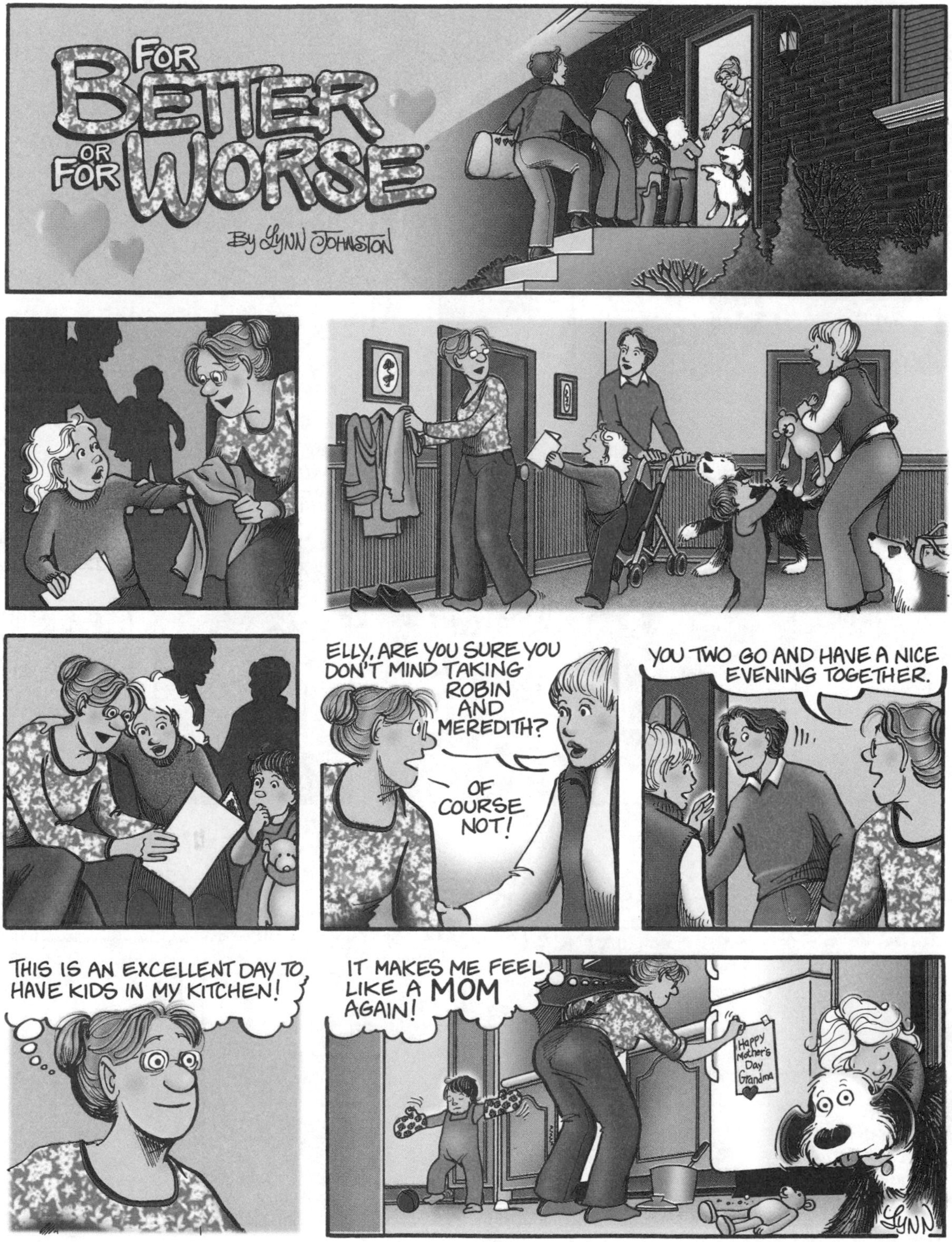
FOR BETTER OR FOR WORSE
BY LYNN JOHNSTON
ELLY, ARE YOU SURE YOU DON'T MIND TAKING ROBIN AND MEREDITH?
OF COURSE NOT!
YOU TWO GO AND HAVE A NICE EVENING TOGETHER.
THIS IS AN EXCELLENT DAY TO HAVE KIDS IN MY KITCHEN!
IT MAKES ME FEEL LIKE A MOM AGAIN!
Happy Mother's Day Grandma
LYNN

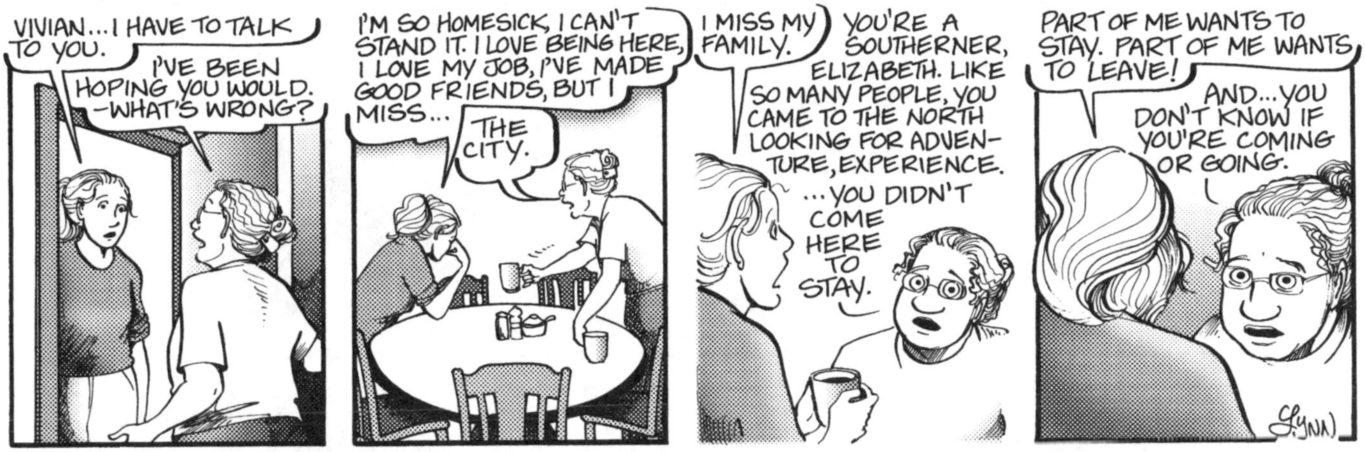
VIVIAN... I HAVE TO TALK TO YOU.
I'VE BEEN HOPING YOU WOULD. -WHAT'S WRONG?
I'M SO HOMESICK, I CAN'T STAND IT. I LOVE BEING HERE, I LOVE MY JOB, I'VE MADE GOOD FRIENDS, BUT I MISS...
THE CITY.
I MISS MY FAMILY.
YOU'RE A SOUTHERNER, ELIZABETH. LIKE SO MANY PEOPLE, YOU CAME TO THE NORTH LOOKING FOR ADVENTURE, EXPERIENCE.
...YOU DIDN'T COME HERE TO STAY.
PART OF ME WANTS TO STAY. PART OF ME WANTS TO LEAVE!
AND...YOU DON'T KNOW IF YOU'RE COMING OR GOING.
LYNN

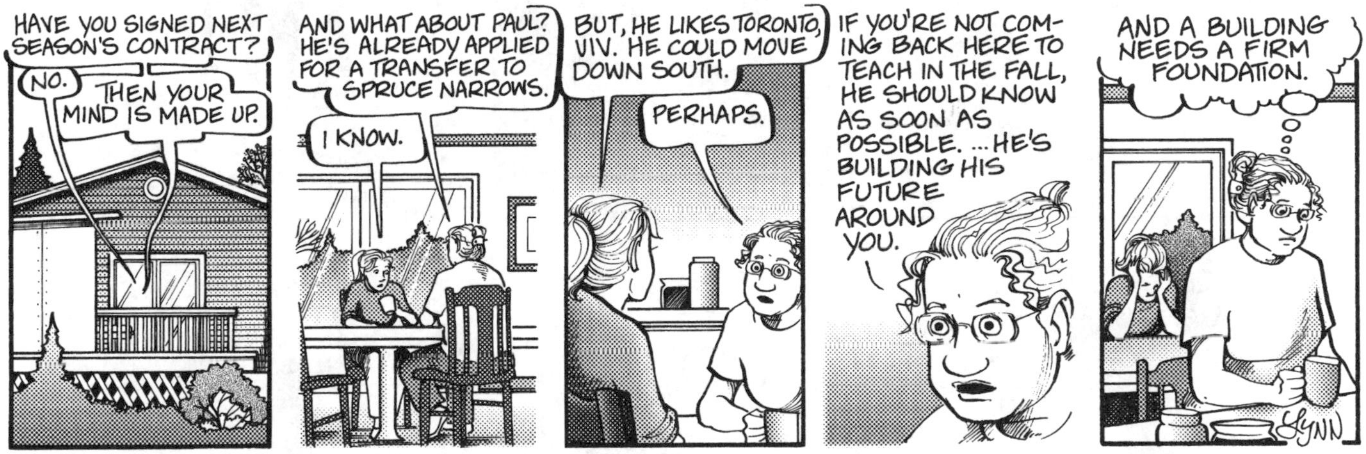
HAVE YOU SIGNED NEXT SEASON'S CONTRACT?
NO.
THEN YOUR MIND IS MADE UP.
AND WHAT ABOUT PAUL? HE'S ALREADY APPLIED FOR A TRANSFER TO SPRUCE NARROWS.
I KNOW.
BUT, HE LIKES TORONTO, VIV. HE COULD MOVE DOWN SOUTH.
PERHAPS.
IF YOU'RE NOT COMING BACK HERE TO TEACH IN THE FALL, HE SHOULD KNOW AS SOON AS POSSIBLE. ...HE'S BUILDING HIS FUTURE AROUND YOU.
AND A BUILDING NEEDS A FIRM FOUNDATION.
LYNN

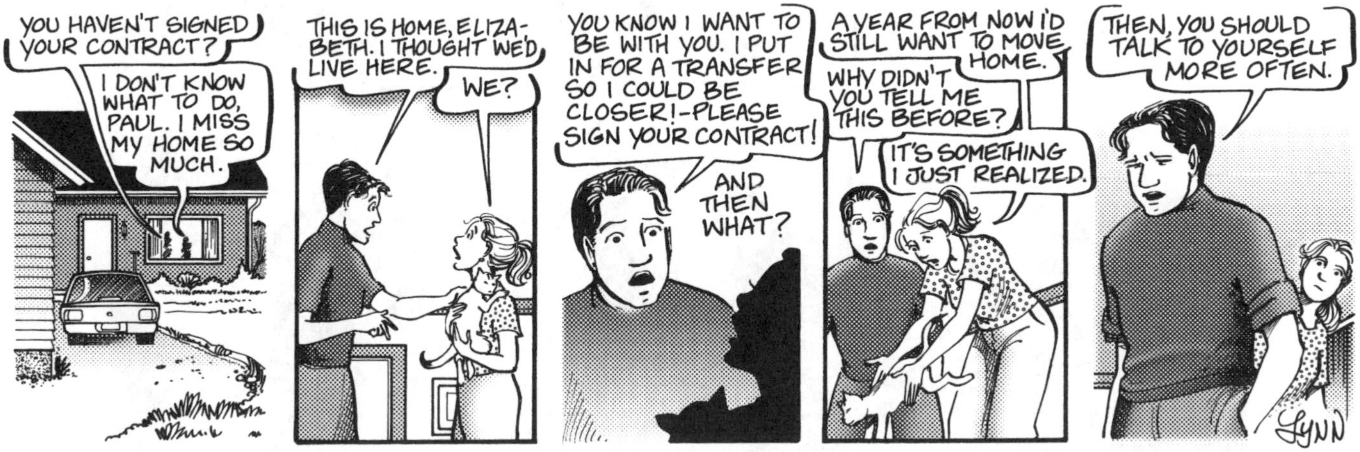
YOU HAVEN'T SIGNED YOUR CONTRACT?
I DON'T KNOW WHAT TO DO, PAUL. I MISS MY HOME SO MUCH.
THIS IS HOME, ELIZABETH. I THOUGHT WE'D LIVE HERE.
WE?
YOU KNOW I WANT TO BE WITH YOU. I PUT IN FOR A TRANSFER SO I COULD BE CLOSER! -PLEASE SIGN YOUR CONTRACT!
AND THEN WHAT?
A YEAR FROM NOW I'D STILL WANT TO MOVE HOME.
WHY DIDN'T YOU TELL ME THIS BEFORE?
IT'S SOMETHING I JUST REALIZED.
THEN, YOU SHOULD TALK TO YOURSELF MORE OFTEN.
LYNN

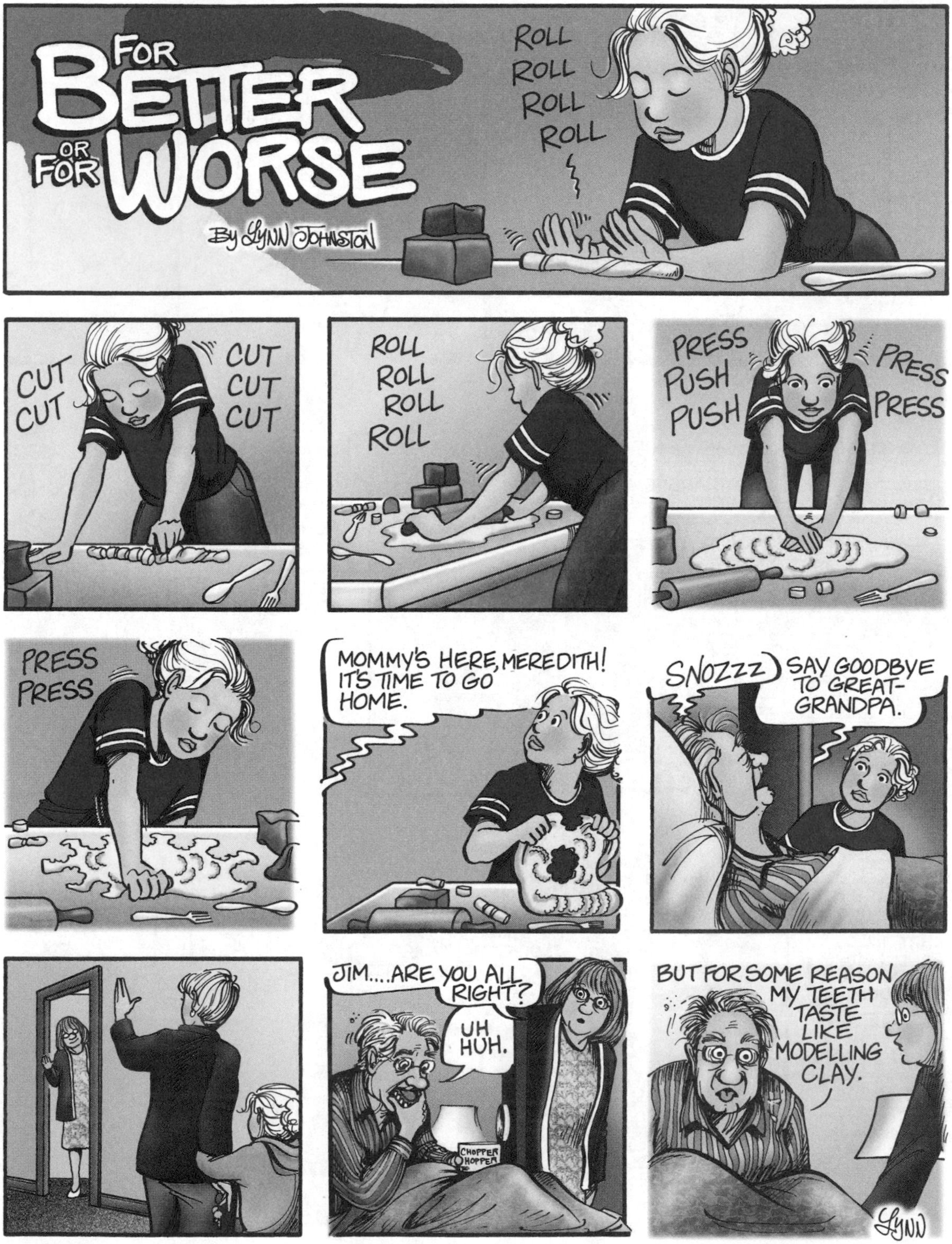
FOR BETTER OR FOR WORSE
By Lynn Johnston
ROLL ROLL ROLL ROLL
CUT CUT
CUT CUT CUT
ROLL ROLL ROLL ROLL
PRESS PUSH PUSH
PRESS PRESS
PRESS PRESS
MOMMY'S HERE, MEREDITH! IT'S TIME TO GO HOME.
SNOZZZ
SAY GOODBYE TO GREAT-GRANDPA.
JIM....ARE YOU ALL RIGHT?
UH HUH.
CHOPPER HOPPER
BUT FOR SOME REASON MY TEETH TASTE LIKE MODELLING CLAY.
Lynn

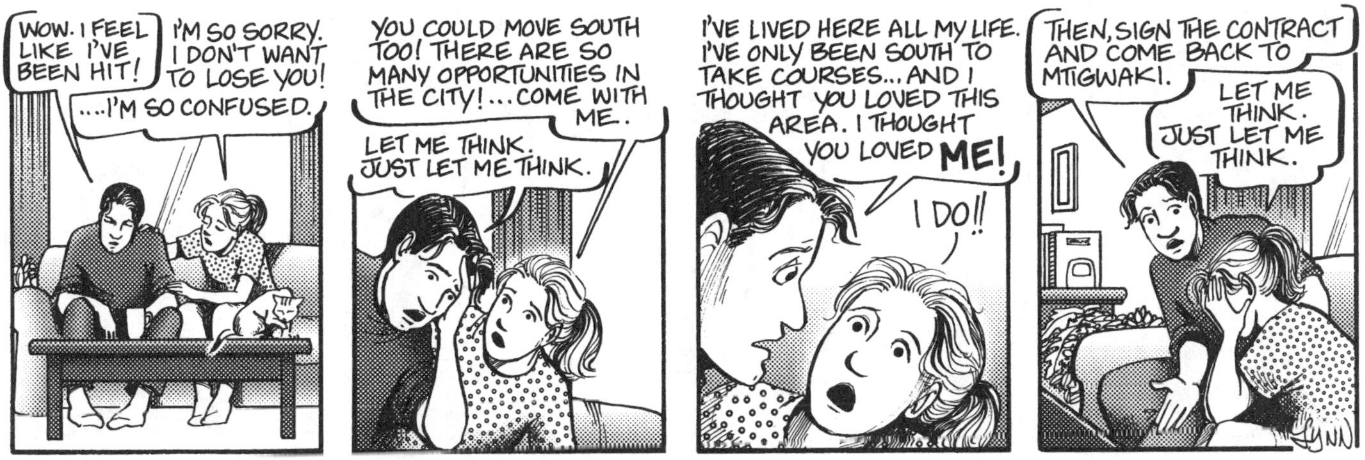
WOW. I FEEL LIKE I'VE BEEN HIT!
I'M SO SORRY. I DON'T WANT TO LOSE YOU!
....I'M SO CONFUSED.
YOU COULD MOVE SOUTH TOO! THERE ARE SO MANY OPPORTUNITIES IN THE CITY!...COME WITH ME.
LET ME THINK. JUST LET ME THINK.
I'VE LIVED HERE ALL MY LIFE. I'VE ONLY BEEN SOUTH TO TAKE COURSES...AND I THOUGHT YOU LOVED THIS AREA. I THOUGHT YOU LOVED ME!
I DO!!
THEN, SIGN THE CONTRACT AND COME BACK TO MTIGWAKI.
LET ME THINK. JUST LET ME THINK.
LYNN

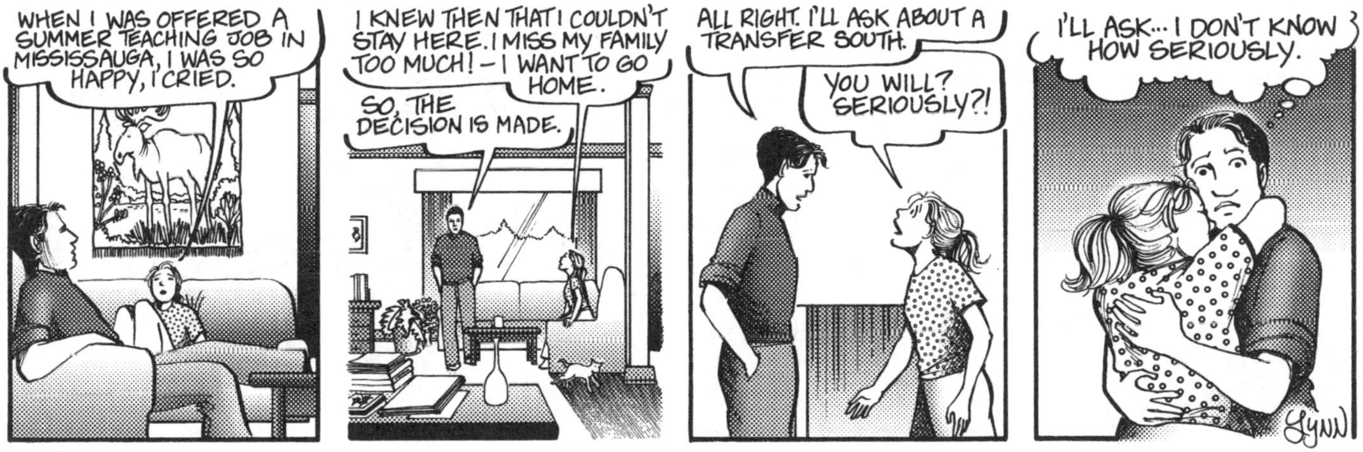
WHEN I WAS OFFERED A SUMMER TEACHING JOB IN MISSISSAUGA, I WAS SO HAPPY, I CRIED.
I KNEW THEN THAT I COULDN'T STAY HERE. I MISS MY FAMILY TOO MUCH! – I WANT TO GO HOME.
SO, THE DECISION IS MADE.
ALL RIGHT. I'LL ASK ABOUT A TRANSFER SOUTH.
YOU WILL? SERIOUSLY?!
I'LL ASK... I DON'T KNOW HOW SERIOUSLY.
LYNN

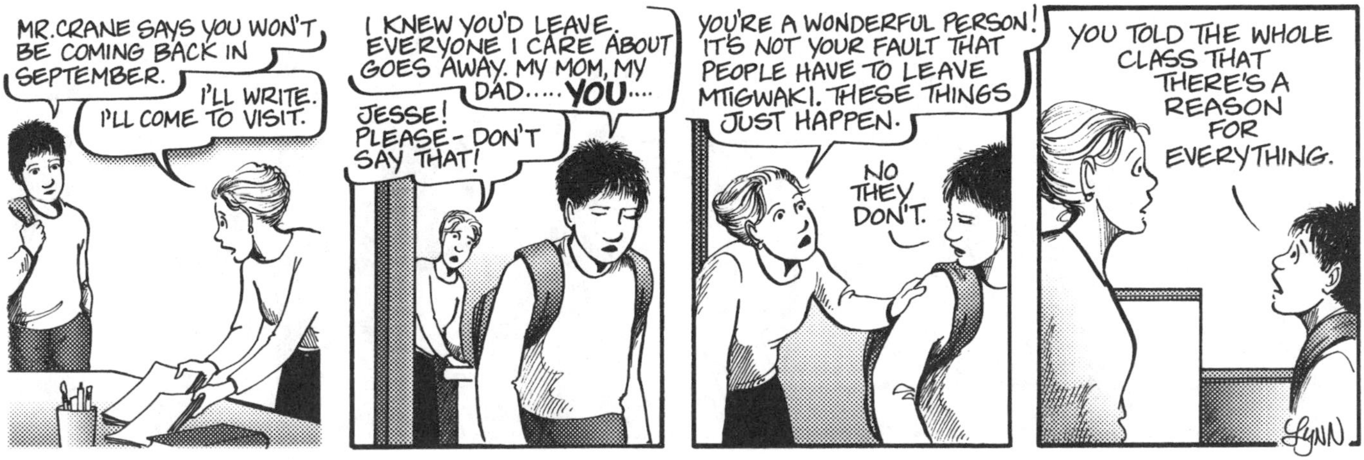
MR. CRANE SAYS YOU WON'T BE COMING BACK IN SEPTEMBER.
I'LL WRITE. I'LL COME TO VISIT.
I KNEW YOU'D LEAVE. EVERYONE I CARE ABOUT GOES AWAY. MY MOM, MY DAD..... YOU....
JESSE! PLEASE- DON'T SAY THAT!
YOU'RE A WONDERFUL PERSON! IT'S NOT YOUR FAULT THAT PEOPLE HAVE TO LEAVE MTIGWAKI. THESE THINGS JUST HAPPEN.
NO THEY DON'T.
YOU TOLD THE WHOLE CLASS THAT THERE'S A REASON FOR EVERYTHING.
LYNN

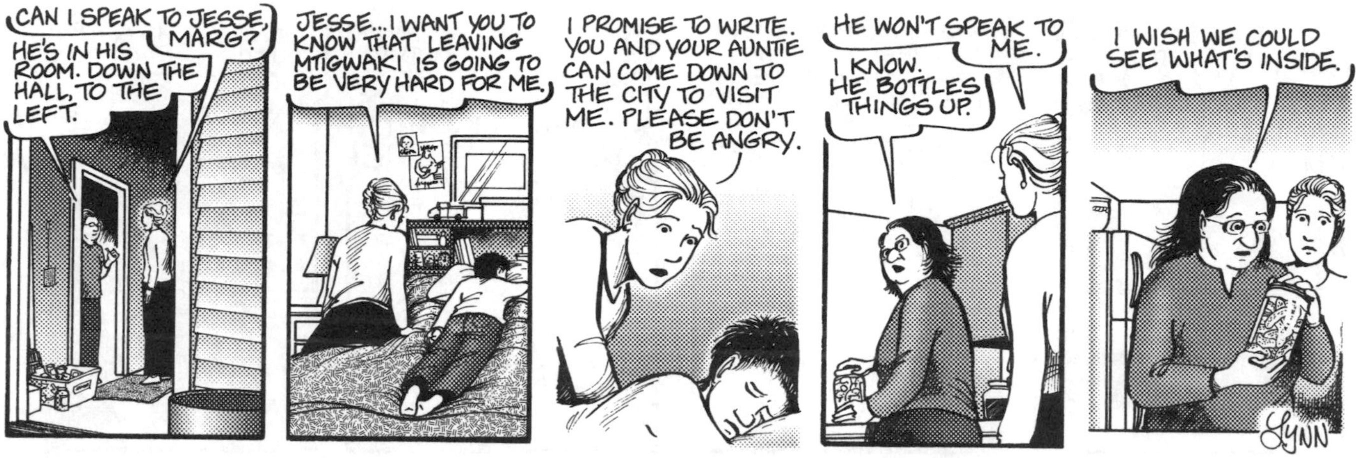
CAN I SPEAK TO JESSE, MARG?
HE'S IN HIS ROOM. DOWN THE HALL, TO THE LEFT.
JESSE...I WANT YOU TO KNOW THAT LEAVING MTIGWAKI IS GOING TO BE VERY HARD FOR ME.
I PROMISE TO WRITE. YOU AND YOUR AUNTIE CAN COME DOWN TO THE CITY TO VISIT ME. PLEASE DON'T BE ANGRY.
HE WON'T SPEAK TO ME.
I KNOW. HE BOTTLES THINGS UP.
I WISH WE COULD SEE WHAT'S INSIDE.
LYNN

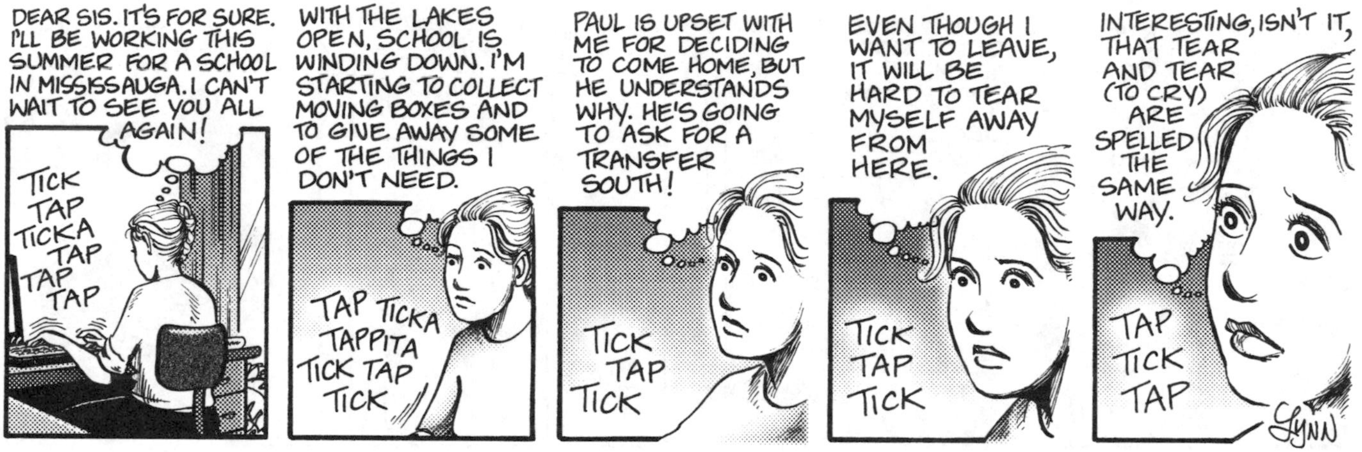
DEAR SIS. IT'S FOR SURE. I'LL BE WORKING THIS SUMMER FOR A SCHOOL IN MISSISSAUGA. I CAN'T WAIT TO SEE YOU ALL AGAIN!
TICK TAP TICKA TAP TAP TAP
WITH THE LAKES OPEN, SCHOOL IS WINDING DOWN. I'M STARTING TO COLLECT MOVING BOXES AND TO GIVE AWAY SOME OF THE THINGS I DON'T NEED.
TAP TICKA TAPPITA TICK TAP TICK
PAUL IS UPSET WITH ME FOR DECIDING TO COME HOME, BUT HE UNDERSTANDS WHY. HE'S GOING TO ASK FOR A TRANSFER SOUTH!
TICK TAP TICK
EVEN THOUGH I WANT TO LEAVE, IT WILL BE HARD TO TEAR MYSELF AWAY FROM HERE.
TICK TAP TICK
INTERESTING, ISN'T IT, THAT TEAR AND TEAR (TO CRY) ARE SPELLED THE SAME WAY.
TAP TICK TAP
LYNN

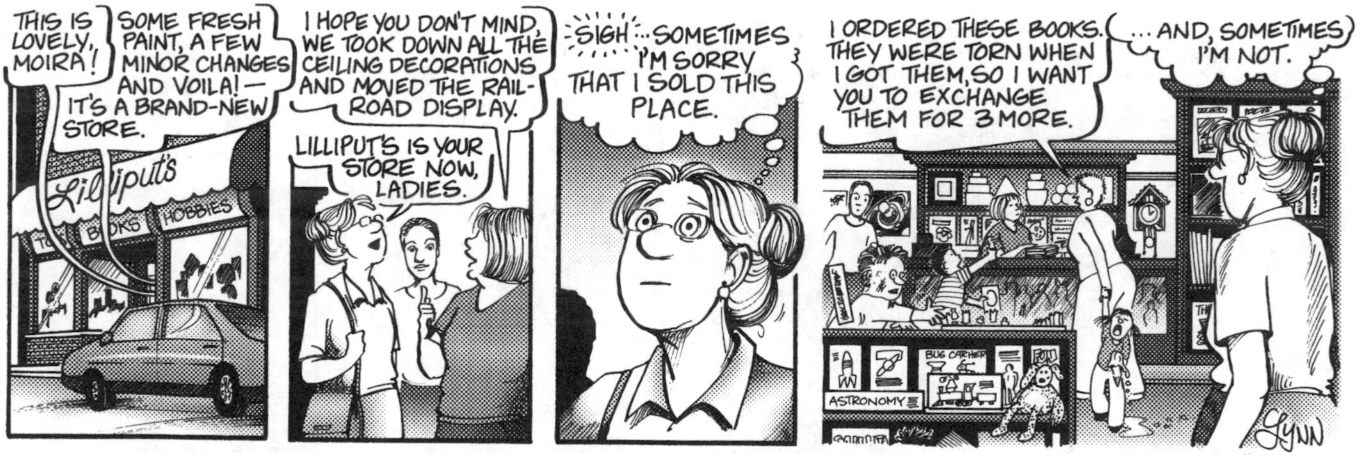
THIS IS LOVELY, MOIRA!
SOME FRESH PAINT, A FEW MINOR CHANGES AND VOILA! — IT'S A BRAND-NEW STORE.
Lilliput's
BOOKS
HOBBIES
I HOPE YOU DON'T MIND, WE TOOK DOWN ALL THE CEILING DECORATIONS AND MOVED THE RAILROAD DISPLAY.
LILLIPUT'S IS YOUR STORE NOW, LADIES.
SIGH ...SOMETIMES I'M SORRY THAT I SOLD THIS PLACE.
I ORDERED THESE BOOKS. THEY WERE TORN WHEN I GOT THEM, SO I WANT YOU TO EXCHANGE THEM FOR 3 MORE.
...AND, SOMETIMES I'M NOT.
BUG CATCHER
ASTRONOMY
LYNN

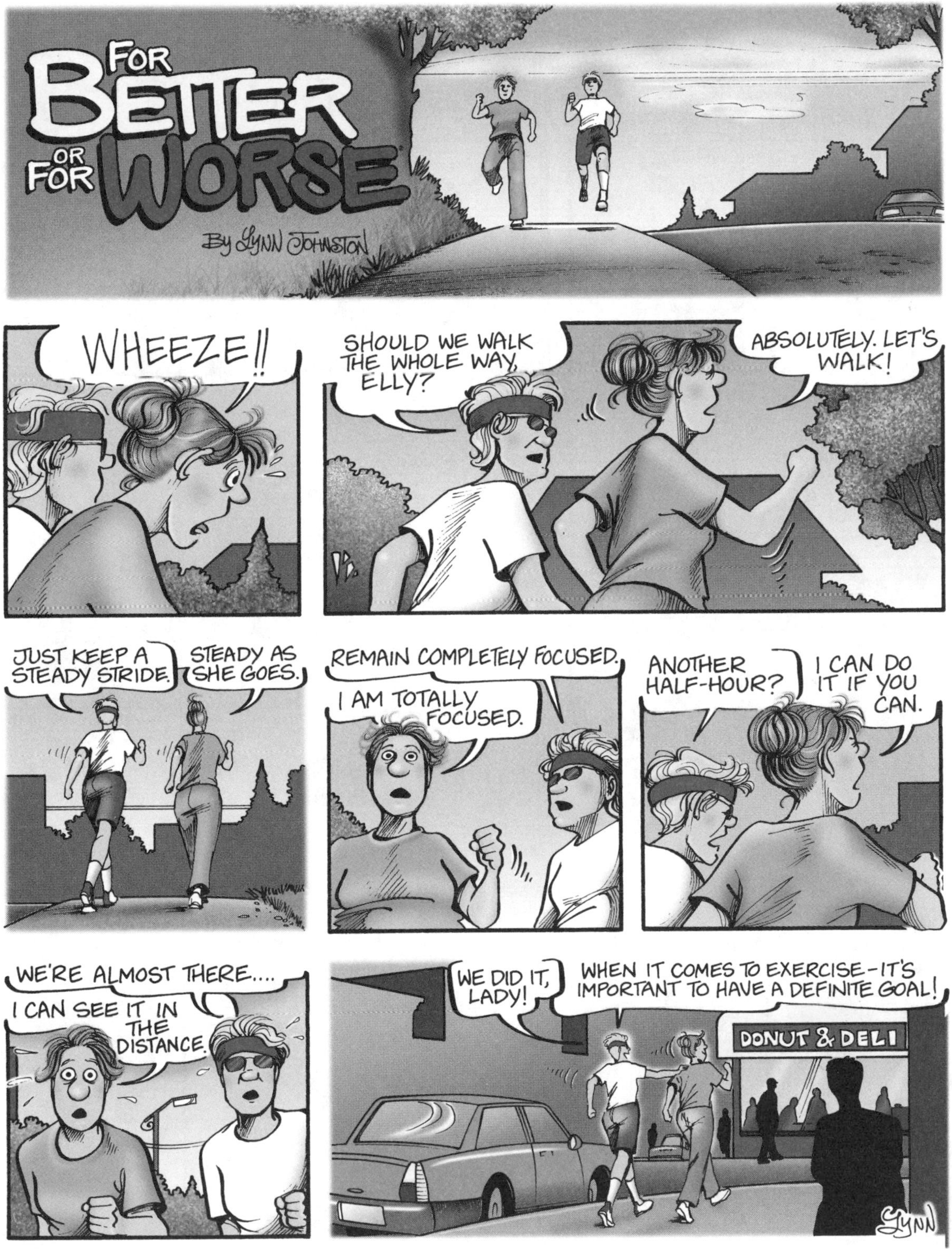
FOR BETTER OR FOR WORSE
BY LYNN JOHNSTON
WHEEZE!!
SHOULD WE WALK THE WHOLE WAY, ELLY?
ABSOLUTELY. LET'S WALK!
JUST KEEP A STEADY STRIDE.
STEADY AS SHE GOES.
REMAIN COMPLETELY FOCUSED.
I AM TOTALLY FOCUSED.
ANOTHER HALF-HOUR?
I CAN DO IT IF YOU CAN.
WE'RE ALMOST THERE....
I CAN SEE IT IN THE DISTANCE.
WE DID IT, LADY!
WHEN IT COMES TO EXERCISE-IT'S IMPORTANT TO HAVE A DEFINITE GOAL!
DONUT & DELI
LYNN

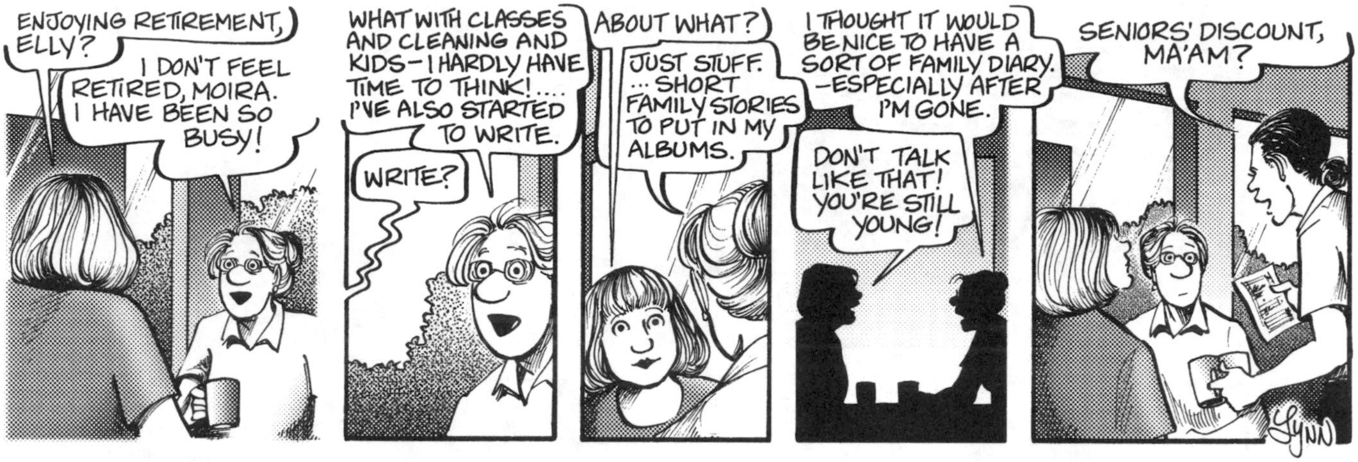
ENJOYING RETIREMENT, ELLY?
I DON'T FEEL RETIRED, MOIRA. I HAVE BEEN SO BUSY!
WHAT WITH CLASSES AND CLEANING AND KIDS–I HARDLY HAVE TIME TO THINK!.... I'VE ALSO STARTED TO WRITE.
WRITE?
ABOUT WHAT?
JUST STUFF. ...SHORT FAMILY STORIES TO PUT IN MY ALBUMS.
I THOUGHT IT WOULD BE NICE TO HAVE A SORT OF FAMILY DIARY. –ESPECIALLY AFTER I'M GONE.
DON'T TALK LIKE THAT! YOU'RE STILL YOUNG!
SENIORS' DISCOUNT, MA'AM?
LYNN

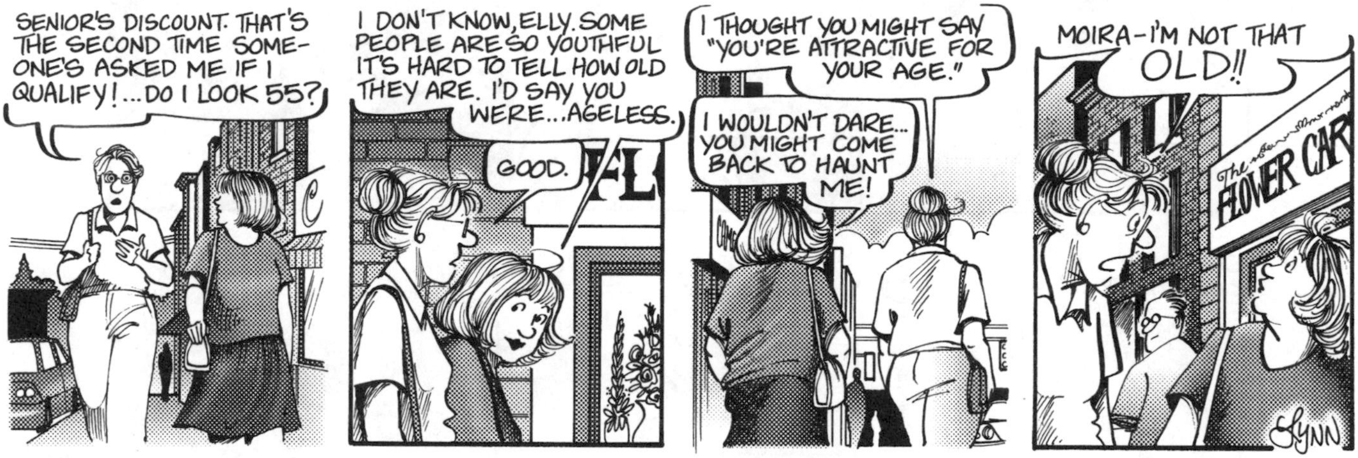
SENIOR'S DISCOUNT. THAT'S THE SECOND TIME SOMEONE'S ASKED ME IF I QUALIFY!...DO I LOOK 55?
I DON'T KNOW, ELLY. SOME PEOPLE ARE SO YOUTHFUL IT'S HARD TO TELL HOW OLD THEY ARE. I'D SAY YOU WERE...AGELESS.
GOOD.
I THOUGHT YOU MIGHT SAY "YOU'RE ATTRACTIVE FOR YOUR AGE."
I WOULDN'T DARE... YOU MIGHT COME BACK TO HAUNT ME!
MOIRA–I'M NOT THAT OLD!!
The FLOWER CART
LYNN

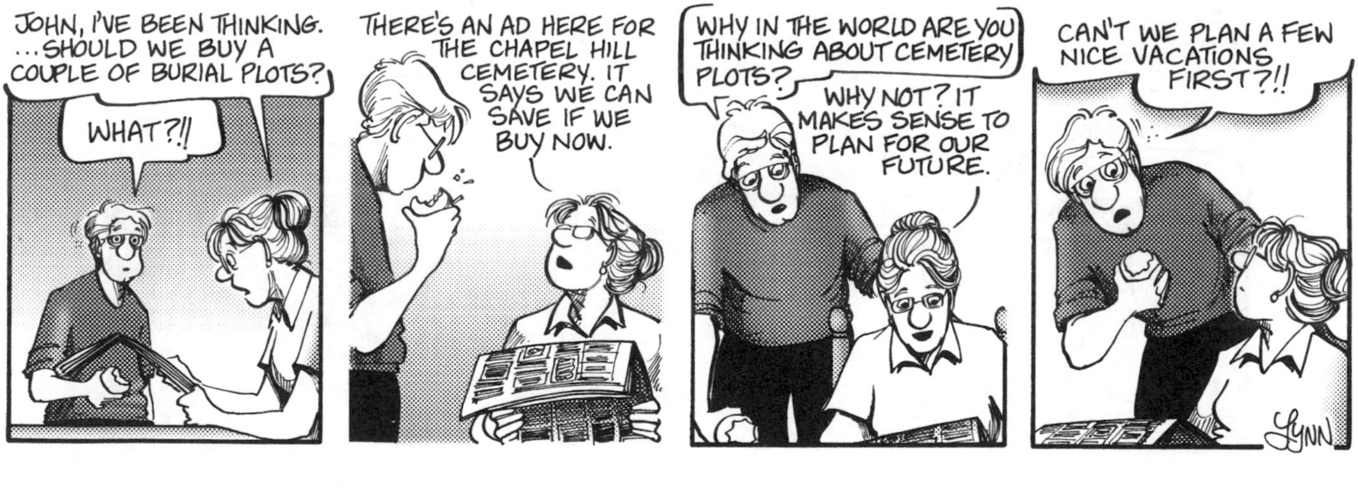
JOHN, I'VE BEEN THINKING. ...SHOULD WE BUY A COUPLE OF BURIAL PLOTS?
WHAT?!!
THERE'S AN AD HERE FOR THE CHAPEL HILL CEMETERY. IT SAYS WE CAN SAVE IF WE BUY NOW.
WHY IN THE WORLD ARE YOU THINKING ABOUT CEMETERY PLOTS?
WHY NOT? IT MAKES SENSE TO PLAN FOR OUR FUTURE.
CAN'T WE PLAN A FEW NICE VACATIONS FIRST?!!
LYNN

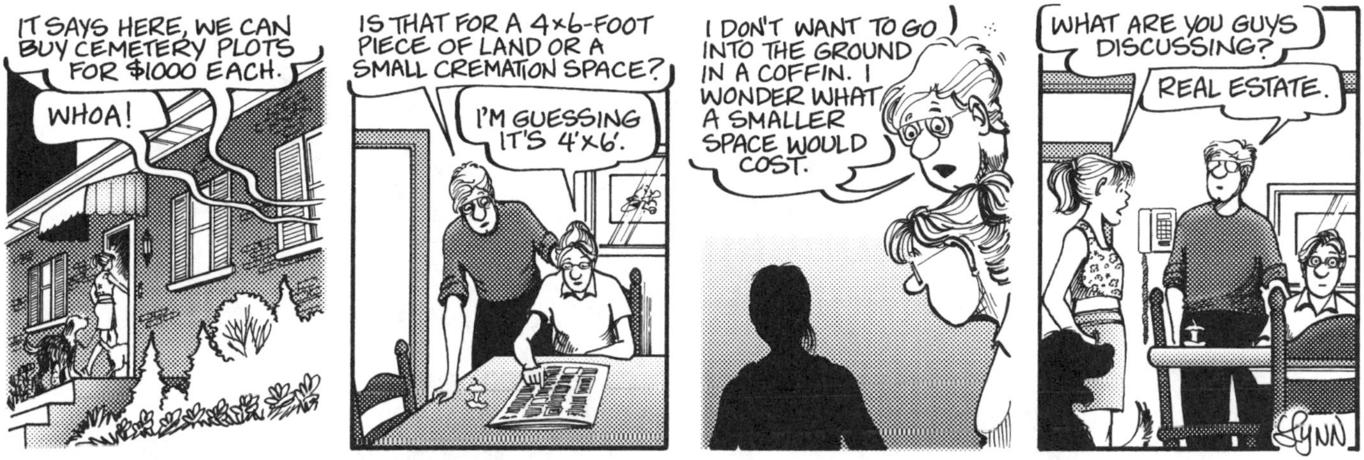
IT SAYS HERE, WE CAN BUY CEMETERY PLOTS FOR $1000 EACH.
WHOA!
IS THAT FOR A 4×6-FOOT PIECE OF LAND OR A SMALL CREMATION SPACE?
I'M GUESSING IT'S 4'×6'.
I DON'T WANT TO GO INTO THE GROUND IN A COFFIN. I WONDER WHAT A SMALLER SPACE WOULD COST.
WHAT ARE YOU GUYS DISCUSSING?
REAL ESTATE.
LYNN

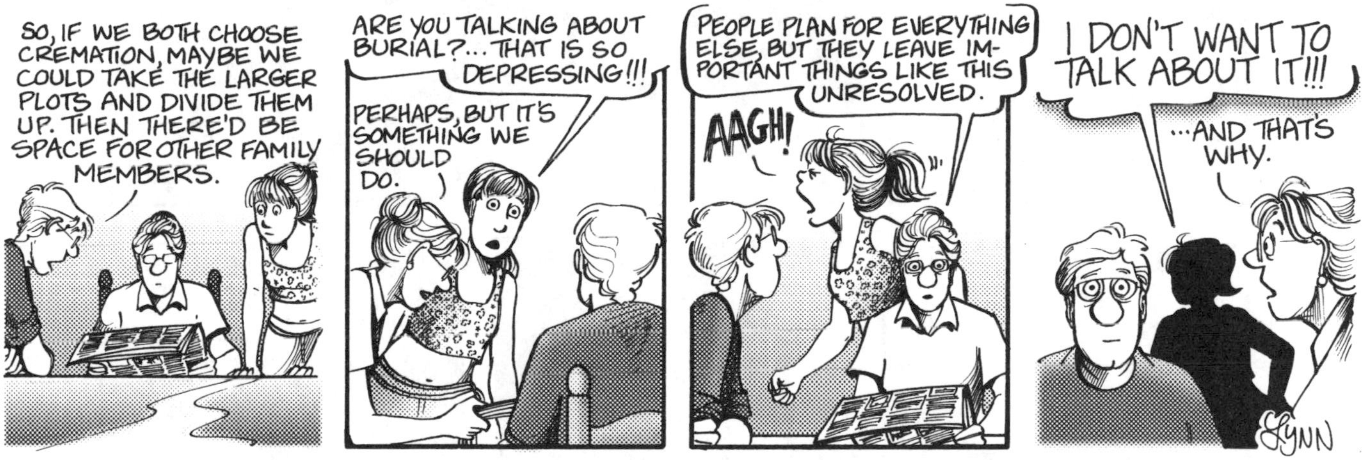
SO, IF WE BOTH CHOOSE CREMATION, MAYBE WE COULD TAKE THE LARGER PLOTS AND DIVIDE THEM UP. THEN THERE'D BE SPACE FOR OTHER FAMILY MEMBERS.
ARE YOU TALKING ABOUT BURIAL?... THAT IS SO DEPRESSING!!!
PERHAPS, BUT IT'S SOMETHING WE SHOULD DO.
PEOPLE PLAN FOR EVERYTHING ELSE, BUT THEY LEAVE IMPORTANT THINGS LIKE THIS UNRESOLVED.
AAGH!
I DON'T WANT TO TALK ABOUT IT!!!
...AND THAT'S WHY.
LYNN

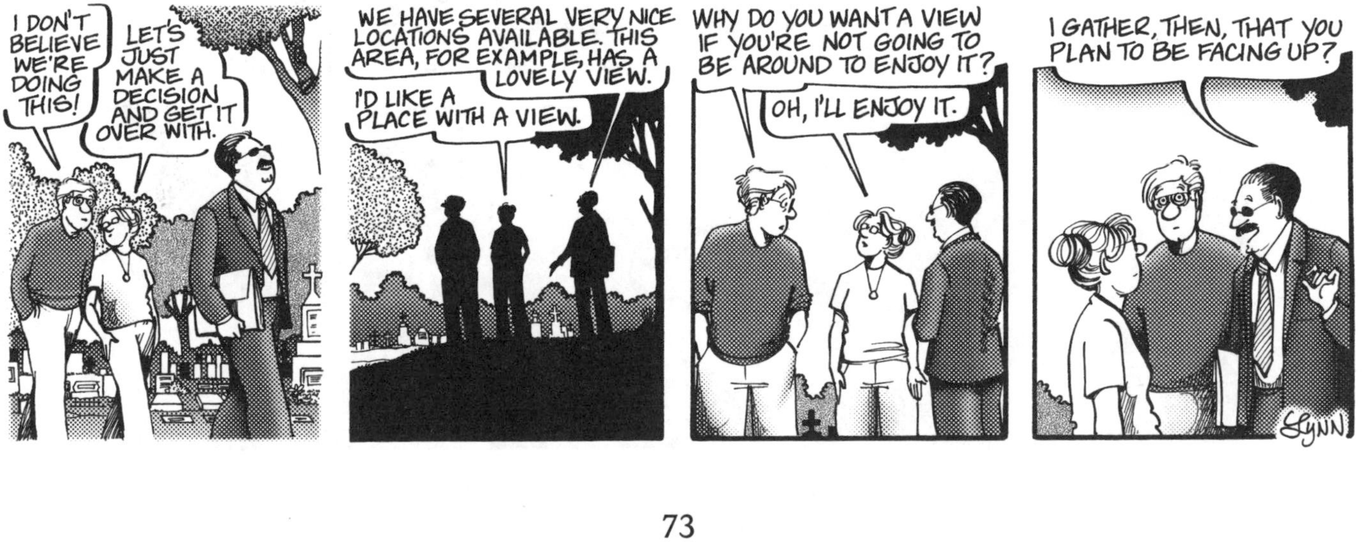
I DON'T BELIEVE WE'RE DOING THIS!
LET'S JUST MAKE A DECISION AND GET IT OVER WITH.
WE HAVE SEVERAL VERY NICE LOCATIONS AVAILABLE. THIS AREA, FOR EXAMPLE, HAS A LOVELY VIEW.
I'D LIKE A PLACE WITH A VIEW.
WHY DO YOU WANT A VIEW IF YOU'RE NOT GOING TO BE AROUND TO ENJOY IT?
OH, I'LL ENJOY IT.
I GATHER, THEN, THAT YOU PLAN TO BE FACING UP?
LYNN

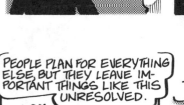

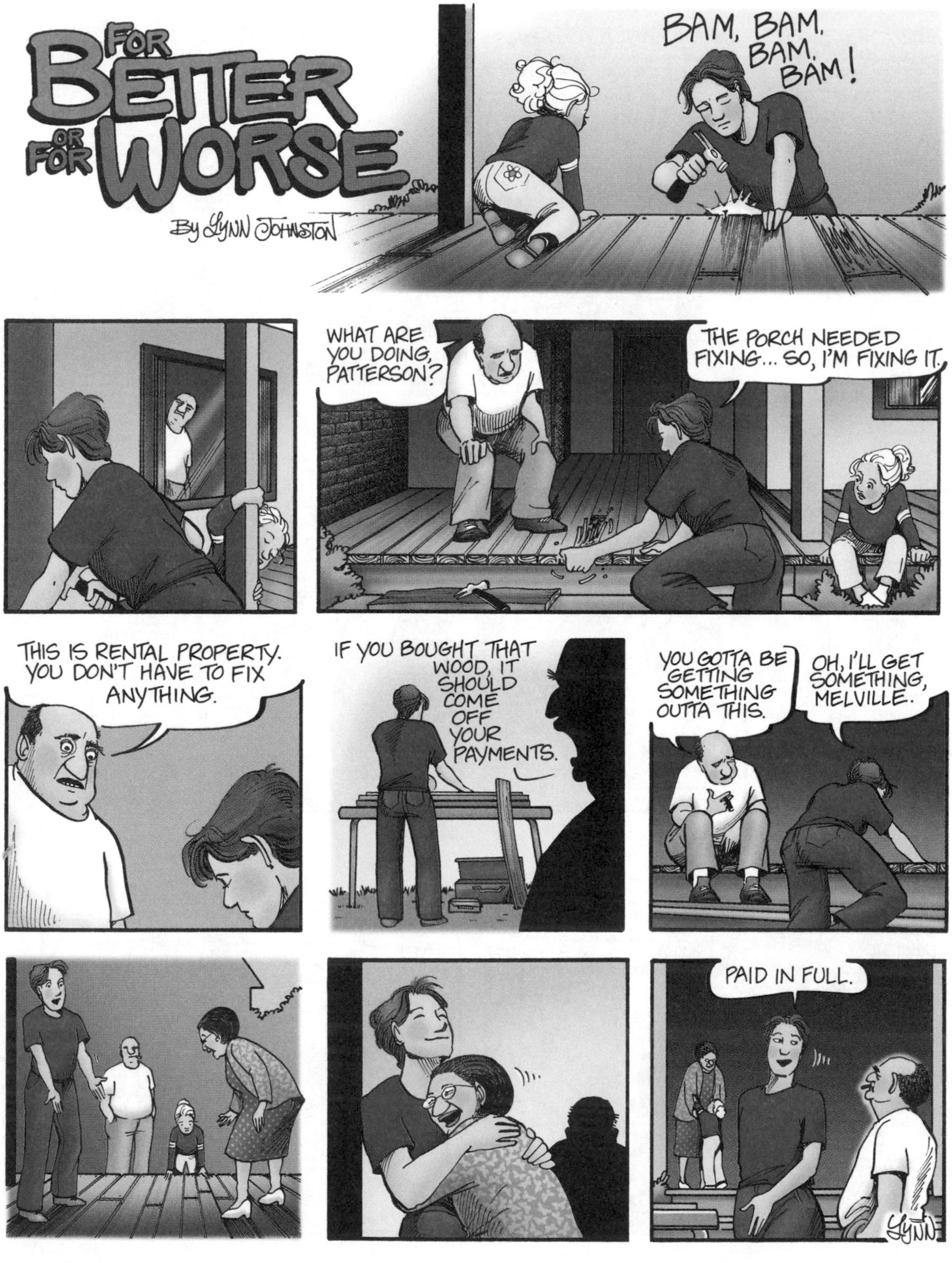
FOR BETTER OR FOR WORSE
BY LYNN JOHNSTON
BAM, BAM. BAM. BAM!
WHAT ARE YOU DOING, PATTERSON?
THE PORCH NEEDED FIXING... SO, I'M FIXING IT.
THIS IS RENTAL PROPERTY. YOU DON'T HAVE TO FIX ANYTHING.
IF YOU BOUGHT THAT WOOD, IT SHOULD COME OFF YOUR PAYMENTS.
YOU GOTTA BE GETTING SOMETHING OUTTA THIS.
OH, I'LL GET SOMETHING, MELVILLE.
PAID IN FULL.
LYNN

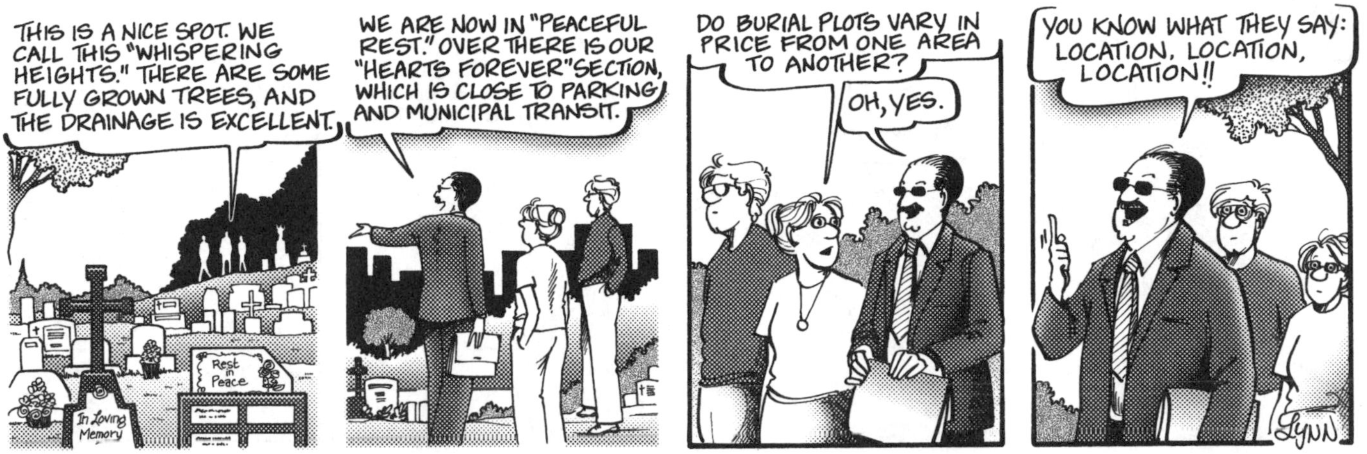
THIS IS A NICE SPOT. WE CALL THIS "WHISPERING HEIGHTS." THERE ARE SOME FULLY GROWN TREES, AND THE DRAINAGE IS EXCELLENT.
Rest in Peace
In Loving Memory
WE ARE NOW IN "PEACEFUL REST." OVER THERE IS OUR "HEARTS FOREVER" SECTION, WHICH IS CLOSE TO PARKING AND MUNICIPAL TRANSIT.
DO BURIAL PLOTS VARY IN PRICE FROM ONE AREA TO ANOTHER?
OH, YES.
YOU KNOW WHAT THEY SAY: LOCATION, LOCATION, LOCATION!!
LYNN

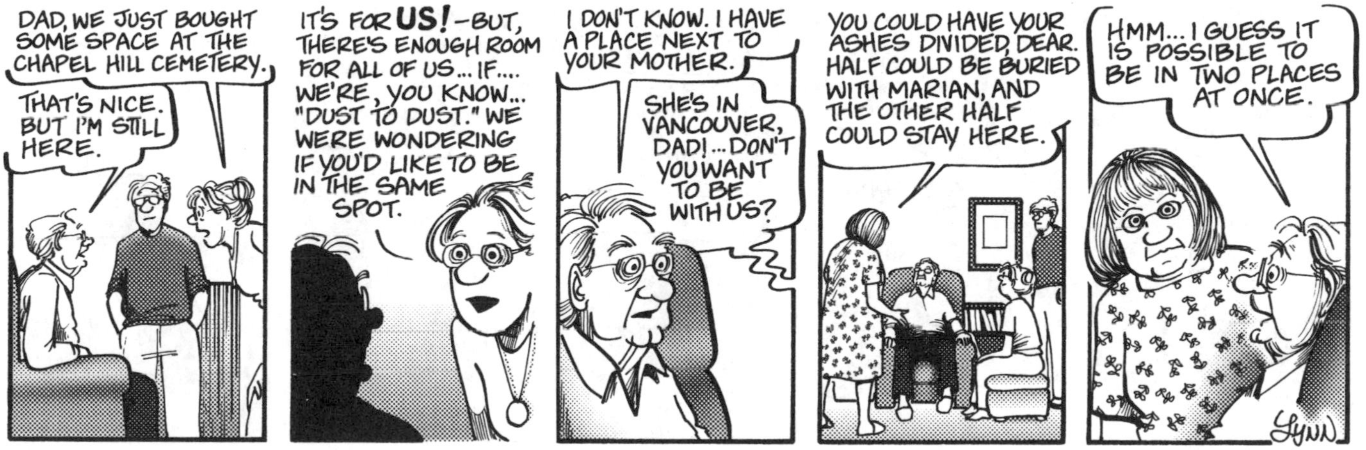
DAD, WE JUST BOUGHT SOME SPACE AT THE CHAPEL HILL CEMETERY.
THAT'S NICE. BUT I'M STILL HERE.
IT'S FOR US! –BUT, THERE'S ENOUGH ROOM FOR ALL OF US... IF.... WE'RE, YOU KNOW... "DUST TO DUST." WE WERE WONDERING IF YOU'D LIKE TO BE IN THE SAME SPOT.
I DON'T KNOW. I HAVE A PLACE NEXT TO YOUR MOTHER.
SHE'S IN VANCOUVER, DAD!... DON'T YOU WANT TO BE WITH US?
YOU COULD HAVE YOUR ASHES DIVIDED, DEAR. HALF COULD BE BURIED WITH MARIAN, AND THE OTHER HALF COULD STAY HERE.
HMM... I GUESS IT IS POSSIBLE TO BE IN TWO PLACES AT ONCE.
LYNN

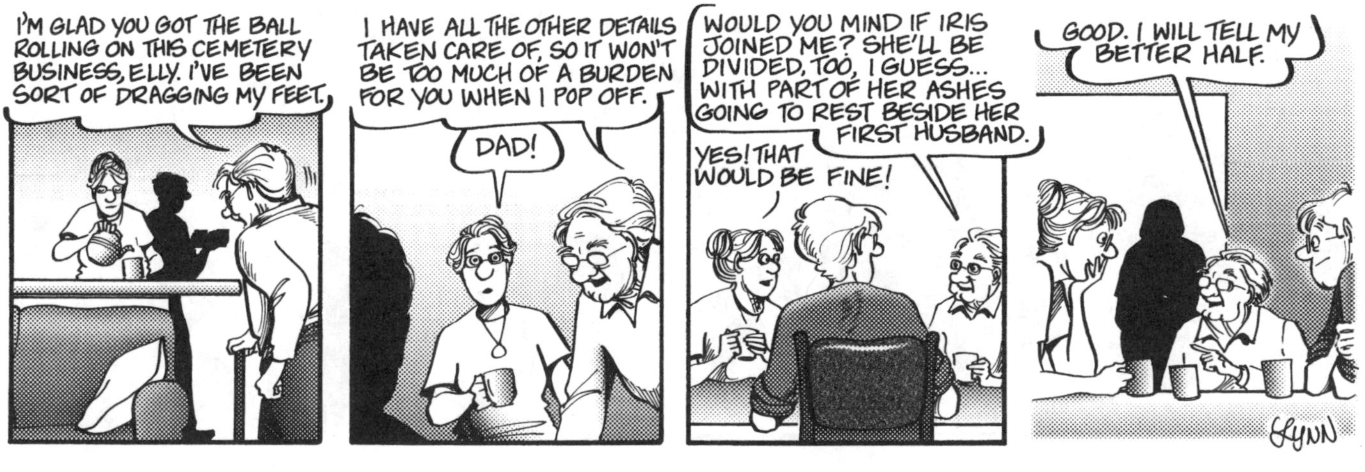
I'M GLAD YOU GOT THE BALL ROLLING ON THIS CEMETERY BUSINESS, ELLY. I'VE BEEN SORT OF DRAGGING MY FEET.
I HAVE ALL THE OTHER DETAILS TAKEN CARE OF, SO IT WON'T BE TOO MUCH OF A BURDEN FOR YOU WHEN I POP OFF.
DAD!
WOULD YOU MIND IF IRIS JOINED ME? SHE'LL BE DIVIDED, TOO, I GUESS... WITH PART OF HER ASHES GOING TO REST BESIDE HER FIRST HUSBAND.
YES! THAT WOULD BE FINE!
GOOD. I WILL TELL MY BETTER HALF.
LYNN

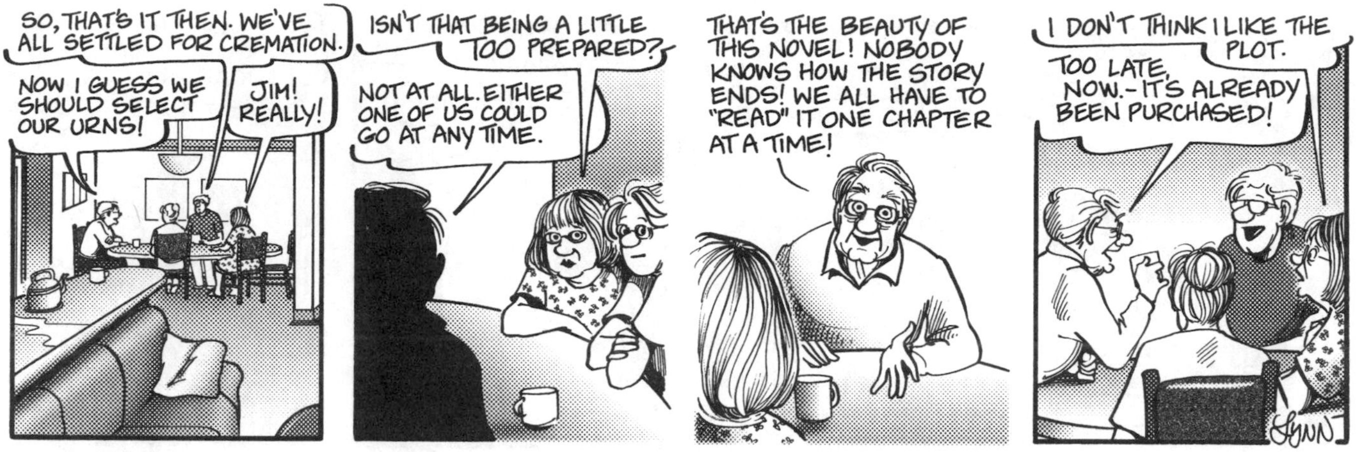
SO, THAT'S IT THEN. WE'VE ALL SETTLED FOR CREMATION.
NOW I GUESS WE SHOULD SELECT OUR URNS!
JIM! REALLY!
ISN'T THAT BEING A LITTLE TOO PREPARED?
NOT AT ALL. EITHER ONE OF US COULD GO AT ANY TIME.
THAT'S THE BEAUTY OF THIS NOVEL! NOBODY KNOWS HOW THE STORY ENDS! WE ALL HAVE TO "READ" IT ONE CHAPTER AT A TIME!
I DON'T THINK I LIKE THE PLOT.
TOO LATE, NOW.- IT'S ALREADY BEEN PURCHASED!
LYNN

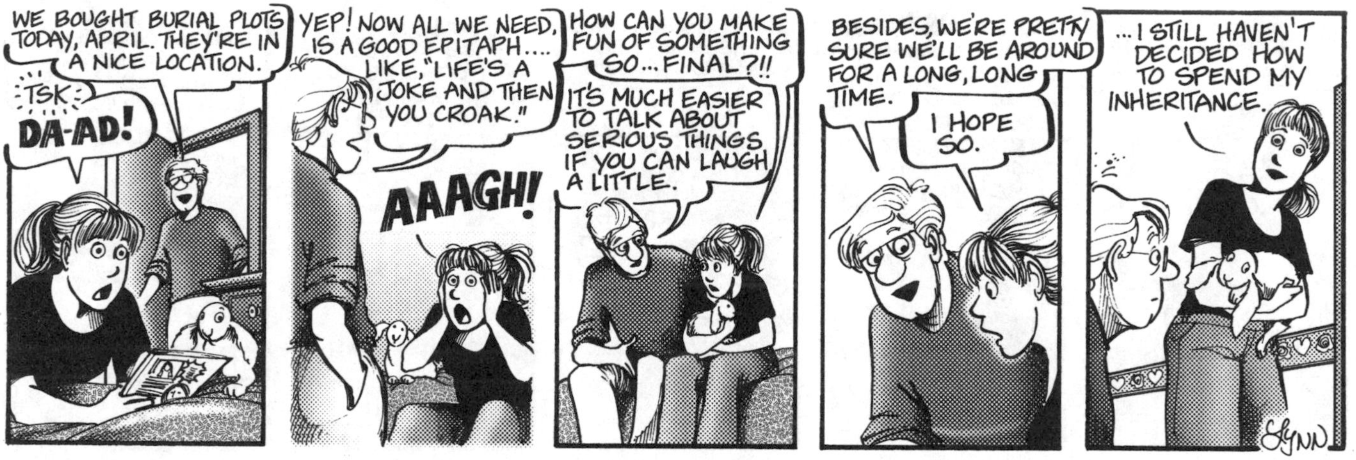
WE BOUGHT BURIAL PLOTS TODAY, APRIL. THEY'RE IN A NICE LOCATION.
TSK
DA-AD!
YEP! NOW ALL WE NEED, IS A GOOD EPITAPH.... LIKE, "LIFE'S A JOKE AND THEN YOU CROAK."
AAAGH!
HOW CAN YOU MAKE FUN OF SOMETHING SO... FINAL?!!
IT'S MUCH EASIER TO TALK ABOUT SERIOUS THINGS IF YOU CAN LAUGH A LITTLE.
BESIDES, WE'RE PRETTY SURE WE'LL BE AROUND FOR A LONG, LONG TIME.
I HOPE SO.
... I STILL HAVEN'T DECIDED HOW TO SPEND MY INHERITANCE.
LYNN

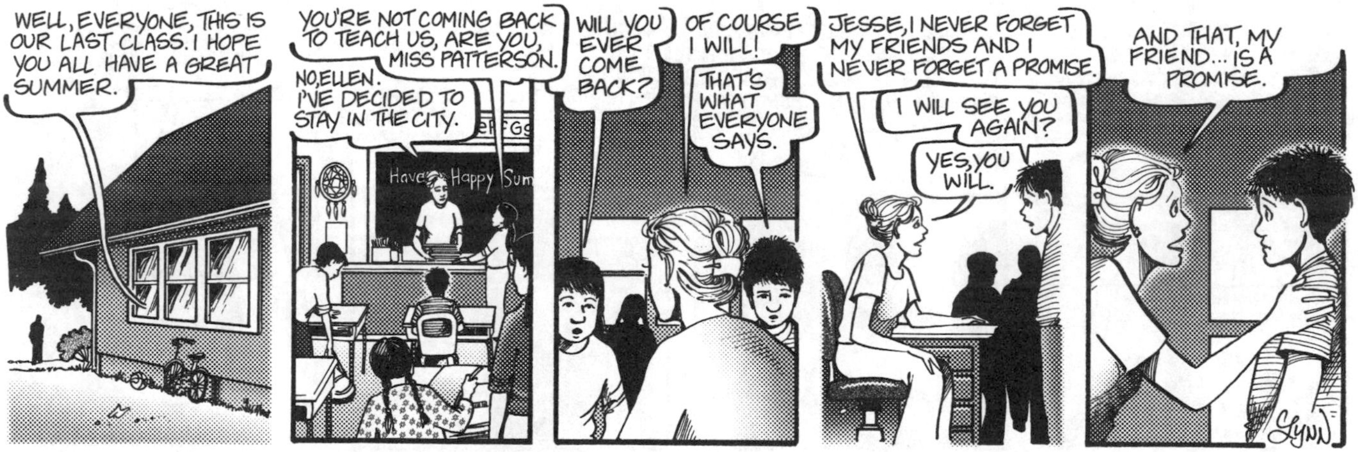
WELL, EVERYONE, THIS IS OUR LAST CLASS. I HOPE YOU ALL HAVE A GREAT SUMMER.
YOU'RE NOT COMING BACK TO TEACH US, ARE YOU, MISS PATTERSON.
NO, ELLEN. I'VE DECIDED TO STAY IN THE CITY.
Have a Happy Sum
WILL YOU EVER COME BACK?
OF COURSE I WILL!
THAT'S WHAT EVERYONE SAYS.
JESSE, I NEVER FORGET MY FRIENDS AND I NEVER FORGET A PROMISE.
I WILL SEE YOU AGAIN?
YES, YOU WILL.
AND THAT, MY FRIEND... IS A PROMISE.
LYNN

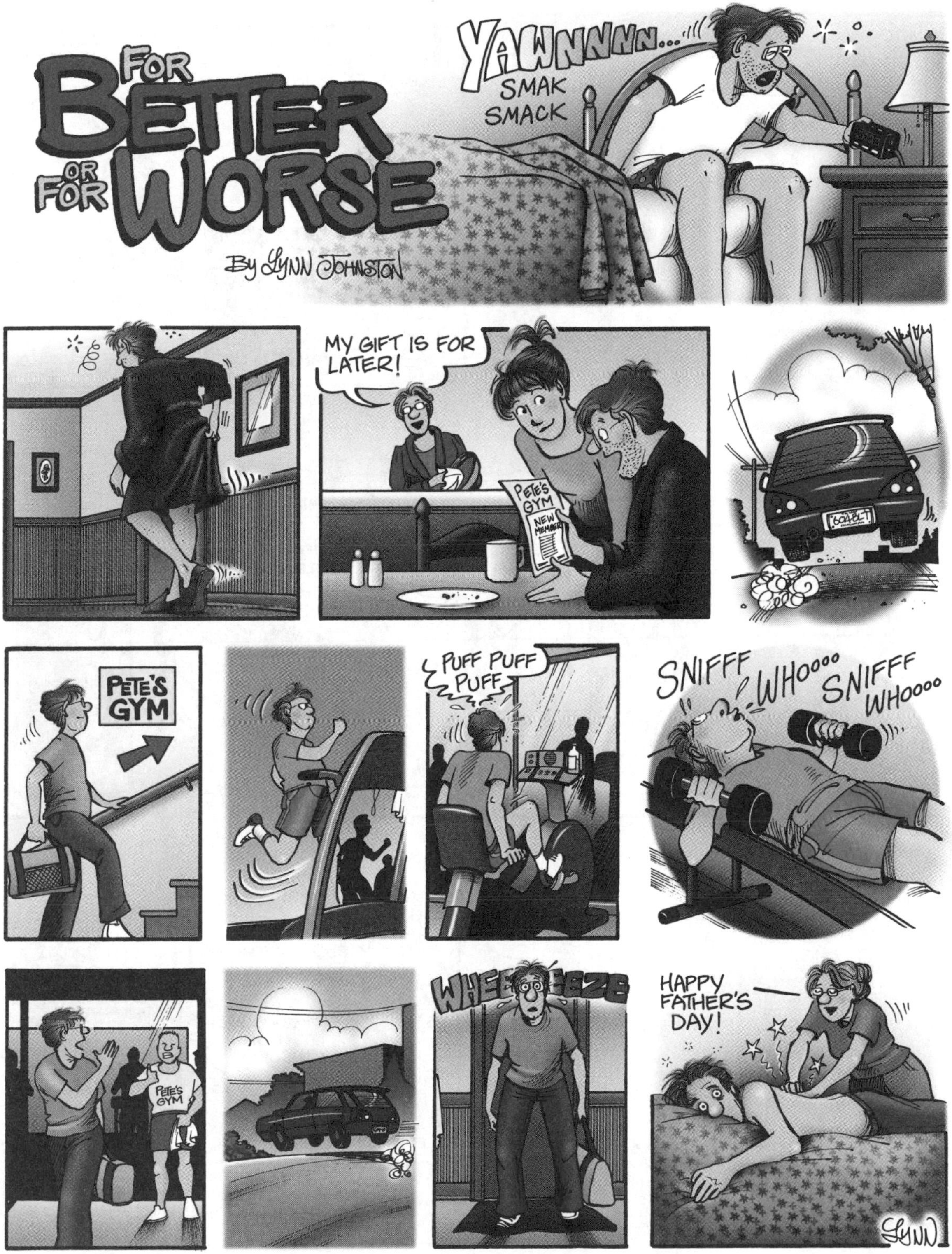
FOR BETTER OR FOR WORSE
By Lynn Johnston
YAWNNNNN...
SMAK
SMACK
MY GIFT IS FOR LATER!
PETE'S GYM
NEW MEMBER
PETE'S GYM
PUFF PUFF PUFF
SNIFFF WHOooo SNIFFF WHOooo
PETE'S GYM
HAPPY FATHER'S DAY!
LYNN

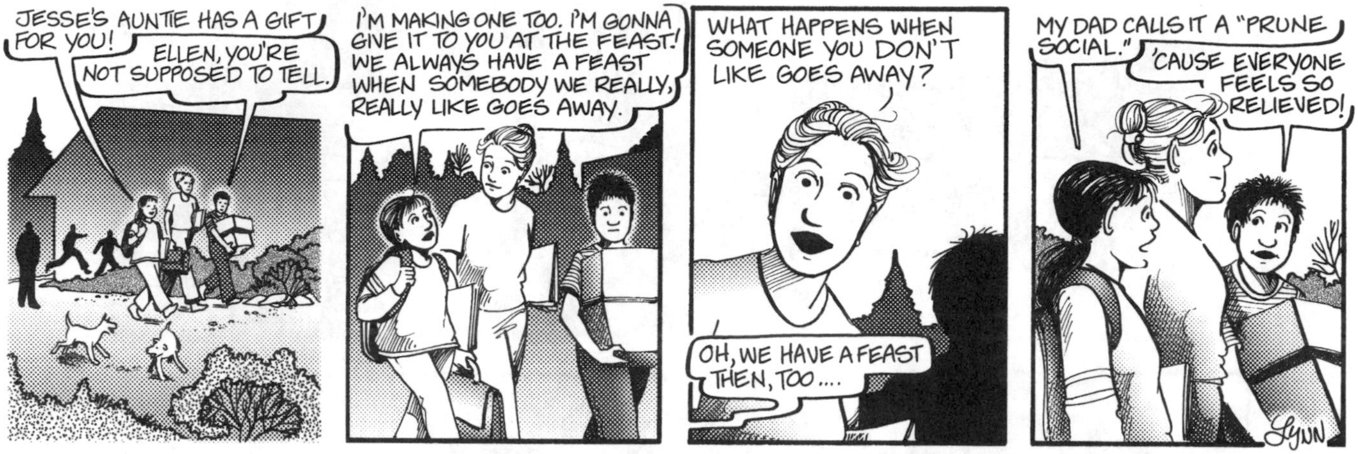
JESSE'S AUNTIE HAS A GIFT FOR YOU!
ELLEN, YOU'RE NOT SUPPOSED TO TELL.
I'M MAKING ONE TOO. I'M GONNA GIVE IT TO YOU AT THE FEAST! WE ALWAYS HAVE A FEAST WHEN SOMEBODY WE REALLY, REALLY LIKE GOES AWAY.
WHAT HAPPENS WHEN SOMEONE YOU DON'T LIKE GOES AWAY?
OH, WE HAVE A FEAST THEN, TOO....
MY DAD CALLS IT A "PRUNE SOCIAL."
'CAUSE EVERYONE FEELS SO RELIEVED!
LYNN

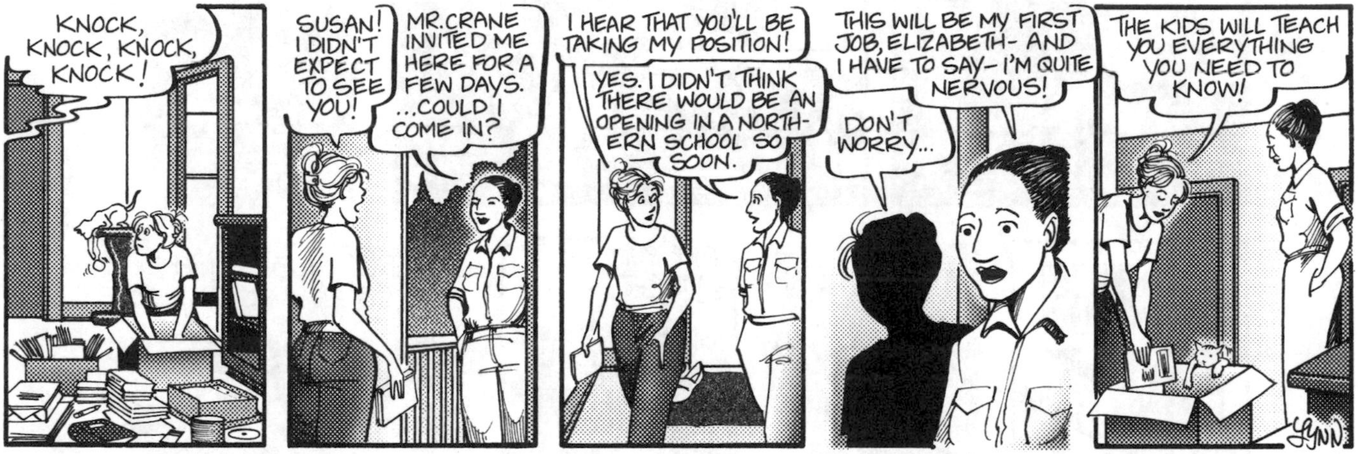
KNOCK, KNOCK, KNOCK, KNOCK!
SUSAN! I DIDN'T EXPECT TO SEE YOU!
MR. CRANE INVITED ME HERE FOR A FEW DAYS. ...COULD I COME IN?
I HEAR THAT YOU'LL BE TAKING MY POSITION!
YES. I DIDN'T THINK THERE WOULD BE AN OPENING IN A NORTHERN SCHOOL SO SOON.
THIS WILL BE MY FIRST JOB, ELIZABETH- AND I HAVE TO SAY- I'M QUITE NERVOUS!
DON'T WORRY...
THE KIDS WILL TEACH YOU EVERYTHING YOU NEED TO KNOW!
LYNN

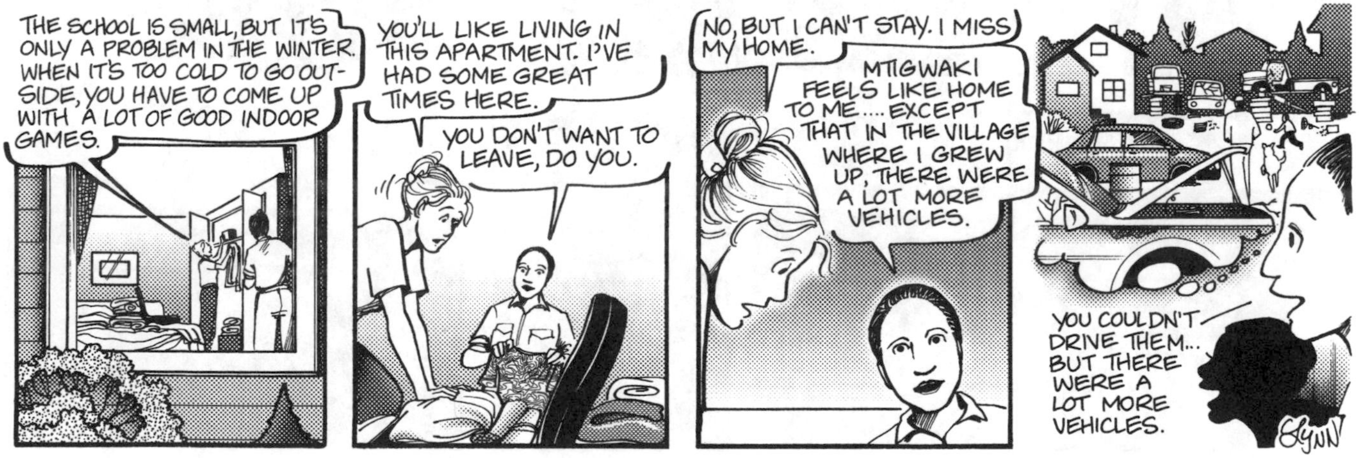
THE SCHOOL IS SMALL, BUT IT'S ONLY A PROBLEM IN THE WINTER. WHEN IT'S TOO COLD TO GO OUTSIDE, YOU HAVE TO COME UP WITH A LOT OF GOOD INDOOR GAMES.
YOU'LL LIKE LIVING IN THIS APARTMENT. I'VE HAD SOME GREAT TIMES HERE.
YOU DON'T WANT TO LEAVE, DO YOU.
NO, BUT I CAN'T STAY. I MISS MY HOME.
MTIGWAKI FEELS LIKE HOME TO ME.... EXCEPT THAT IN THE VILLAGE WHERE I GREW UP, THERE WERE A LOT MORE VEHICLES.
YOU COULDN'T DRIVE THEM... BUT THERE WERE A LOT MORE VEHICLES.
LYNN

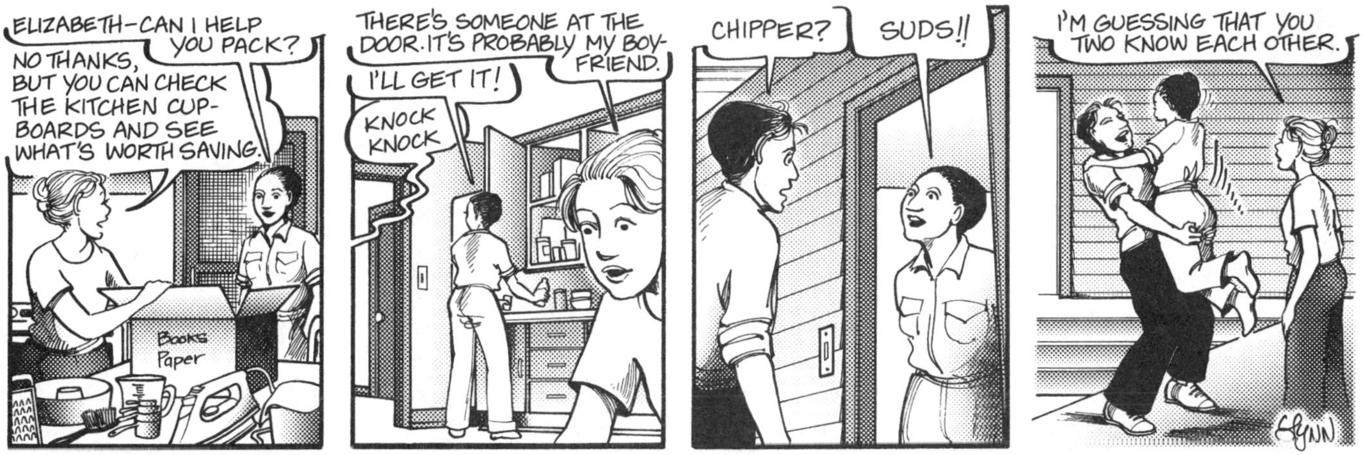
ELIZABETH—CAN I HELP YOU PACK?
NO THANKS, BUT YOU CAN CHECK THE KITCHEN CUPBOARDS AND SEE WHAT'S WORTH SAVING.
Books
Paper
THERE'S SOMEONE AT THE DOOR. IT'S PROBABLY MY BOYFRIEND.
I'LL GET IT!
KNOCK KNOCK
CHIPPER?
SUDS!!
I'M GUESSING THAT YOU TWO KNOW EACH OTHER.
LYNN

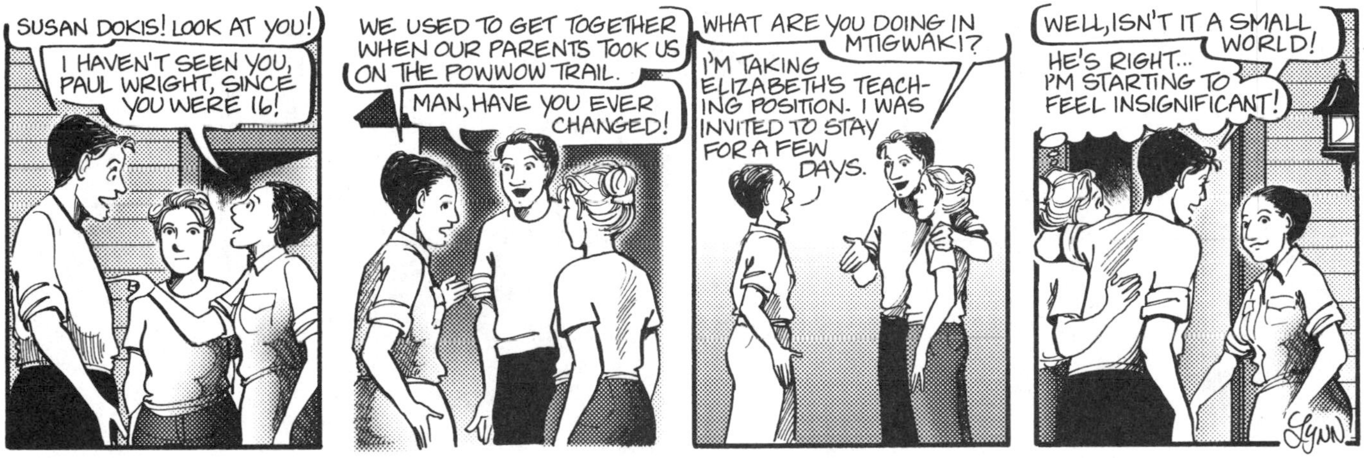
SUSAN DOKIS! LOOK AT YOU!
I HAVEN'T SEEN YOU, PAUL WRIGHT, SINCE YOU WERE 16!
WE USED TO GET TOGETHER WHEN OUR PARENTS TOOK US ON THE POWWOW TRAIL.
MAN, HAVE YOU EVER CHANGED!
WHAT ARE YOU DOING IN MTIGWAKI?
I'M TAKING ELIZABETH'S TEACHING POSITION. I WAS INVITED TO STAY FOR A FEW DAYS.
WELL, ISN'T IT A SMALL WORLD!
HE'S RIGHT... I'M STARTING TO FEEL INSIGNIFICANT!
LYNN

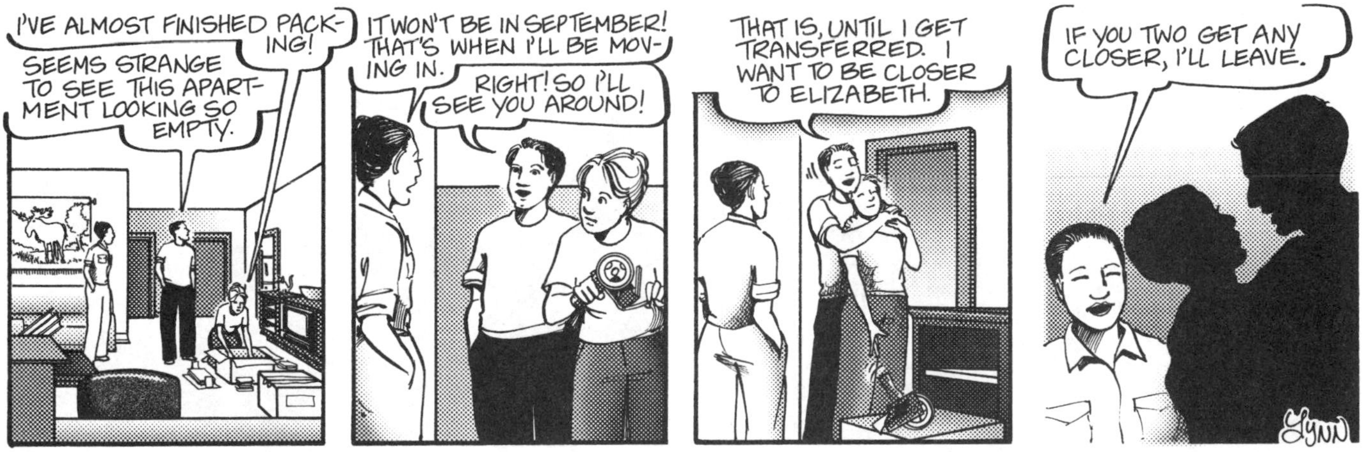
I'VE ALMOST FINISHED PACKING!
SEEMS STRANGE TO SEE THIS APARTMENT LOOKING SO EMPTY.
IT WON'T BE IN SEPTEMBER! THAT'S WHEN I'LL BE MOVING IN.
RIGHT! SO I'LL SEE YOU AROUND!
THAT IS, UNTIL I GET TRANSFERRED. I WANT TO BE CLOSER TO ELIZABETH.
IF YOU TWO GET ANY CLOSER, I'LL LEAVE.
LYNN

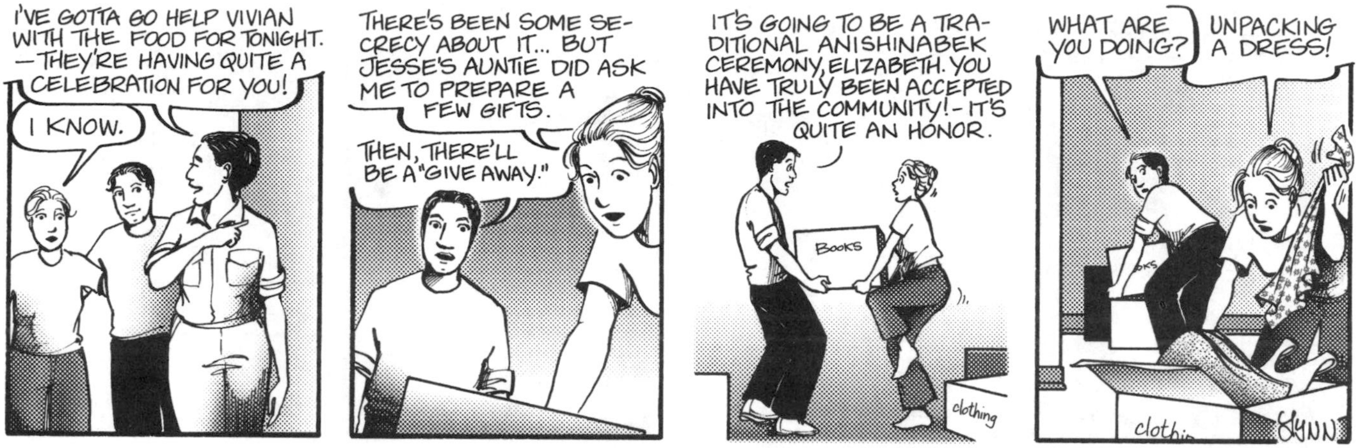
I'VE GOTTA GO HELP VIVIAN WITH THE FOOD FOR TONIGHT. — THEY'RE HAVING QUITE A CELEBRATION FOR YOU!
I KNOW.
THERE'S BEEN SOME SECRECY ABOUT IT... BUT JESSE'S AUNTIE DID ASK ME TO PREPARE A FEW GIFTS.
THEN, THERE'LL BE A "GIVE AWAY."
IT'S GOING TO BE A TRADITIONAL ANISHINABEK CEREMONY, ELIZABETH. YOU HAVE TRULY BEEN ACCEPTED INTO THE COMMUNITY! - IT'S QUITE AN HONOR.
BOOKS
clothing
WHAT ARE YOU DOING?
UNPACKING A DRESS!
clothi
LYNN

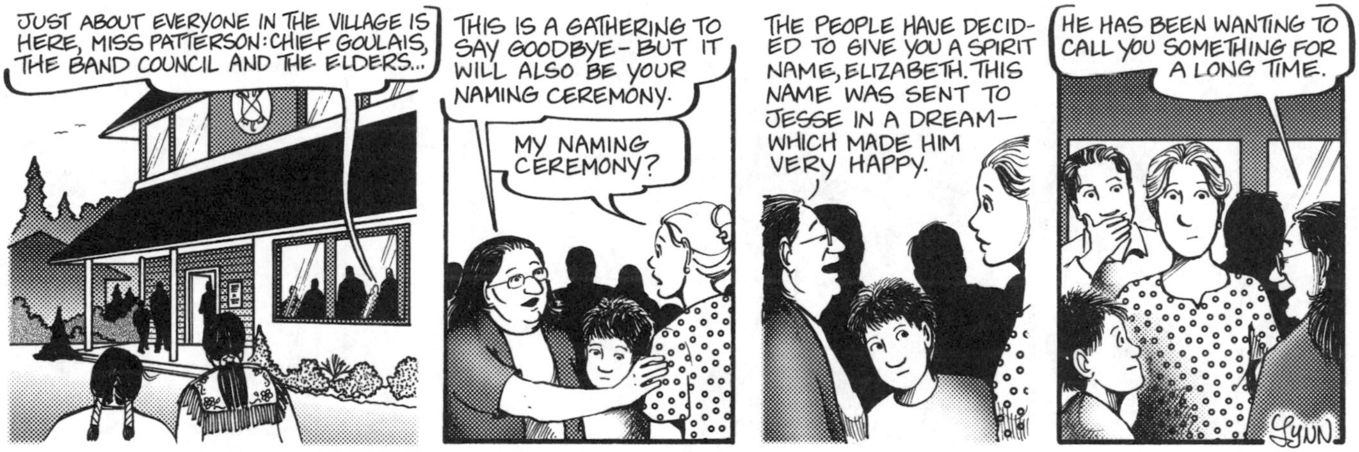
JUST ABOUT EVERYONE IN THE VILLAGE IS HERE, MISS PATTERSON: CHIEF GOULAIS, THE BAND COUNCIL AND THE ELDERS...
THIS IS A GATHERING TO SAY GOODBYE - BUT IT WILL ALSO BE YOUR NAMING CEREMONY.
MY NAMING CEREMONY?
THE PEOPLE HAVE DECIDED TO GIVE YOU A SPIRIT NAME, ELIZABETH. THIS NAME WAS SENT TO JESSE IN A DREAM— WHICH MADE HIM VERY HAPPY.
HE HAS BEEN WANTING TO CALL YOU SOMETHING FOR A LONG TIME.
LYNN

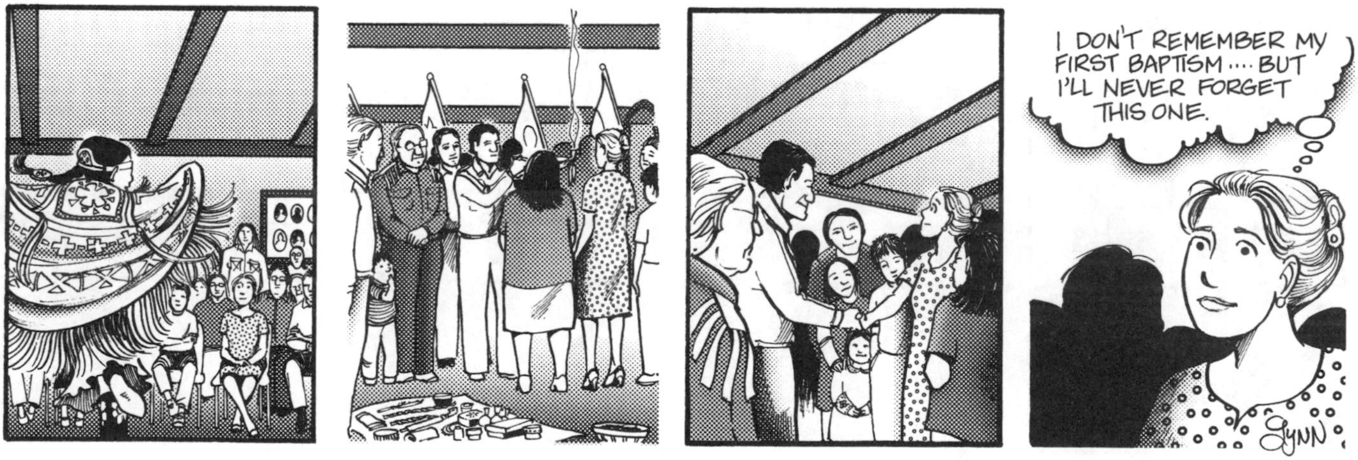
I DON'T REMEMBER MY FIRST BAPTISM.... BUT I'LL NEVER FORGET THIS ONE.
LYNN

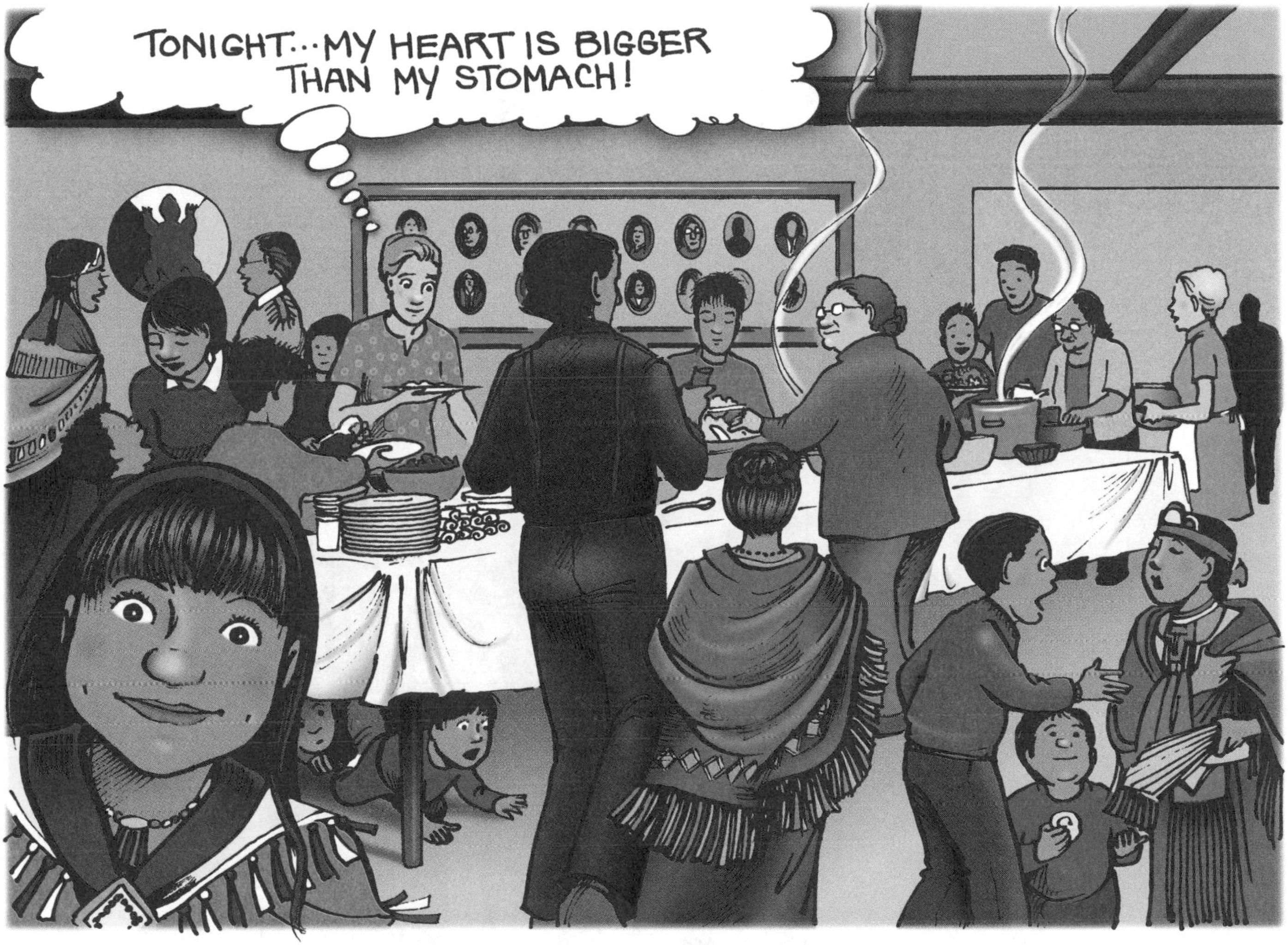
TONIGHT... MY HEART IS BIGGER THAN MY STOMACH!

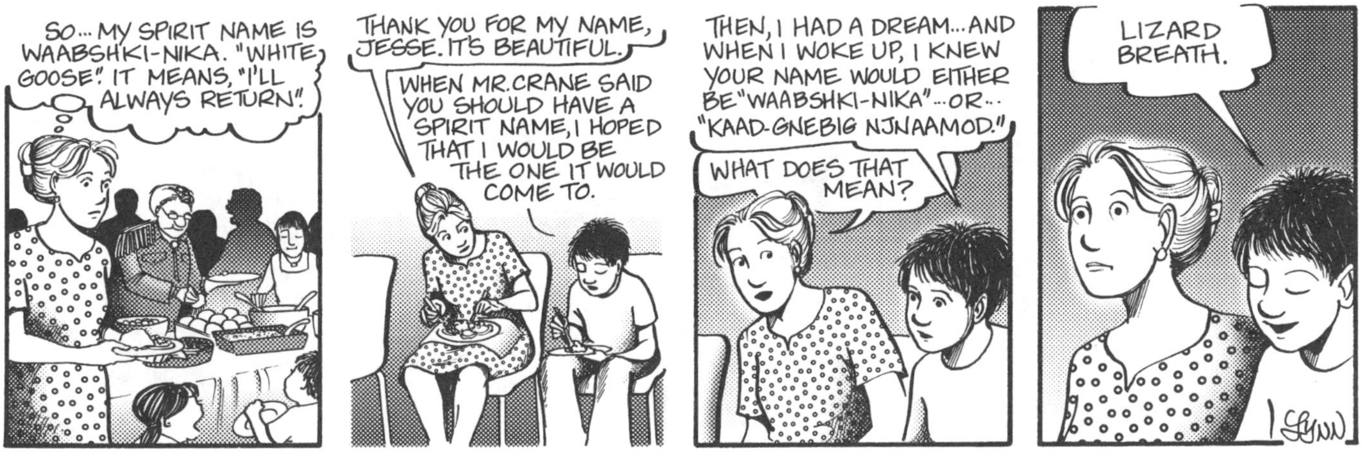
SO... MY SPIRIT NAME IS WAABSHKI-NIKA. "WHITE GOOSE." IT MEANS, "I'LL ALWAYS RETURN."
THANK YOU FOR MY NAME, JESSE. IT'S BEAUTIFUL.
WHEN MR. CRANE SAID YOU SHOULD HAVE A SPIRIT NAME, I HOPED THAT I WOULD BE THE ONE IT WOULD COME TO.
THEN, I HAD A DREAM... AND WHEN I WOKE UP, I KNEW YOUR NAME WOULD EITHER BE "WAABSHKI-NIKA"... OR... "KAAD-GNEBIG NJNAAMOD."
WHAT DOES THAT MEAN?
LIZARD BREATH.
LYNN

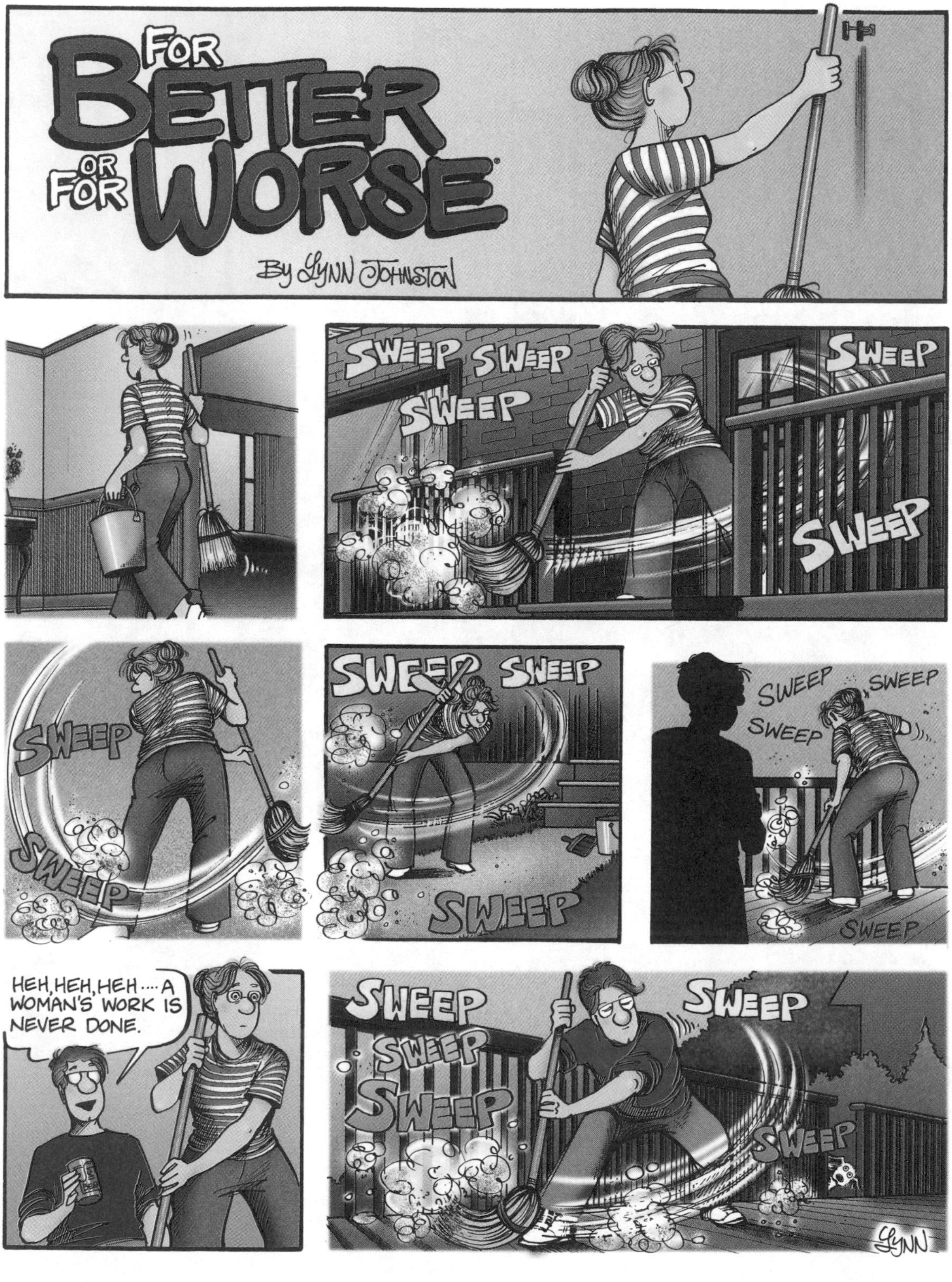
FOR BETTER OR FOR WORSE
BY LYNN JOHNSTON
SWEEP SWEEP
SWEEP
SWEEP
SWEEP
SWEEP
SWEEP
SWEEP
SWEEP SWEEP
SWEEP
SWEEP
SWEEP
SWEEP
SWEEP
SWEEP
HEH, HEH, HEH.... A WOMAN'S WORK IS NEVER DONE.
SWEEP
SWEEP
SWEEP
SWEEP
SWEEP
LYNN

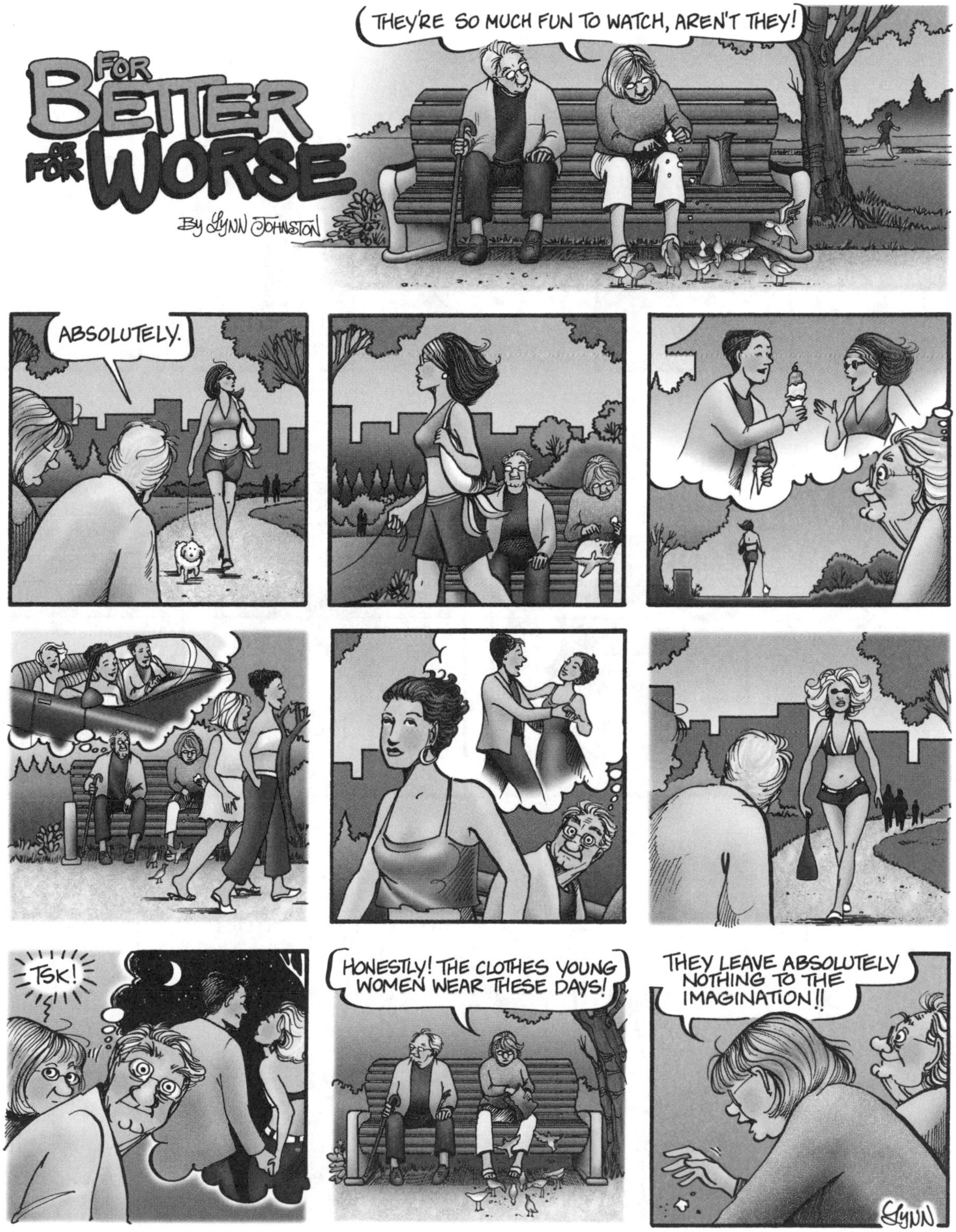
FOR BETTER OR FOR WORSE
BY LYNN JOHNSTON
THEY'RE SO MUCH FUN TO WATCH, AREN'T THEY!
ABSOLUTELY.
TSK!
HONESTLY! THE CLOTHES YOUNG WOMEN WEAR THESE DAYS!
THEY LEAVE ABSOLUTELY NOTHING TO THE IMAGINATION!!
LYNN

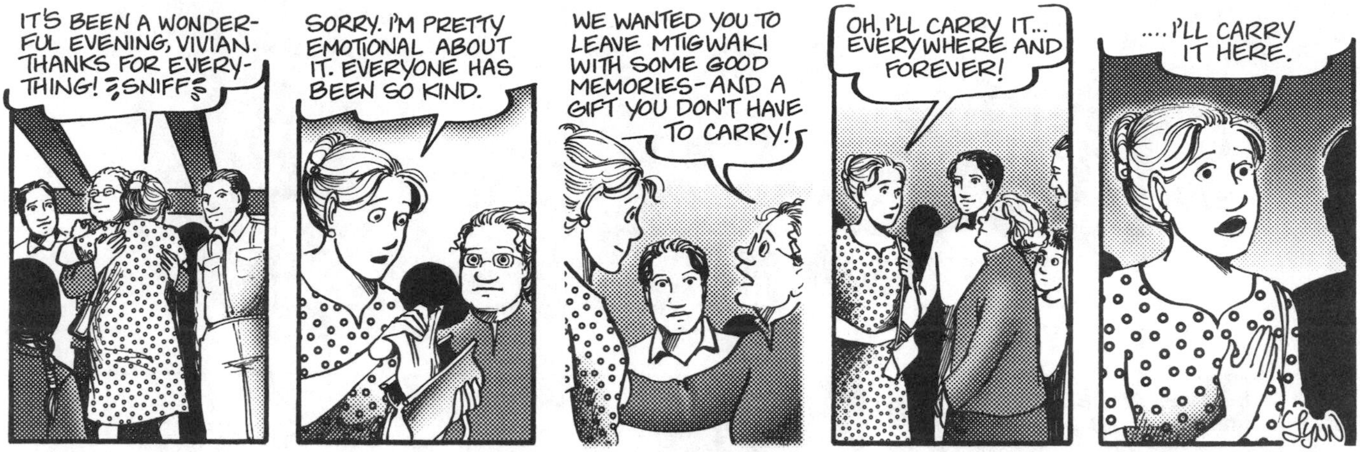
IT'S BEEN A WONDERFUL EVENING, VIVIAN. THANKS FOR EVERYTHING! ≈SNIFF≈
SORRY. I'M PRETTY EMOTIONAL ABOUT IT. EVERYONE HAS BEEN SO KIND.
WE WANTED YOU TO LEAVE MTIGWAKI WITH SOME GOOD MEMORIES- AND A GIFT YOU DON'T HAVE TO CARRY!
OH, I'LL CARRY IT... EVERYWHERE AND FOREVER!
....I'LL CARRY IT HERE.
LYNN

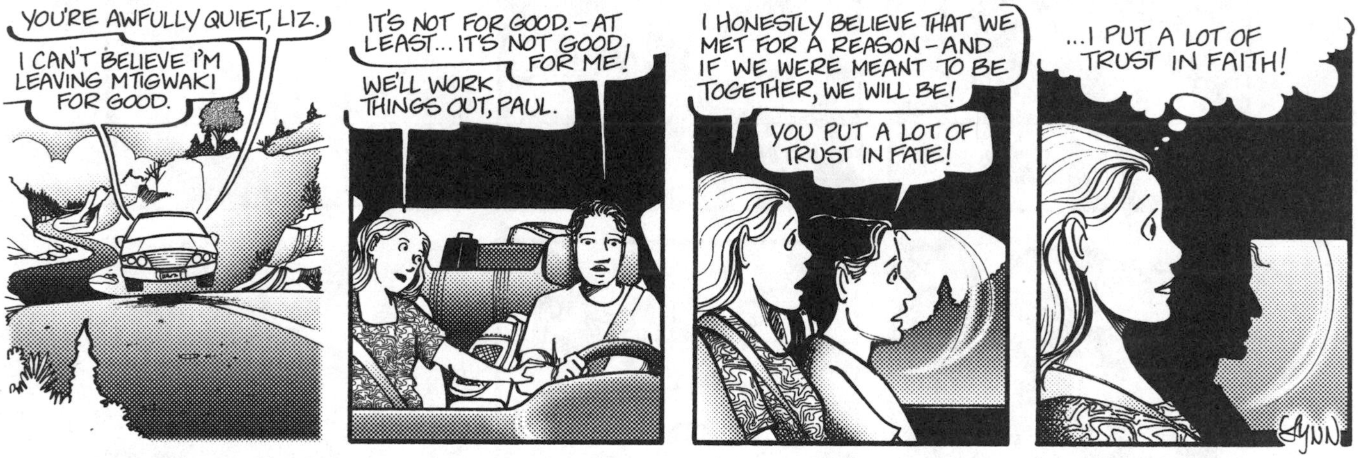
YOU'RE AWFULLY QUIET, LIZ.
I CAN'T BELIEVE I'M LEAVING MTIGWAKI FOR GOOD.
IT'S NOT FOR GOOD. - AT LEAST... IT'S NOT GOOD FOR ME!
WE'LL WORK THINGS OUT, PAUL.
I HONESTLY BELIEVE THAT WE MET FOR A REASON - AND IF WE WERE MEANT TO BE TOGETHER, WE WILL BE!
YOU PUT A LOT OF TRUST IN FATE!
...I PUT A LOT OF TRUST IN FAITH!
LYNN

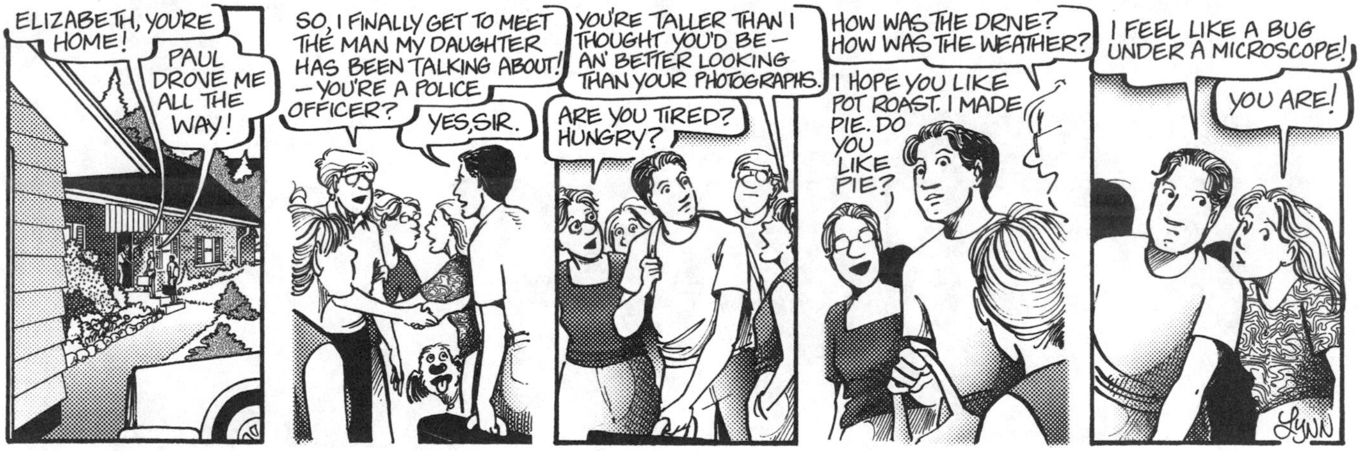
ELIZABETH, YOU'RE HOME!
PAUL DROVE ME ALL THE WAY!
SO, I FINALLY GET TO MEET THE MAN MY DAUGHTER HAS BEEN TALKING ABOUT! - YOU'RE A POLICE OFFICER?
YES, SIR.
YOU'RE TALLER THAN I THOUGHT YOU'D BE - AN' BETTER LOOKING THAN YOUR PHOTOGRAPHS.
ARE YOU TIRED? HUNGRY?
HOW WAS THE DRIVE? HOW WAS THE WEATHER?
I HOPE YOU LIKE POT ROAST. I MADE PIE. DO YOU LIKE PIE?
I FEEL LIKE A BUG UNDER A MICROSCOPE!
YOU ARE!
LYNN

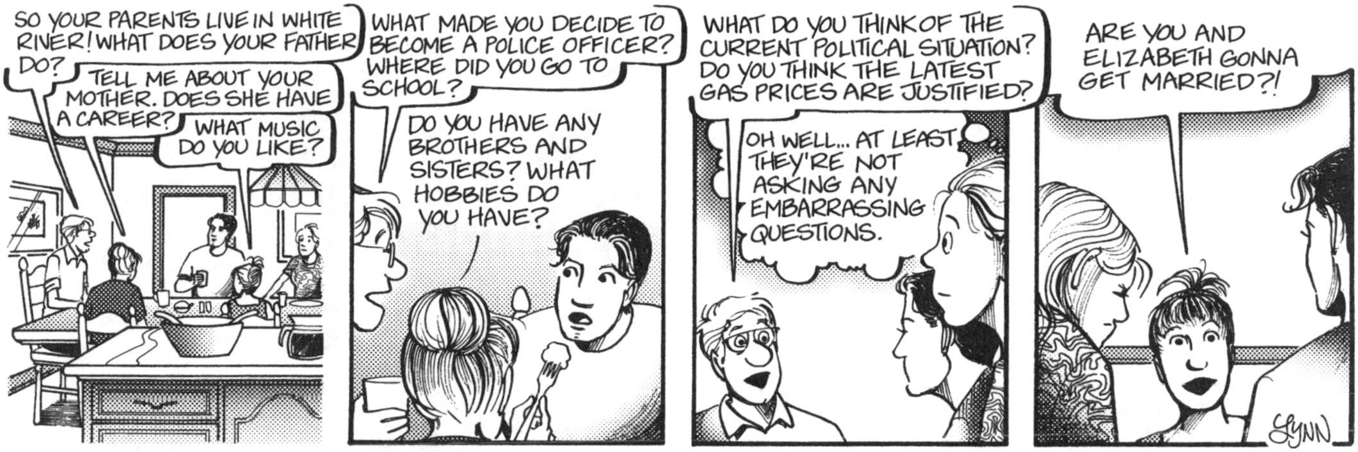
SO YOUR PARENTS LIVE IN WHITE RIVER! WHAT DOES YOUR FATHER DO?
TELL ME ABOUT YOUR MOTHER. DOES SHE HAVE A CAREER?
WHAT MUSIC DO YOU LIKE?
WHAT MADE YOU DECIDE TO BECOME A POLICE OFFICER? WHERE DID YOU GO TO SCHOOL?
DO YOU HAVE ANY BROTHERS AND SISTERS? WHAT HOBBIES DO YOU HAVE?
WHAT DO YOU THINK OF THE CURRENT POLITICAL SITUATION? DO YOU THINK THE LATEST GAS PRICES ARE JUSTIFIED?
OH WELL... AT LEAST THEY'RE NOT ASKING ANY EMBARRASSING QUESTIONS.
ARE YOU AND ELIZABETH GONNA GET MARRIED?!
LYNN

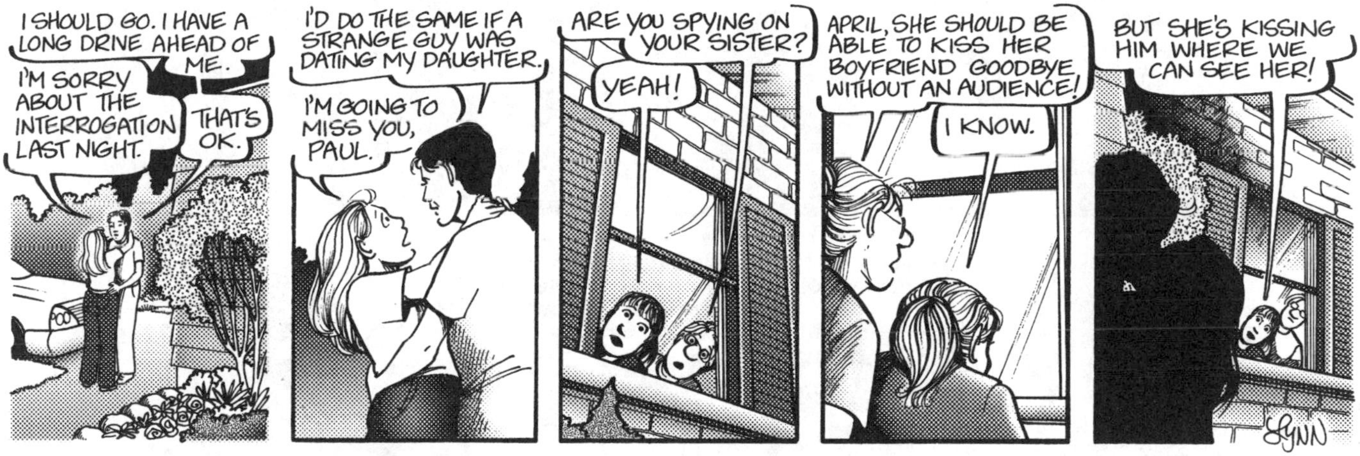
I SHOULD GO. I HAVE A LONG DRIVE AHEAD OF ME.
I'M SORRY ABOUT THE INTERROGATION LAST NIGHT.
THAT'S OK.
I'D DO THE SAME IF A STRANGE GUY WAS DATING MY DAUGHTER.
I'M GOING TO MISS YOU, PAUL.
ARE YOU SPYING ON YOUR SISTER?
YEAH!
APRIL, SHE SHOULD BE ABLE TO KISS HER BOYFRIEND GOODBYE WITHOUT AN AUDIENCE!
I KNOW.
BUT SHE'S KISSING HIM WHERE WE CAN SEE HER!
LYNN

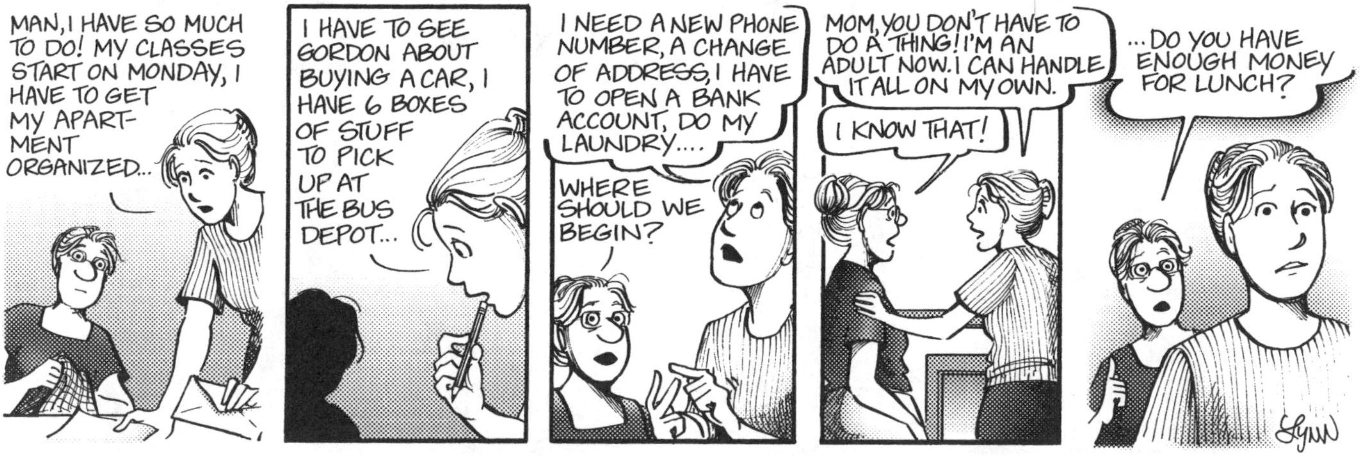
MAN, I HAVE SO MUCH TO DO! MY CLASSES START ON MONDAY, I HAVE TO GET MY APARTMENT ORGANIZED...
I HAVE TO SEE GORDON ABOUT BUYING A CAR, I HAVE 6 BOXES OF STUFF TO PICK UP AT THE BUS DEPOT...
I NEED A NEW PHONE NUMBER, A CHANGE OF ADDRESS, I HAVE TO OPEN A BANK ACCOUNT, DO MY LAUNDRY....
WHERE SHOULD WE BEGIN?
MOM, YOU DON'T HAVE TO DO A THING! I'M AN ADULT NOW. I CAN HANDLE IT ALL ON MY OWN.
I KNOW THAT!
...DO YOU HAVE ENOUGH MONEY FOR LUNCH?
LYNN

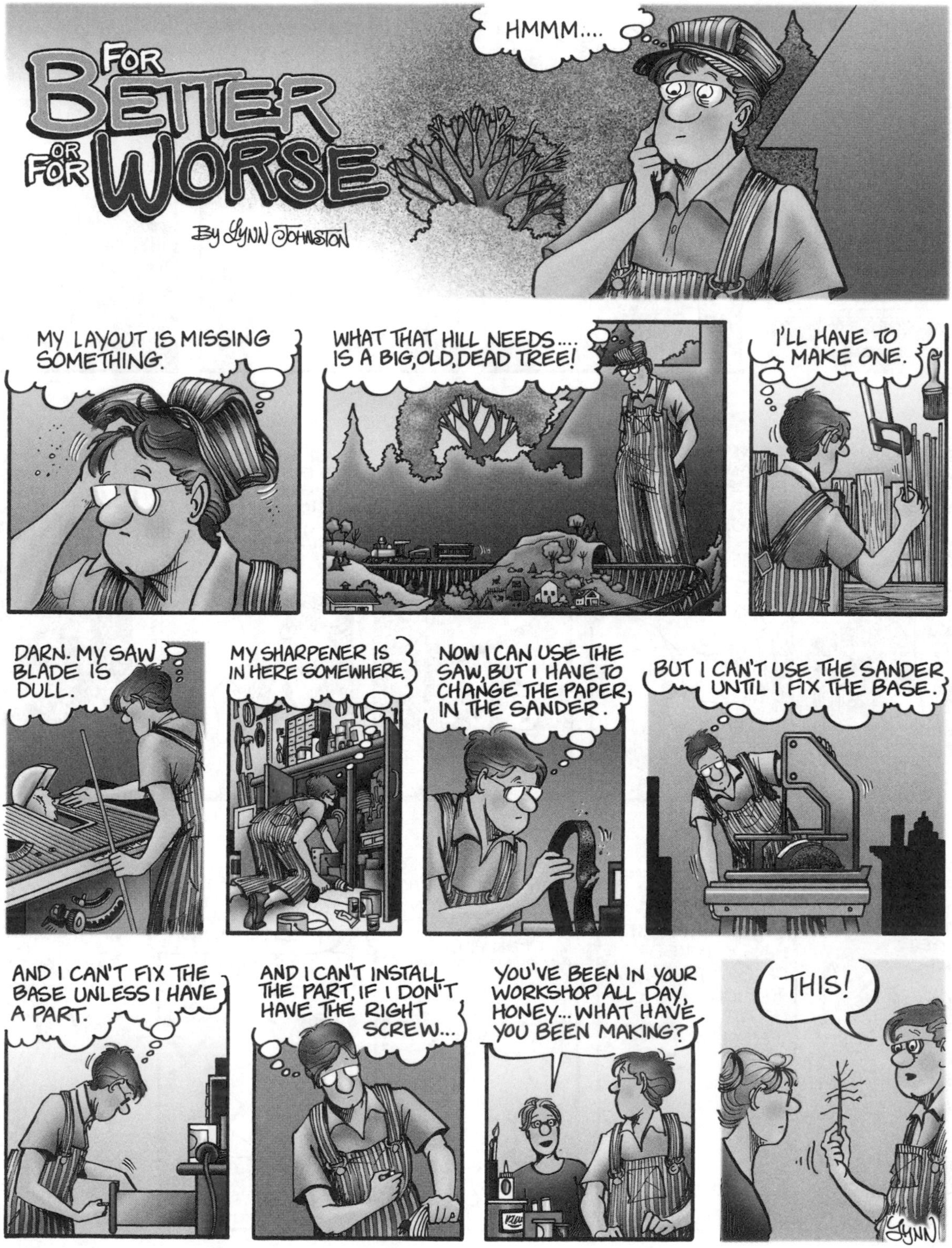
HMMM....
FOR BETTER OR FOR WORSE
BY LYNN JOHNSTON
MY LAYOUT IS MISSING SOMETHING.
WHAT THAT HILL NEEDS.... IS A BIG, OLD, DEAD TREE!
I'LL HAVE TO MAKE ONE.
DARN. MY SAW BLADE IS DULL.
MY SHARPENER IS IN HERE SOMEWHERE.
NOW I CAN USE THE SAW, BUT I HAVE TO CHANGE THE PAPER IN THE SANDER.
BUT I CAN'T USE THE SANDER UNTIL I FIX THE BASE.
AND I CAN'T FIX THE BASE UNLESS I HAVE A PART.
AND I CAN'T INSTALL THE PART, IF I DON'T HAVE THE RIGHT SCREW...
YOU'VE BEEN IN YOUR WORKSHOP ALL DAY, HONEY... WHAT HAVE YOU BEEN MAKING?
THIS!
LYNN

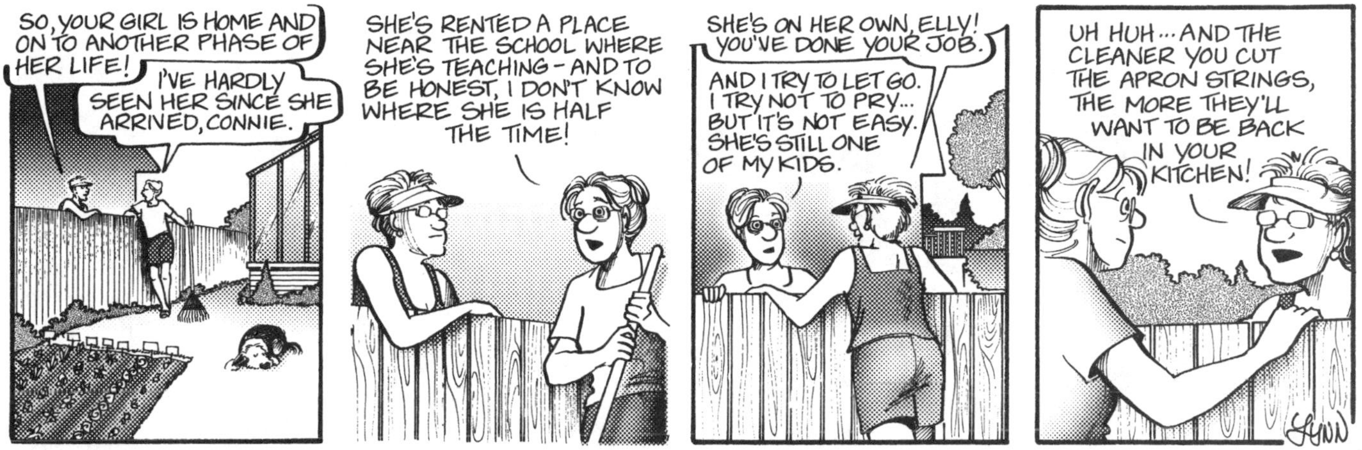
SO, YOUR GIRL IS HOME AND ON TO ANOTHER PHASE OF HER LIFE!
I'VE HARDLY SEEN HER SINCE SHE ARRIVED, CONNIE.
SHE'S RENTED A PLACE NEAR THE SCHOOL WHERE SHE'S TEACHING - AND TO BE HONEST, I DON'T KNOW WHERE SHE IS HALF THE TIME!
SHE'S ON HER OWN, ELLY! YOU'VE DONE YOUR JOB.
AND I TRY TO LET GO. I TRY NOT TO PRY... BUT IT'S NOT EASY. SHE'S STILL ONE OF MY KIDS.
UH HUH... AND THE CLEANER YOU CUT THE APRON STRINGS, THE MORE THEY'LL WANT TO BE BACK IN YOUR KITCHEN!
LYNN

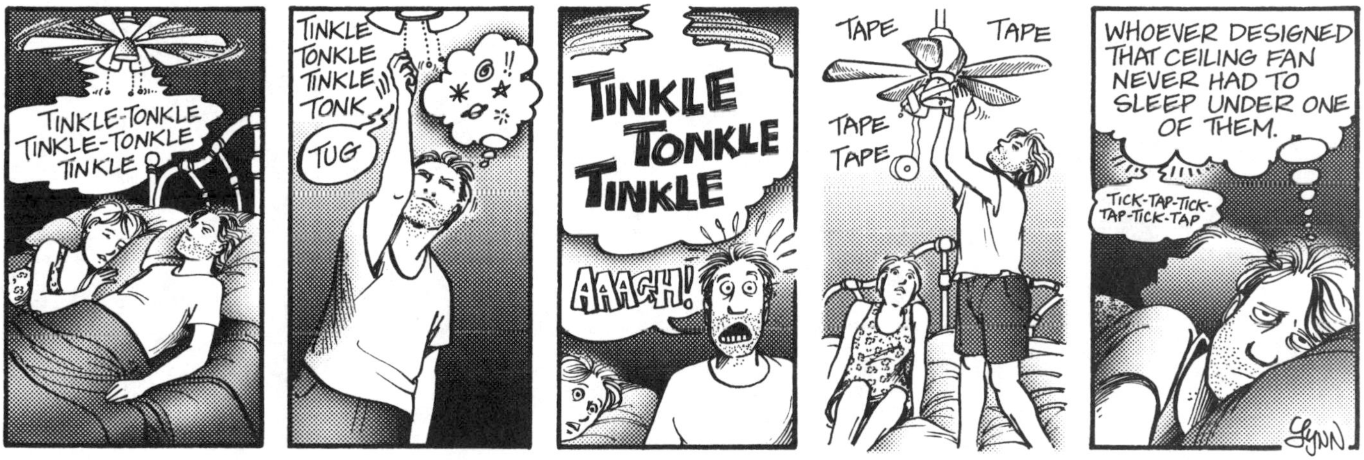
TINKLE-TONKLE TINKLE-TONKLE TINKLE
TINKLE TONKLE TINKLE TONK
TUG
TINKLE TONKLE TINKLE
AAAGH!
TAPE
TAPE
TAPE
TAPE
WHOEVER DESIGNED THAT CEILING FAN NEVER HAD TO SLEEP UNDER ONE OF THEM.
TICK-TAP-TICK-TAP-TICK-TAP
LYNN

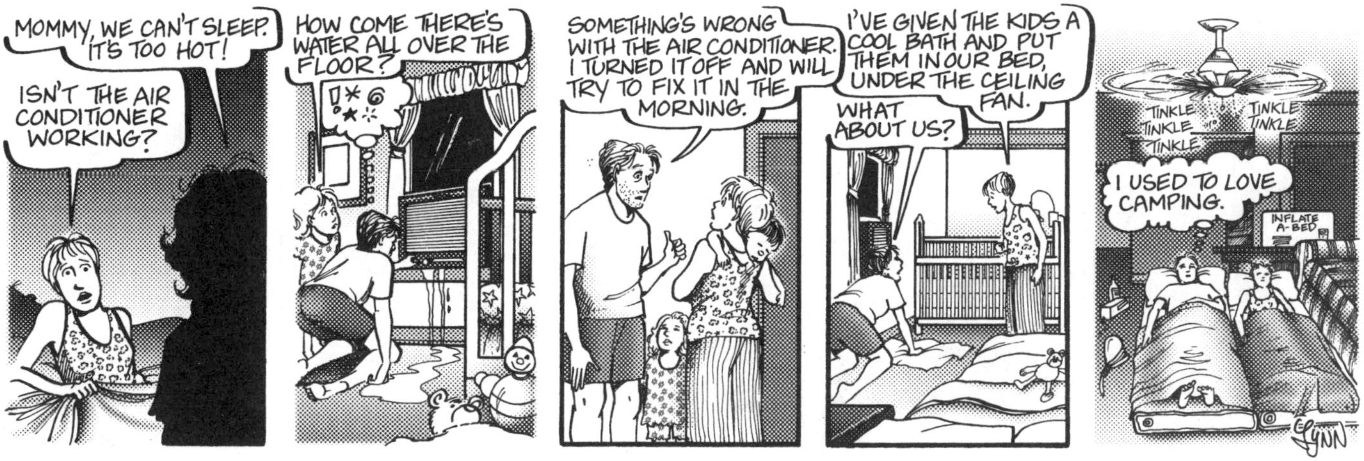
MOMMY, WE CAN'T SLEEP. IT'S TOO HOT!
ISN'T THE AIR CONDITIONER WORKING?
HOW COME THERE'S WATER ALL OVER THE FLOOR?
SOMETHING'S WRONG WITH THE AIR CONDITIONER. I TURNED IT OFF AND WILL TRY TO FIX IT IN THE MORNING.
I'VE GIVEN THE KIDS A COOL BATH AND PUT THEM IN OUR BED, UNDER THE CEILING FAN.
WHAT ABOUT US?
TINKLE TINKLE TINKLE
TINKLE TINKLE
I USED TO LOVE CAMPING.
INFLATE A-BED
LYNN

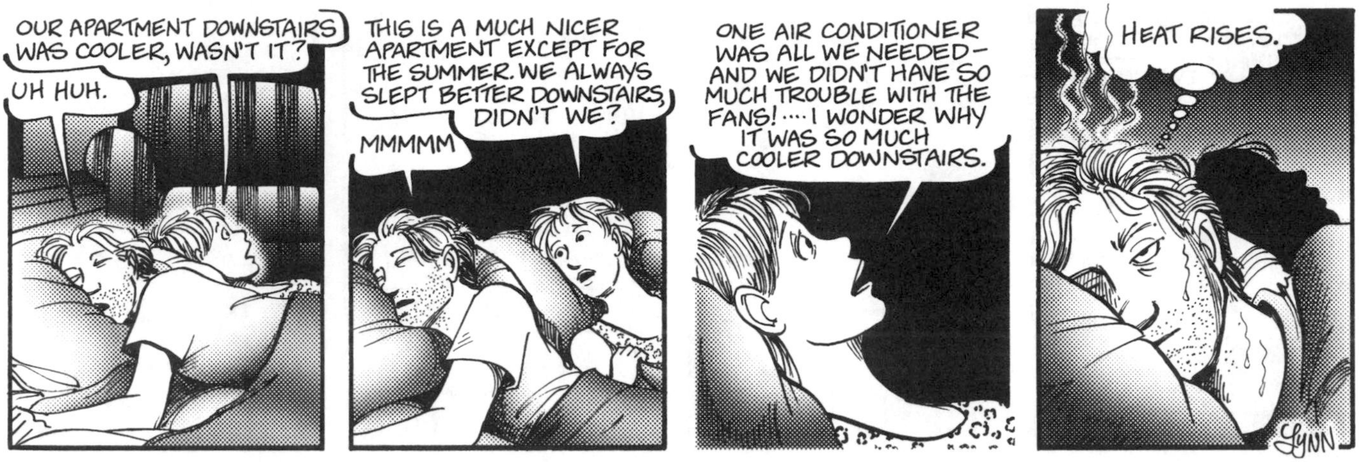
OUR APARTMENT DOWNSTAIRS WAS COOLER, WASN'T IT?
UH HUH.
THIS IS A MUCH NICER APARTMENT EXCEPT FOR THE SUMMER. WE ALWAYS SLEPT BETTER DOWNSTAIRS, DIDN'T WE?
MMMMM
ONE AIR CONDITIONER WAS ALL WE NEEDED– AND WE DIDN'T HAVE SO MUCH TROUBLE WITH THE FANS! .... I WONDER WHY IT WAS SO MUCH COOLER DOWNSTAIRS.
HEAT RISES.
LYNN

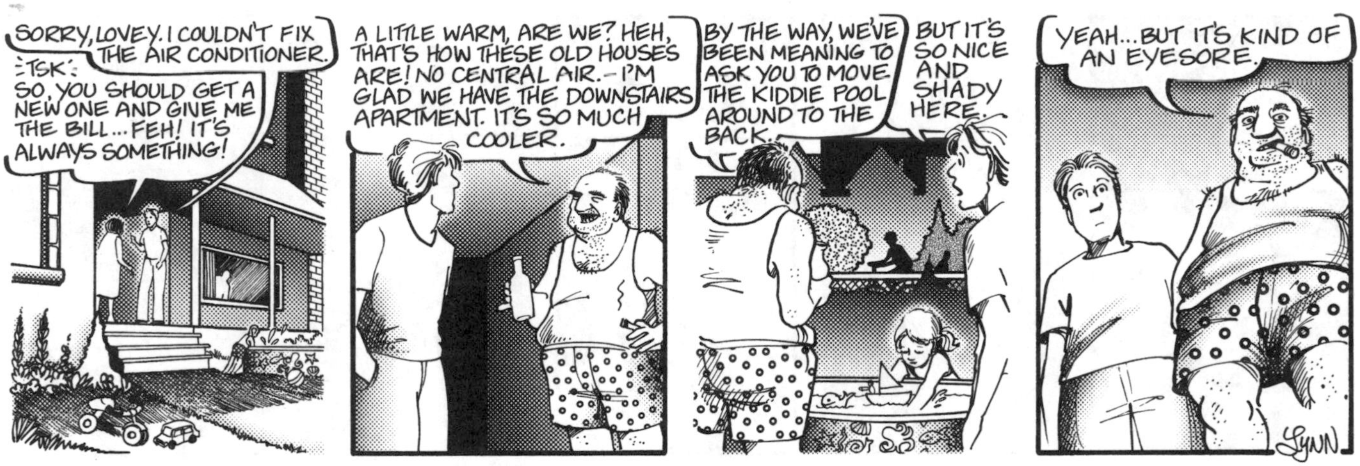
SORRY, LOVEY. I COULDN'T FIX THE AIR CONDITIONER.
TSK
SO, YOU SHOULD GET A NEW ONE AND GIVE ME THE BILL... FEH! IT'S ALWAYS SOMETHING!
A LITTLE WARM, ARE WE? HEH, THAT'S HOW THESE OLD HOUSES ARE! NO CENTRAL AIR.– I'M GLAD WE HAVE THE DOWNSTAIRS APARTMENT. IT'S SO MUCH COOLER.
BY THE WAY, WE'VE BEEN MEANING TO ASK YOU TO MOVE THE KIDDIE POOL AROUND TO THE BACK.
BUT IT'S SO NICE AND SHADY HERE.
YEAH... BUT IT'S KIND OF AN EYESORE.
LYNN

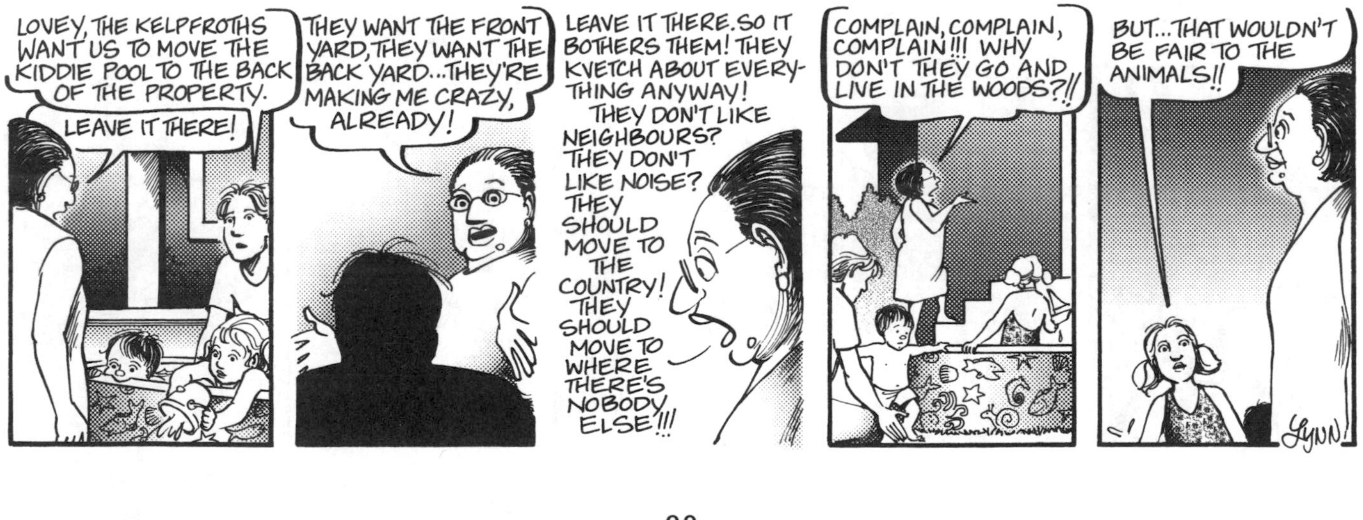
LOVEY, THE KELPFROTHS WANT US TO MOVE THE KIDDIE POOL TO THE BACK OF THE PROPERTY.
LEAVE IT THERE!
THEY WANT THE FRONT YARD, THEY WANT THE BACK YARD... THEY'RE MAKING ME CRAZY, ALREADY!
LEAVE IT THERE. SO IT BOTHERS THEM! THEY KVETCH ABOUT EVERYTHING ANYWAY! THEY DON'T LIKE NEIGHBOURS? THEY DON'T LIKE NOISE? THEY SHOULD MOVE TO THE COUNTRY! THEY SHOULD MOVE TO WHERE THERE'S NOBODY ELSE!!!
COMPLAIN, COMPLAIN, COMPLAIN!!! WHY DON'T THEY GO AND LIVE IN THE WOODS?!!
BUT... THAT WOULDN'T BE FAIR TO THE ANIMALS!!
LYNN

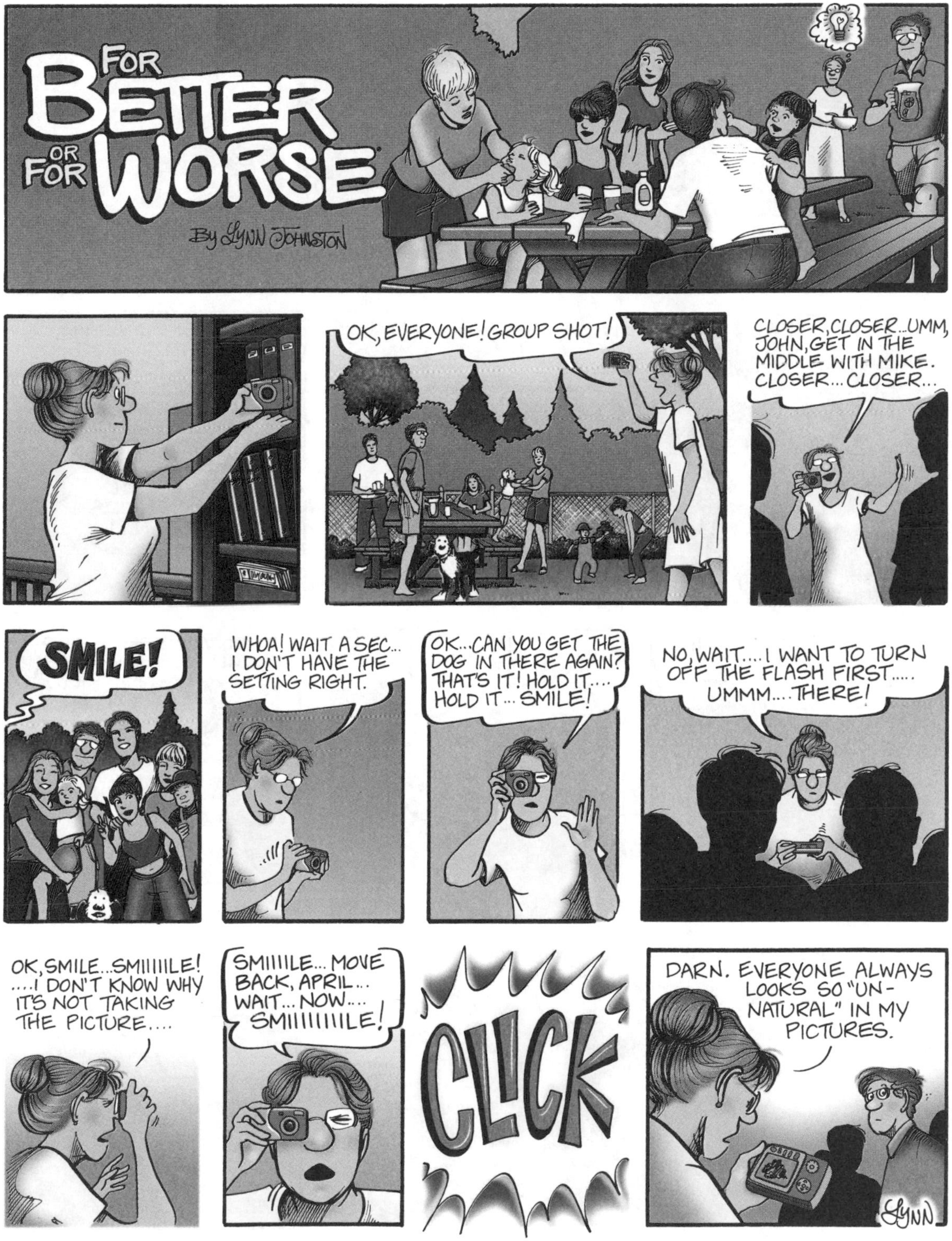
FOR BETTER OR FOR WORSE
BY LYNN JOHNSTON
OK, EVERYONE! GROUP SHOT!
CLOSER, CLOSER...UMM, JOHN, GET IN THE MIDDLE WITH MIKE. CLOSER... CLOSER...
SMILE!
WHOA! WAIT A SEC... I DON'T HAVE THE SETTING RIGHT.
OK...CAN YOU GET THE DOG IN THERE AGAIN? THAT'S IT! HOLD IT.... HOLD IT... SMILE!
NO, WAIT.... I WANT TO TURN OFF THE FLASH FIRST..... UMMM.... THERE!
OK, SMILE...SMIIIIILE! ....I DON'T KNOW WHY IT'S NOT TAKING THE PICTURE....
SMIIIILE... MOVE BACK, APRIL... WAIT... NOW.... SMIIIIIIIILE!
CLICK
DARN. EVERYONE ALWAYS LOOKS SO "UN-NATURAL" IN MY PICTURES.
LYNN

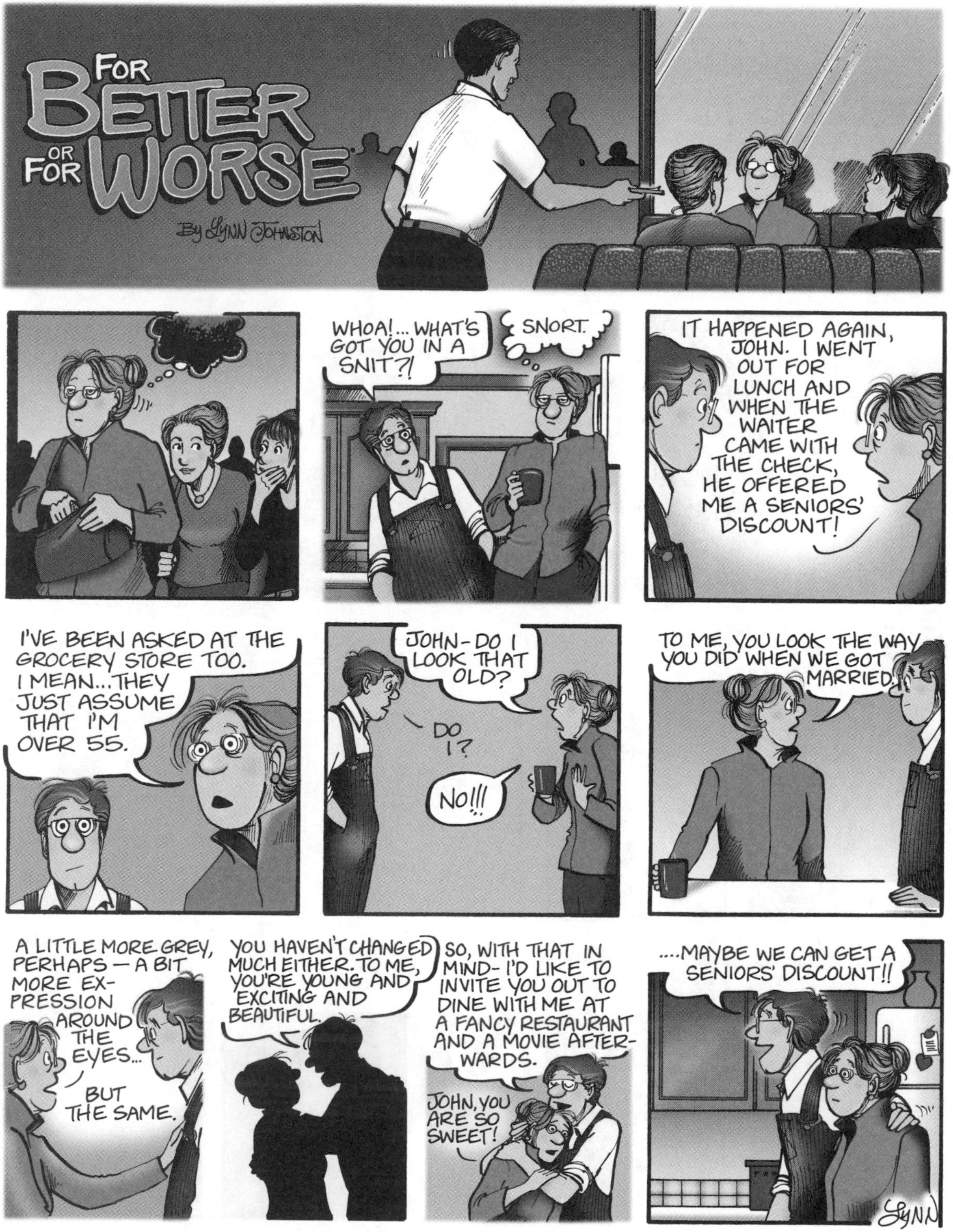
FOR BETTER OR FOR WORSE
By Lynn Johnston
WHOA!... WHAT'S GOT YOU IN A SNIT?!
SNORT.
IT HAPPENED AGAIN, JOHN. I WENT OUT FOR LUNCH AND WHEN THE WAITER CAME WITH THE CHECK, HE OFFERED ME A SENIORS' DISCOUNT!
I'VE BEEN ASKED AT THE GROCERY STORE TOO. I MEAN... THEY JUST ASSUME THAT I'M OVER 55.
JOHN- DO I LOOK THAT OLD?
DO I?
NO!!!
TO ME, YOU LOOK THE WAY YOU DID WHEN WE GOT MARRIED.
A LITTLE MORE GREY, PERHAPS — A BIT MORE EX-PRESSION AROUND THE EYES...
BUT THE SAME.
YOU HAVEN'T CHANGED MUCH EITHER. TO ME, YOU'RE YOUNG AND EXCITING AND BEAUTIFUL.
SO, WITH THAT IN MIND- I'D LIKE TO INVITE YOU OUT TO DINE WITH ME AT A FANCY RESTAURANT AND A MOVIE AFTER-WARDS.
JOHN, YOU ARE SO SWEET!
....MAYBE WE CAN GET A SENIORS' DISCOUNT!!
LYNN

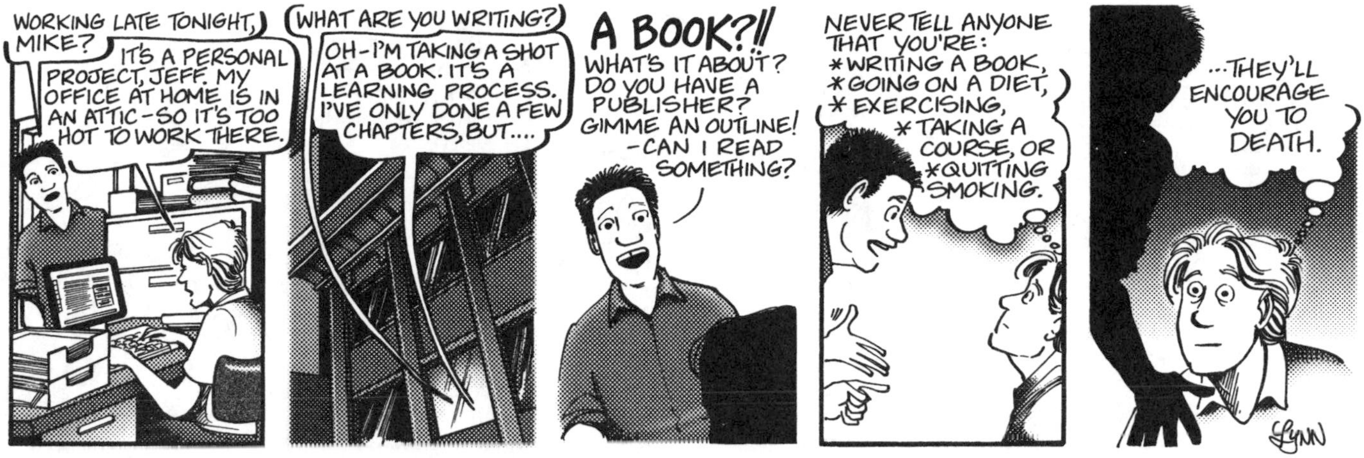
WORKING LATE TONIGHT, MIKE?
IT'S A PERSONAL PROJECT, JEFF. MY OFFICE AT HOME IS IN AN ATTIC - SO IT'S TOO HOT TO WORK THERE.
WHAT ARE YOU WRITING?
OH - I'M TAKING A SHOT AT A BOOK. IT'S A LEARNING PROCESS. I'VE ONLY DONE A FEW CHAPTERS, BUT....
A BOOK?!!
WHAT'S IT ABOUT? DO YOU HAVE A PUBLISHER? GIMME AN OUTLINE! - CAN I READ SOMETHING?
NEVER TELL ANYONE THAT YOU'RE:
* WRITING A BOOK,
* GOING ON A DIET,
* EXERCISING,
* TAKING A COURSE, OR
* QUITTING SMOKING.
...THEY'LL ENCOURAGE YOU TO DEATH.
Lynn

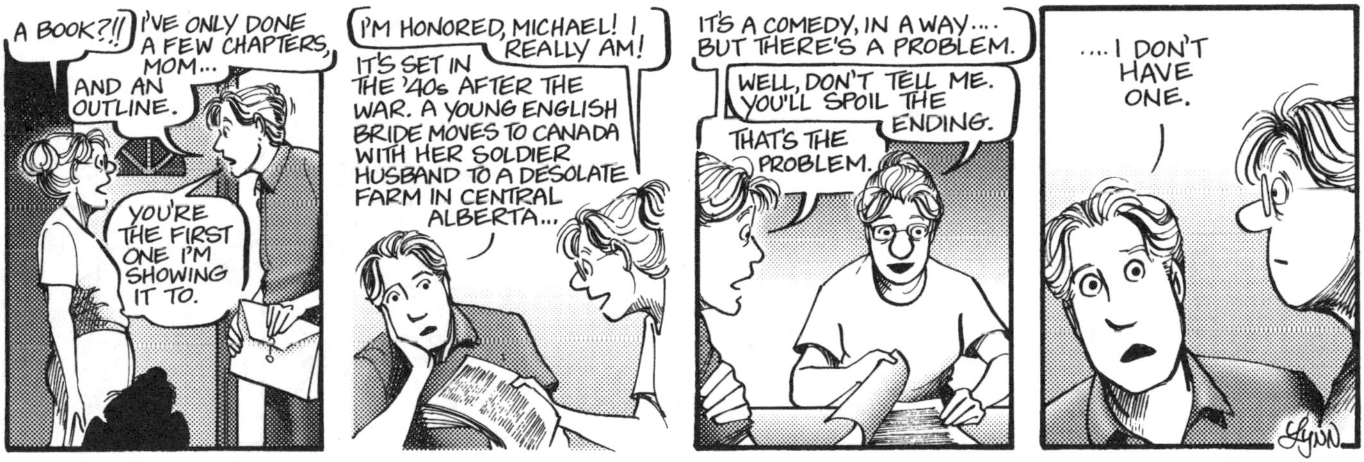
A BOOK?!!
I'VE ONLY DONE A FEW CHAPTERS, MOM...
AND AN OUTLINE.
YOU'RE THE FIRST ONE I'M SHOWING IT TO.
I'M HONORED, MICHAEL! I REALLY AM!
IT'S SET IN THE '40s AFTER THE WAR. A YOUNG ENGLISH BRIDE MOVES TO CANADA WITH HER SOLDIER HUSBAND TO A DESOLATE FARM IN CENTRAL ALBERTA...
IT'S A COMEDY, IN A WAY.... BUT THERE'S A PROBLEM.
WELL, DON'T TELL ME. YOU'LL SPOIL THE ENDING.
THAT'S THE PROBLEM.
.... I DON'T HAVE ONE.
Lynn

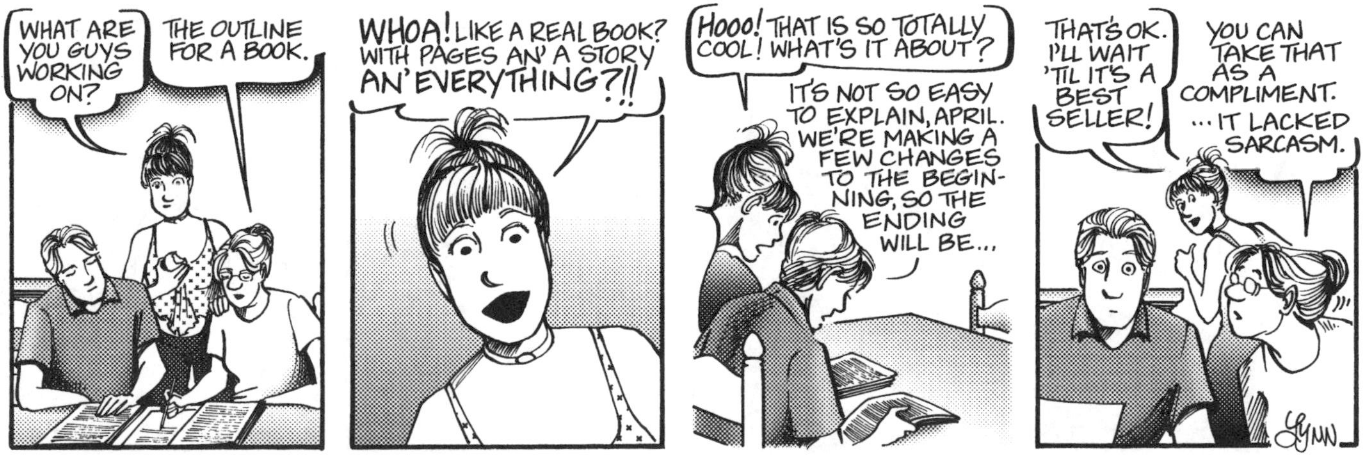
WHAT ARE YOU GUYS WORKING ON?
THE OUTLINE FOR A BOOK.
WHOA! LIKE A REAL BOOK? WITH PAGES AN' A STORY AN' EVERYTHING?!!
HOOO! THAT IS SO TOTALLY COOL! WHAT'S IT ABOUT?
IT'S NOT SO EASY TO EXPLAIN, APRIL. WE'RE MAKING A FEW CHANGES TO THE BEGINNING, SO THE ENDING WILL BE...
THAT'S OK. I'LL WAIT 'TIL IT'S A BEST SELLER!
YOU CAN TAKE THAT AS A COMPLIMENT. ...IT LACKED SARCASM.
Lynn

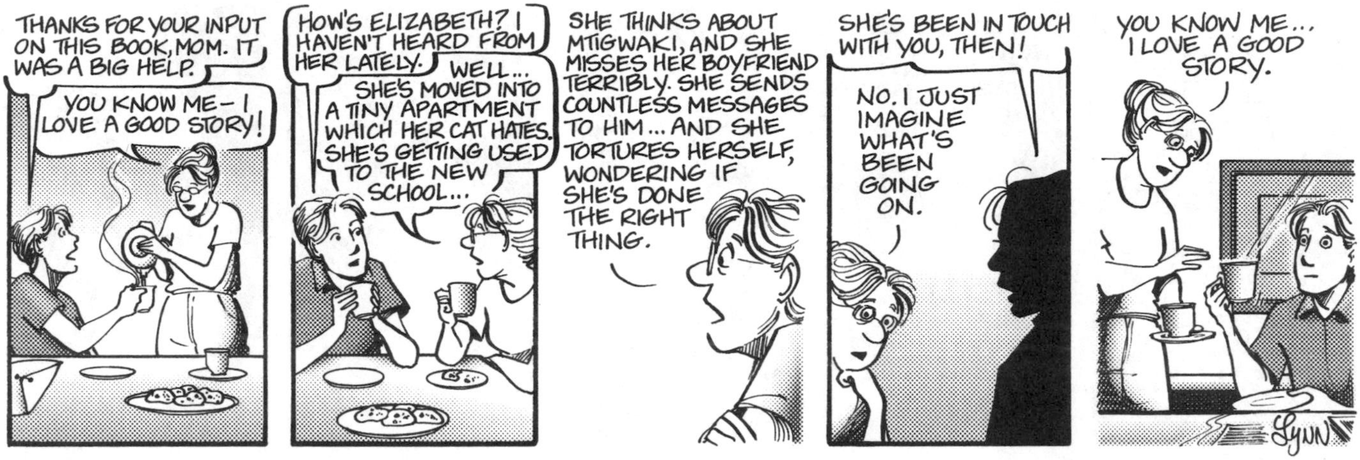
THANKS FOR YOUR INPUT ON THIS BOOK, MOM. IT WAS A BIG HELP.
YOU KNOW ME– I LOVE A GOOD STORY!
HOW'S ELIZABETH? I HAVEN'T HEARD FROM HER LATELY.
WELL... SHE'S MOVED INTO A TINY APARTMENT WHICH HER CAT HATES. SHE'S GETTING USED TO THE NEW SCHOOL...
SHE THINKS ABOUT MTIGWAKI, AND SHE MISSES HER BOYFRIEND TERRIBLY. SHE SENDS COUNTLESS MESSAGES TO HIM... AND SHE TORTURES HERSELF, WONDERING IF SHE'S DONE THE RIGHT THING.
SHE'S BEEN IN TOUCH WITH YOU, THEN!
NO. I JUST IMAGINE WHAT'S BEEN GOING ON.
YOU KNOW ME... I LOVE A GOOD STORY.
LYNN

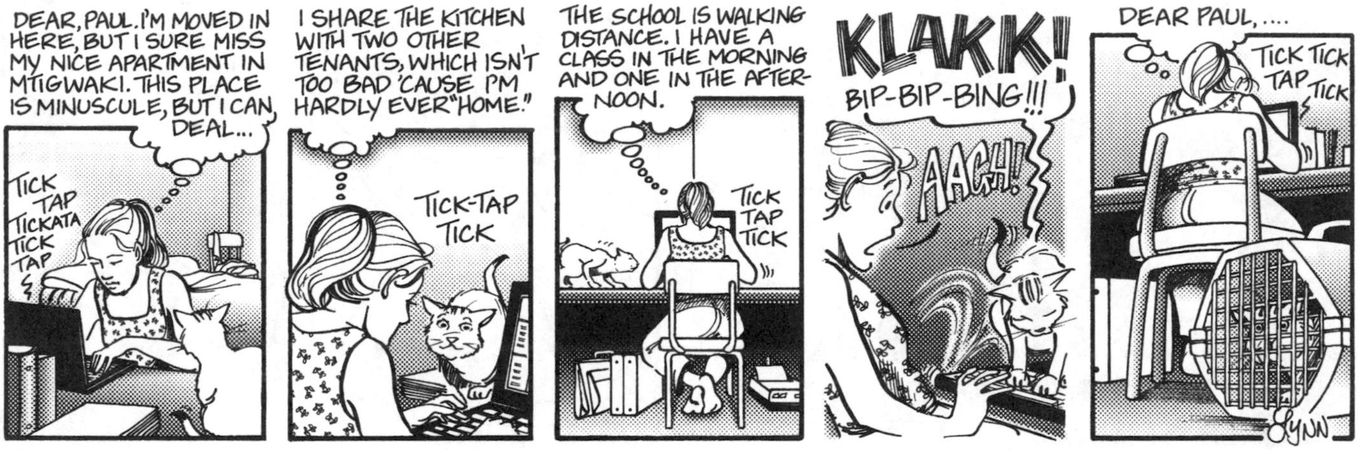
DEAR, PAUL. I'M MOVED IN HERE, BUT I SURE MISS MY NICE APARTMENT IN MTIGWAKI. THIS PLACE IS MINUSCULE, BUT I CAN DEAL...
TICK TAP TICKATA TICK TAP
I SHARE THE KITCHEN WITH TWO OTHER TENANTS, WHICH ISN'T TOO BAD 'CAUSE I'M HARDLY EVER "HOME."
TICK-TAP TICK
THE SCHOOL IS WALKING DISTANCE. I HAVE A CLASS IN THE MORNING AND ONE IN THE AFTERNOON.
TICK TAP TICK
KLAKK!
BIP-BIP-BING!!!
AACH!
DEAR PAUL, ...
TICK TICK TAP TICK
LYNN

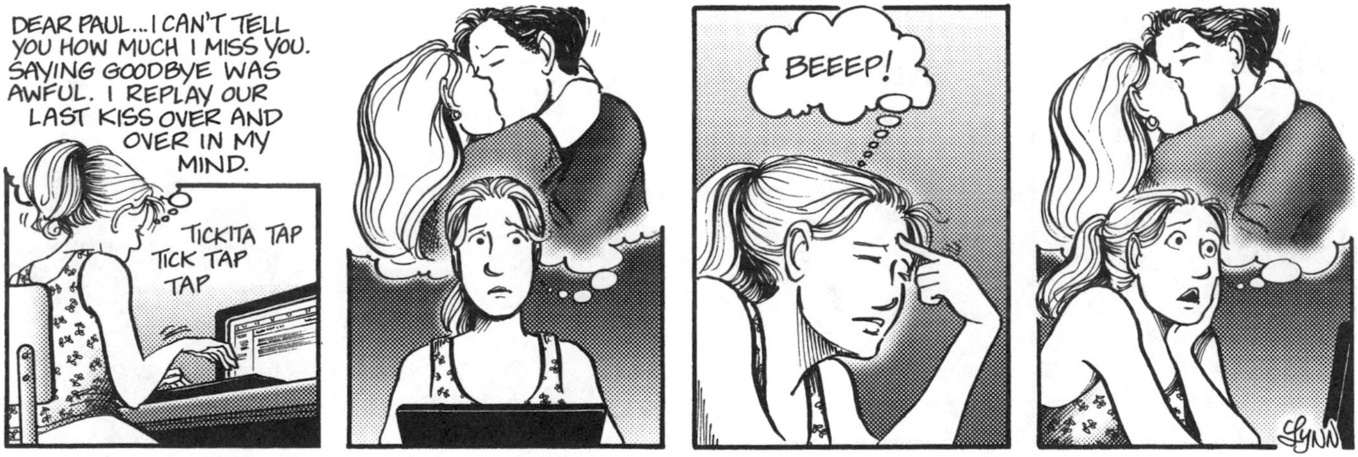
DEAR PAUL... I CAN'T TELL YOU HOW MUCH I MISS YOU. SAYING GOODBYE WAS AWFUL. I REPLAY OUR LAST KISS OVER AND OVER IN MY MIND.
TICKITA TAP TICK TAP TAP
BEEEP!
LYNN

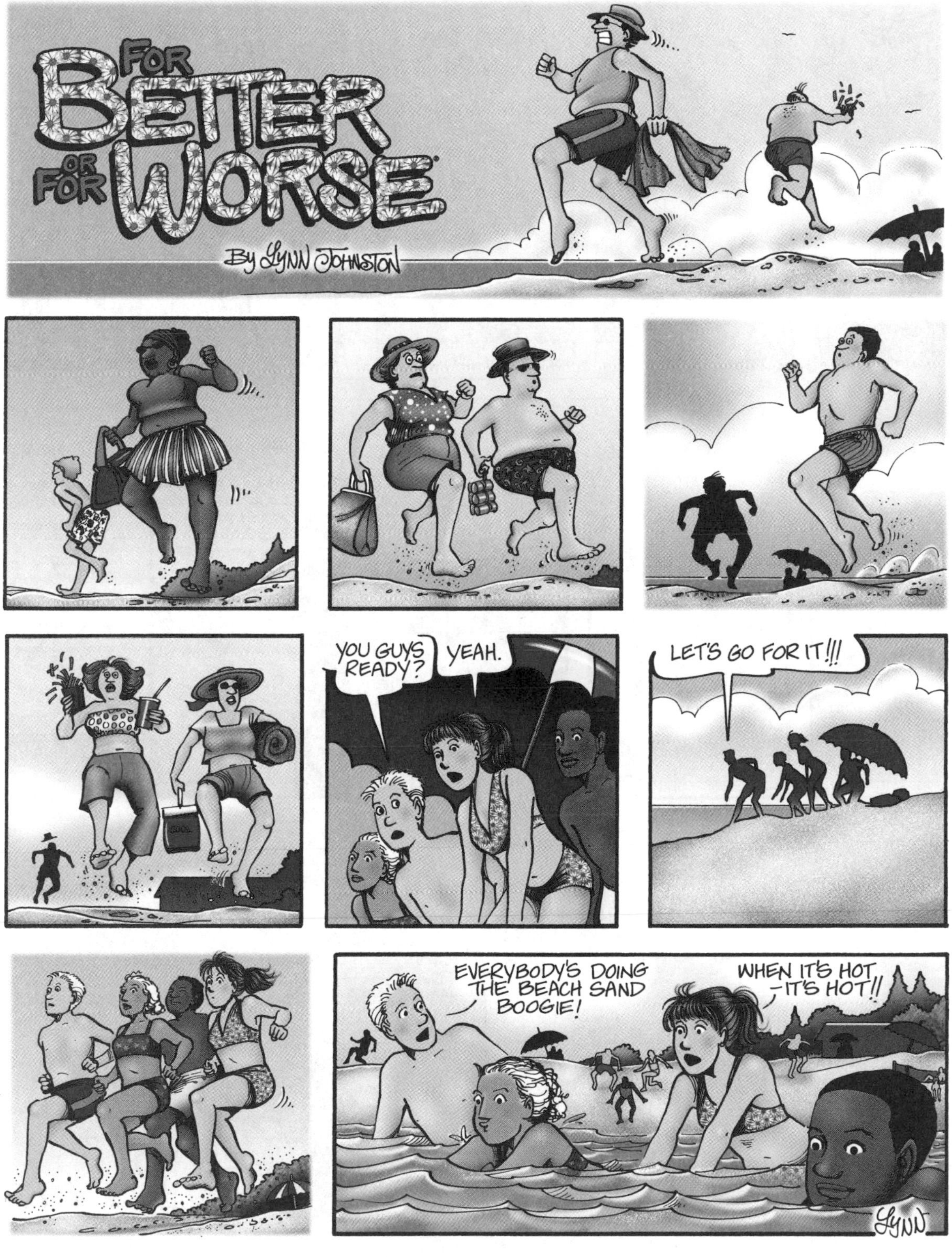
FOR BETTER OR FOR WORSE
BY LYNN JOHNSTON
COOL
YOU GUYS READY?
YEAH.
LET'S GO FOR IT!!!
EVERYBODY'S DOING THE BEACH SAND BOOGIE!
WHEN IT'S HOT, IT'S HOT!!
LYNN

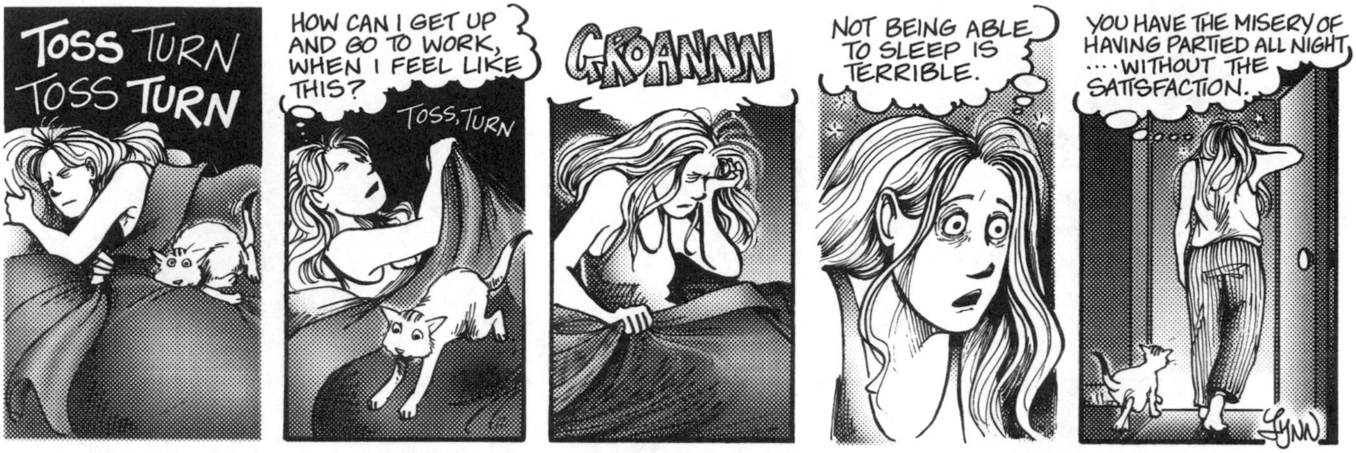
TOSS TURN
TOSS TURN
HOW CAN I GET UP AND GO TO WORK, WHEN I FEEL LIKE THIS?
TOSS, TURN
GROANNN
NOT BEING ABLE TO SLEEP IS TERRIBLE.
YOU HAVE THE MISERY OF HAVING PARTIED ALL NIGHT, ...WITHOUT THE SATISFACTION.
LYNN

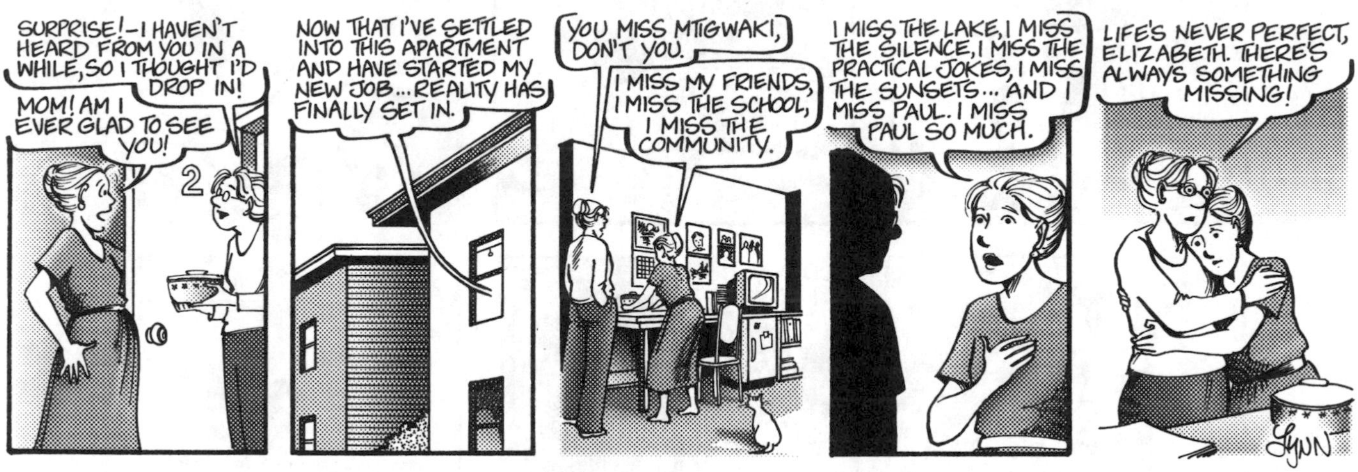
SURPRISE! – I HAVEN'T HEARD FROM YOU IN A WHILE, SO I THOUGHT I'D DROP IN!
MOM! AM I EVER GLAD TO SEE YOU!
2
NOW THAT I'VE SETTLED INTO THIS APARTMENT AND HAVE STARTED MY NEW JOB... REALITY HAS FINALLY SET IN.
YOU MISS MTIGWAKI, DON'T YOU.
I MISS MY FRIENDS, I MISS THE SCHOOL, I MISS THE COMMUNITY.
I MISS THE LAKE, I MISS THE SILENCE, I MISS THE PRACTICAL JOKES, I MISS THE SUNSETS... AND I MISS PAUL. I MISS PAUL SO MUCH.
LIFE'S NEVER PERFECT, ELIZABETH. THERE'S ALWAYS SOMETHING MISSING!
LYNN

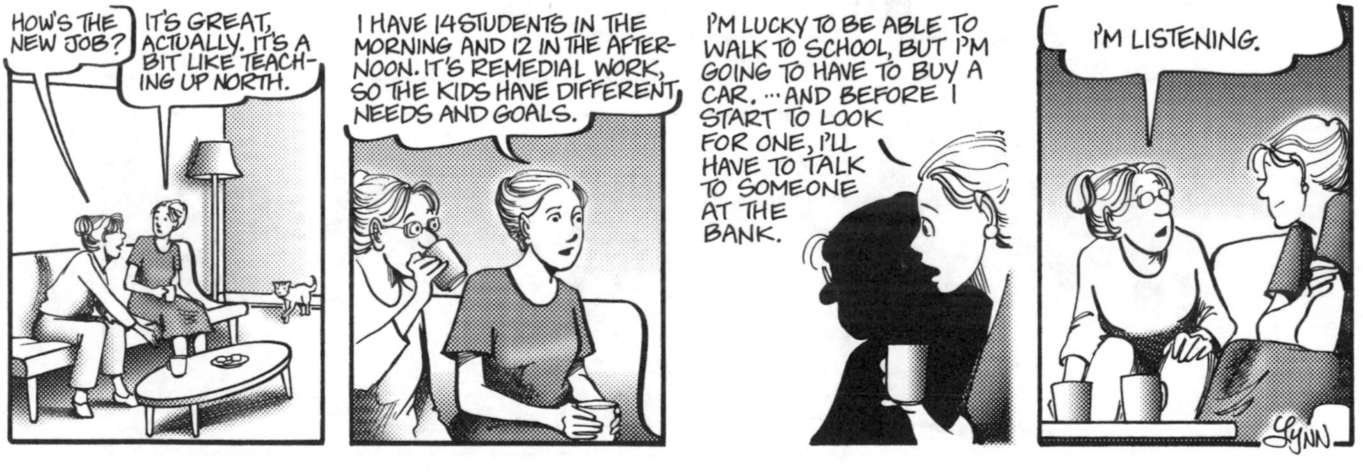
HOW'S THE NEW JOB?
IT'S GREAT, ACTUALLY. IT'S A BIT LIKE TEACHING UP NORTH.
I HAVE 14 STUDENTS IN THE MORNING AND 12 IN THE AFTERNOON. IT'S REMEDIAL WORK, SO THE KIDS HAVE DIFFERENT NEEDS AND GOALS.
I'M LUCKY TO BE ABLE TO WALK TO SCHOOL, BUT I'M GOING TO HAVE TO BUY A CAR. ... AND BEFORE I START TO LOOK FOR ONE, I'LL HAVE TO TALK TO SOMEONE AT THE BANK.
I'M LISTENING.
LYNN

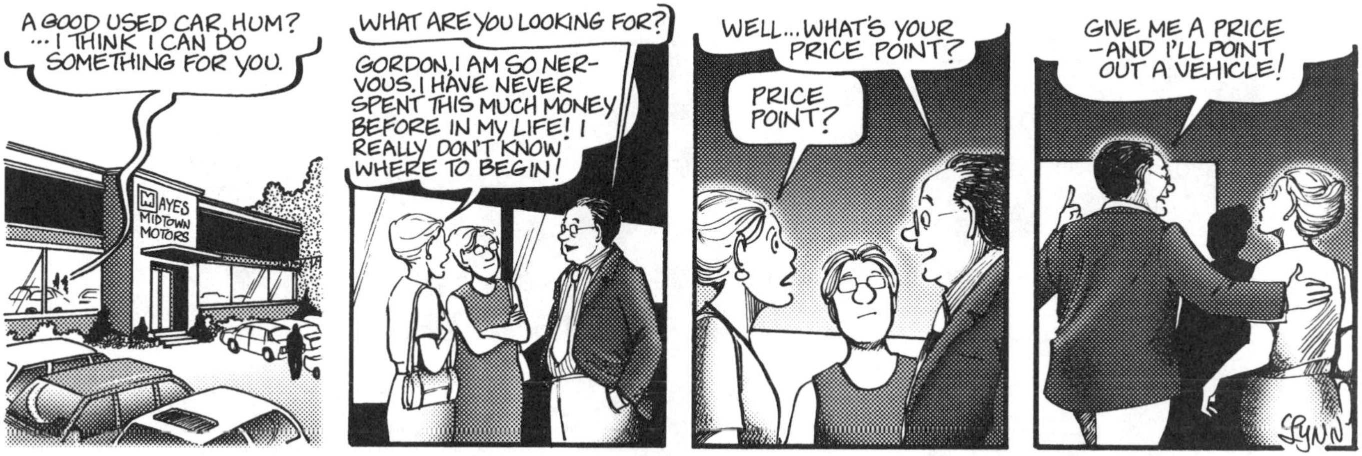
A GOOD USED CAR, HUM? ...I THINK I CAN DO SOMETHING FOR YOU.
MAYES MIDTOWN MOTORS
WHAT ARE YOU LOOKING FOR?
GORDON, I AM SO NERVOUS. I HAVE NEVER SPENT THIS MUCH MONEY BEFORE IN MY LIFE! I REALLY DON'T KNOW WHERE TO BEGIN!
WELL... WHAT'S YOUR PRICE POINT?
PRICE POINT?
GIVE ME A PRICE -AND I'LL POINT OUT A VEHICLE!
LYNN

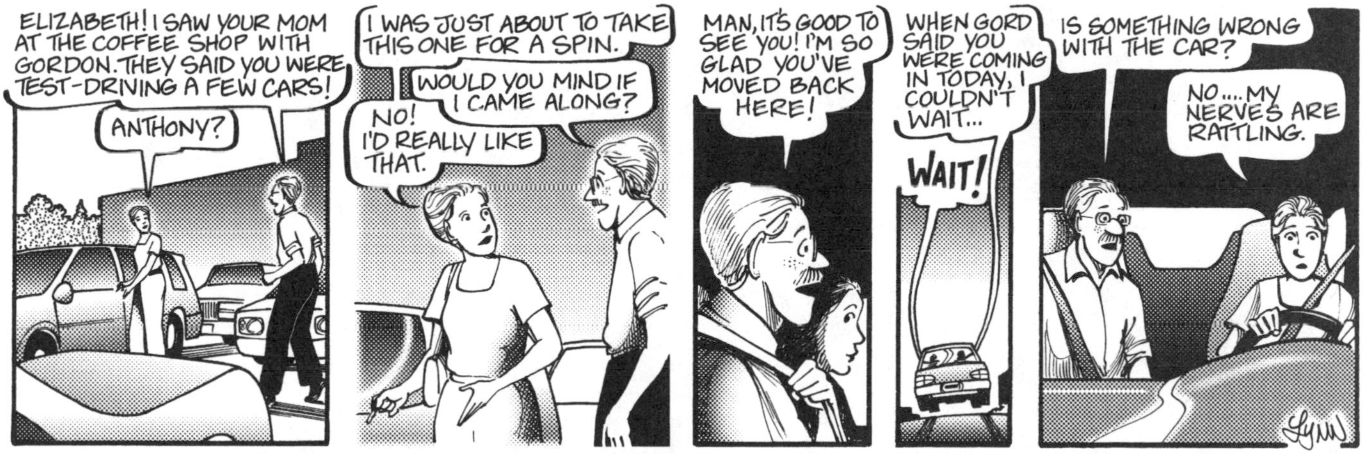
ELIZABETH! I SAW YOUR MOM AT THE COFFEE SHOP WITH GORDON. THEY SAID YOU WERE TEST-DRIVING A FEW CARS!
ANTHONY?
I WAS JUST ABOUT TO TAKE THIS ONE FOR A SPIN.
WOULD YOU MIND IF I CAME ALONG?
NO! I'D REALLY LIKE THAT.
MAN, IT'S GOOD TO SEE YOU! I'M SO GLAD YOU'VE MOVED BACK HERE!
WHEN GORD SAID YOU WERE COMING IN TODAY, I COULDN'T WAIT...
WAIT!
IS SOMETHING WRONG WITH THE CAR?
NO.... MY NERVES ARE RATTLING.
LYNN

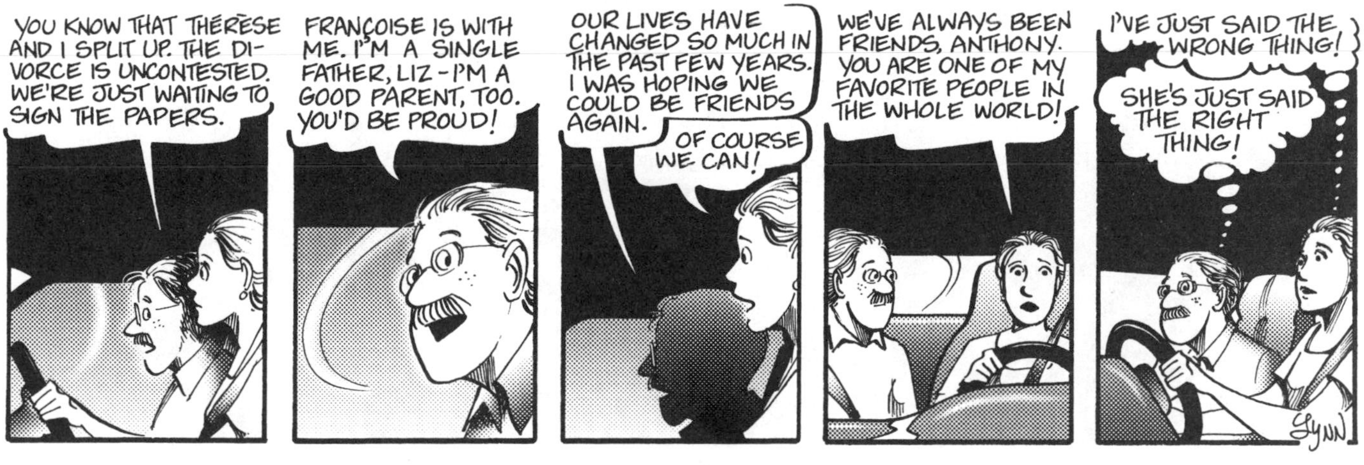
YOU KNOW THAT THÉRÈSE AND I SPLIT UP. THE DIVORCE IS UNCONTESTED. WE'RE JUST WAITING TO SIGN THE PAPERS.
FRANÇOISE IS WITH ME. I'M A SINGLE FATHER, LIZ - I'M A GOOD PARENT, TOO. YOU'D BE PROUD!
OUR LIVES HAVE CHANGED SO MUCH IN THE PAST FEW YEARS. I WAS HOPING WE COULD BE FRIENDS AGAIN.
OF COURSE WE CAN!
WE'VE ALWAYS BEEN FRIENDS, ANTHONY. YOU ARE ONE OF MY FAVORITE PEOPLE IN THE WHOLE WORLD!
I'VE JUST SAID THE WRONG THING!
SHE'S JUST SAID THE RIGHT THING!
LYNN

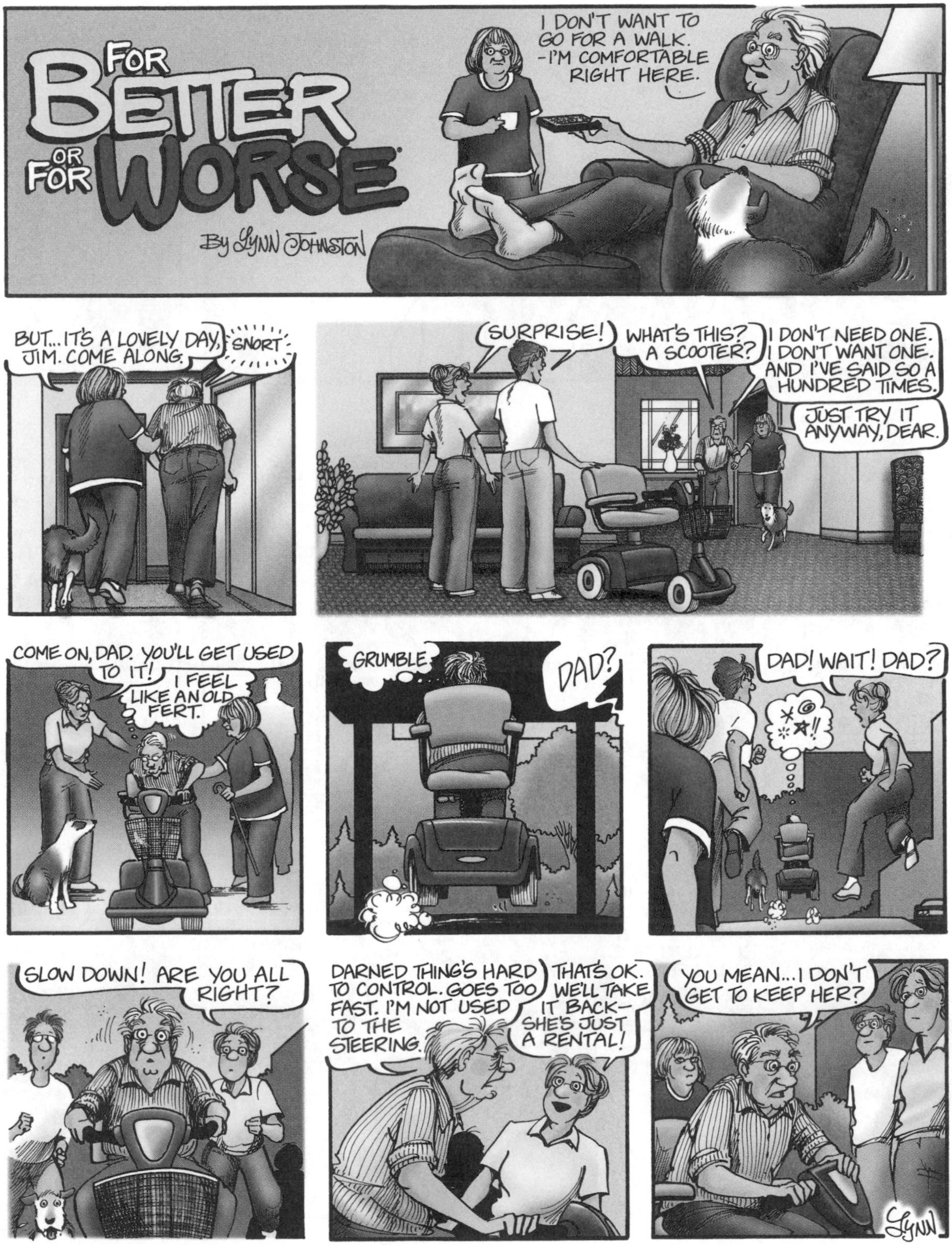

FOR BETTER OR FOR WORSE
By Lynn Johnston
I DON'T WANT TO GO FOR A WALK. -I'M COMFORTABLE RIGHT HERE.
BUT... IT'S A LOVELY DAY, JIM. COME ALONG.
SNORT
SURPRISE!
WHAT'S THIS? A SCOOTER?
I DON'T NEED ONE. I DON'T WANT ONE. AND I'VE SAID SO A HUNDRED TIMES.
JUST TRY IT ANYWAY, DEAR.
COME ON, DAD. YOU'LL GET USED TO IT!
I FEEL LIKE AN OLD FERT.
GRUMBLE
DAD?
DAD! WAIT! DAD?
SLOW DOWN! ARE YOU ALL RIGHT?
DARNED THING'S HARD TO CONTROL. GOES TOO FAST. I'M NOT USED TO THE STEERING.
THAT'S OK. WE'LL TAKE IT BACK– SHE'S JUST A RENTAL!
YOU MEAN... I DON'T GET TO KEEP HER?
LYNN

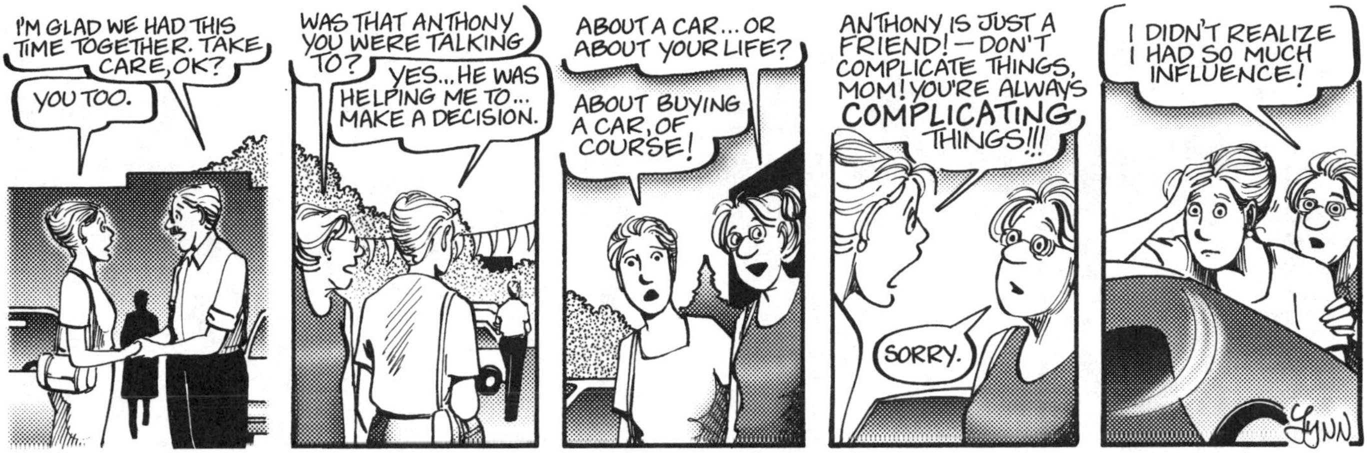
I'M GLAD WE HAD THIS TIME TOGETHER. TAKE CARE, OK?
YOU TOO.
WAS THAT ANTHONY YOU WERE TALKING TO?
YES... HE WAS HELPING ME TO... MAKE A DECISION.
ABOUT A CAR... OR ABOUT YOUR LIFE?
ABOUT BUYING A CAR, OF COURSE!
ANTHONY IS JUST A FRIEND! — DON'T COMPLICATE THINGS, MOM! YOU'RE ALWAYS COMPLICATING THINGS!!!
SORRY.
I DIDN'T REALIZE I HAD SO MUCH INFLUENCE!
LYNN

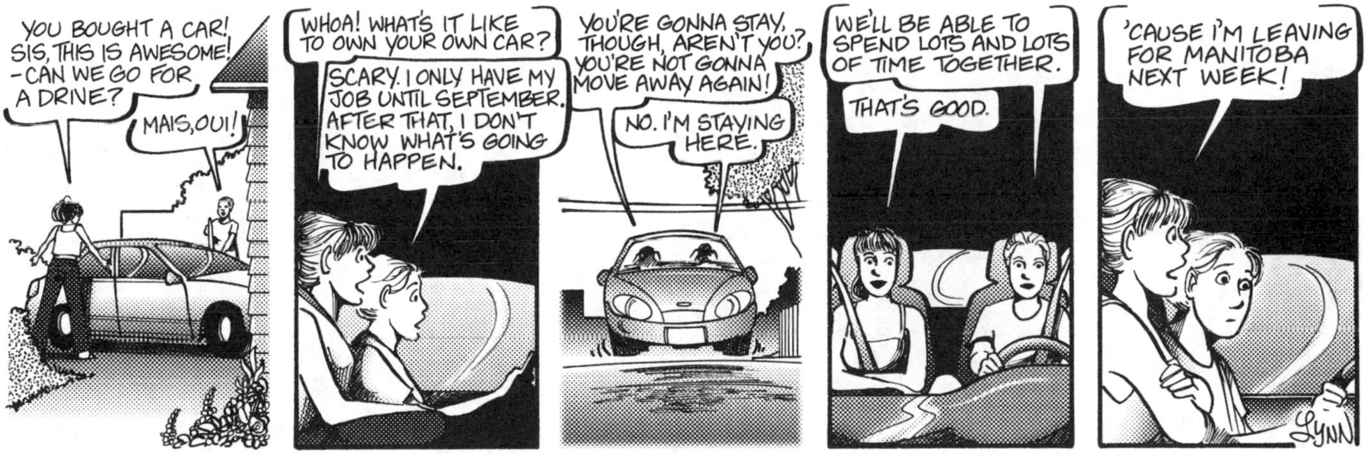
YOU BOUGHT A CAR! SIS, THIS IS AWESOME! -CAN WE GO FOR A DRIVE?
MAIS, OUI!
WHOA! WHAT'S IT LIKE TO OWN YOUR OWN CAR?
SCARY. I ONLY HAVE MY JOB UNTIL SEPTEMBER. AFTER THAT, I DON'T KNOW WHAT'S GOING TO HAPPEN.
YOU'RE GONNA STAY, THOUGH, AREN'T YOU? YOU'RE NOT GONNA MOVE AWAY AGAIN!
NO. I'M STAYING HERE.
WE'LL BE ABLE TO SPEND LOTS AND LOTS OF TIME TOGETHER.
THAT'S GOOD.
'CAUSE I'M LEAVING FOR MANITOBA NEXT WEEK!
LYNN

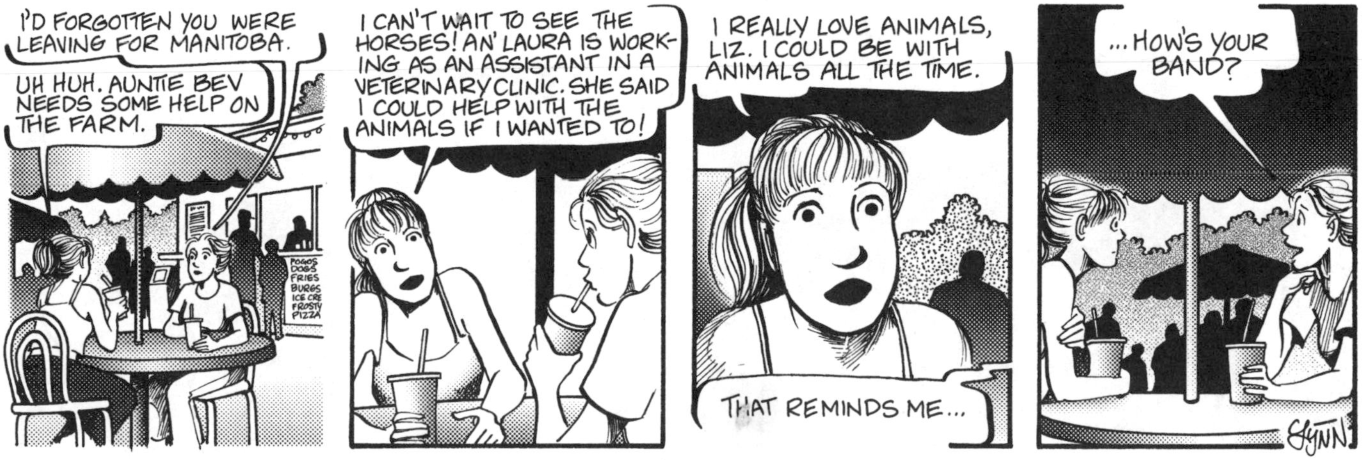
I'D FORGOTTEN YOU WERE LEAVING FOR MANITOBA.
UH HUH. AUNTIE BEV NEEDS SOME HELP ON THE FARM.
POGOS
DOGS
FRIES
BURGS
FROSTY
PIZZA
I CAN'T WAIT TO SEE THE HORSES! AN' LAURA IS WORKING AS AN ASSISTANT IN A VETERINARY CLINIC. SHE SAID I COULD HELP WITH THE ANIMALS IF I WANTED TO!
I REALLY LOVE ANIMALS, LIZ. I COULD BE WITH ANIMALS ALL THE TIME.
THAT REMINDS ME...
... HOW'S YOUR BAND?
LYNN

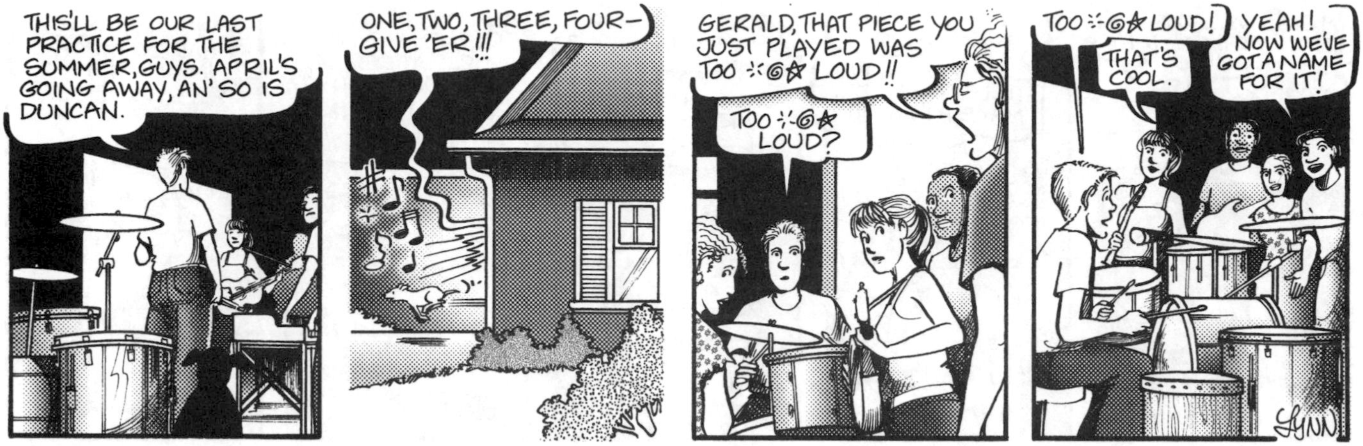
THIS'LL BE OUR LAST PRACTICE FOR THE SUMMER, GUYS. APRIL'S GOING AWAY, AN' SO IS DUNCAN.
ONE, TWO, THREE, FOUR— GIVE 'ER!!!
GERALD, THAT PIECE YOU JUST PLAYED WAS TOO *@☆ LOUD!!
TOO *@☆ LOUD?
TOO *@☆ LOUD!
THAT'S COOL.
YEAH! NOW WE'VE GOT A NAME FOR IT!
LYNN

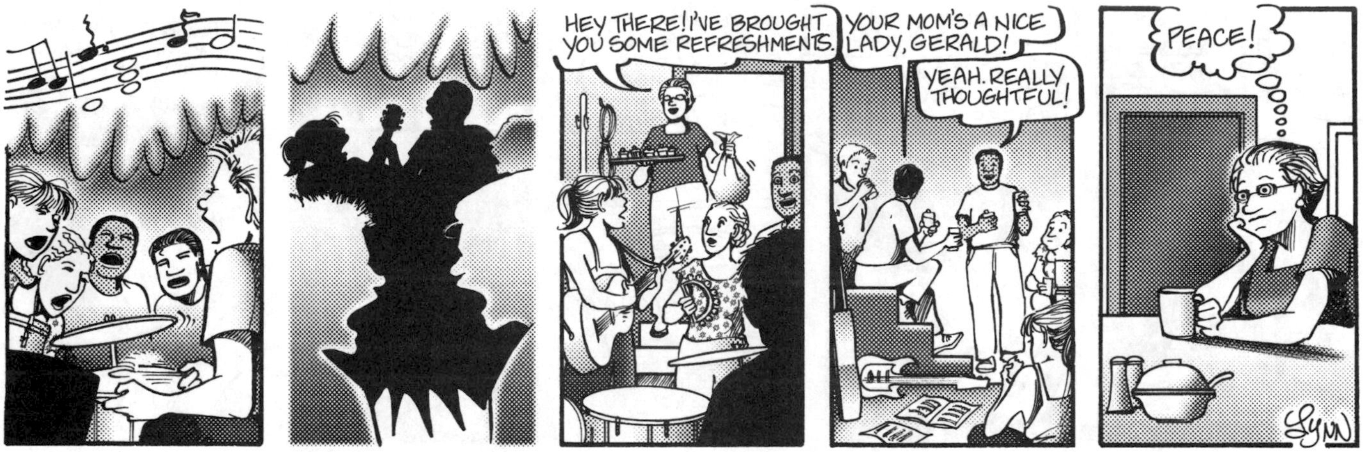
HEY THERE! I'VE BROUGHT YOU SOME REFRESHMENTS.
YOUR MOM'S A NICE LADY, GERALD!
YEAH. REALLY THOUGHTFUL!
PEACE!
LYNN

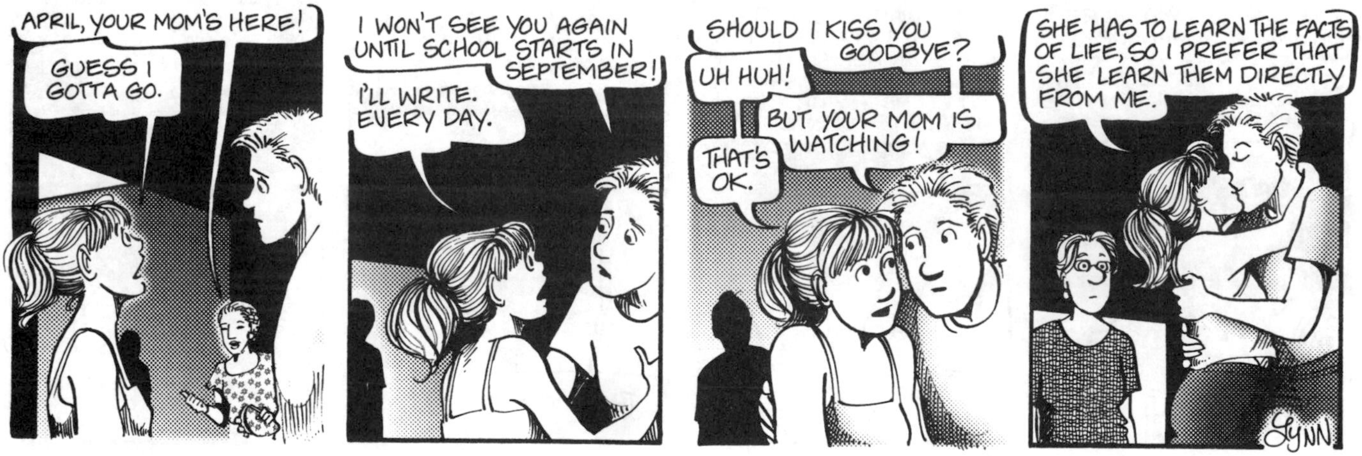
APRIL, YOUR MOM'S HERE!
GUESS I GOTTA GO.
I WON'T SEE YOU AGAIN UNTIL SCHOOL STARTS IN SEPTEMBER!
I'LL WRITE. EVERY DAY.
SHOULD I KISS YOU GOODBYE?
UH HUH!
BUT YOUR MOM IS WATCHING!
THAT'S OK.
SHE HAS TO LEARN THE FACTS OF LIFE, SO I PREFER THAT SHE LEARN THEM DIRECTLY FROM ME.
LYNN

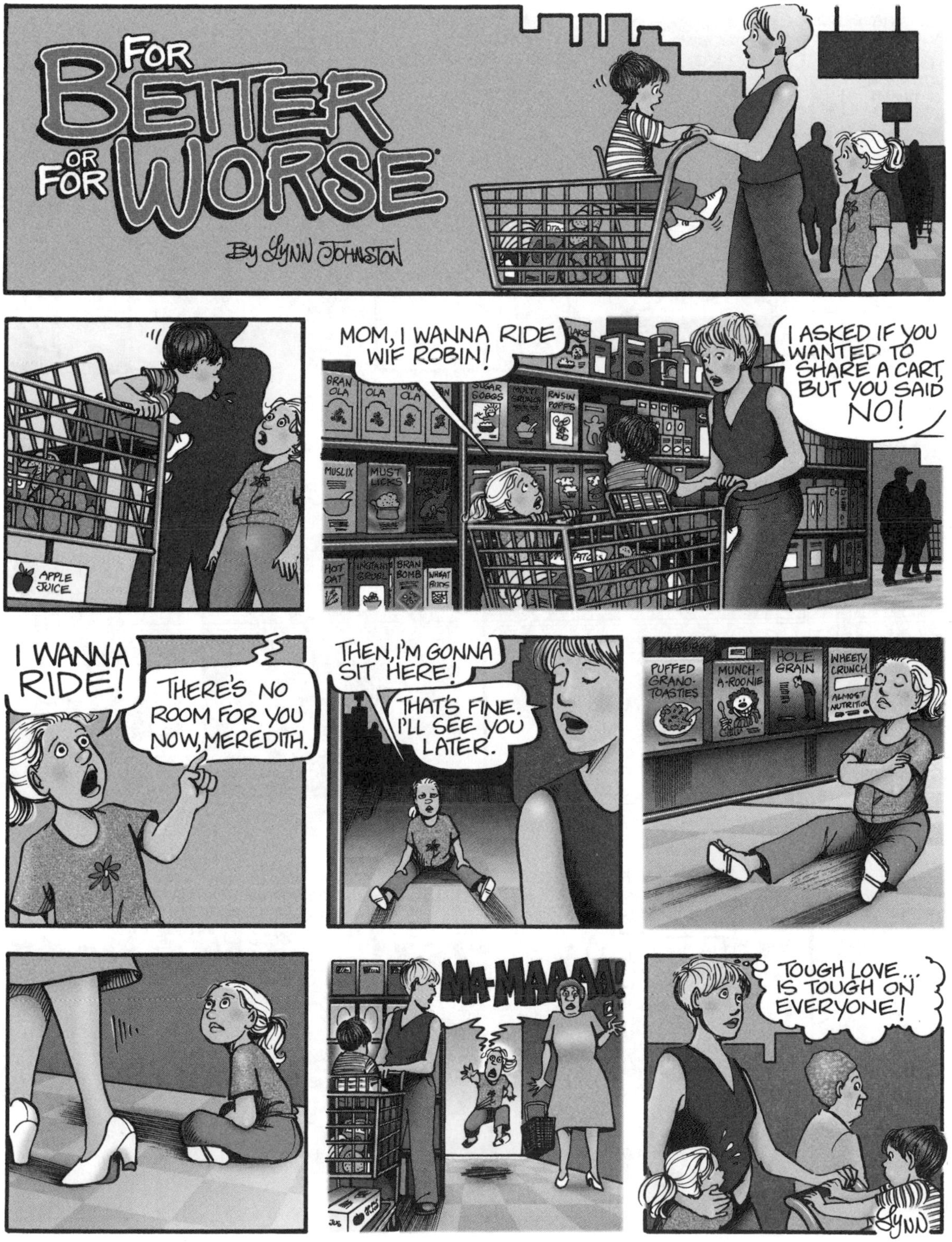
FOR BETTER OR FOR WORSE
By Lynn Johnston
APPLE JUICE
MOM, I WANNA RIDE WIF ROBIN!
I ASKED IF YOU WANTED TO SHARE A CART, BUT YOU SAID NO!
I WANNA RIDE!
THERE'S NO ROOM FOR YOU NOW, MEREDITH.
THEN, I'M GONNA SIT HERE!
THAT'S FINE. I'LL SEE YOU LATER.
PUFFED GRANO-TOASTIES
MUNCH-A-ROONIE
HOLE GRAIN
WHEETY CRUNCH
MA-MAAAA!
TOUGH LOVE... IS TOUGH ON EVERYONE!
Lynn

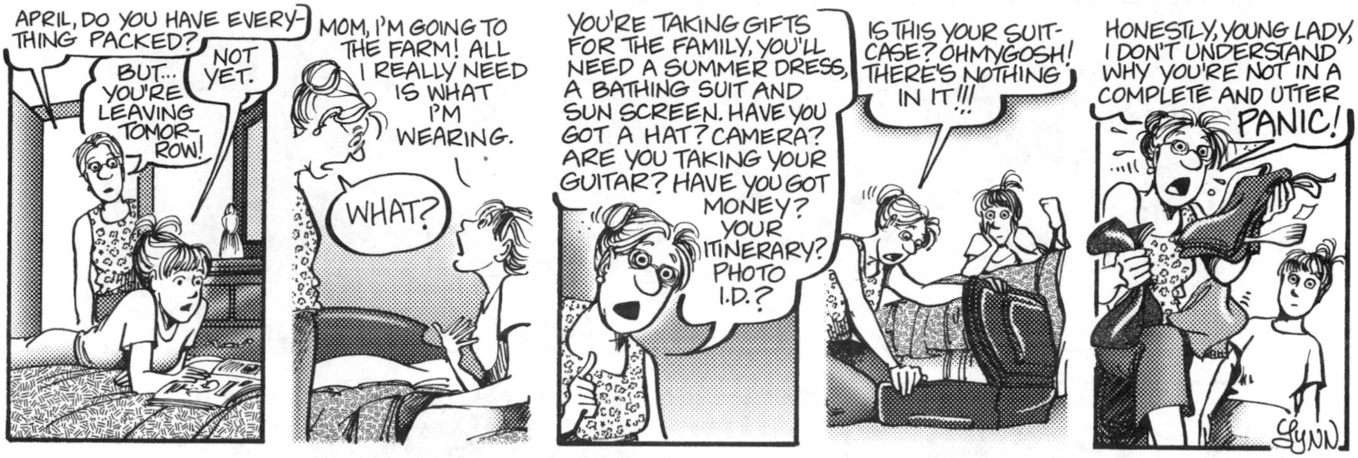
APRIL, DO YOU HAVE EVERY-THING PACKED?
NOT YET.
BUT... YOU'RE LEAVING TOMOR-ROW!
MOM, I'M GOING TO THE FARM! ALL I REALLY NEED IS WHAT I'M WEARING.
WHAT?
YOU'RE TAKING GIFTS FOR THE FAMILY, YOU'LL NEED A SUMMER DRESS, A BATHING SUIT AND SUN SCREEN. HAVE YOU GOT A HAT? CAMERA? ARE YOU TAKING YOUR GUITAR? HAVE YOU GOT MONEY? YOUR ITINERARY? PHOTO I.D.?
IS THIS YOUR SUIT-CASE? OHMYGOSH! THERE'S NOTHING IN IT!!!
HONESTLY, YOUNG LADY, I DON'T UNDERSTAND WHY YOU'RE NOT IN A COMPLETE AND UTTER PANIC!
LYNN

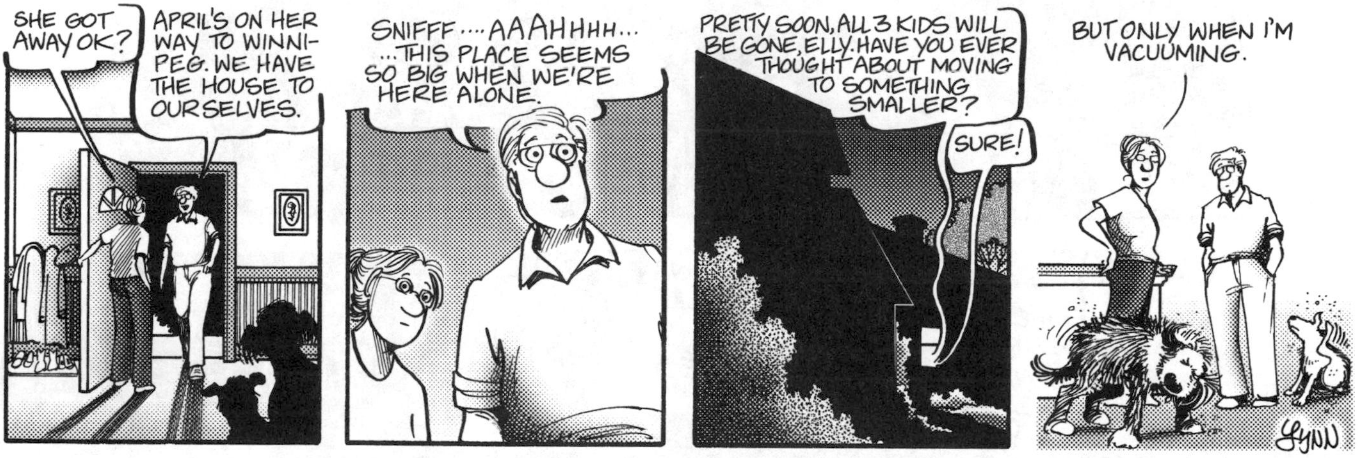
SHE GOT AWAY OK?
APRIL'S ON HER WAY TO WINNI-PEG. WE HAVE THE HOUSE TO OURSELVES.
SNIFFF.... AAAHHHH... ...THIS PLACE SEEMS SO BIG WHEN WE'RE HERE ALONE.
PRETTY SOON, ALL 3 KIDS WILL BE GONE, ELLY. HAVE YOU EVER THOUGHT ABOUT MOVING TO SOMETHING SMALLER?
SURE!
BUT ONLY WHEN I'M VACUUMING.
LYNN

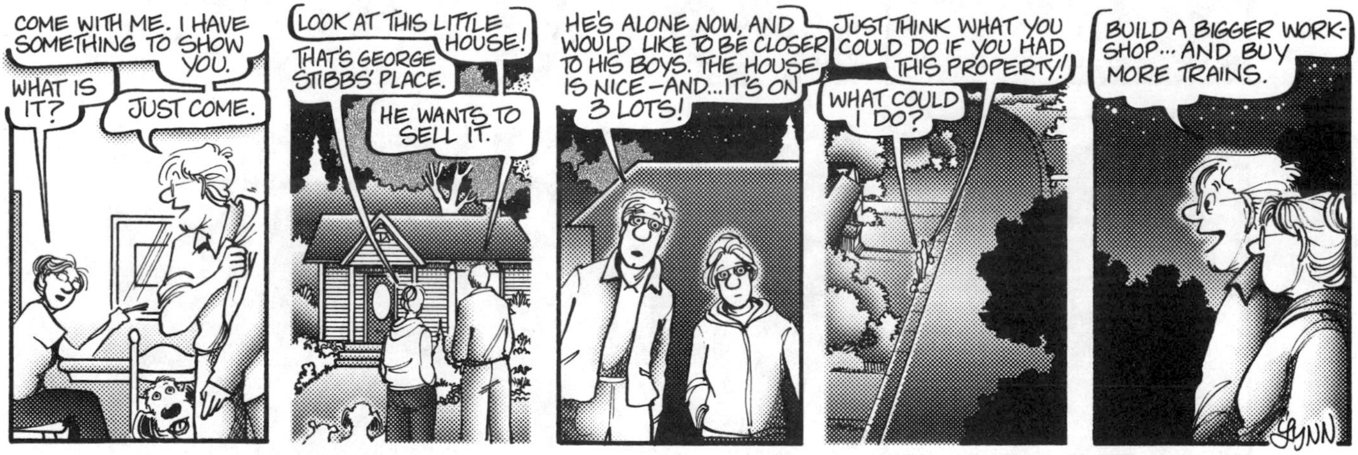
COME WITH ME. I HAVE SOMETHING TO SHOW YOU.
WHAT IS IT?
JUST COME.
LOOK AT THIS LITTLE HOUSE!
THAT'S GEORGE STIBBS' PLACE.
HE WANTS TO SELL IT.
HE'S ALONE NOW, AND WOULD LIKE TO BE CLOSER TO HIS BOYS. THE HOUSE IS NICE—AND... IT'S ON 3 LOTS!
JUST THINK WHAT YOU COULD DO IF YOU HAD THIS PROPERTY!
WHAT COULD I DO?
BUILD A BIGGER WORK-SHOP... AND BUY MORE TRAINS.
LYNN

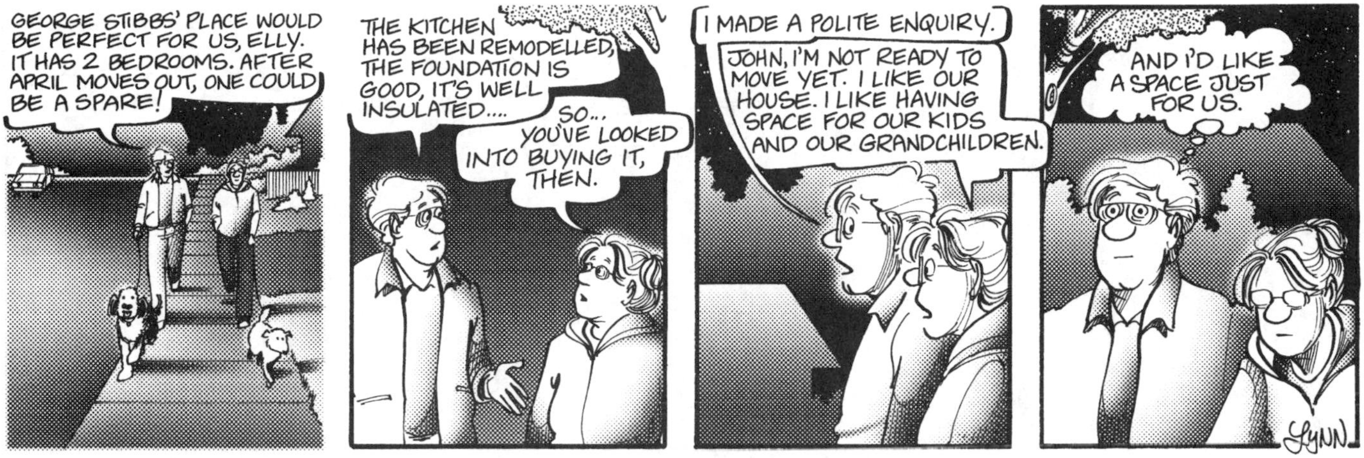
GEORGE STIBBS' PLACE WOULD BE PERFECT FOR US, ELLY. IT HAS 2 BEDROOMS. AFTER APRIL MOVES OUT, ONE COULD BE A SPARE!
THE KITCHEN HAS BEEN REMODELLED, THE FOUNDATION IS GOOD, IT'S WELL INSULATED....
SO... YOU'VE LOOKED INTO BUYING IT, THEN.
I MADE A POLITE ENQUIRY.
JOHN, I'M NOT READY TO MOVE YET. I LIKE OUR HOUSE. I LIKE HAVING SPACE FOR OUR KIDS AND OUR GRANDCHILDREN.
AND I'D LIKE A SPACE JUST FOR US.
LYNN

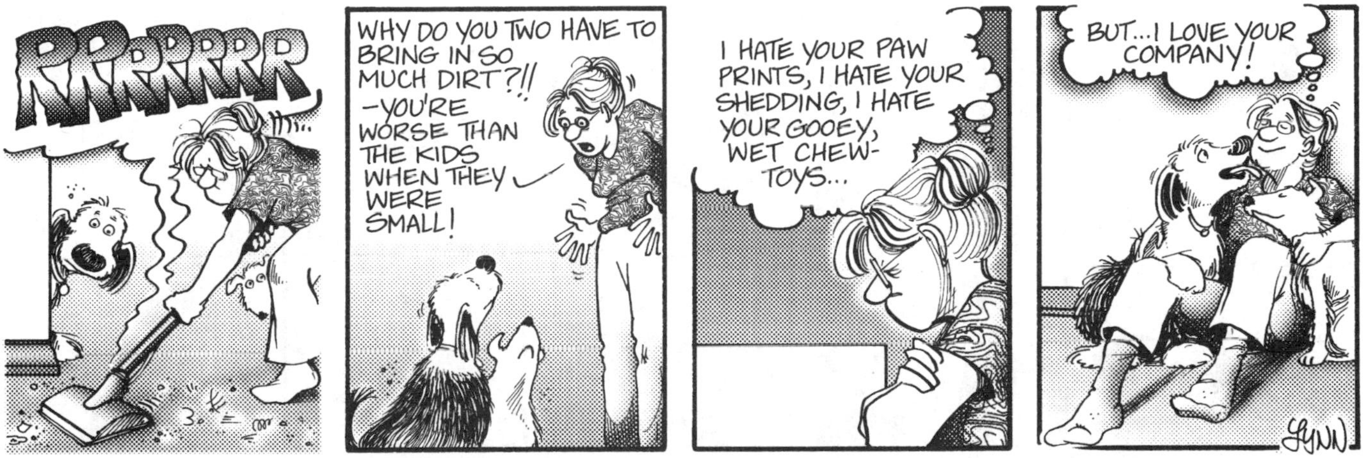
RRRRRRR
WHY DO YOU TWO HAVE TO BRING IN SO MUCH DIRT?!! —YOU'RE WORSE THAN THE KIDS WHEN THEY WERE SMALL!
I HATE YOUR PAW PRINTS, I HATE YOUR SHEDDING, I HATE YOUR GOOEY, WET CHEW-TOYS...
BUT...I LOVE YOUR COMPANY!
LYNN

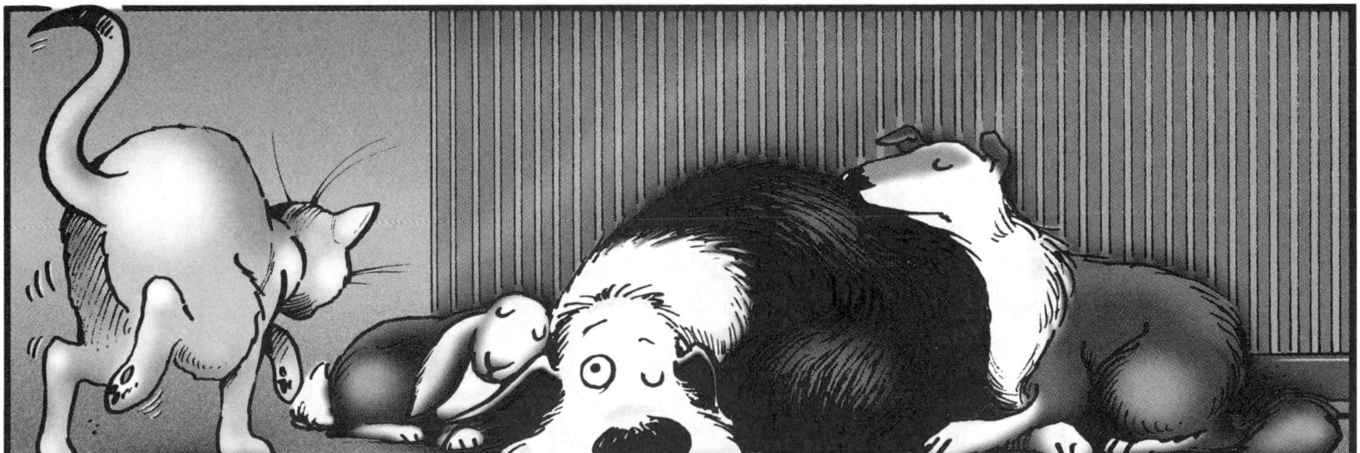

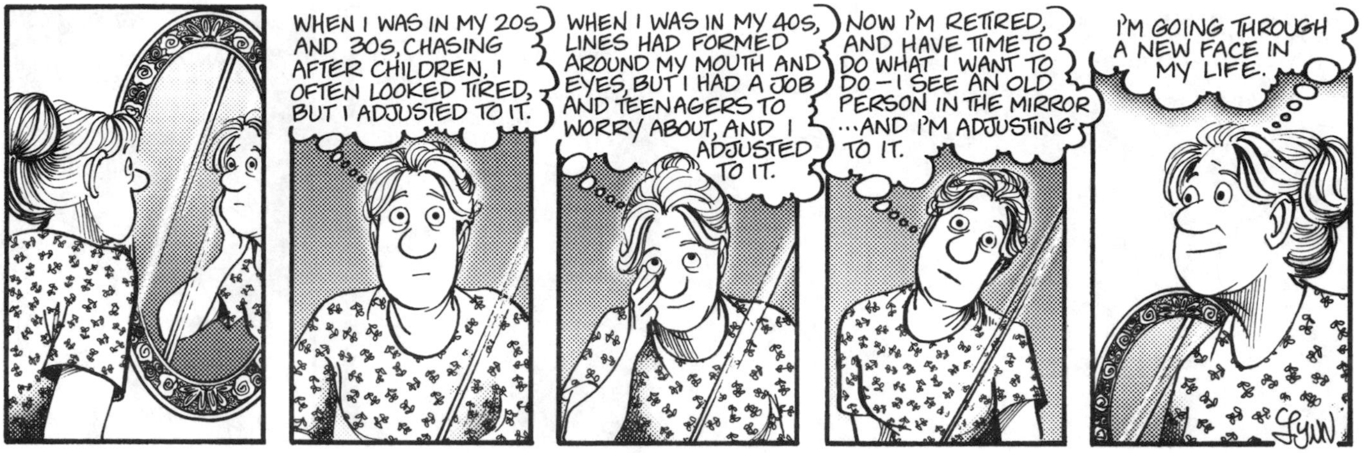
WHEN I WAS IN MY 20s AND 30s, CHASING AFTER CHILDREN, I OFTEN LOOKED TIRED, BUT I ADJUSTED TO IT.
WHEN I WAS IN MY 40s, LINES HAD FORMED AROUND MY MOUTH AND EYES, BUT I HAD A JOB AND TEENAGERS TO WORRY ABOUT, AND I ADJUSTED TO IT.
NOW I'M RETIRED, AND HAVE TIME TO DO WHAT I WANT TO DO – I SEE AN OLD PERSON IN THE MIRROR ...AND I'M ADJUSTING TO IT.
I'M GOING THROUGH A NEW FACE IN MY LIFE.

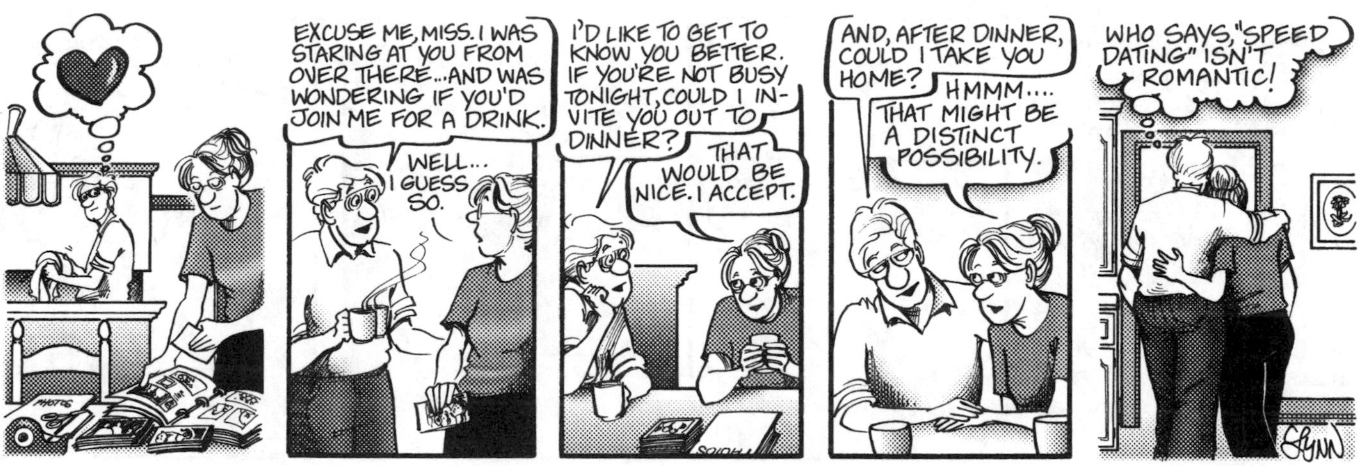
EXCUSE ME, MISS. I WAS STARING AT YOU FROM OVER THERE...AND WAS WONDERING IF YOU'D JOIN ME FOR A DRINK.
WELL... I GUESS SO.
I'D LIKE TO GET TO KNOW YOU BETTER. IF YOU'RE NOT BUSY TONIGHT, COULD I INVITE YOU OUT TO DINNER?
THAT WOULD BE NICE. I ACCEPT.
AND, AFTER DINNER, COULD I TAKE YOU HOME?
HMMM.... THAT MIGHT BE A DISTINCT POSSIBILITY.
WHO SAYS, "SPEED DATING" ISN'T ROMANTIC!

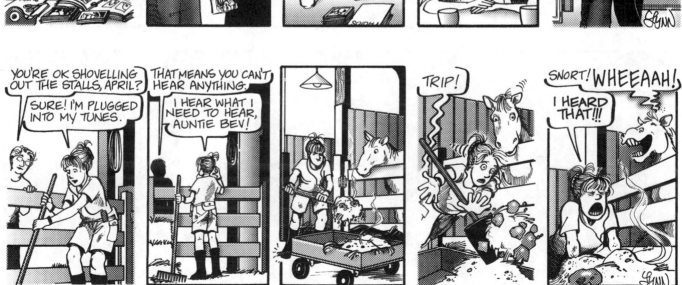

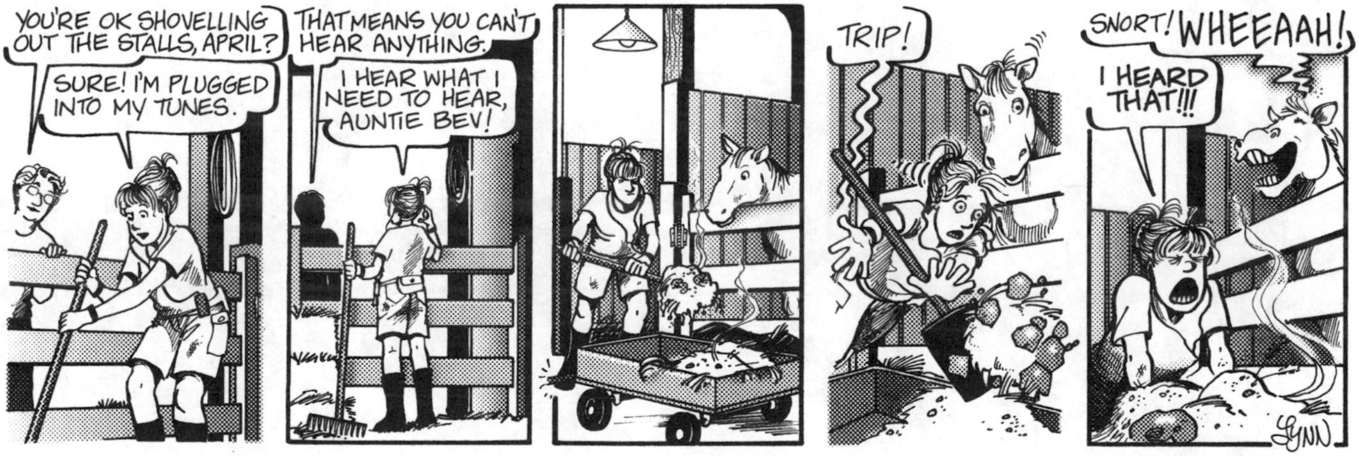
YOU'RE OK SHOVELLING OUT THE STALLS, APRIL?
SURE! I'M PLUGGED INTO MY TUNES.
THAT MEANS YOU CAN'T HEAR ANYTHING.
I HEAR WHAT I NEED TO HEAR, AUNTIE BEV!
TRIP!
SNORT! WHEEAAH!
I HEARD THAT!!!

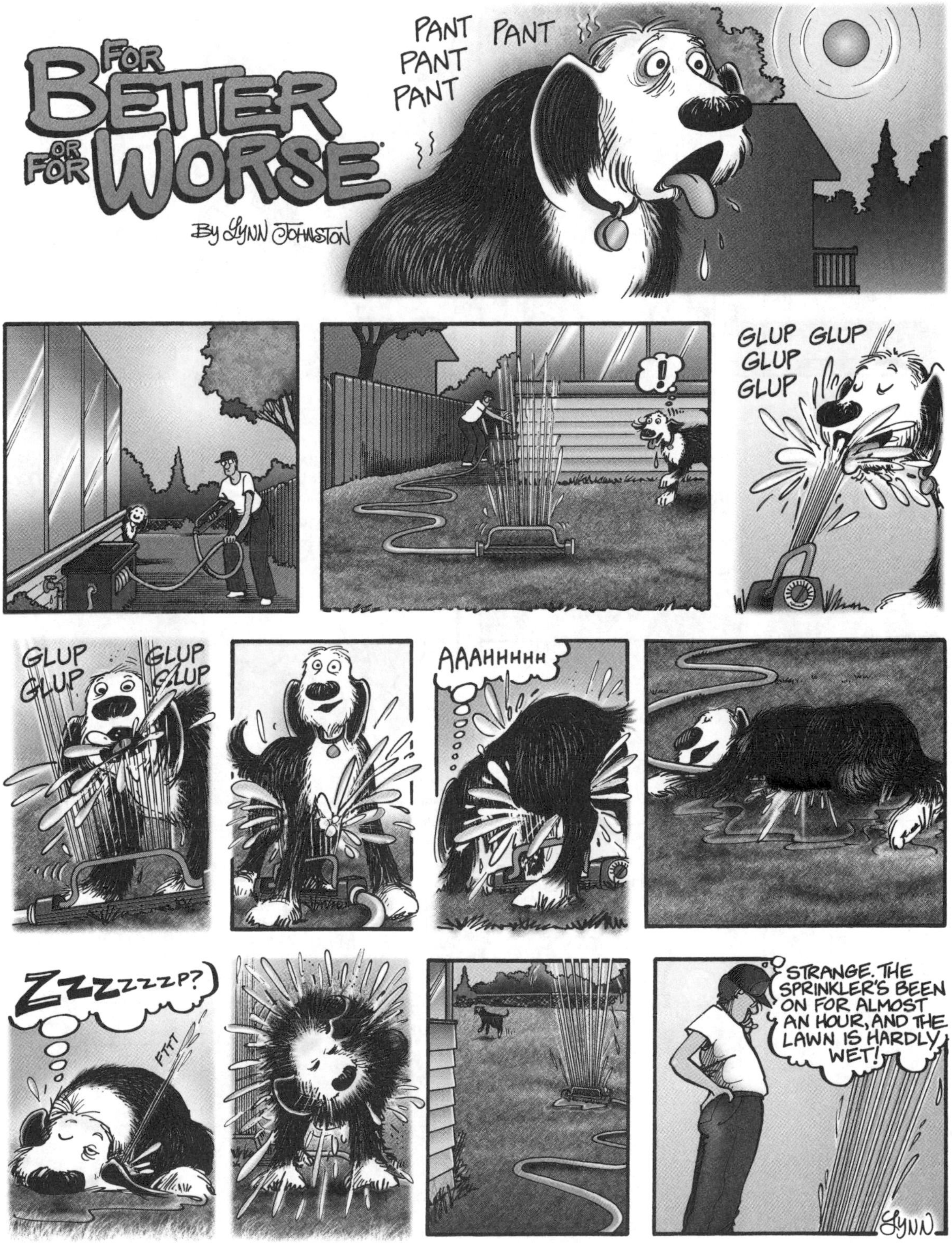
FOR BETTER OR FOR WORSE
BY LYNN JOHNSTON
PANT PANT PANT PANT
!
GLUP GLUP GLUP GLUP
GLUP GLUP GLUP GLUP
AAAHHHHH
ZZZzzzzp?
STRANGE. THE SPRINKLER'S BEEN ON FOR ALMOST AN HOUR, AND THE LAWN IS HARDLY WET!
LYNN

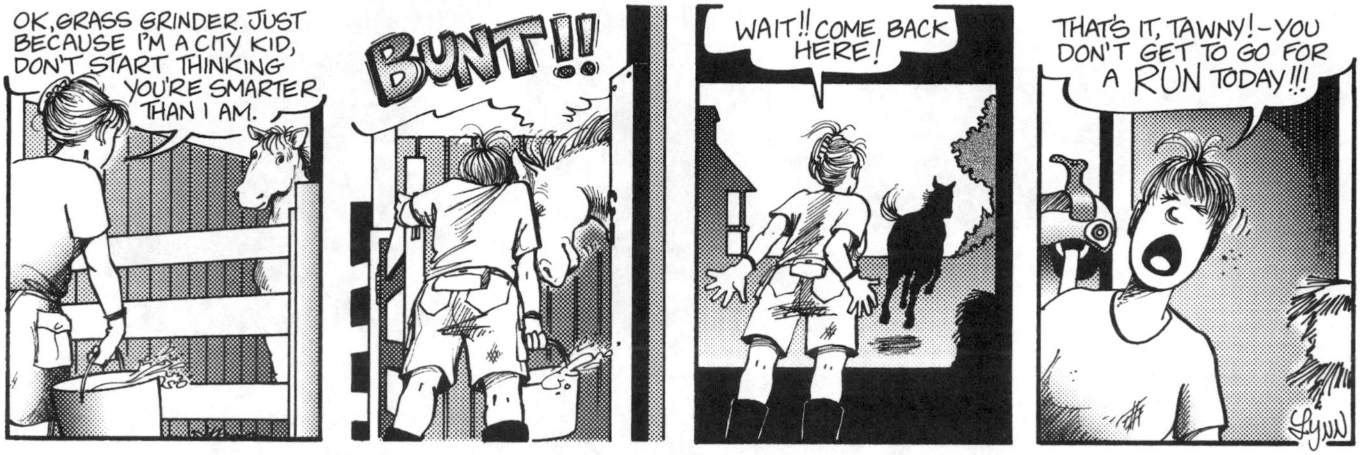
OK, GRASS GRINDER. JUST BECAUSE I'M A CITY KID, DON'T START THINKING YOU'RE SMARTER THAN I AM.
BUNT!!
WAIT!! COME BACK HERE!
THAT'S IT, TAWNY! - YOU DON'T GET TO GO FOR A RUN TODAY!!!
LYNN

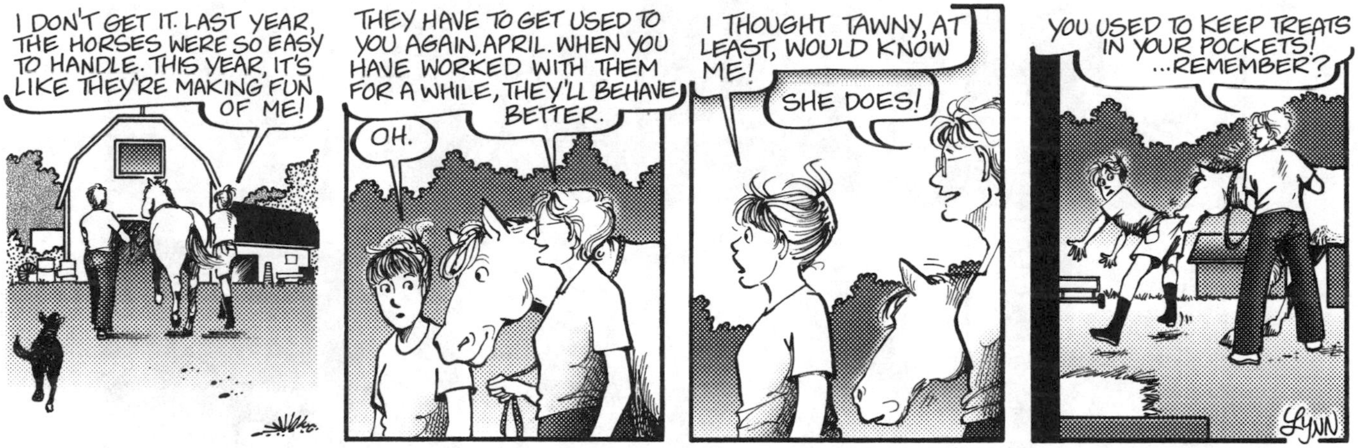
I DON'T GET IT. LAST YEAR, THE HORSES WERE SO EASY TO HANDLE. THIS YEAR, IT'S LIKE THEY'RE MAKING FUN OF ME!
THEY HAVE TO GET USED TO YOU AGAIN, APRIL. WHEN YOU HAVE WORKED WITH THEM FOR A WHILE, THEY'LL BEHAVE BETTER.
OH.
I THOUGHT TAWNY, AT LEAST, WOULD KNOW ME!
SHE DOES!
YOU USED TO KEEP TREATS IN YOUR POCKETS! ...REMEMBER?
LYNN

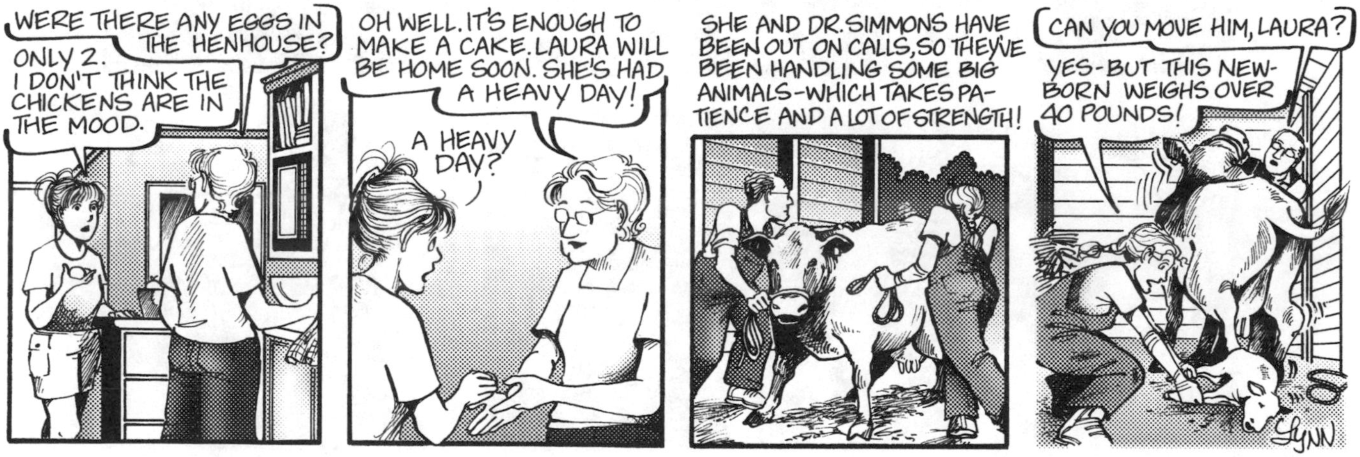
WERE THERE ANY EGGS IN THE HENHOUSE?
ONLY 2. I DON'T THINK THE CHICKENS ARE IN THE MOOD.
OH WELL. IT'S ENOUGH TO MAKE A CAKE. LAURA WILL BE HOME SOON. SHE'S HAD A HEAVY DAY!
A HEAVY DAY?
SHE AND DR. SIMMONS HAVE BEEN OUT ON CALLS, SO THEY'VE BEEN HANDLING SOME BIG ANIMALS - WHICH TAKES PATIENCE AND A LOT OF STRENGTH!
CAN YOU MOVE HIM, LAURA?
YES - BUT THIS NEWBORN WEIGHS OVER 40 POUNDS!
LYNN

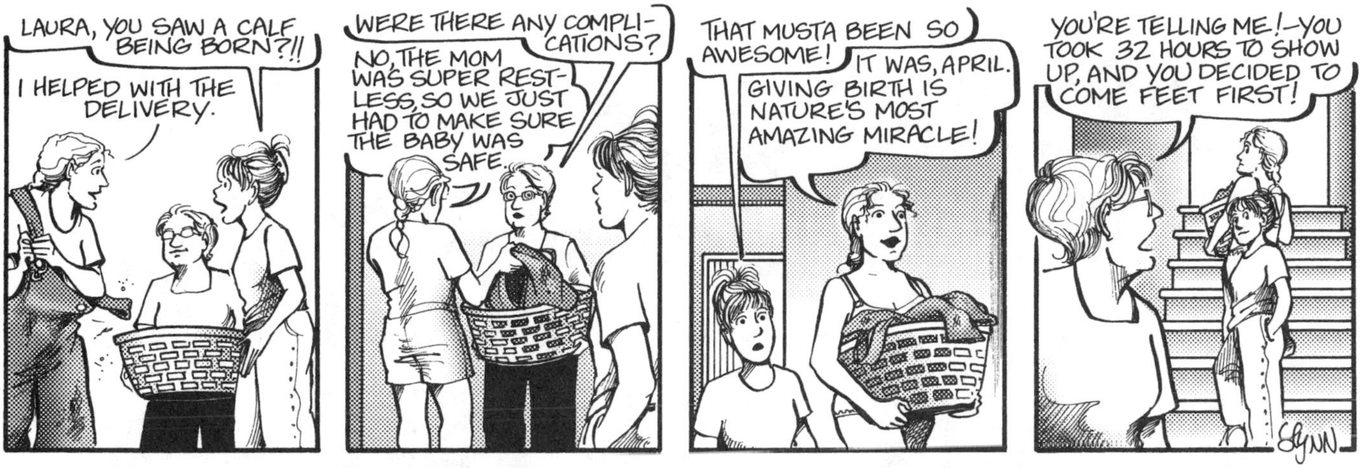
LAURA, YOU SAW A CALF BEING BORN?!!
I HELPED WITH THE DELIVERY.
WERE THERE ANY COMPLICATIONS?
NO, THE MOM WAS SUPER RESTLESS, SO WE JUST HAD TO MAKE SURE THE BABY WAS SAFE.
THAT MUSTA BEEN SO AWESOME!
IT WAS, APRIL. GIVING BIRTH IS NATURE'S MOST AMAZING MIRACLE!
YOU'RE TELLING ME!—YOU TOOK 32 HOURS TO SHOW UP, AND YOU DECIDED TO COME FEET FIRST!
Lynn

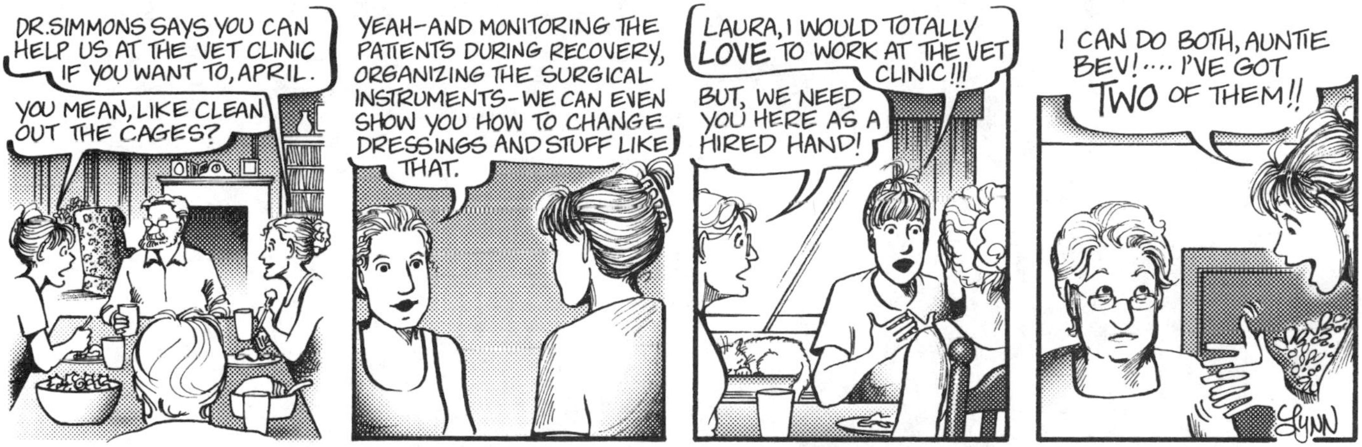
DR. SIMMONS SAYS YOU CAN HELP US AT THE VET CLINIC IF YOU WANT TO, APRIL.
YOU MEAN, LIKE CLEAN OUT THE CAGES?
YEAH—AND MONITORING THE PATIENTS DURING RECOVERY, ORGANIZING THE SURGICAL INSTRUMENTS—WE CAN EVEN SHOW YOU HOW TO CHANGE DRESSINGS AND STUFF LIKE THAT.
LAURA, I WOULD TOTALLY LOVE TO WORK AT THE VET CLINIC!!!
BUT, WE NEED YOU HERE AS A HIRED HAND!
I CAN DO BOTH, AUNTIE BEV!.... I'VE GOT TWO OF THEM!!
Lynn

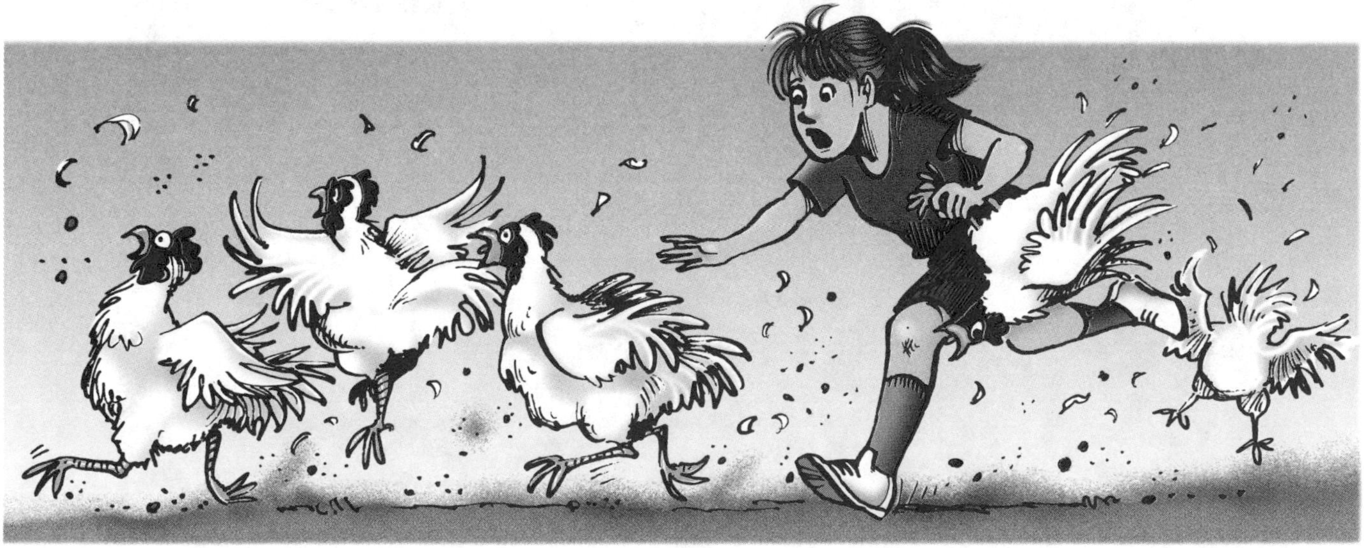

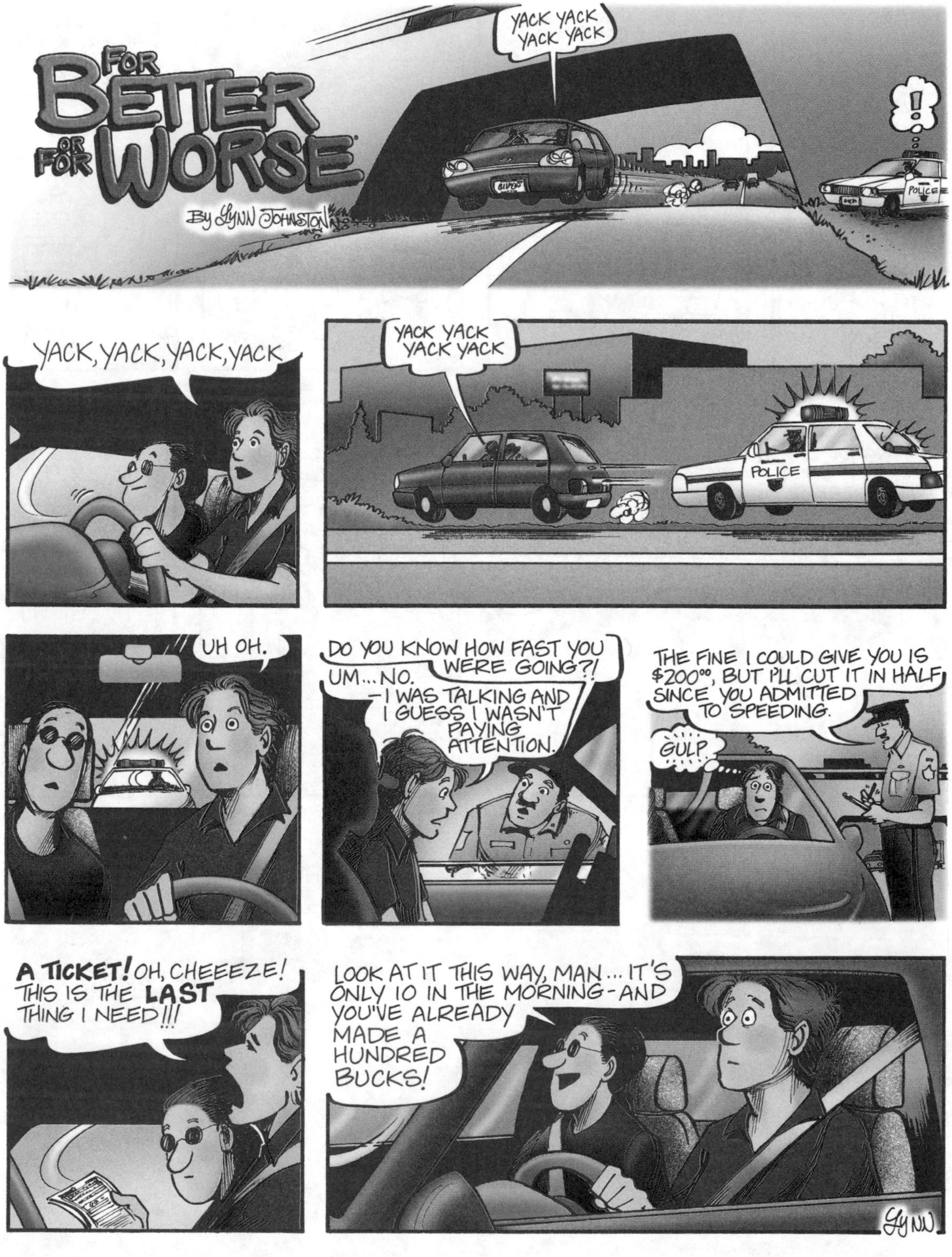
FOR BETTER OR FOR WORSE
By Lynn Johnston
YACK YACK YACK YACK
!
YACK, YACK, YACK, YACK
YACK YACK YACK YACK
POLICE
UH OH.
DO YOU KNOW HOW FAST YOU WERE GOING?!
UM... NO. —I WAS TALKING AND I GUESS I WASN'T PAYING ATTENTION.
THE FINE I COULD GIVE YOU IS $200.00, BUT I'LL CUT IT IN HALF SINCE YOU ADMITTED TO SPEEDING.
GULP
A TICKET! OH, CHEEEZE! THIS IS THE LAST THING I NEED!!!
LOOK AT IT THIS WAY, MAN... IT'S ONLY 10 IN THE MORNING - AND YOU'VE ALREADY MADE A HUNDRED BUCKS!
LYNN

DEAR GERALD, HOW'S IT GOING? UNCLE DANNY'S LETTING ME DRIVE THE TRACTOR LOTS THIS YEAR AN' I'M LOOKING AFTER THE HORSES.

TICK, TAP TAPPITA TICK

THERE'S NO PIGS HERE ANYMORE, BUT WE'VE GOT 6 CHICKENS AND A ROOSTER THAT'LL CHASE YOU IF YOU GET TOO CLOSE.

MY COUSIN, LAURA, IS GONNA BE A VETERINARIAN. SHE'S WORKING AS AN ASSISTANT AT THE CLINIC HERE, AND SHE SAID I COULD HELP!

SIMMONS ANIMAL HOSPITAL

ENTRANCE

SO FAR, I'VE JUST BEEN ORGANIZING THE SUPPLIES, WHICH IS SUPER INTERESTING.

STERILIZER

VET INJECT

THOSE SYRINGES ARE ONLY USED ON VERY LARGE ANIMALS, APRIL!

BIO TRAX INJECTA

Lynn

WE'LL DO THE SURGERY THIS AFTERNOON, MRS. PRESCOTT, AND WE'LL LET YOU KNOW WHEN CLOVER IS READY TO COME HOME.

FOR THEIR SAKE VACCINATE

HEARTWORM PRECAUTION

WHAT KIND OF SURGERY ARE YOU GONNA DO?

WE'RE GOING TO REMOVE HER UTERUS, SO SHE WON'T HAVE PUPPIES.

OH, YOU MEAN—SHE'S GONNA GET "FIXED"!

THAT'S NOT THE WORD WE USE, APRIL.

WE LIKE TO CALL A SPAYED A SPAYED!

Lynn

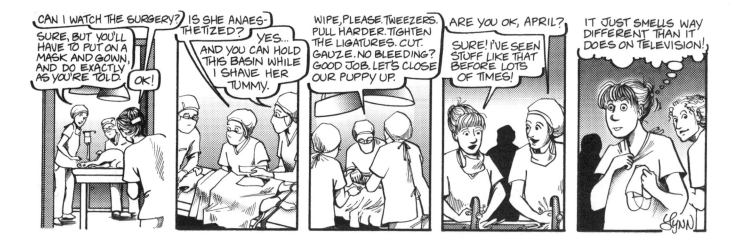

CAN I WATCH THE SURGERY?

SURE, BUT YOU'LL HAVE TO PUT ON A MASK AND GOWN, AND DO EXACTLY AS YOU'RE TOLD.

OK!

IS SHE ANAESTHETIZED?

YES... AND YOU CAN HOLD THIS BASIN WHILE I SHAVE HER TUMMY.

WIPE, PLEASE. TWEEZERS. PULL HARDER. TIGHTEN THE LIGATURES. CUT. GAUZE. NO BLEEDING? GOOD JOB. LET'S CLOSE OUR PUPPY UP.

ARE YOU OK, APRIL?

SURE! I'VE SEEN STUFF LIKE THAT BEFORE LOTS OF TIMES!

IT JUST SMELLS WAY DIFFERENT THAN IT DOES ON TELEVISION!

Lynn

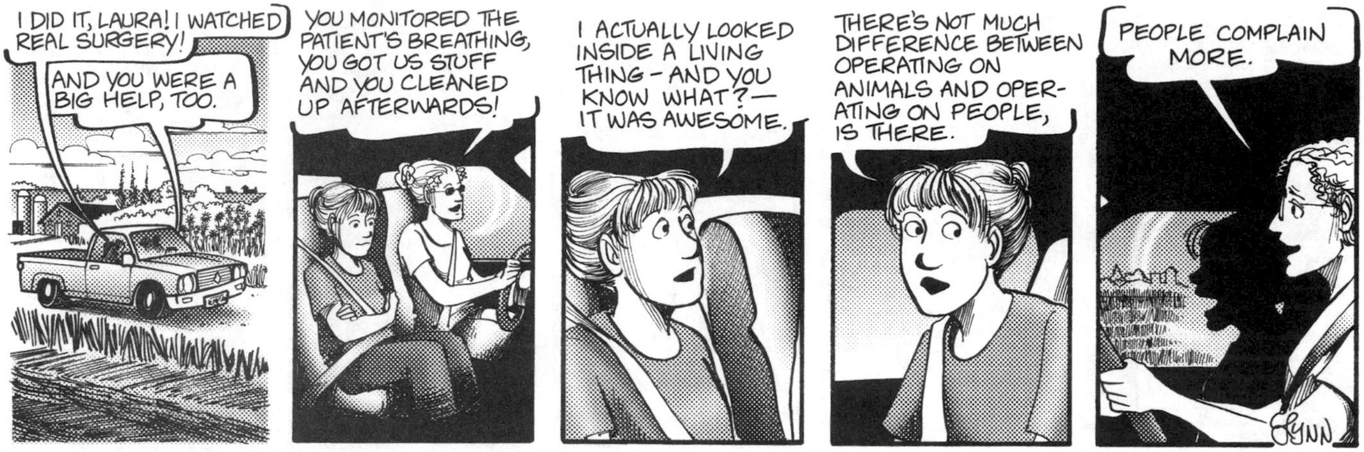
I DID IT, LAURA! I WATCHED REAL SURGERY!
AND YOU WERE A BIG HELP, TOO.
YOU MONITORED THE PATIENT'S BREATHING, YOU GOT US STUFF AND YOU CLEANED UP AFTERWARDS!
I ACTUALLY LOOKED INSIDE A LIVING THING – AND YOU KNOW WHAT? — IT WAS AWESOME.
THERE'S NOT MUCH DIFFERENCE BETWEEN OPERATING ON ANIMALS AND OPERATING ON PEOPLE, IS THERE.
PEOPLE COMPLAIN MORE.
LYNN

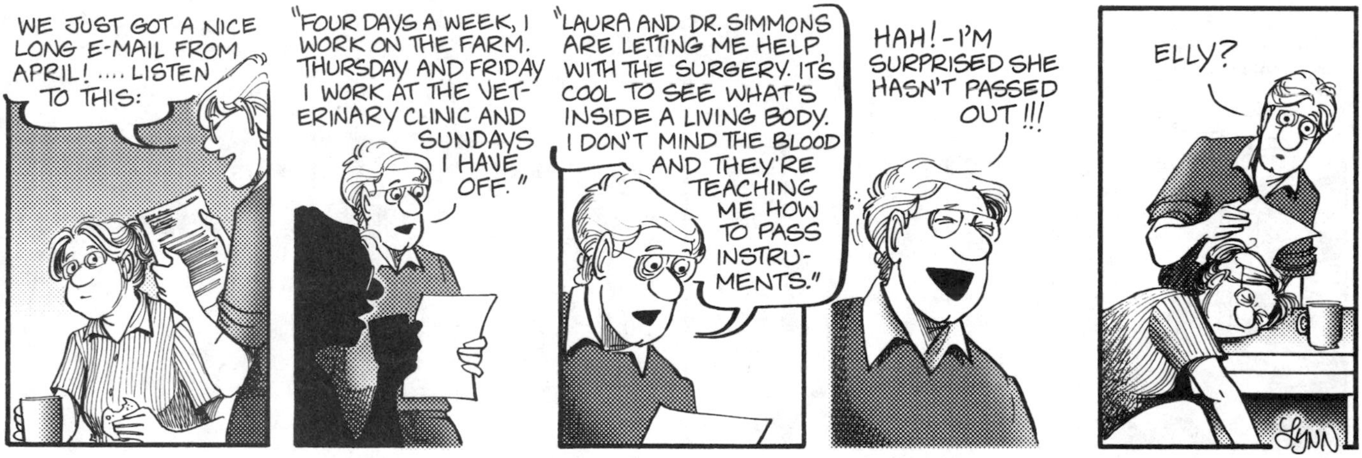
WE JUST GOT A NICE LONG E-MAIL FROM APRIL! .... LISTEN TO THIS:
"FOUR DAYS A WEEK, I WORK ON THE FARM. THURSDAY AND FRIDAY I WORK AT THE VETERINARY CLINIC AND SUNDAYS I HAVE OFF."
"LAURA AND DR. SIMMONS ARE LETTING ME HELP WITH THE SURGERY. IT'S COOL TO SEE WHAT'S INSIDE A LIVING BODY. I DON'T MIND THE BLOOD AND THEY'RE TEACHING ME HOW TO PASS INSTRUMENTS."
HAH! - I'M SURPRISED SHE HASN'T PASSED OUT !!!
ELLY?
LYNN

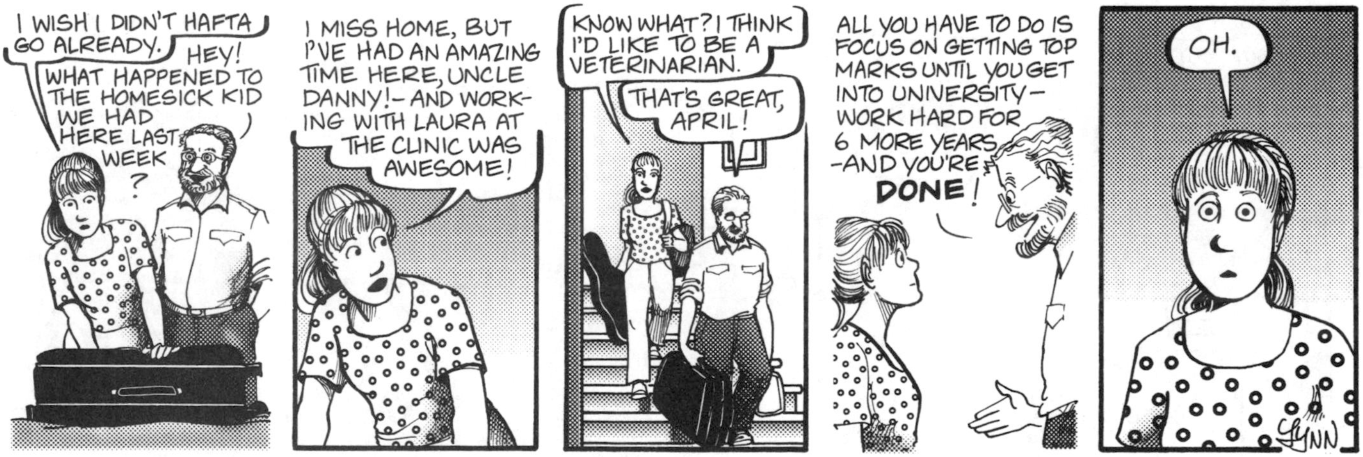
I WISH I DIDN'T HAFTA GO ALREADY.
HEY! WHAT HAPPENED TO THE HOMESICK KID WE HAD HERE LAST WEEK ?
I MISS HOME, BUT I'VE HAD AN AMAZING TIME HERE, UNCLE DANNY! – AND WORKING WITH LAURA AT THE CLINIC WAS AWESOME!
KNOW WHAT? I THINK I'D LIKE TO BE A VETERINARIAN.
THAT'S GREAT, APRIL!
ALL YOU HAVE TO DO IS FOCUS ON GETTING TOP MARKS UNTIL YOU GET INTO UNIVERSITY – WORK HARD FOR 6 MORE YEARS -AND YOU'RE DONE!
OH.
LYNN

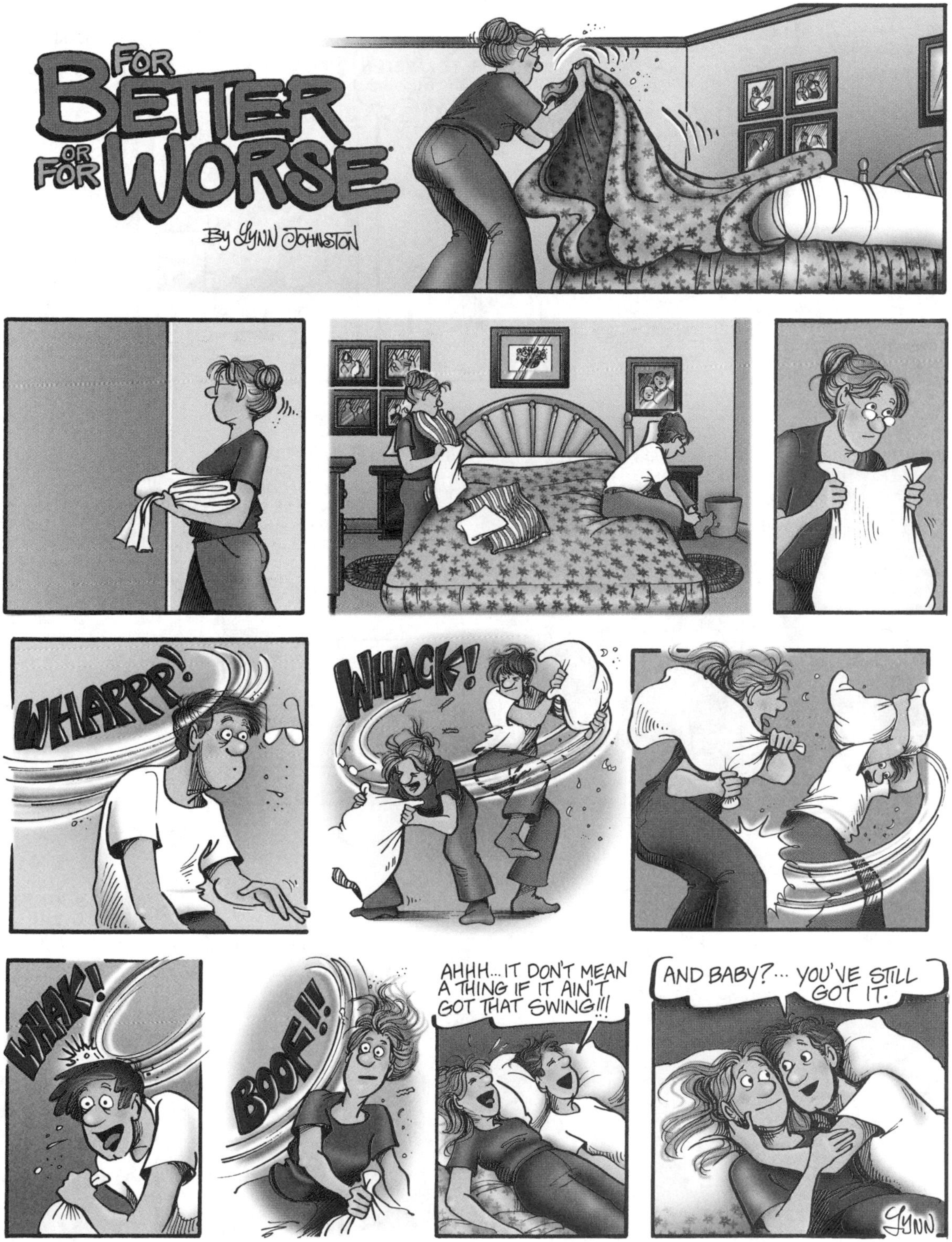
FOR BETTER OR FOR WORSE
BY LYNN JOHNSTON
WHARPP!
WHACK!
WHAK!
BOOF!!!
AHHH... IT DON'T MEAN A THING IF IT AIN'T GOT THAT SWING!!!
AND BABY?... YOU'VE STILL GOT IT.
LYNN

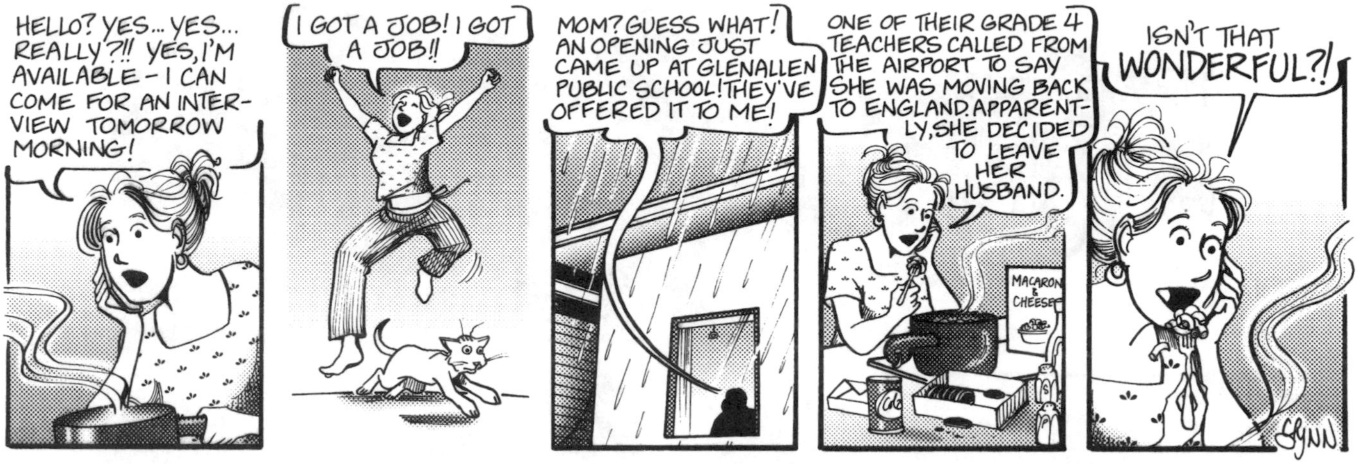
HELLO? YES... YES... REALLY?!! YES, I'M AVAILABLE - I CAN COME FOR AN INTERVIEW TOMORROW MORNING!
I GOT A JOB! I GOT A JOB!!
MOM? GUESS WHAT! AN OPENING JUST CAME UP AT GLENALLEN PUBLIC SCHOOL! THEY'VE OFFERED IT TO ME!
ONE OF THEIR GRADE 4 TEACHERS CALLED FROM THE AIRPORT TO SAY SHE WAS MOVING BACK TO ENGLAND. APPARENTLY, SHE DECIDED TO LEAVE HER HUSBAND.
ISN'T THAT WONDERFUL?!

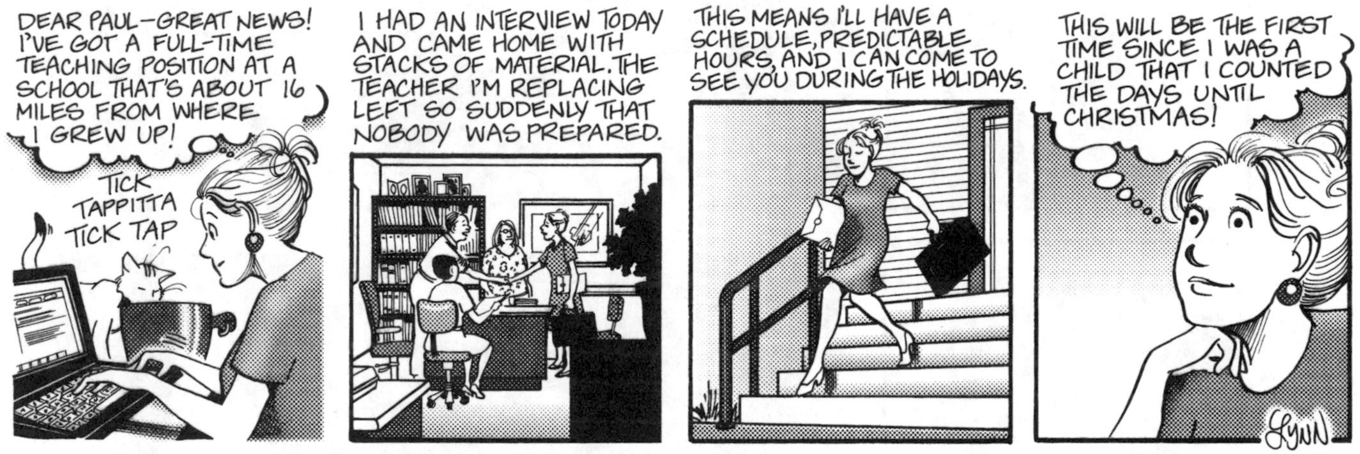
DEAR PAUL—GREAT NEWS! I'VE GOT A FULL-TIME TEACHING POSITION AT A SCHOOL THAT'S ABOUT 16 MILES FROM WHERE I GREW UP!
TICK TAPPITTA TICK TAP
I HAD AN INTERVIEW TODAY AND CAME HOME WITH STACKS OF MATERIAL. THE TEACHER I'M REPLACING LEFT SO SUDDENLY THAT NOBODY WAS PREPARED.
THIS MEANS I'LL HAVE A SCHEDULE, PREDICTABLE HOURS, AND I CAN COME TO SEE YOU DURING THE HOLIDAYS.
THIS WILL BE THE FIRST TIME SINCE I WAS A CHILD THAT I COUNTED THE DAYS UNTIL CHRISTMAS!

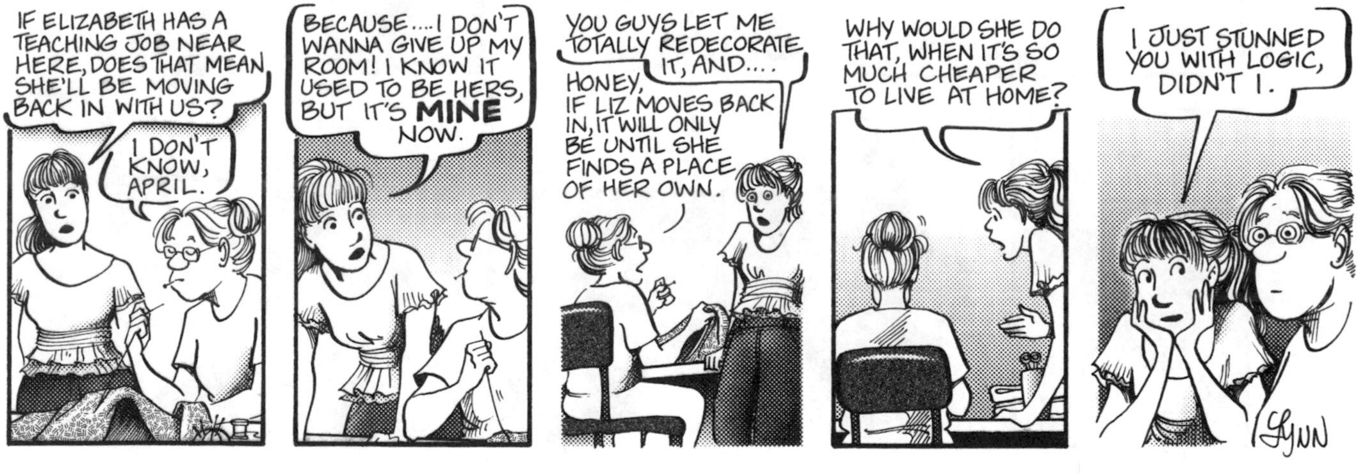
IF ELIZABETH HAS A TEACHING JOB NEAR HERE, DOES THAT MEAN SHE'LL BE MOVING BACK IN WITH US?
I DON'T KNOW, APRIL.
BECAUSE.... I DON'T WANNA GIVE UP MY ROOM! I KNOW IT USED TO BE HERS, BUT IT'S MINE NOW.
YOU GUYS LET ME TOTALLY REDECORATE IT, AND....
HONEY, IF LIZ MOVES BACK IN, IT WILL ONLY BE UNTIL SHE FINDS A PLACE OF HER OWN.
WHY WOULD SHE DO THAT, WHEN IT'S SO MUCH CHEAPER TO LIVE AT HOME?
I JUST STUNNED YOU WITH LOGIC, DIDN'T I.

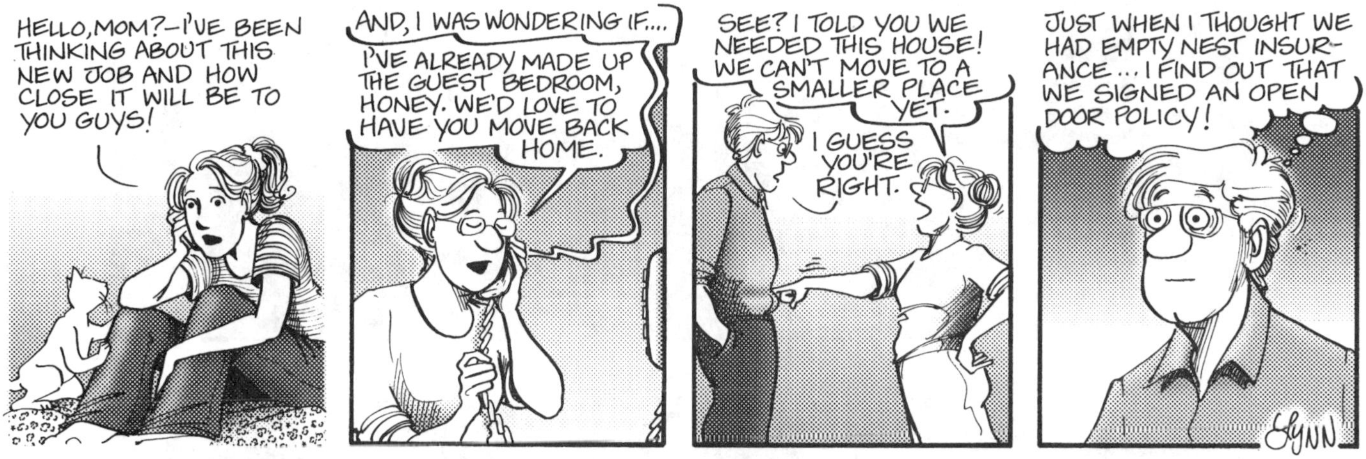
HELLO, MOM? – I'VE BEEN THINKING ABOUT THIS NEW JOB AND HOW CLOSE IT WILL BE TO YOU GUYS!
AND, I WAS WONDERING IF....
I'VE ALREADY MADE UP THE GUEST BEDROOM, HONEY. WE'D LOVE TO HAVE YOU MOVE BACK HOME.
SEE? I TOLD YOU WE NEEDED THIS HOUSE! WE CAN'T MOVE TO A SMALLER PLACE YET.
I GUESS YOU'RE RIGHT.
JUST WHEN I THOUGHT WE HAD EMPTY NEST INSURANCE ... I FIND OUT THAT WE SIGNED AN OPEN DOOR POLICY!
LYNN

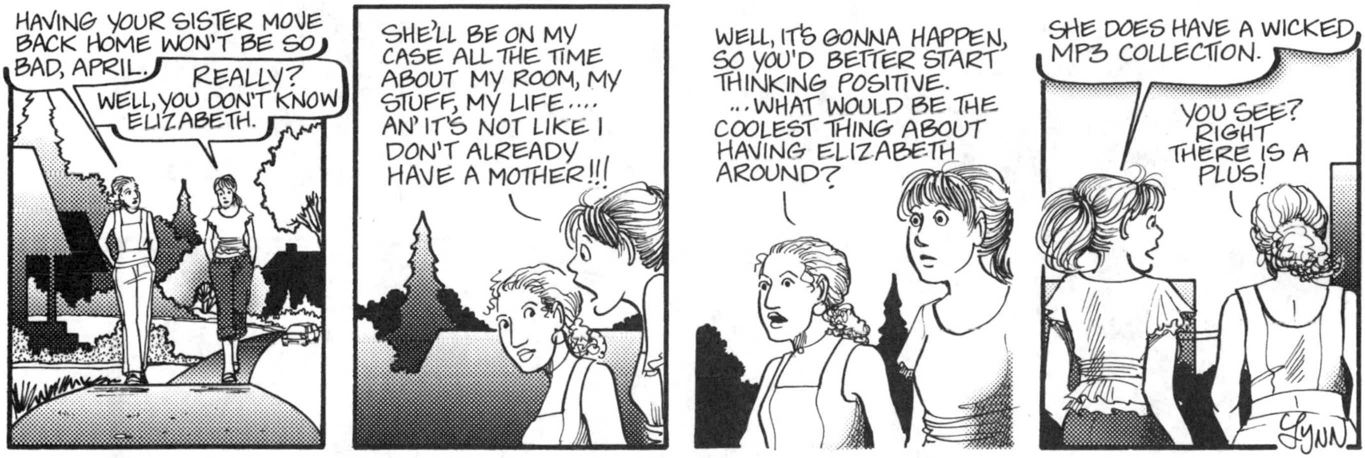
HAVING YOUR SISTER MOVE BACK HOME WON'T BE SO BAD, APRIL.
REALLY? WELL, YOU DON'T KNOW ELIZABETH.
SHE'LL BE ON MY CASE ALL THE TIME ABOUT MY ROOM, MY STUFF, MY LIFE.... AN' IT'S NOT LIKE I DON'T ALREADY HAVE A MOTHER!!!
WELL, IT'S GONNA HAPPEN, SO YOU'D BETTER START THINKING POSITIVE. ... WHAT WOULD BE THE COOLEST THING ABOUT HAVING ELIZABETH AROUND?
SHE DOES HAVE A WICKED MP3 COLLECTION.
YOU SEE? RIGHT THERE IS A PLUS!
LYNN

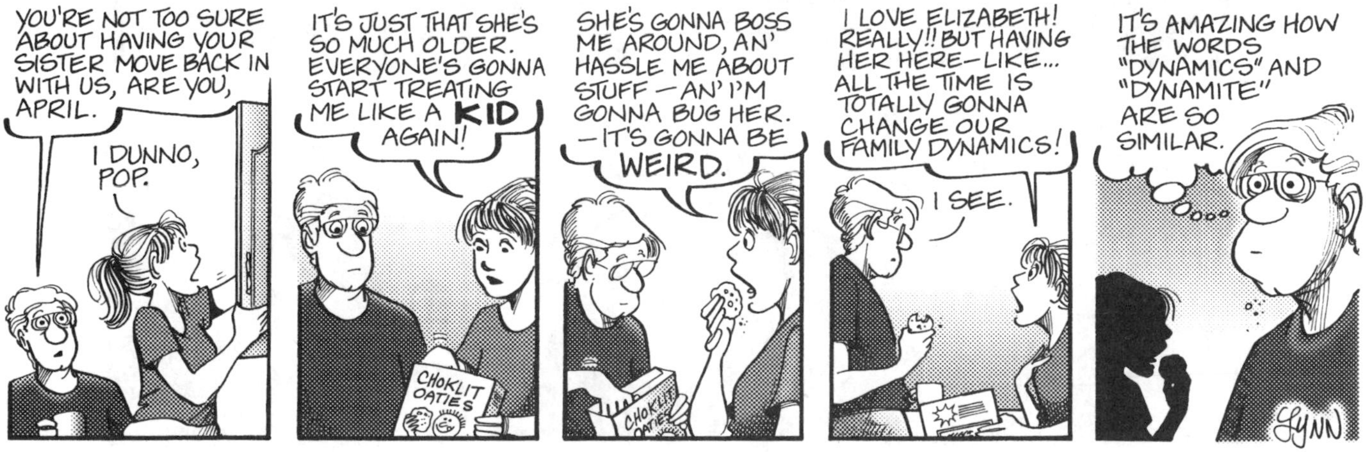
YOU'RE NOT TOO SURE ABOUT HAVING YOUR SISTER MOVE BACK IN WITH US, ARE YOU, APRIL.
I DUNNO, POP.
IT'S JUST THAT SHE'S SO MUCH OLDER. EVERYONE'S GONNA START TREATING ME LIKE A KID AGAIN!
CHOKLIT OATIES
SHE'S GONNA BOSS ME AROUND, AN' HASSLE ME ABOUT STUFF – AN' I'M GONNA BUG HER. – IT'S GONNA BE WEIRD.
CHOKLIT OATIES
I LOVE ELIZABETH! REALLY!! BUT HAVING HER HERE – LIKE... ALL THE TIME IS TOTALLY GONNA CHANGE OUR FAMILY DYNAMICS!
I SEE.
IT'S AMAZING HOW THE WORDS "DYNAMICS" AND "DYNAMITE" ARE SO SIMILAR.
LYNN

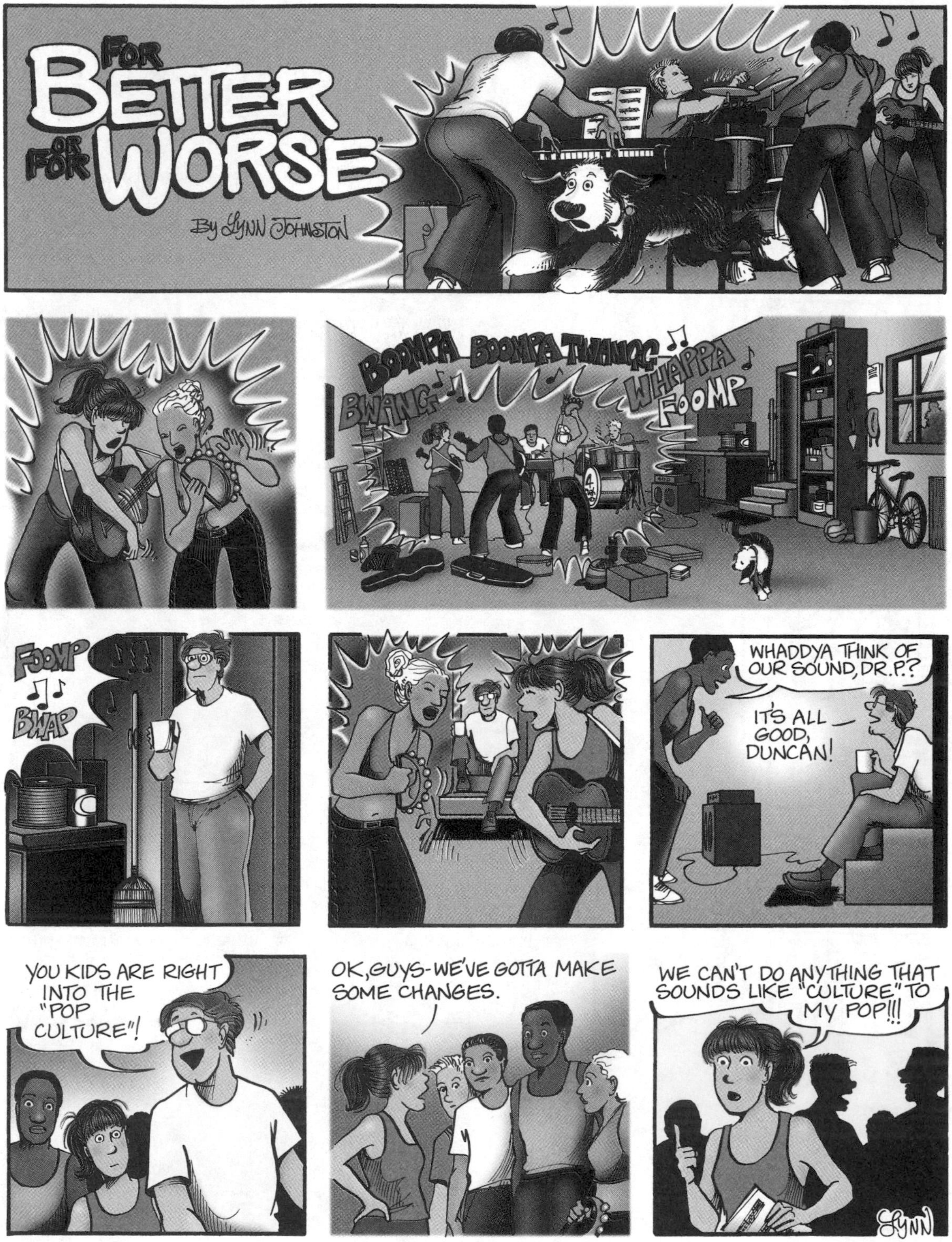
FOR BETTER OR FOR WORSE
BY LYNN JOHNSTON
BOOMPA BOOMPA TWANGG
WHAPPA
BWANG
FOOMP
FOOMP
BWAP
WHADDYA THINK OF OUR SOUND, DR. P.?
IT'S ALL GOOD, DUNCAN!
YOU KIDS ARE RIGHT INTO THE "POP CULTURE"!
OK, GUYS- WE'VE GOTTA MAKE SOME CHANGES.
WE CAN'T DO ANYTHING THAT SOUNDS LIKE "CULTURE" TO MY POP!!!
LYNN

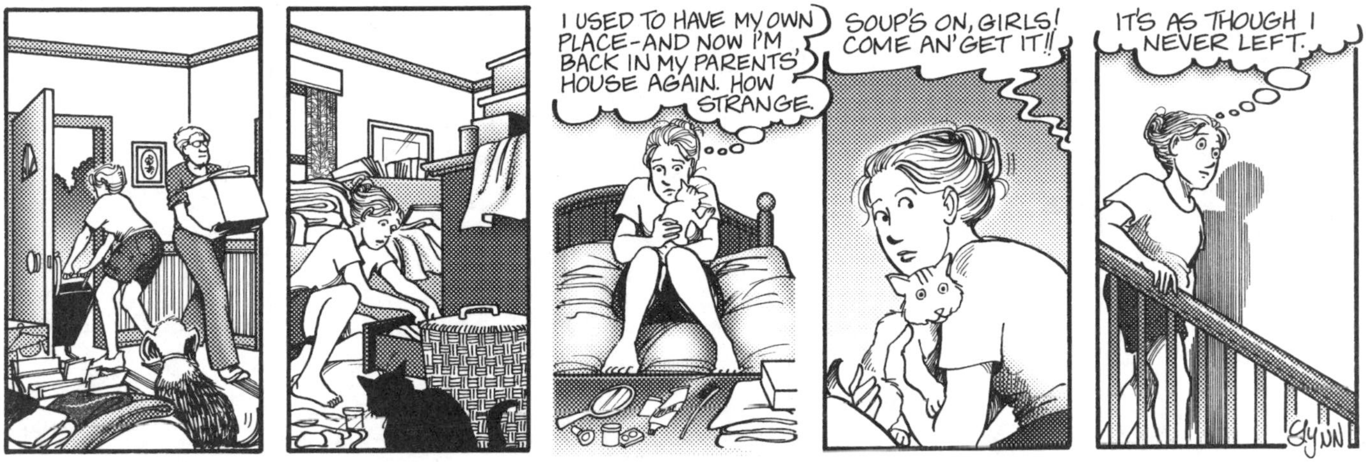
I USED TO HAVE MY OWN PLACE-AND NOW I'M BACK IN MY PARENTS' HOUSE AGAIN. HOW STRANGE.
SOUP'S ON, GIRLS! COME AN' GET IT!!
IT'S AS THOUGH I NEVER LEFT.
LYNN

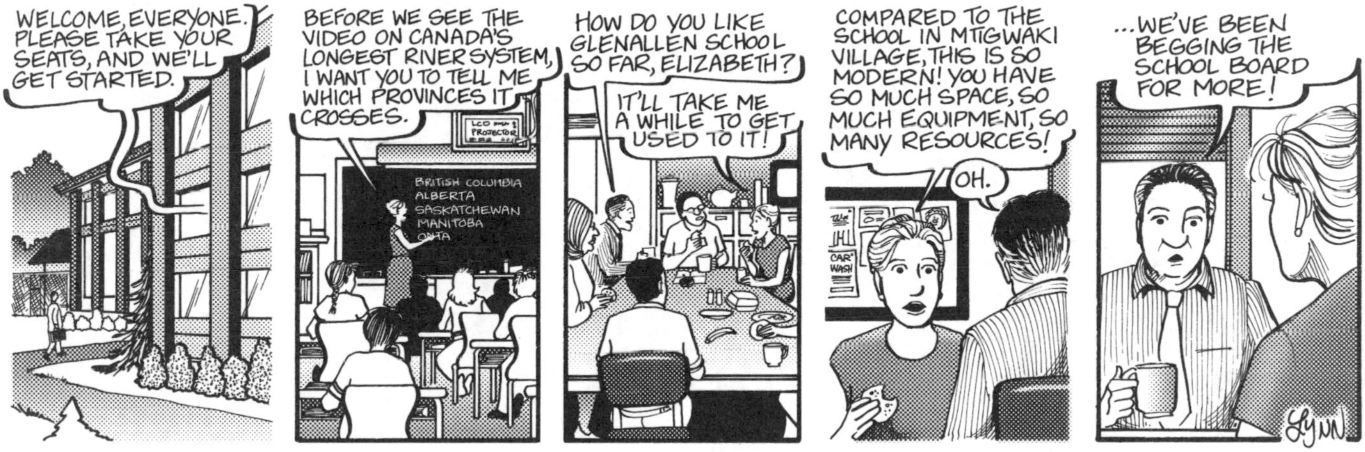
WELCOME, EVERYONE. PLEASE TAKE YOUR SEATS, AND WE'LL GET STARTED.
BEFORE WE SEE THE VIDEO ON CANADA'S LONGEST RIVER SYSTEM, I WANT YOU TO TELL ME WHICH PROVINCES IT CROSSES.
BRITISH COLUMBIA
ALBERTA
SASKATCHEWAN
MANITOBA
ONTA
HOW DO YOU LIKE GLENALLEN SCHOOL SO FAR, ELIZABETH?
IT'LL TAKE ME A WHILE TO GET USED TO IT!
COMPARED TO THE SCHOOL IN MTIGWAKI VILLAGE, THIS IS SO MODERN! YOU HAVE SO MUCH SPACE, SO MUCH EQUIPMENT, SO MANY RESOURCES!
OH.
CAR WASH
...WE'VE BEEN BEGGING THE SCHOOL BOARD FOR MORE!
LYNN

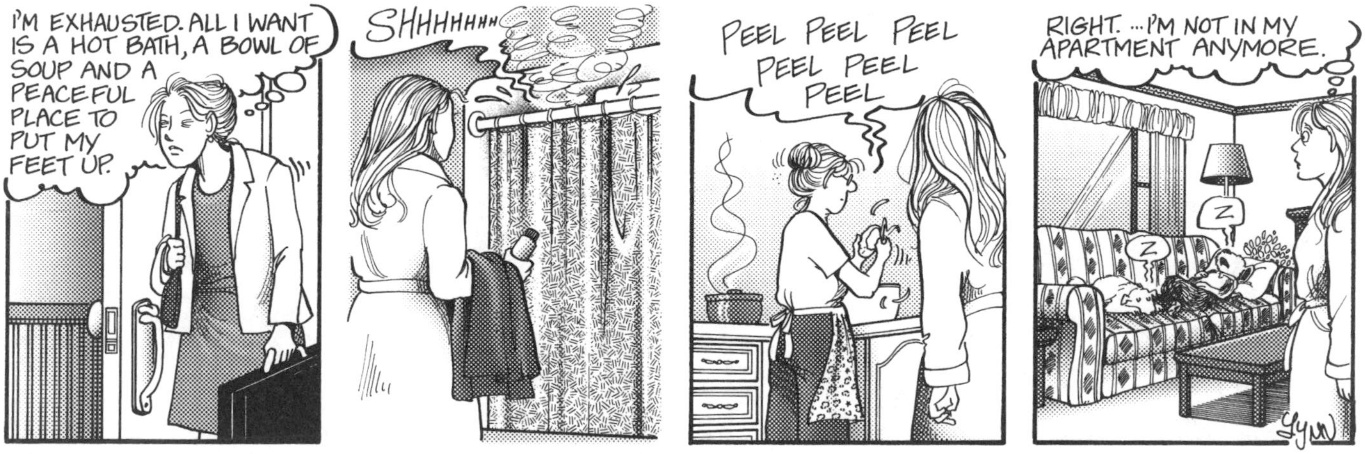
I'M EXHAUSTED. ALL I WANT IS A HOT BATH, A BOWL OF SOUP AND A PEACEFUL PLACE TO PUT MY FEET UP.
SHHHHHHH
PEEL PEEL PEEL PEEL PEEL PEEL
RIGHT. ...I'M NOT IN MY APARTMENT ANYMORE.
Z
Z
LYNN

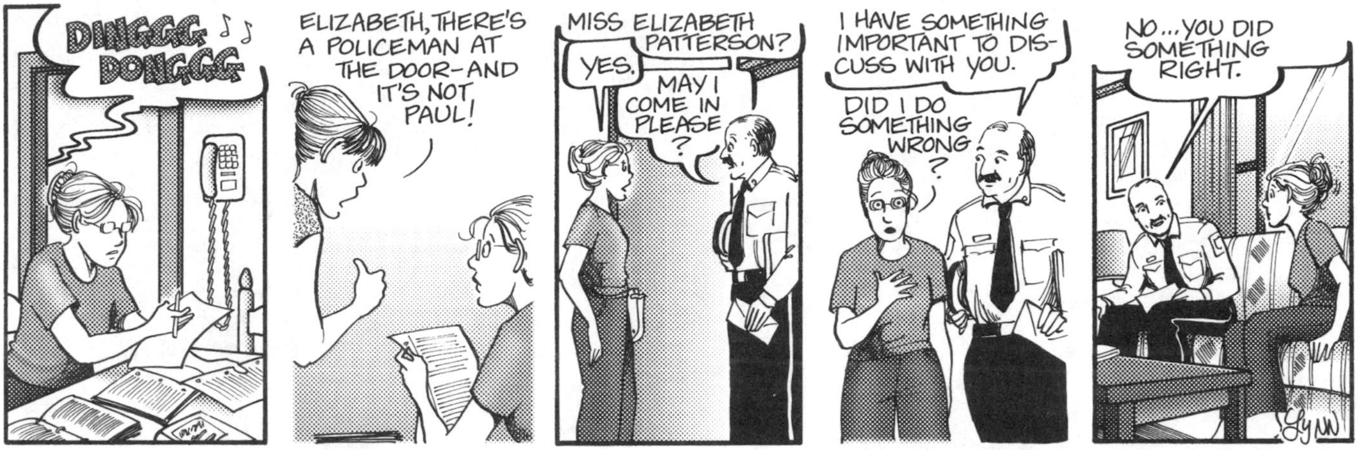
DINGGG DONGGG
ELIZABETH, THERE'S A POLICEMAN AT THE DOOR-AND IT'S NOT PAUL!
MISS ELIZABETH PATTERSON?
YES.
MAY I COME IN PLEASE?
I HAVE SOMETHING IMPORTANT TO DISCUSS WITH YOU.
DID I DO SOMETHING WRONG?
NO...YOU DID SOMETHING RIGHT.
LYNN

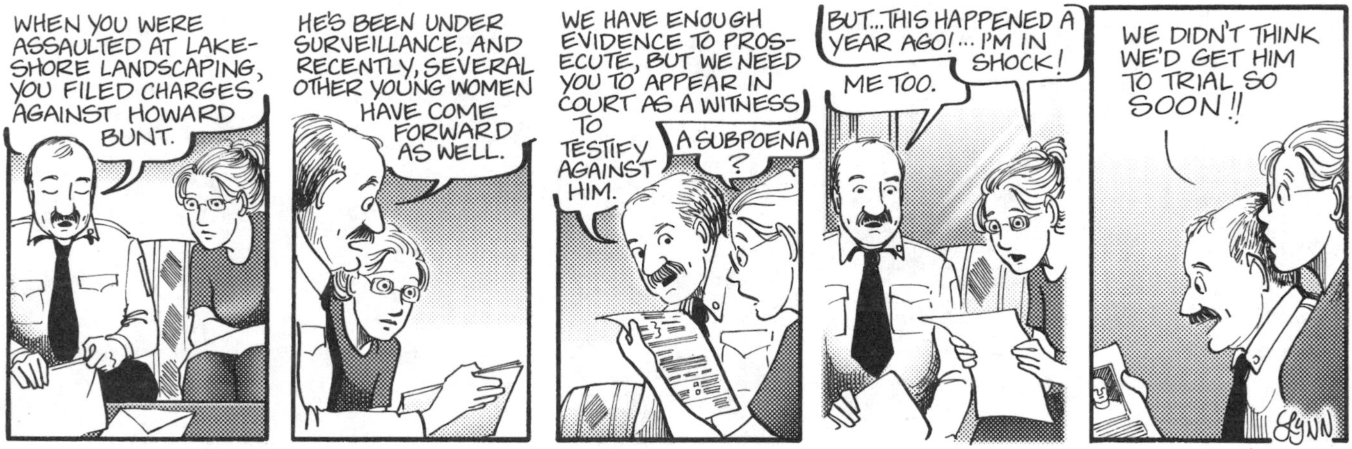
WHEN YOU WERE ASSAULTED AT LAKESHORE LANDSCAPING, YOU FILED CHARGES AGAINST HOWARD BUNT.
HE'S BEEN UNDER SURVEILLANCE, AND RECENTLY, SEVERAL OTHER YOUNG WOMEN HAVE COME FORWARD AS WELL.
WE HAVE ENOUGH EVIDENCE TO PROSECUTE, BUT WE NEED YOU TO APPEAR IN COURT AS A WITNESS TO TESTIFY AGAINST HIM.
A SUBPOENA?
BUT...THIS HAPPENED A YEAR AGO!...I'M IN SHOCK!
ME TOO.
WE DIDN'T THINK WE'D GET HIM TO TRIAL SO SOON!!
LYNN

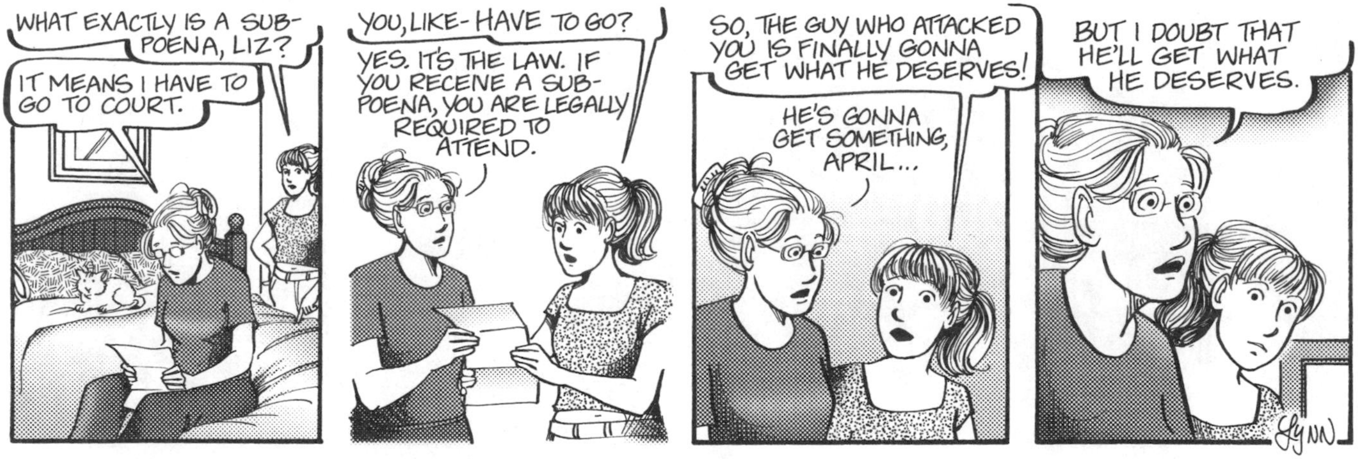
WHAT EXACTLY IS A SUBPOENA, LIZ?
IT MEANS I HAVE TO GO TO COURT.
YOU, LIKE- HAVE TO GO?
YES. IT'S THE LAW. IF YOU RECEIVE A SUBPOENA, YOU ARE LEGALLY REQUIRED TO ATTEND.
SO, THE GUY WHO ATTACKED YOU IS FINALLY GONNA GET WHAT HE DESERVES!
HE'S GONNA GET SOMETHING, APRIL...
BUT I DOUBT THAT HE'LL GET WHAT HE DESERVES.
LYNN

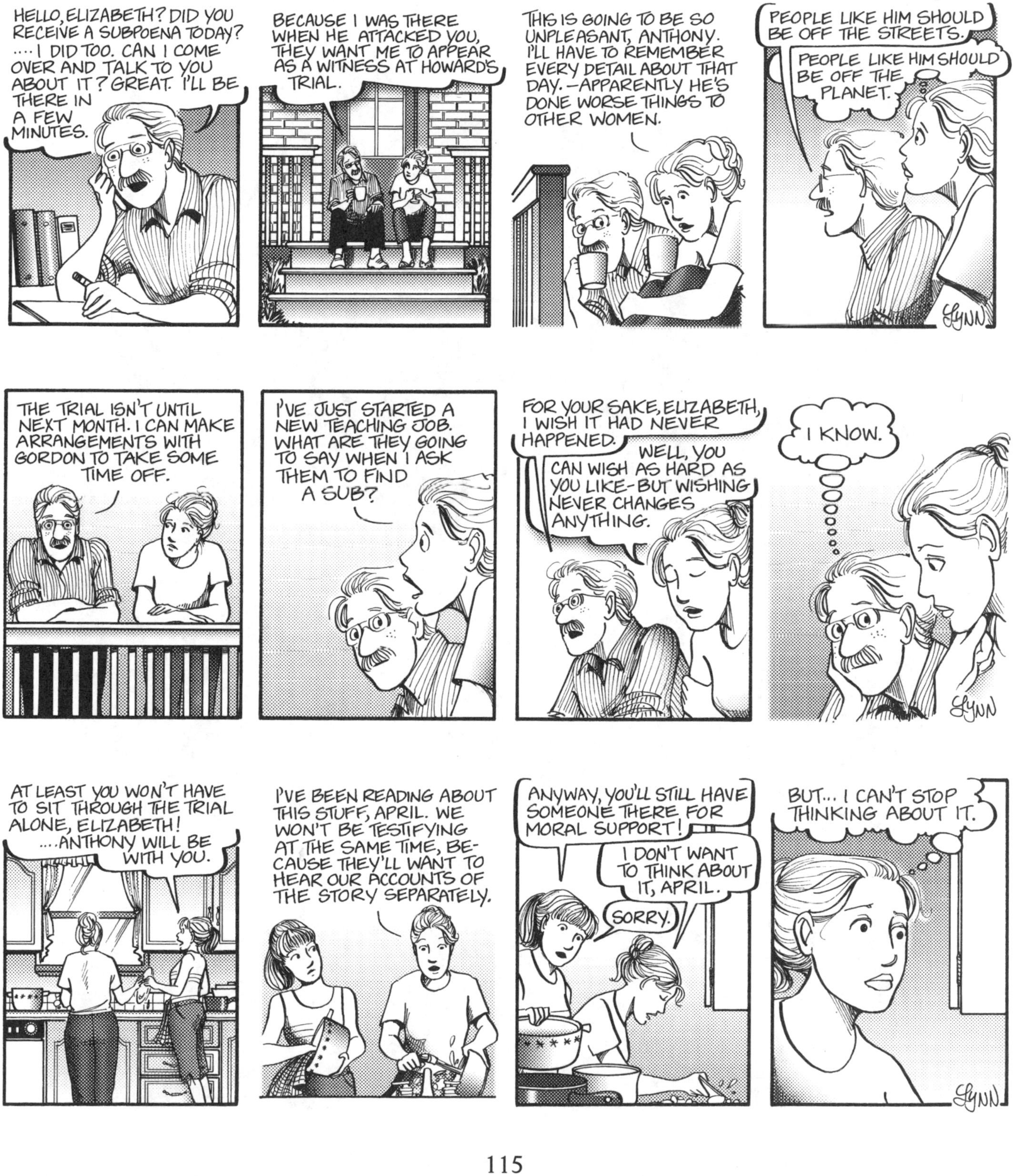
HELLO, ELIZABETH? DID YOU RECEIVE A SUBPOENA TODAY? ....I DID TOO. CAN I COME OVER AND TALK TO YOU ABOUT IT? GREAT. I'LL BE THERE IN A FEW MINUTES.
BECAUSE I WAS THERE WHEN HE ATTACKED YOU, THEY WANT ME TO APPEAR AS A WITNESS AT HOWARD'S TRIAL.
THIS IS GOING TO BE SO UNPLEASANT, ANTHONY. I'LL HAVE TO REMEMBER EVERY DETAIL ABOUT THAT DAY. —APPARENTLY HE'S DONE WORSE THINGS TO OTHER WOMEN.
PEOPLE LIKE HIM SHOULD BE OFF THE STREETS.
PEOPLE LIKE HIM SHOULD BE OFF THE PLANET.
LYNN
THE TRIAL ISN'T UNTIL NEXT MONTH. I CAN MAKE ARRANGEMENTS WITH GORDON TO TAKE SOME TIME OFF.
I'VE JUST STARTED A NEW TEACHING JOB. WHAT ARE THEY GOING TO SAY WHEN I ASK THEM TO FIND A SUB?
FOR YOUR SAKE, ELIZABETH, I WISH IT HAD NEVER HAPPENED.
WELL, YOU CAN WISH AS HARD AS YOU LIKE- BUT WISHING NEVER CHANGES ANYTHING.
I KNOW.
LYNN
AT LEAST YOU WON'T HAVE TO SIT THROUGH THE TRIAL ALONE, ELIZABETH! ....ANTHONY WILL BE WITH YOU.
I'VE BEEN READING ABOUT THIS STUFF, APRIL. WE WON'T BE TESTIFYING AT THE SAME TIME, BECAUSE THEY'LL WANT TO HEAR OUR ACCOUNTS OF THE STORY SEPARATELY.
ANYWAY, YOU'LL STILL HAVE SOMEONE THERE FOR MORAL SUPPORT!
I DON'T WANT TO THINK ABOUT IT, APRIL.
SORRY.
BUT... I CAN'T STOP THINKING ABOUT IT.
LYNN

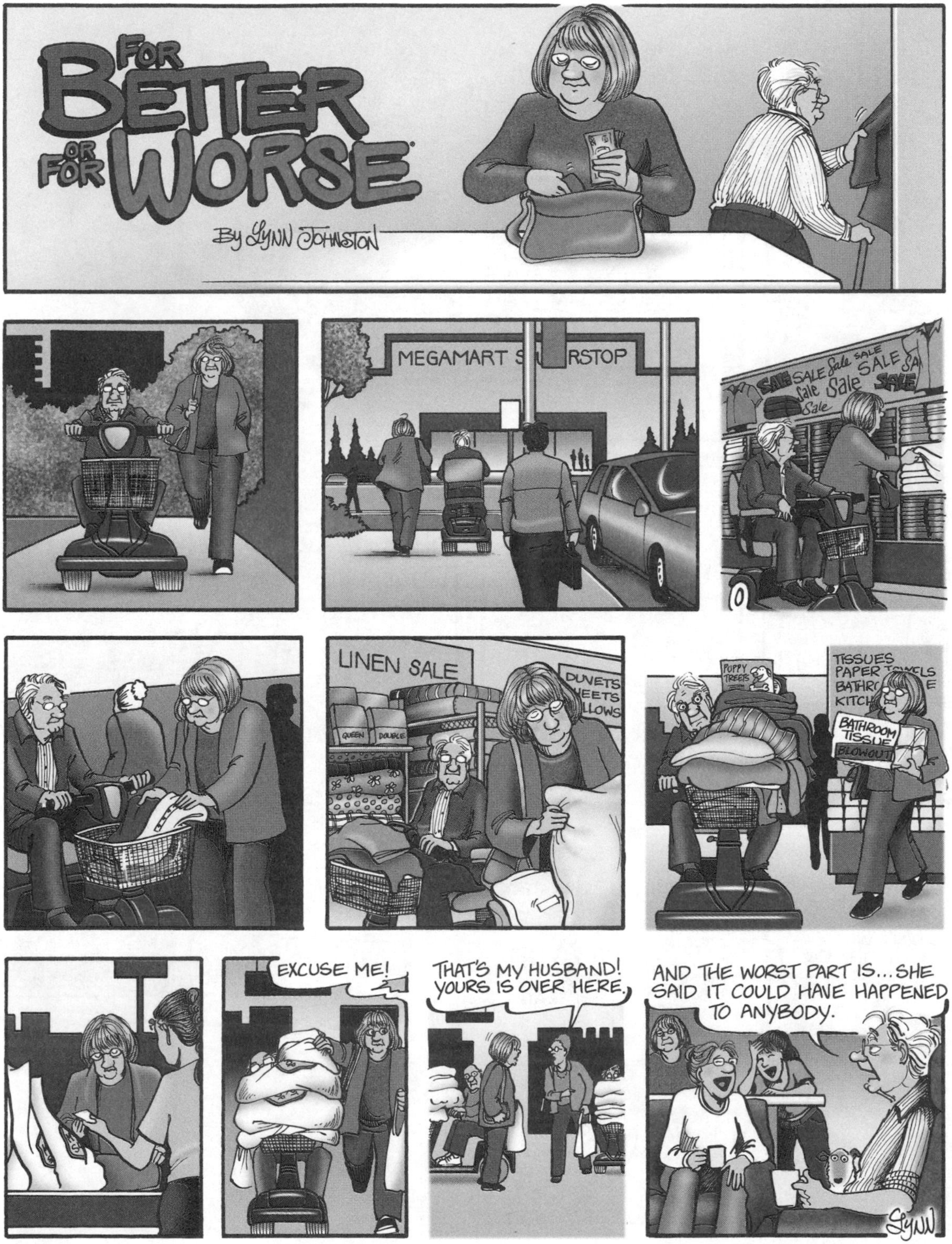
FOR BETTER OR FOR WORSE
By Lynn Johnston
MEGAMART S RSTOP
SALE SALE Sale SALE Sale SALE SALE Sale Sale
LINEN SALE
QUEEN
DOUBLE
DUVETS
EETS
LLOWS
POPPY TREETS
TISSUES
PAPER TOWELS
BATHRO
KITCH
BATHROOM TISSUE BLOWOUT
EXCUSE ME!
THAT'S MY HUSBAND! YOURS IS OVER HERE.
AND THE WORST PART IS... SHE SAID IT COULD HAVE HAPPENED TO ANYBODY.
LYNN

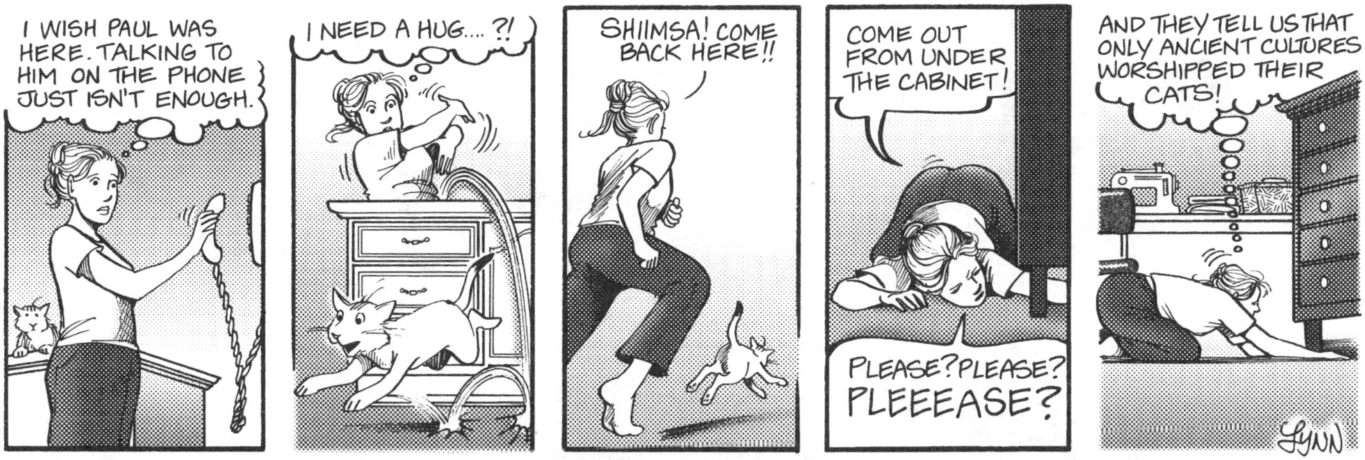
I WISH PAUL WAS HERE. TALKING TO HIM ON THE PHONE JUST ISN'T ENOUGH.
I NEED A HUG....?!
SHIIMSA! COME BACK HERE!!
COME OUT FROM UNDER THE CABINET!
PLEASE? PLEASE? PLEEEASE?
AND THEY TELL US THAT ONLY ANCIENT CULTURES WORSHIPPED THEIR CATS!
LYNN

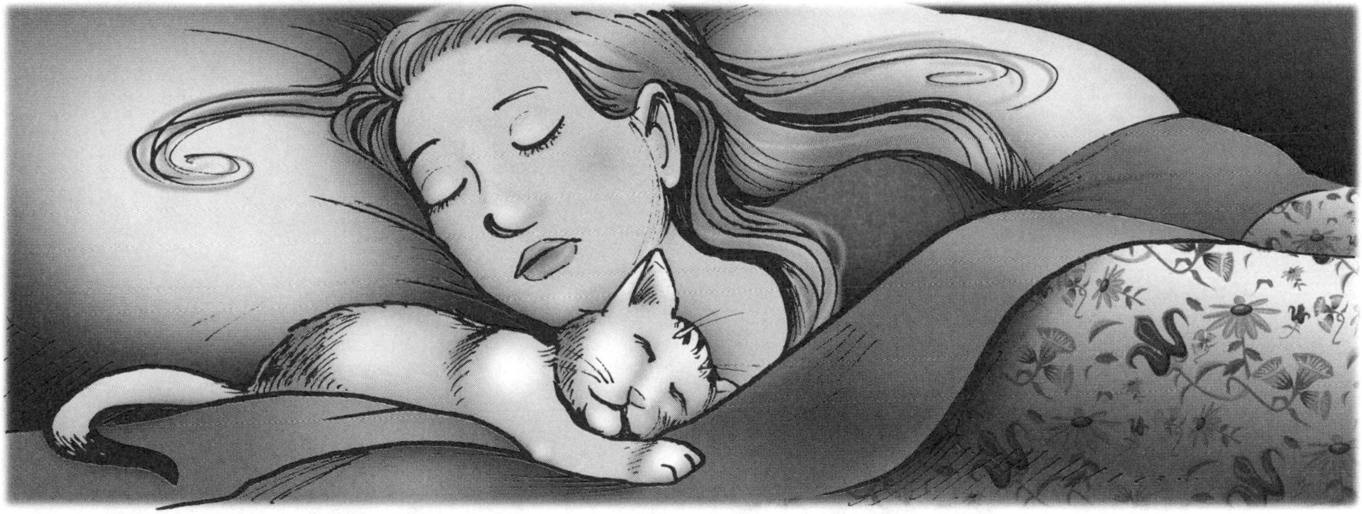

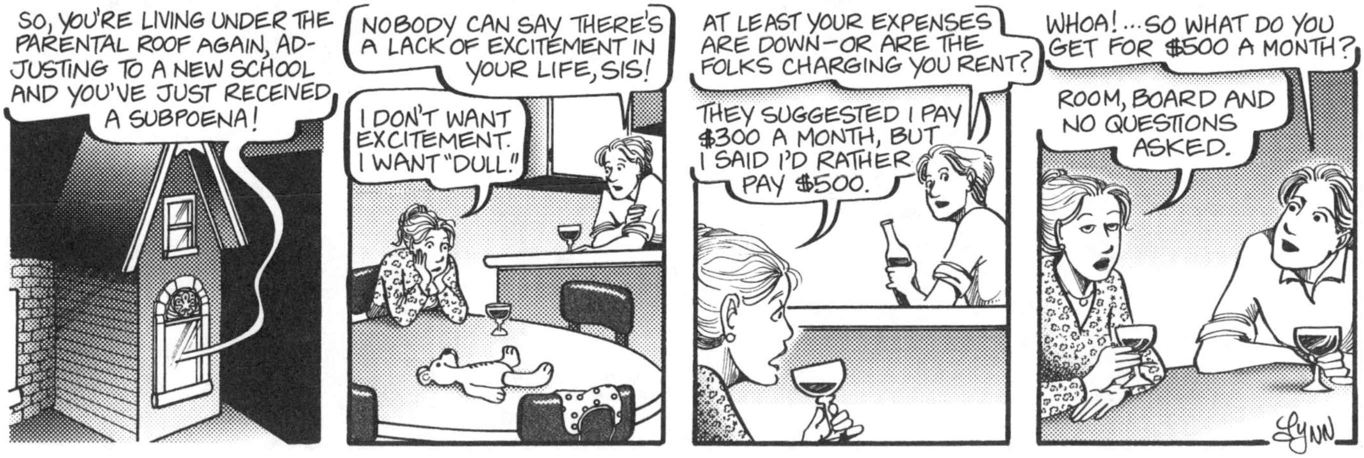
SO, YOU'RE LIVING UNDER THE PARENTAL ROOF AGAIN, ADJUSTING TO A NEW SCHOOL AND YOU'VE JUST RECEIVED A SUBPOENA!
NOBODY CAN SAY THERE'S A LACK OF EXCITEMENT IN YOUR LIFE, SIS!
I DON'T WANT EXCITEMENT. I WANT "DULL."
AT LEAST YOUR EXPENSES ARE DOWN—OR ARE THE FOLKS CHARGING YOU RENT?
THEY SUGGESTED I PAY $300 A MONTH, BUT I SAID I'D RATHER PAY $500.
WHOA! ... SO WHAT DO YOU GET FOR $500 A MONTH?
ROOM, BOARD AND NO QUESTIONS ASKED.
LYNN

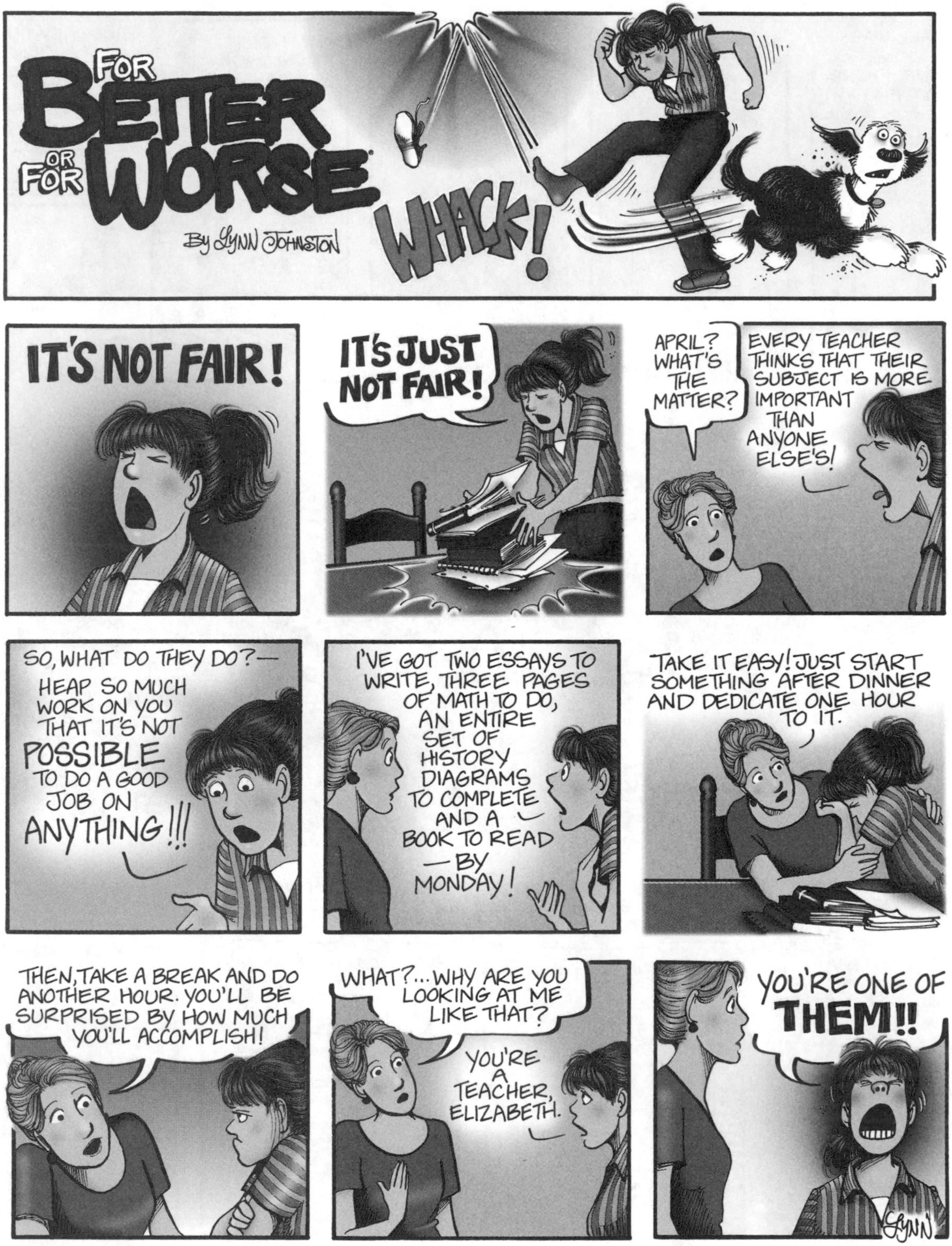
FOR BETTER OR FOR WORSE
BY LYNN JOHNSTON
WHACK!
IT'S NOT FAIR!
IT'S JUST NOT FAIR!
APRIL? WHAT'S THE MATTER?
EVERY TEACHER THINKS THAT THEIR SUBJECT IS MORE IMPORTANT THAN ANYONE ELSE'S!
SO, WHAT DO THEY DO?— HEAP SO MUCH WORK ON YOU THAT IT'S NOT POSSIBLE TO DO A GOOD JOB ON ANYTHING!!!
I'VE GOT TWO ESSAYS TO WRITE, THREE PAGES OF MATH TO DO, AN ENTIRE SET OF HISTORY DIAGRAMS TO COMPLETE AND A BOOK TO READ —BY MONDAY!
TAKE IT EASY! JUST START SOMETHING AFTER DINNER AND DEDICATE ONE HOUR TO IT.
THEN, TAKE A BREAK AND DO ANOTHER HOUR. YOU'LL BE SURPRISED BY HOW MUCH YOU'LL ACCOMPLISH!
WHAT?... WHY ARE YOU LOOKING AT ME LIKE THAT?
YOU'RE A TEACHER, ELIZABETH.
YOU'RE ONE OF THEM!!
LYNN

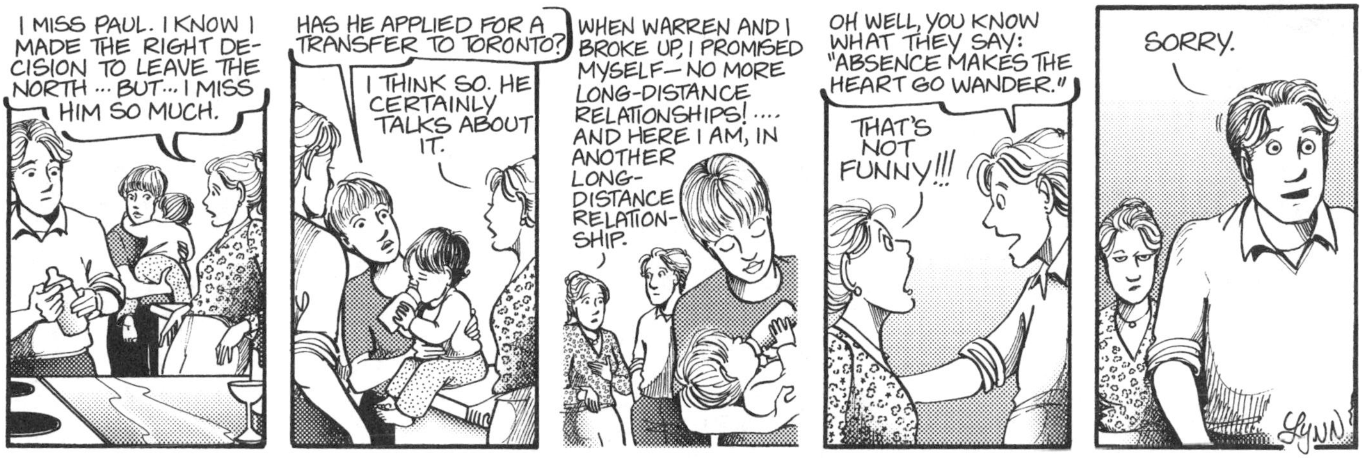
I MISS PAUL. I KNOW I MADE THE RIGHT DECISION TO LEAVE THE NORTH ... BUT... I MISS HIM SO MUCH.
HAS HE APPLIED FOR A TRANSFER TO TORONTO?
I THINK SO. HE CERTAINLY TALKS ABOUT IT.
WHEN WARREN AND I BROKE UP, I PROMISED MYSELF— NO MORE LONG-DISTANCE RELATIONSHIPS! .... AND HERE I AM, IN ANOTHER LONG-DISTANCE RELATIONSHIP.
OH WELL, YOU KNOW WHAT THEY SAY: "ABSENCE MAKES THE HEART GO WANDER."
THAT'S NOT FUNNY!!!
SORRY.
LYNN

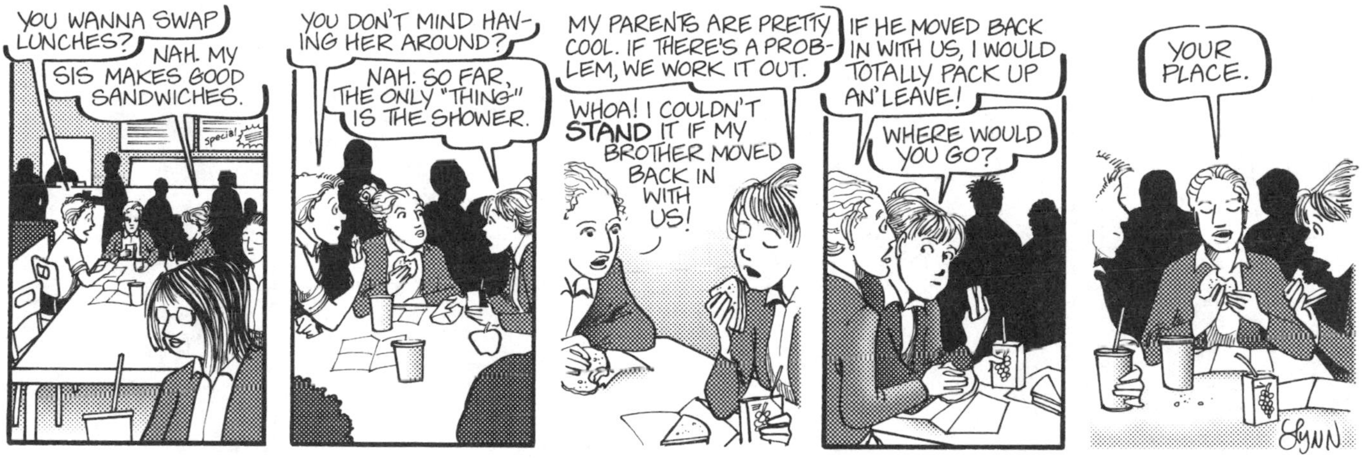
YOU WANNA SWAP LUNCHES?
NAH. MY SIS MAKES GOOD SANDWICHES.
Special
YOU DON'T MIND HAVING HER AROUND?
NAH. SO FAR, THE ONLY "THING" IS THE SHOWER.
MY PARENTS ARE PRETTY COOL. IF THERE'S A PROBLEM, WE WORK IT OUT.
WHOA! I COULDN'T **STAND** IT IF MY BROTHER MOVED BACK IN WITH US!
IF HE MOVED BACK IN WITH US, I WOULD TOTALLY PACK UP AN' LEAVE!
WHERE WOULD YOU GO?
YOUR PLACE.
LYNN

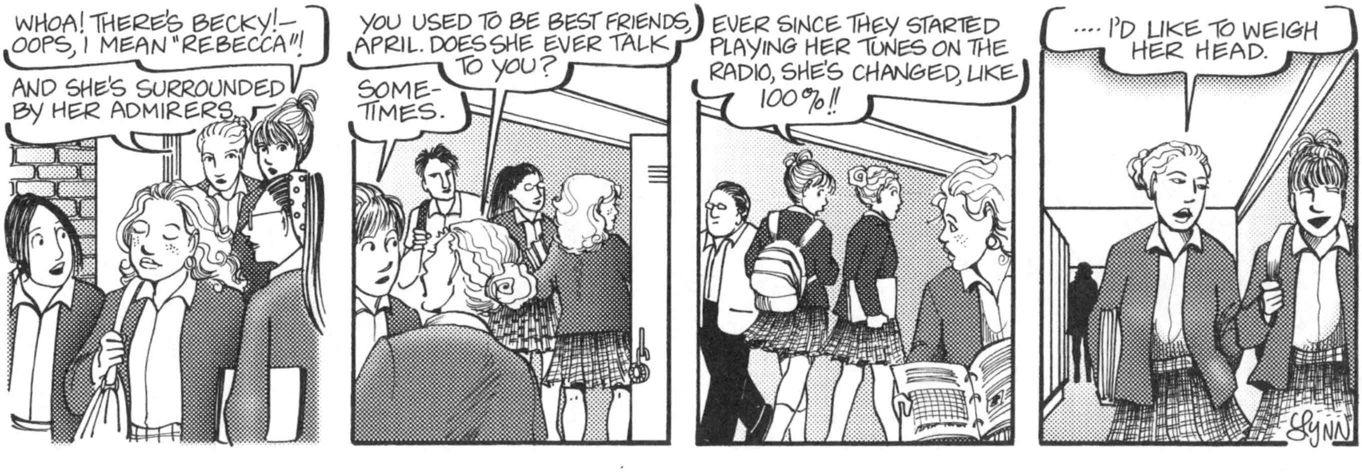
WHOA! THERE'S BECKY!— OOPS, I MEAN "REBECCA"!
AND SHE'S SURROUNDED BY HER ADMIRERS.
YOU USED TO BE BEST FRIENDS, APRIL. DOES SHE EVER TALK TO YOU?
SOMETIMES.
EVER SINCE THEY STARTED PLAYING HER TUNES ON THE RADIO, SHE'S CHANGED, LIKE 100%!!
.... I'D LIKE TO WEIGH HER HEAD.
LYNN

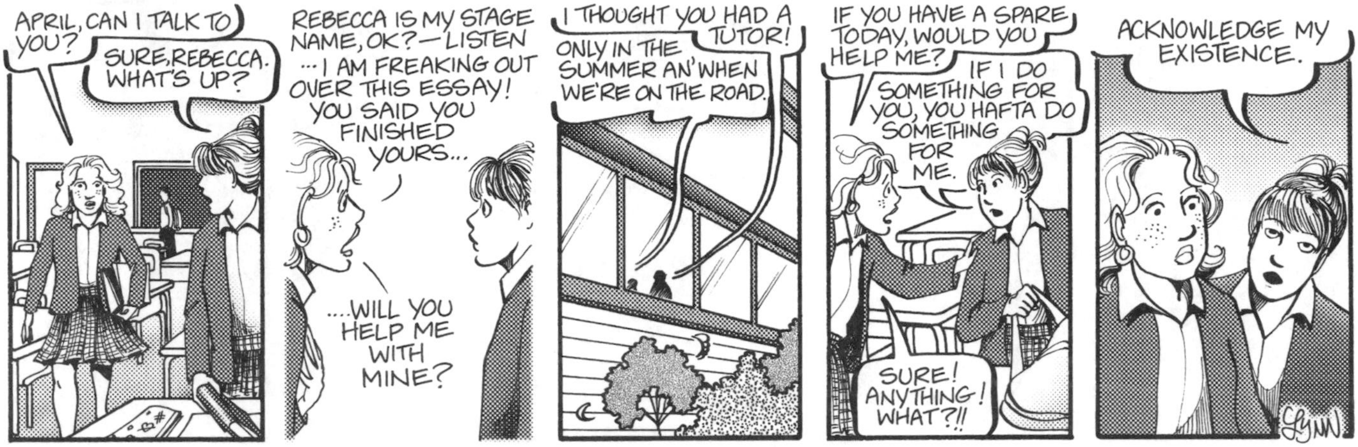
APRIL, CAN I TALK TO YOU?
SURE, REBECCA. WHAT'S UP?
REBECCA IS MY STAGE NAME, OK?— LISTEN ...I AM FREAKING OUT OVER THIS ESSAY! YOU SAID YOU FINISHED YOURS...
....WILL YOU HELP ME WITH MINE?
I THOUGHT YOU HAD A TUTOR!
ONLY IN THE SUMMER AN' WHEN WE'RE ON THE ROAD.
IF YOU HAVE A SPARE TODAY, WOULD YOU HELP ME?
IF I DO SOMETHING FOR YOU, YOU HAFTA DO SOMETHING FOR ME.
SURE! ANYTHING! WHAT?!!
ACKNOWLEDGE MY EXISTENCE.
LYNN

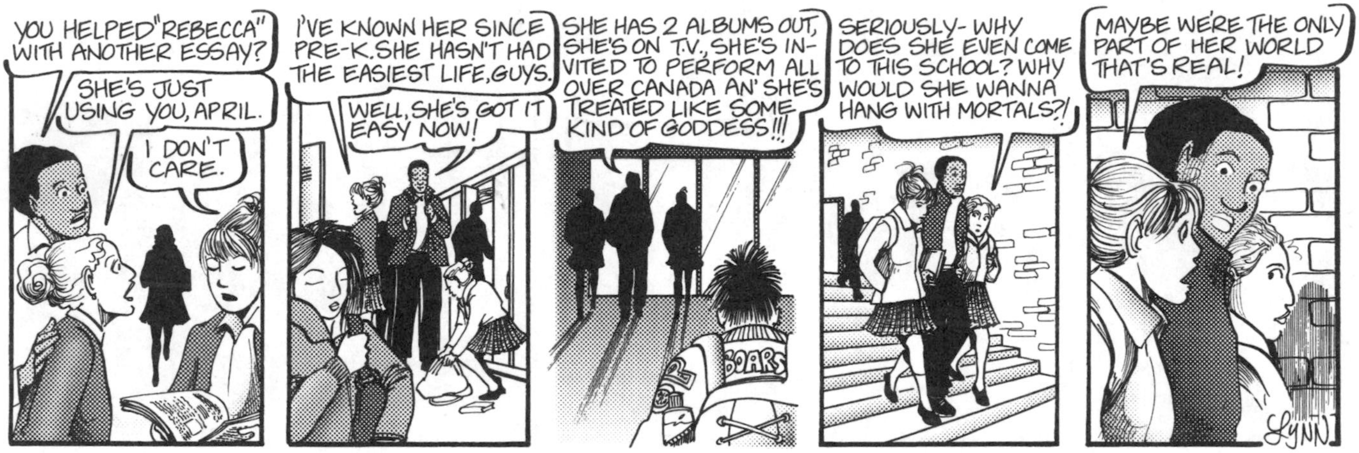
YOU HELPED "REBECCA" WITH ANOTHER ESSAY?
SHE'S JUST USING YOU, APRIL.
I DON'T CARE.
I'VE KNOWN HER SINCE PRE-K. SHE HASN'T HAD THE EASIEST LIFE, GUYS.
WELL, SHE'S GOT IT EASY NOW!
SHE HAS 2 ALBUMS OUT, SHE'S ON T.V., SHE'S INVITED TO PERFORM ALL OVER CANADA AN' SHE'S TREATED LIKE SOME KIND OF GODDESS!!!
BOARS
SERIOUSLY- WHY DOES SHE EVEN COME TO THIS SCHOOL? WHY WOULD SHE WANNA HANG WITH MORTALS?!
MAYBE WE'RE THE ONLY PART OF HER WORLD THAT'S REAL!
LYNN

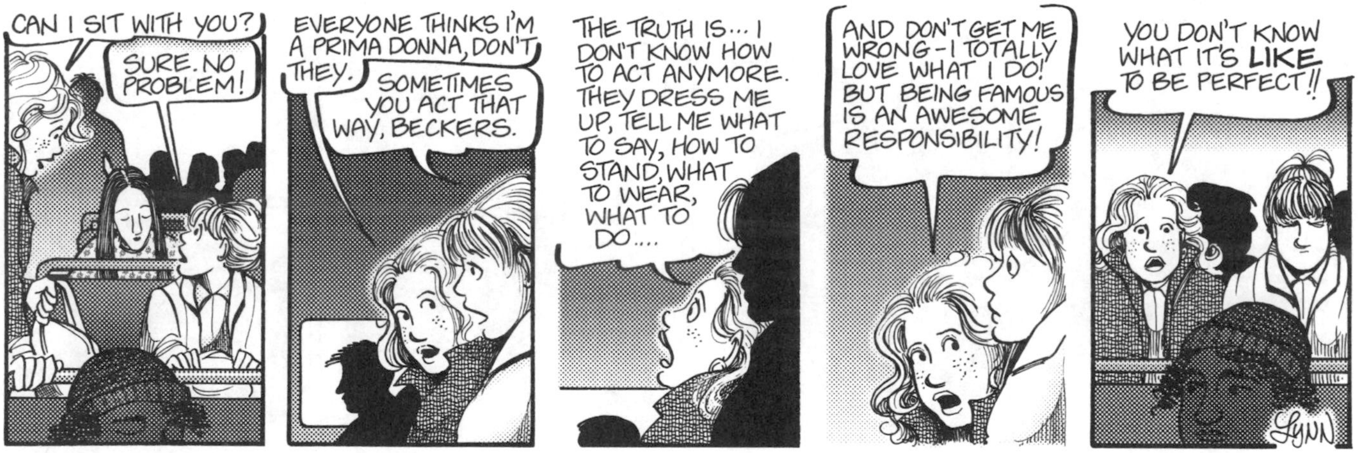
CAN I SIT WITH YOU?
SURE. NO PROBLEM!
EVERYONE THINKS I'M A PRIMA DONNA, DON'T THEY.
SOMETIMES YOU ACT THAT WAY, BECKERS.
THE TRUTH IS... I DON'T KNOW HOW TO ACT ANYMORE. THEY DRESS ME UP, TELL ME WHAT TO SAY, HOW TO STAND, WHAT TO WEAR, WHAT TO DO....
AND DON'T GET ME WRONG - I TOTALLY LOVE WHAT I DO! BUT BEING FAMOUS IS AN AWESOME RESPONSIBILITY!
YOU DON'T KNOW WHAT IT'S LIKE TO BE PERFECT!!
LYNN

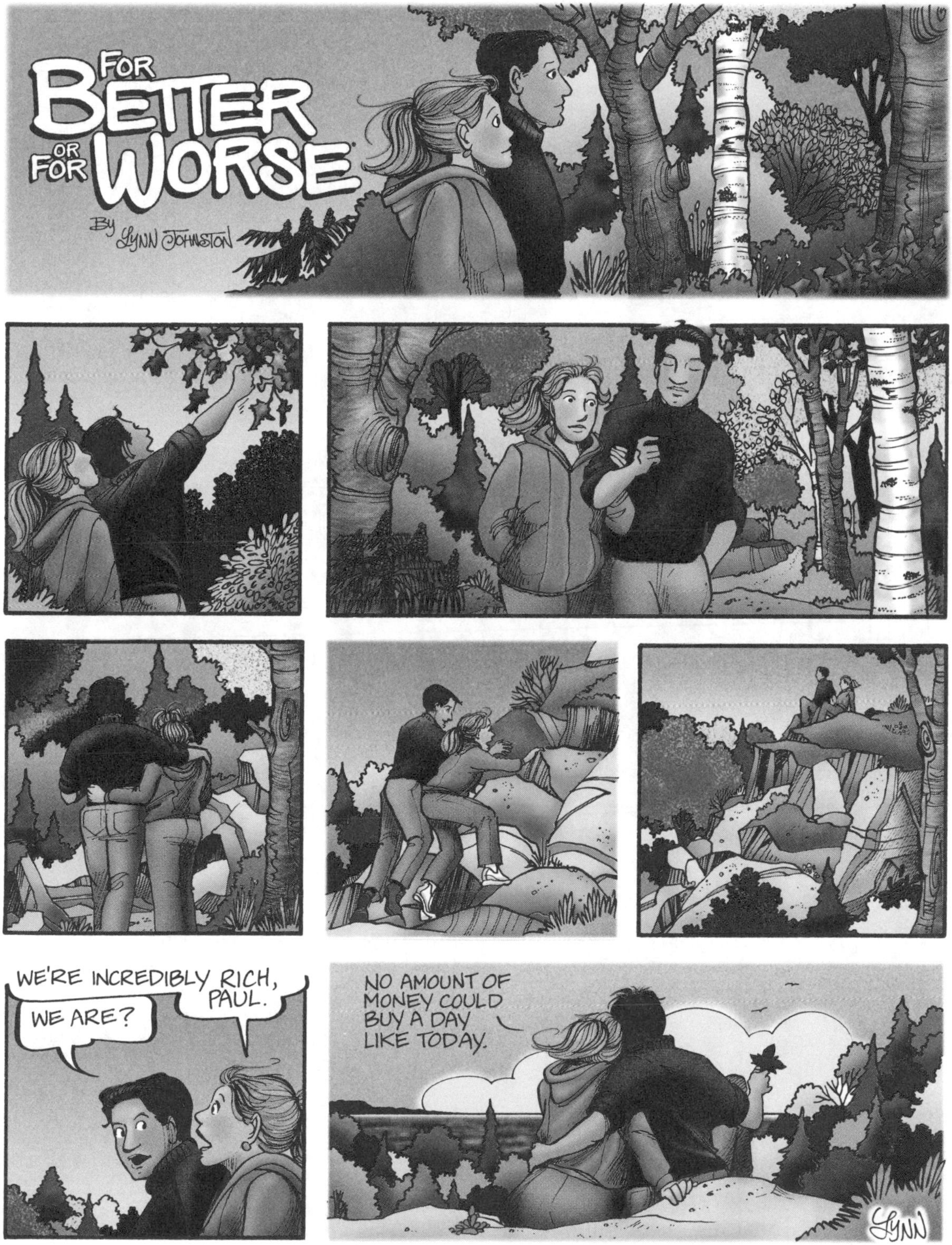
FOR BETTER OR FOR WORSE
BY LYNN JOHNSTON
WE'RE INCREDIBLY RICH, PAUL.
WE ARE?
NO AMOUNT OF MONEY COULD BUY A DAY LIKE TODAY.
LYNN

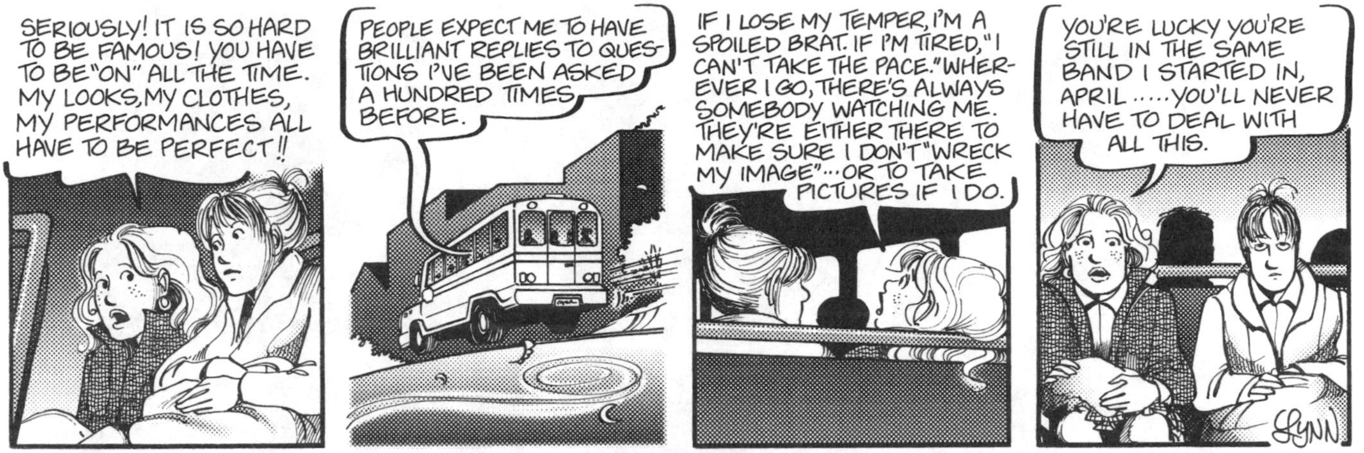
SERIOUSLY! IT IS SO HARD TO BE FAMOUS! YOU HAVE TO BE "ON" ALL THE TIME. MY LOOKS, MY CLOTHES, MY PERFORMANCES ALL HAVE TO BE PERFECT!!
PEOPLE EXPECT ME TO HAVE BRILLIANT REPLIES TO QUESTIONS I'VE BEEN ASKED A HUNDRED TIMES BEFORE.
IF I LOSE MY TEMPER, I'M A SPOILED BRAT. IF I'M TIRED, "I CAN'T TAKE THE PACE." WHEREVER I GO, THERE'S ALWAYS SOMEBODY WATCHING ME. THEY'RE EITHER THERE TO MAKE SURE I DON'T "WRECK MY IMAGE"... OR TO TAKE PICTURES IF I DO.
YOU'RE LUCKY YOU'RE STILL IN THE SAME BAND I STARTED IN, APRIL ..... YOU'LL NEVER HAVE TO DEAL WITH ALL THIS.
LYNN

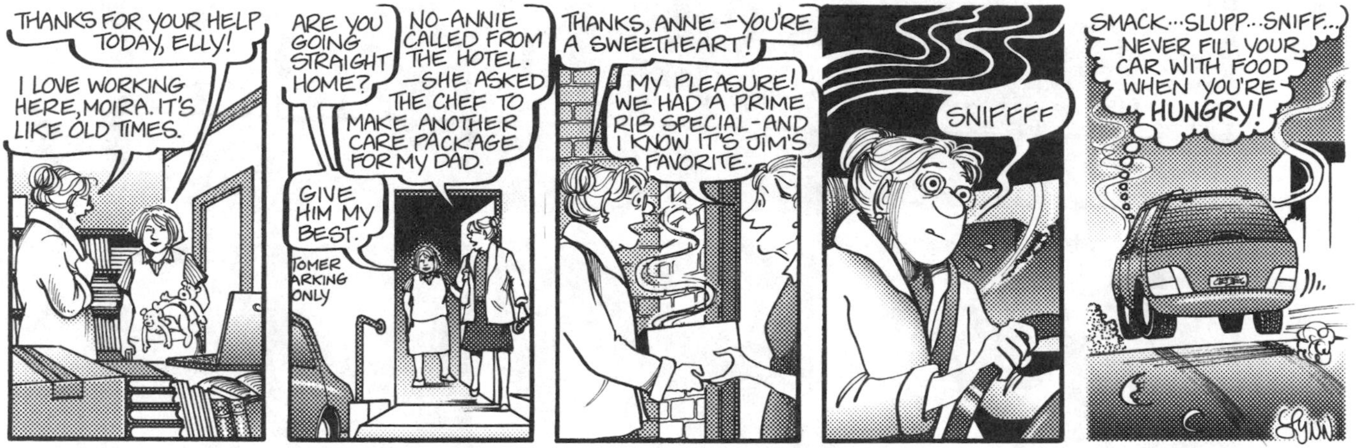
THANKS FOR YOUR HELP TODAY, ELLY!
I LOVE WORKING HERE, MOIRA. IT'S LIKE OLD TIMES.
ARE YOU GOING STRAIGHT HOME?
NO-ANNIE CALLED FROM THE HOTEL. -SHE ASKED THE CHEF TO MAKE ANOTHER CARE PACKAGE FOR MY DAD.
GIVE HIM MY BEST.
THANKS, ANNE -YOU'RE A SWEETHEART!
MY PLEASURE! WE HAD A PRIME RIB SPECIAL-AND I KNOW IT'S JIM'S FAVORITE.
SNIFFFF
SMACK...SLUPP...SNIFF... -NEVER FILL YOUR CAR WITH FOOD WHEN YOU'RE HUNGRY!
LYNN

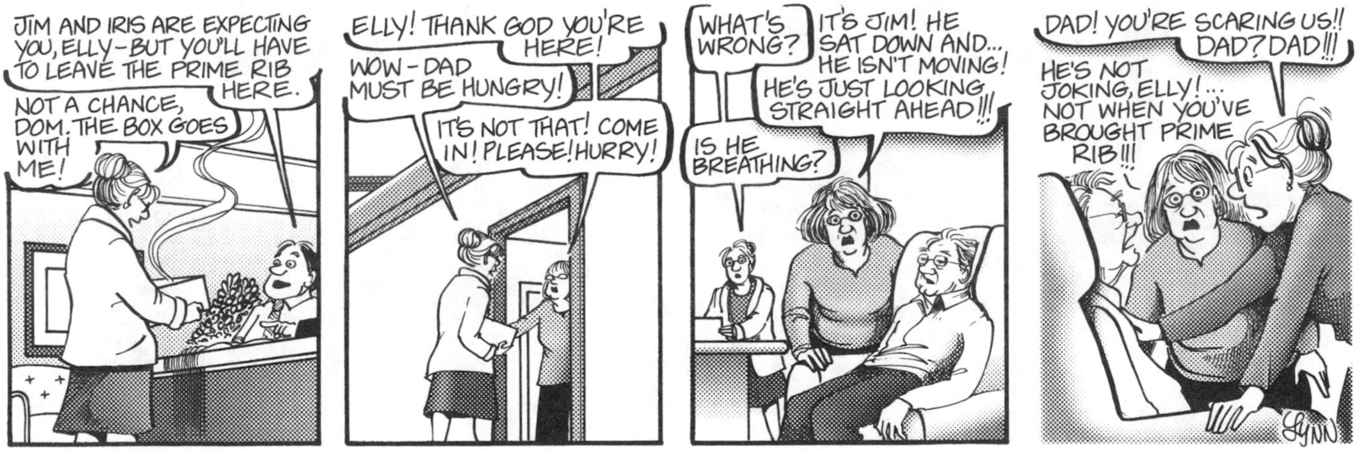
JIM AND IRIS ARE EXPECTING YOU, ELLY-BUT YOU'LL HAVE TO LEAVE THE PRIME RIB HERE.
NOT A CHANCE, DOM. THE BOX GOES WITH ME!
ELLY! THANK GOD YOU'RE HERE!
WOW-DAD MUST BE HUNGRY!
IT'S NOT THAT! COME IN! PLEASE! HURRY!
WHAT'S WRONG?
IT'S JIM! HE SAT DOWN AND... HE ISN'T MOVING! HE'S JUST LOOKING STRAIGHT AHEAD!!!
IS HE BREATHING?
DAD! YOU'RE SCARING US!! DAD? DAD!!!
HE'S NOT JOKING, ELLY!... NOT WHEN YOU'VE BROUGHT PRIME RIB!!!
LYNN

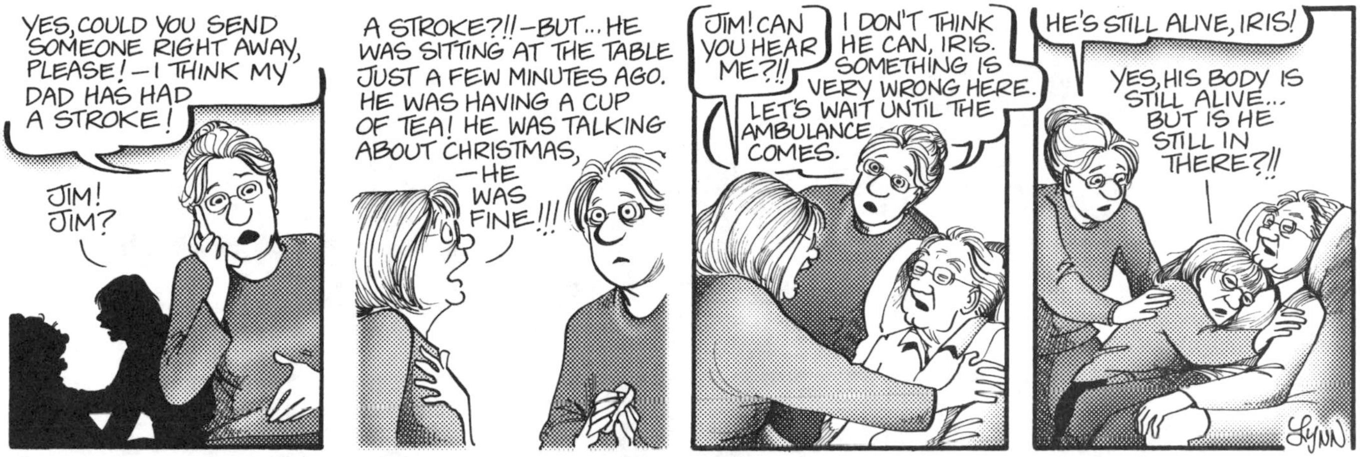
YES, COULD YOU SEND SOMEONE RIGHT AWAY, PLEASE! – I THINK MY DAD HAS HAD A STROKE!
JIM! JIM?
A STROKE?!! –BUT... HE WAS SITTING AT THE TABLE JUST A FEW MINUTES AGO. HE WAS HAVING A CUP OF TEA! HE WAS TALKING ABOUT CHRISTMAS,
–HE WAS FINE!!!
JIM! CAN YOU HEAR ME?!!
I DON'T THINK HE CAN, IRIS. SOMETHING IS VERY WRONG HERE.
LET'S WAIT UNTIL THE AMBULANCE COMES.
HE'S STILL ALIVE, IRIS!
YES, HIS BODY IS STILL ALIVE... BUT IS HE STILL IN THERE?!!
LYNN

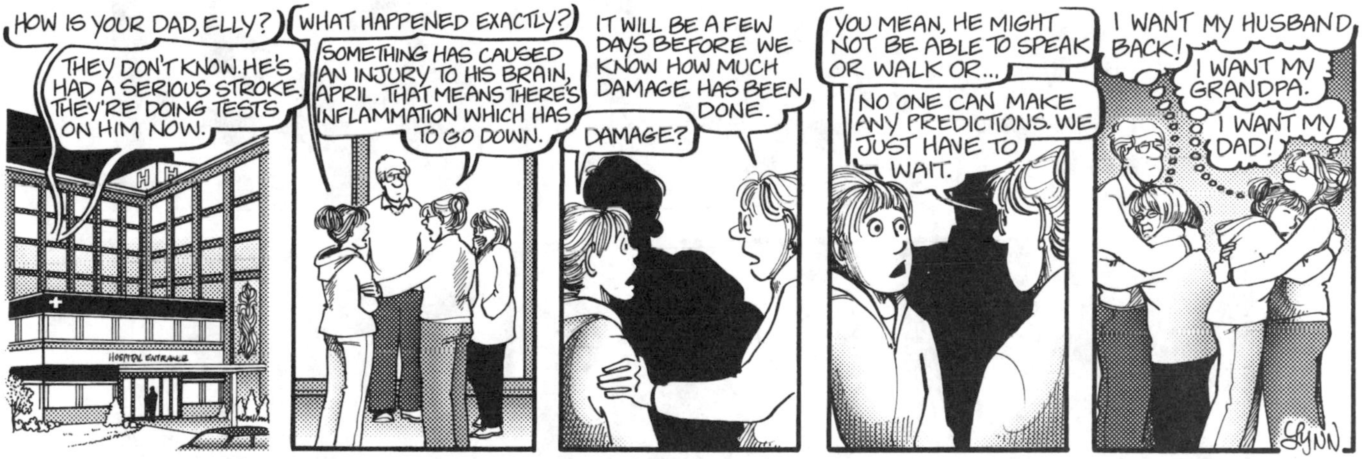
HOW IS YOUR DAD, ELLY?
THEY DON'T KNOW. HE'S HAD A SERIOUS STROKE. THEY'RE DOING TESTS ON HIM NOW.
HOSPITAL ENTRANCE
WHAT HAPPENED EXACTLY?
SOMETHING HAS CAUSED AN INJURY TO HIS BRAIN, APRIL. THAT MEANS THERE'S INFLAMMATION WHICH HAS TO GO DOWN.
IT WILL BE A FEW DAYS BEFORE WE KNOW HOW MUCH DAMAGE HAS BEEN DONE.
DAMAGE?
YOU MEAN, HE MIGHT NOT BE ABLE TO SPEAK OR WALK OR...
NO ONE CAN MAKE ANY PREDICTIONS. WE JUST HAVE TO WAIT.
I WANT MY HUSBAND BACK!
I WANT MY GRANDPA.
I WANT MY DAD!
LYNN

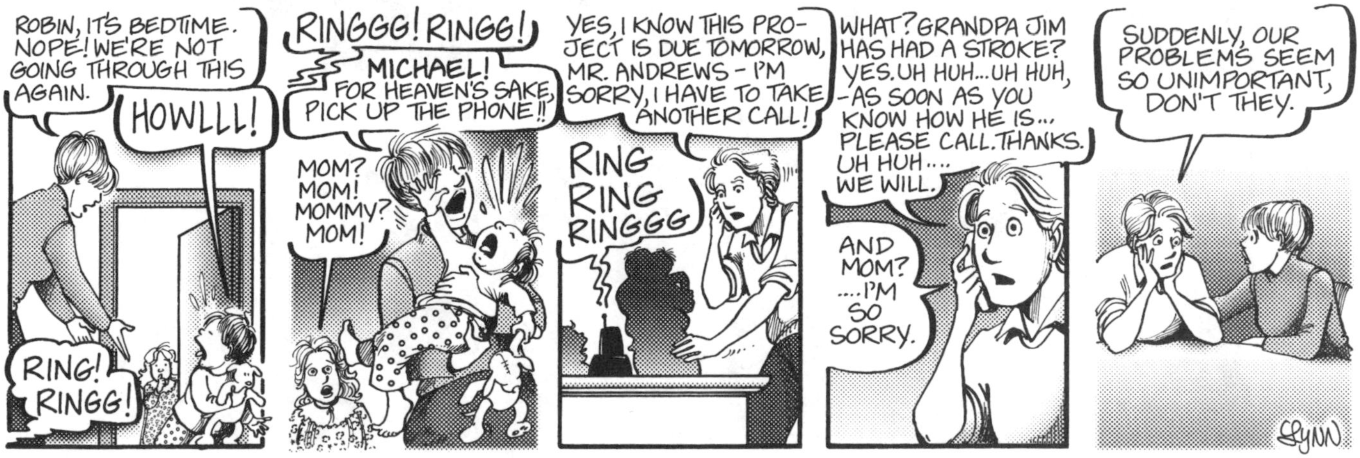
ROBIN, IT'S BEDTIME. NOPE! WE'RE NOT GOING THROUGH THIS AGAIN.
HOWLLL!
RING! RINGG!
RINGGG! RINGG!
MICHAEL! FOR HEAVEN'S SAKE, PICK UP THE PHONE!!
MOM? MOM! MOMMY? MOM!
YES, I KNOW THIS PROJECT IS DUE TOMORROW, MR. ANDREWS – I'M SORRY, I HAVE TO TAKE ANOTHER CALL!
RING RING RINGGG
WHAT? GRANDPA JIM HAS HAD A STROKE? YES. UH HUH... UH HUH, –AS SOON AS YOU KNOW HOW HE IS... PLEASE CALL. THANKS. UH HUH.... WE WILL.
AND MOM? ....I'M SO SORRY.
SUDDENLY, OUR PROBLEMS SEEM SO UNIMPORTANT, DON'T THEY.
LYNN

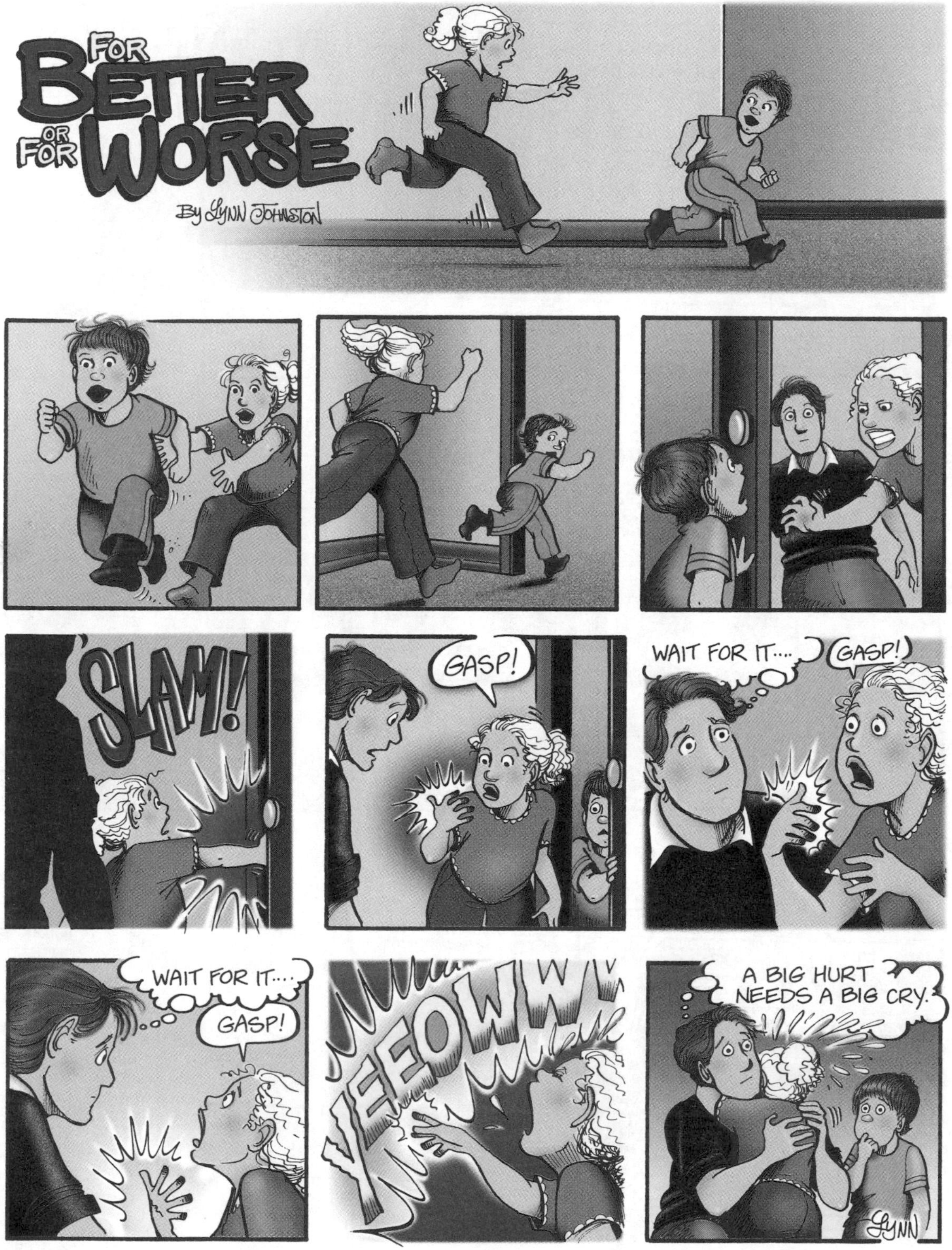
FOR BETTER OR FOR WORSE
BY LYNN JOHNSTON
SLAM!
GASP!
WAIT FOR IT....
GASP!
WAIT FOR IT....
GASP!
YEEOWW!
A BIG HURT NEEDS A BIG CRY.
LYNN

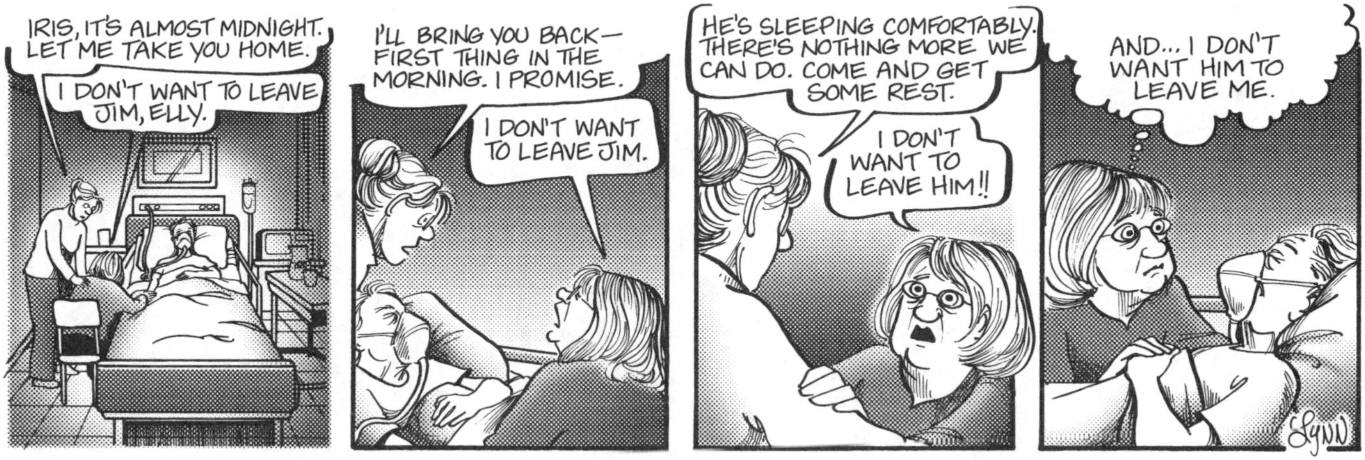
IRIS, IT'S ALMOST MIDNIGHT. LET ME TAKE YOU HOME.
I DON'T WANT TO LEAVE JIM, ELLY.
I'LL BRING YOU BACK— FIRST THING IN THE MORNING. I PROMISE.
I DON'T WANT TO LEAVE JIM.
HE'S SLEEPING COMFORTABLY. THERE'S NOTHING MORE WE CAN DO. COME AND GET SOME REST.
I DON'T WANT TO LEAVE HIM!!
AND... I DON'T WANT HIM TO LEAVE ME.
LYNN

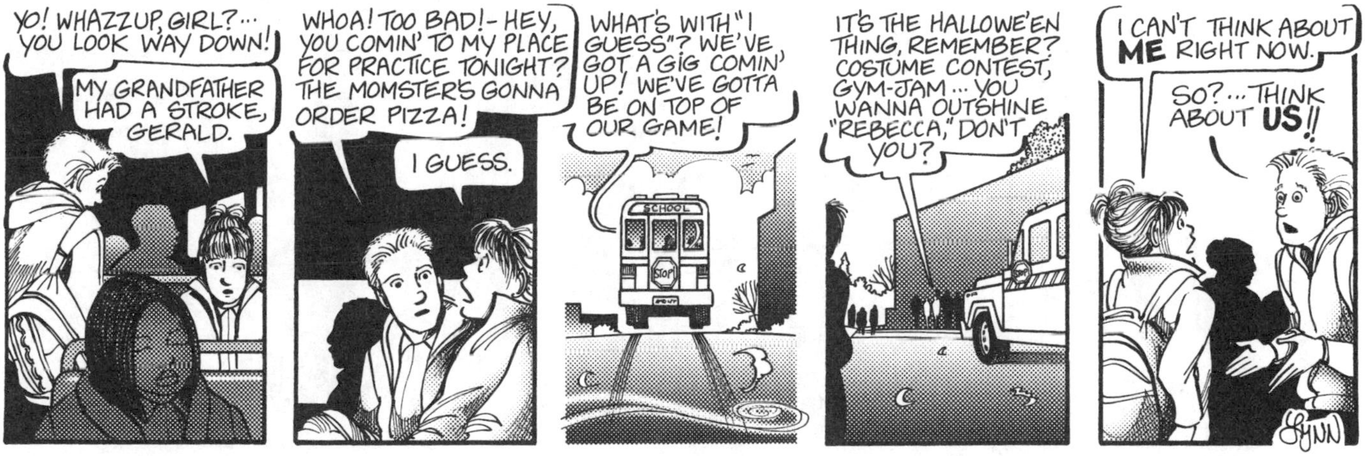
YO! WHAZZUP, GIRL?... YOU LOOK WAY DOWN!
MY GRANDFATHER HAD A STROKE, GERALD.
WHOA! TOO BAD! - HEY, YOU COMIN' TO MY PLACE FOR PRACTICE TONIGHT? THE MOMSTER'S GONNA ORDER PIZZA!
I GUESS.
WHAT'S WITH "I GUESS"? WE'VE GOT A GIG COMIN' UP! WE'VE GOTTA BE ON TOP OF OUR GAME!
SCHOOL
IT'S THE HALLOWE'EN THING, REMEMBER? COSTUME CONTEST, GYM-JAM ... YOU WANNA OUTSHINE "REBECCA," DON'T YOU?
I CAN'T THINK ABOUT **ME** RIGHT NOW.
SO?... THINK ABOUT **US**!!
LYNN

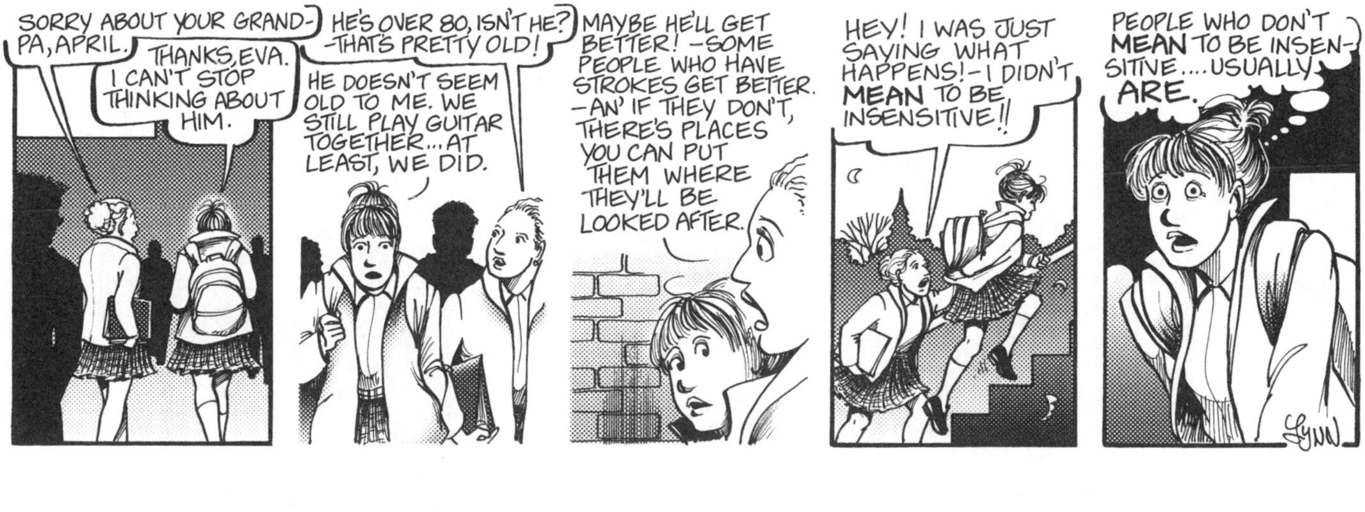
SORRY ABOUT YOUR GRAND-PA, APRIL.
THANKS, EVA. I CAN'T STOP THINKING ABOUT HIM.
HE'S OVER 80, ISN'T HE? -THAT'S PRETTY OLD!
HE DOESN'T SEEM OLD TO ME. WE STILL PLAY GUITAR TOGETHER... AT LEAST, WE DID.
MAYBE HE'LL GET BETTER! -SOME PEOPLE WHO HAVE STROKES GET BETTER. -AN' IF THEY DON'T, THERE'S PLACES YOU CAN PUT THEM WHERE THEY'LL BE LOOKED AFTER.
HEY! I WAS JUST SAYING WHAT HAPPENS! - I DIDN'T **MEAN** TO BE INSENSITIVE!!
PEOPLE WHO DON'T **MEAN** TO BE INSEN-SITIVE.... USUALLY **ARE**.
LYNN

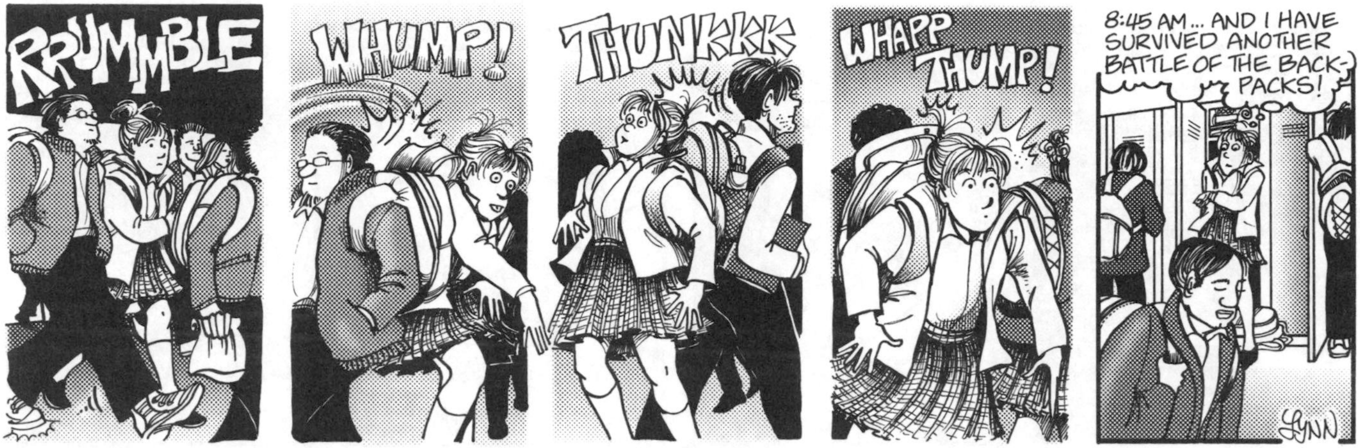
RRUMMBLE
WHUMP!
THUNKKK
WHAPP THUMP!
8:45 AM ... AND I HAVE SURVIVED ANOTHER BATTLE OF THE BACK-PACKS!
LYNN

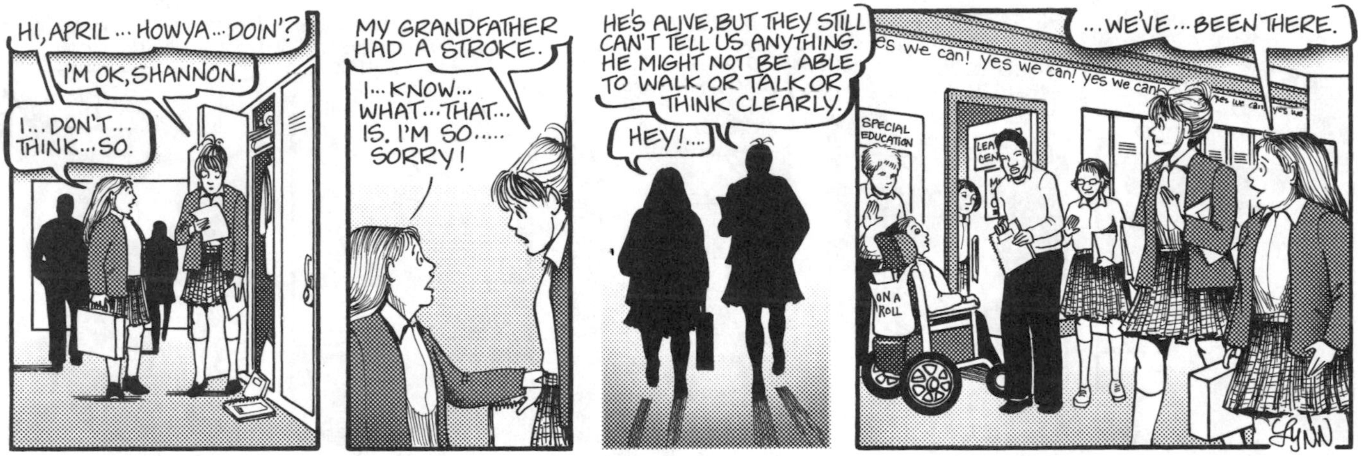
HI, APRIL ... HOWYA ... DOIN'?
I'M OK, SHANNON.
I ... DON'T ... THINK ... SO.
MY GRANDFATHER HAD A STROKE.
I ... KNOW ... WHAT ... THAT ... IS. I'M SO..... SORRY!
HE'S ALIVE, BUT THEY STILL CAN'T TELL US ANYTHING. HE MIGHT NOT BE ABLE TO WALK OR TALK OR THINK CLEARLY.
HEY! ....
... WE'VE ... BEEN THERE.
yes we can! yes we can! yes we can!
SPECIAL EDUCATION
ON A ROLL
LYNN

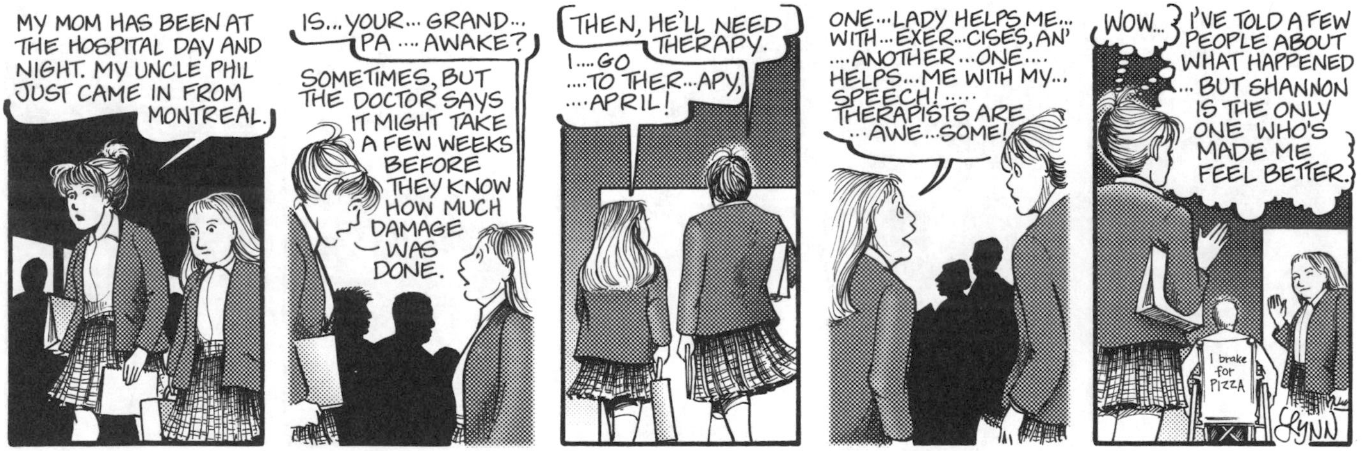
MY MOM HAS BEEN AT THE HOSPITAL DAY AND NIGHT. MY UNCLE PHIL JUST CAME IN FROM MONTREAL.
IS ... YOUR ... GRAND ... PA .... AWAKE?
SOMETIMES, BUT THE DOCTOR SAYS IT MIGHT TAKE A FEW WEEKS BEFORE THEY KNOW HOW MUCH DAMAGE WAS DONE.
THEN, HE'LL NEED THERAPY.
I .... GO .... TO THER ... APY, ... APRIL!
ONE ... LADY HELPS ME ... WITH ... EXER ... CISES, AN' .... ANOTHER ... ONE .... HELPS ... ME WITH MY ... SPEECH! ..... THERAPISTS ARE ... AWE ... SOME!
WOW ...
I'VE TOLD A FEW PEOPLE ABOUT WHAT HAPPENED ... BUT SHANNON IS THE ONLY ONE WHO'S MADE ME FEEL BETTER.
I brake for PIZZA
LYNN

For BETTER or For WORSE
By Lynn Johnston

CLICK!

TWIDDLE... TWIDDLE... TWIDDLE...

TWIDDLE, TWIDDLE, TWIDDLE....

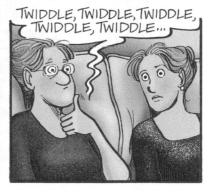

TWIDDLE, TWIDDLE, TWIDDLE, TWIDDLE, TWIDDLE...

TWIDDLE...

MOTHER!!

WHAT?!

WOULD YOU JUST GO TO THE BATHROOM AND **DEAL** WITH THAT THING ?!!!

HMPH... I GET ONE CHIN HAIR AND IT DRIVES MY DAUGHTER CRAZY!

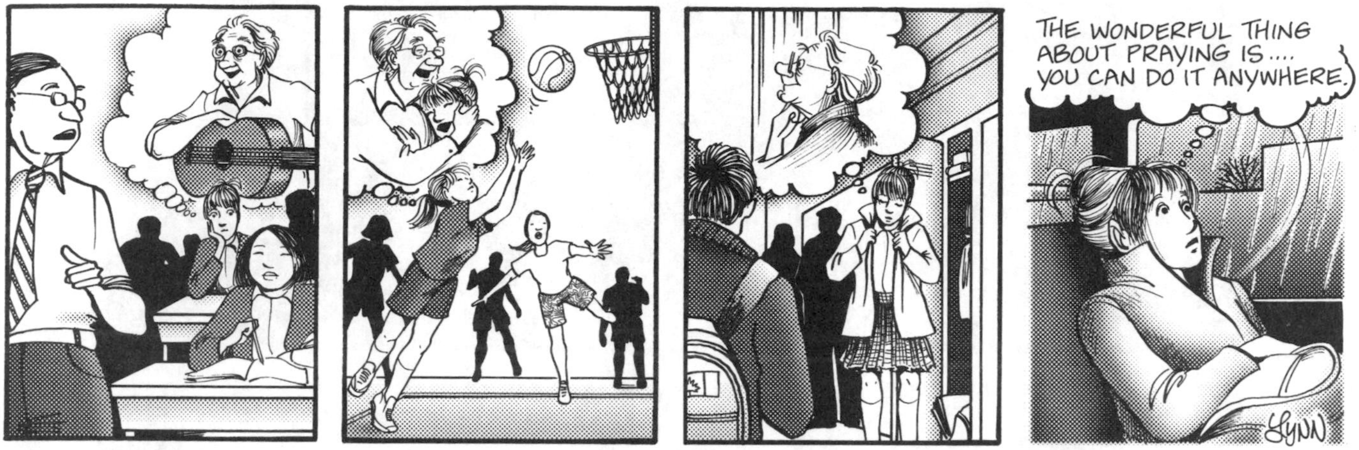
THE WONDERFUL THING ABOUT PRAYING IS.... YOU CAN DO IT ANYWHERE.
LYNN

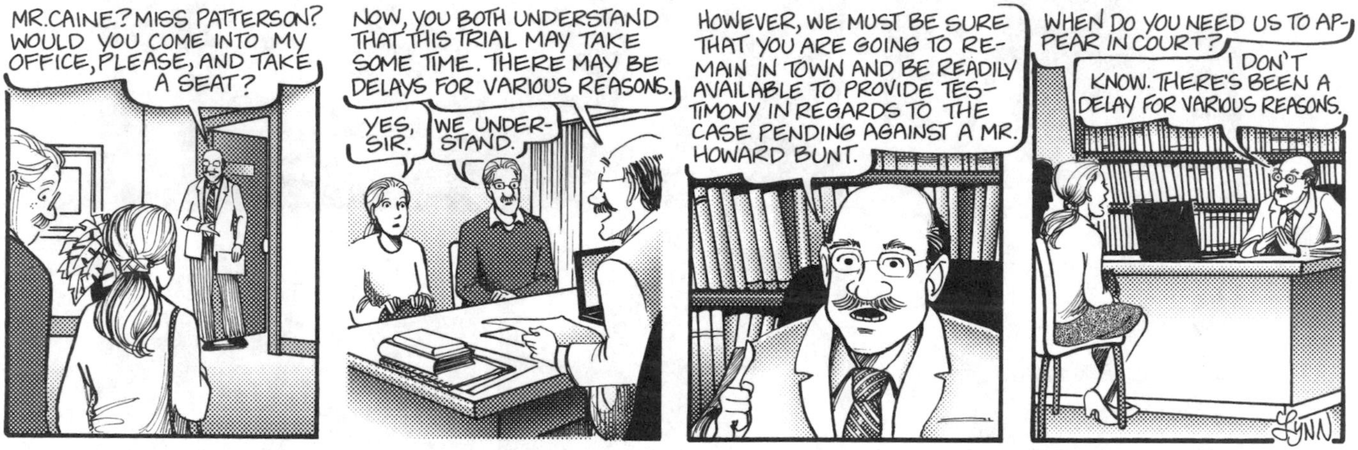
MR.CAINE? MISS PATTERSON? WOULD YOU COME INTO MY OFFICE, PLEASE, AND TAKE A SEAT?
NOW, YOU BOTH UNDERSTAND THAT THIS TRIAL MAY TAKE SOME TIME. THERE MAY BE DELAYS FOR VARIOUS REASONS.
YES, SIR.
WE UNDERSTAND.
HOWEVER, WE MUST BE SURE THAT YOU ARE GOING TO REMAIN IN TOWN AND BE READILY AVAILABLE TO PROVIDE TESTIMONY IN REGARDS TO THE CASE PENDING AGAINST A MR. HOWARD BUNT.
WHEN DO YOU NEED US TO APPEAR IN COURT?
I DON'T KNOW. THERE'S BEEN A DELAY FOR VARIOUS REASONS.
LYNN

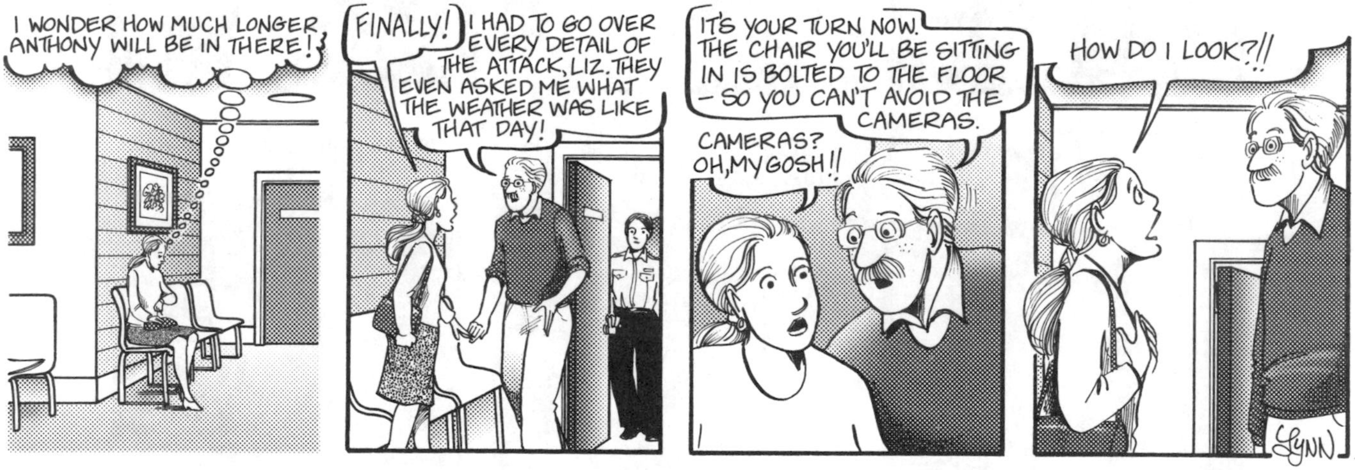
I WONDER HOW MUCH LONGER ANTHONY WILL BE IN THERE!
FINALLY!
I HAD TO GO OVER EVERY DETAIL OF THE ATTACK, LIZ. THEY EVEN ASKED ME WHAT THE WEATHER WAS LIKE THAT DAY!
IT'S YOUR TURN NOW. THE CHAIR YOU'LL BE SITTING IN IS BOLTED TO THE FLOOR – SO YOU CAN'T AVOID THE CAMERAS.
CAMERAS? OH, MY GOSH!!
HOW DO I LOOK?!!
LYNN

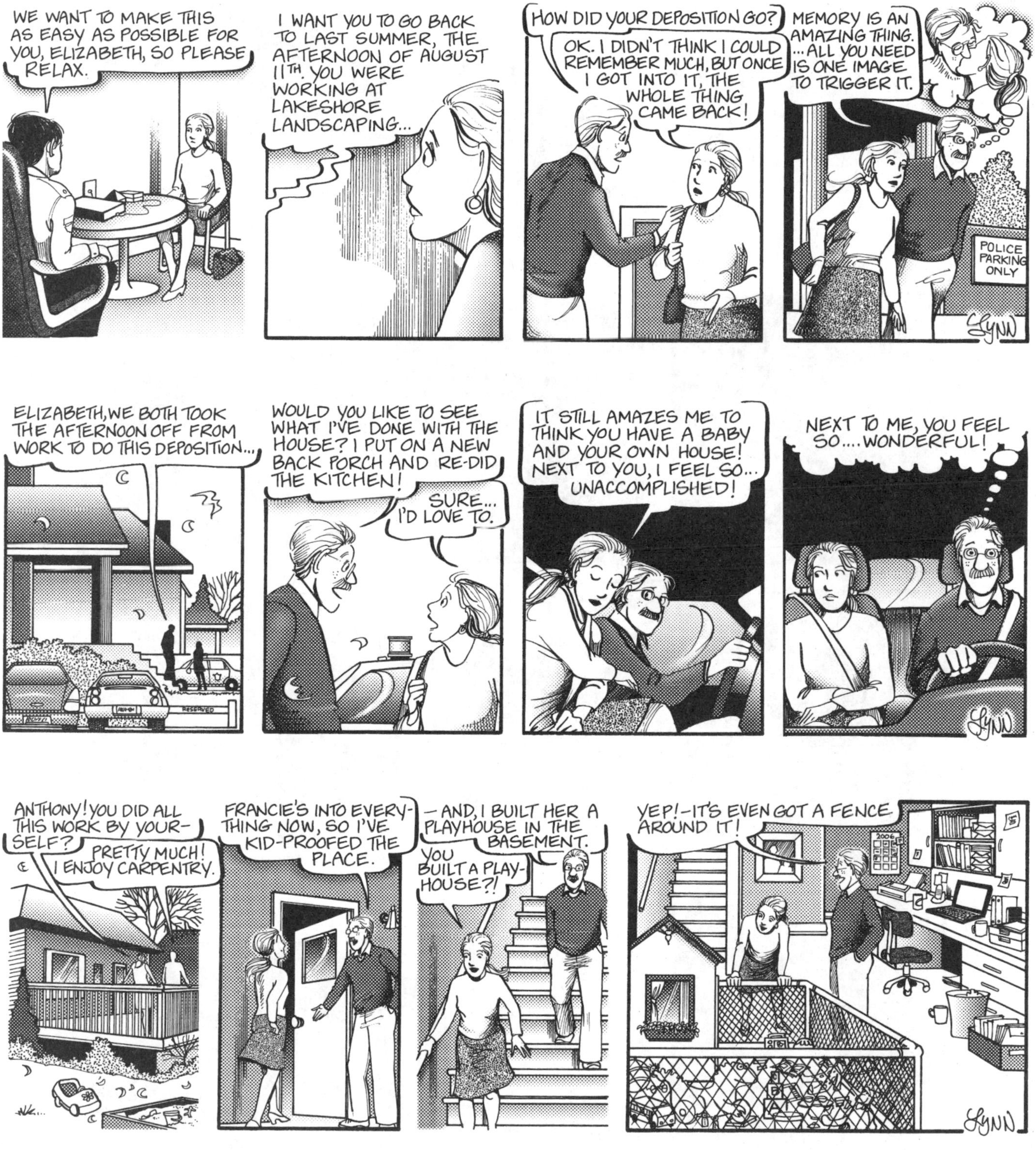
WE WANT TO MAKE THIS AS EASY AS POSSIBLE FOR YOU, ELIZABETH, SO PLEASE RELAX.
I WANT YOU TO GO BACK TO LAST SUMMER, THE AFTERNOON OF AUGUST 11TH. YOU WERE WORKING AT LAKESHORE LANDSCAPING...
HOW DID YOUR DEPOSITION GO?
OK. I DIDN'T THINK I COULD REMEMBER MUCH, BUT ONCE I GOT INTO IT, THE WHOLE THING CAME BACK!
MEMORY IS AN AMAZING THING. ...ALL YOU NEED IS ONE IMAGE TO TRIGGER IT.
POLICE PARKING ONLY
LYNN
ELIZABETH, WE BOTH TOOK THE AFTERNOON OFF FROM WORK TO DO THIS DEPOSITION...
WOULD YOU LIKE TO SEE WHAT I'VE DONE WITH THE HOUSE? I PUT ON A NEW BACK PORCH AND RE-DID THE KITCHEN!
SURE... I'D LOVE TO.
IT STILL AMAZES ME TO THINK YOU HAVE A BABY AND YOUR OWN HOUSE! NEXT TO YOU, I FEEL SO... UNACCOMPLISHED!
NEXT TO ME, YOU FEEL SO.... WONDERFUL!
LYNN
ANTHONY! YOU DID ALL THIS WORK BY YOURSELF?
PRETTY MUCH! I ENJOY CARPENTRY.
FRANCIE'S INTO EVERYTHING NOW, SO I'VE KID-PROOFED THE PLACE.
—AND, I BUILT HER A PLAYHOUSE IN THE BASEMENT.
YOU BUILT A PLAYHOUSE?!
YEP! —IT'S EVEN GOT A FENCE AROUND IT!
2006
LYNN

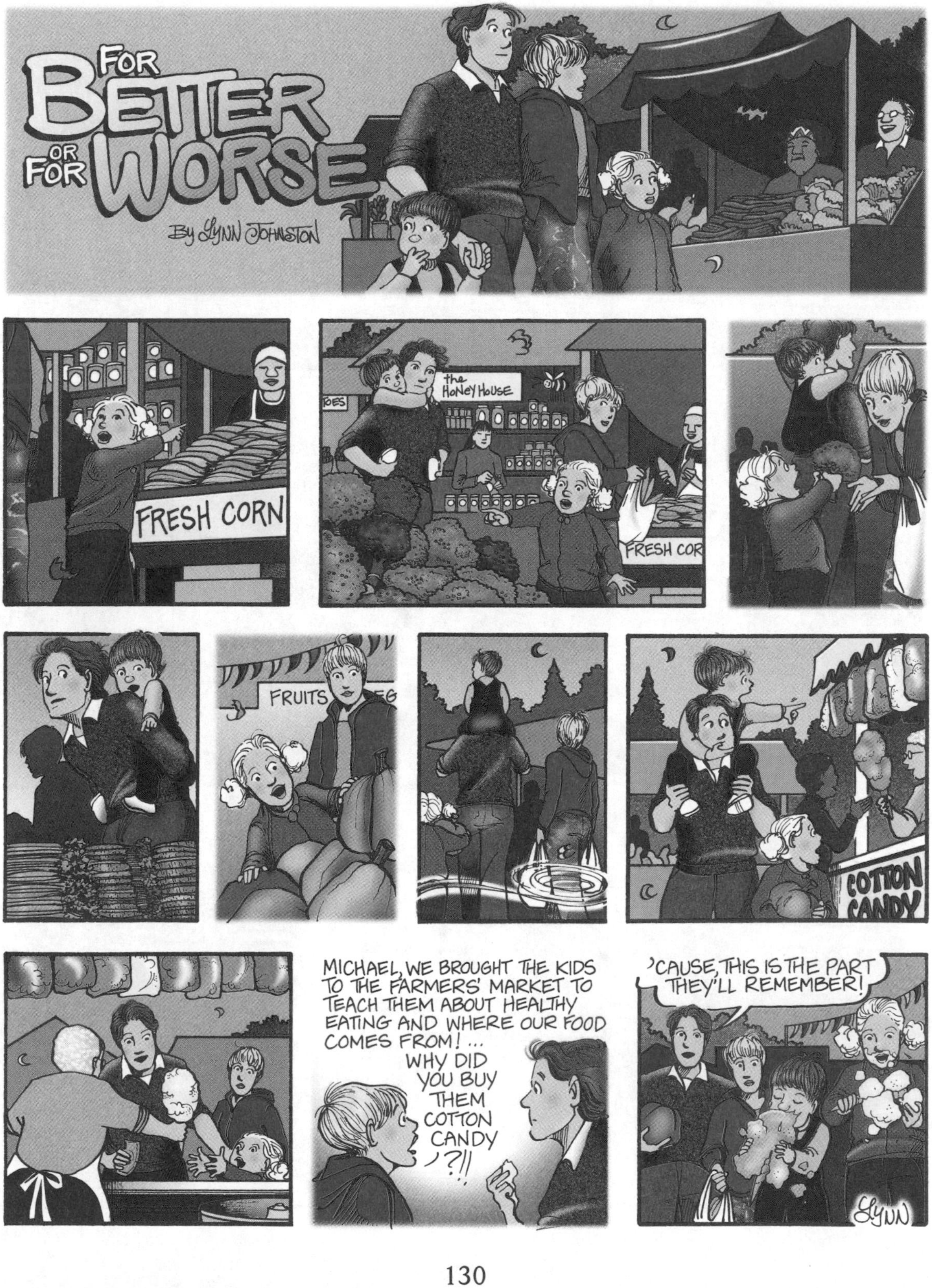
FOR BETTER OR FOR WORSE
By Lynn Johnston
FRESH CORN
the Honey House
TOES
FRESH COR
FRUITS
EG
COTTON CANDY
MICHAEL, WE BROUGHT THE KIDS TO THE FARMERS' MARKET TO TEACH THEM ABOUT HEALTHY EATING AND WHERE OUR FOOD COMES FROM! ...
WHY DID YOU BUY THEM COTTON CANDY ?!!
'CAUSE, THIS IS THE PART THEY'LL REMEMBER!
Lynn

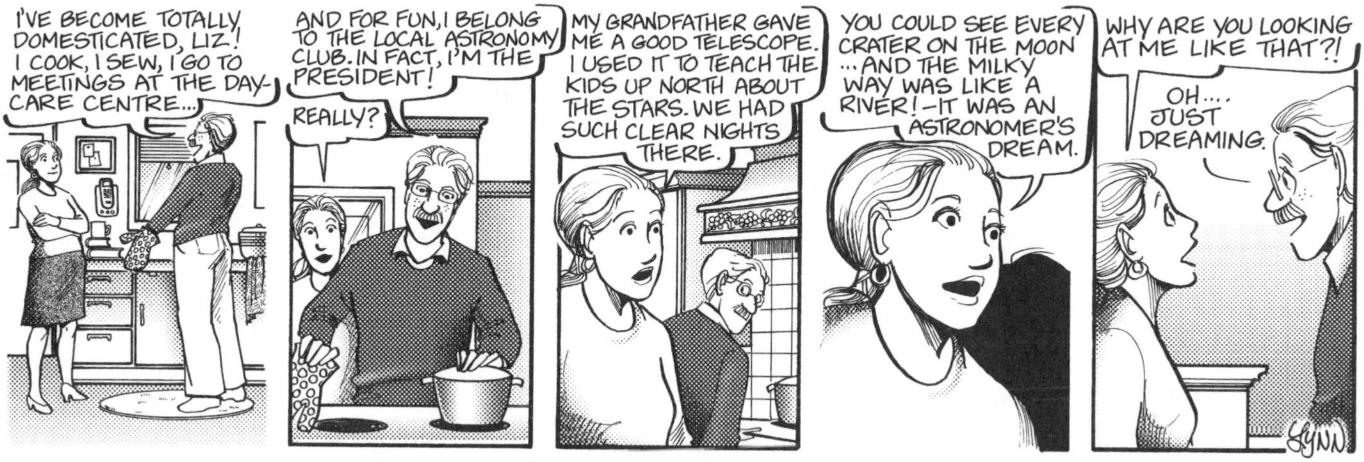
I'VE BECOME TOTALLY DOMESTICATED, LIZ! I COOK, I SEW, I GO TO MEETINGS AT THE DAY-CARE CENTRE...
AND FOR FUN, I BELONG TO THE LOCAL ASTRONOMY CLUB. IN FACT, I'M THE PRESIDENT!
REALLY?
MY GRANDFATHER GAVE ME A GOOD TELESCOPE. I USED IT TO TEACH THE KIDS UP NORTH ABOUT THE STARS. WE HAD SUCH CLEAR NIGHTS THERE.
YOU COULD SEE EVERY CRATER ON THE MOON ...AND THE MILKY WAY WAS LIKE A RIVER! –IT WAS AN ASTRONOMER'S DREAM.
WHY ARE YOU LOOKING AT ME LIKE THAT?!
OH.... JUST DREAMING.
LYNN

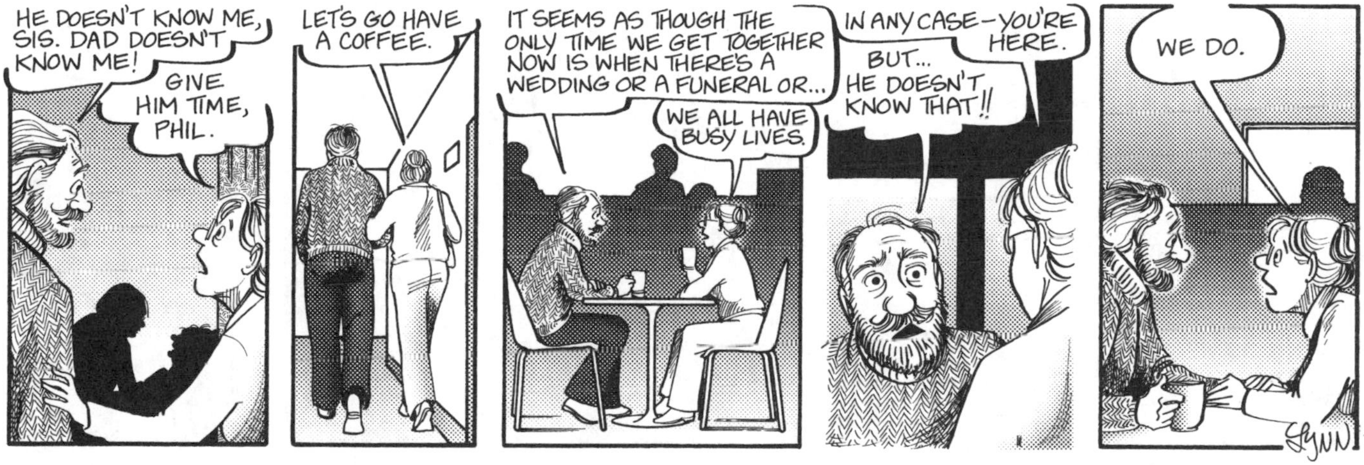
HE DOESN'T KNOW ME, SIS. DAD DOESN'T KNOW ME!
GIVE HIM TIME, PHIL.
LET'S GO HAVE A COFFEE.
IT SEEMS AS THOUGH THE ONLY TIME WE GET TOGETHER NOW IS WHEN THERE'S A WEDDING OR A FUNERAL OR...
WE ALL HAVE BUSY LIVES.
IN ANY CASE–YOU'RE HERE.
BUT... HE DOESN'T KNOW THAT!!
WE DO.
LYNN

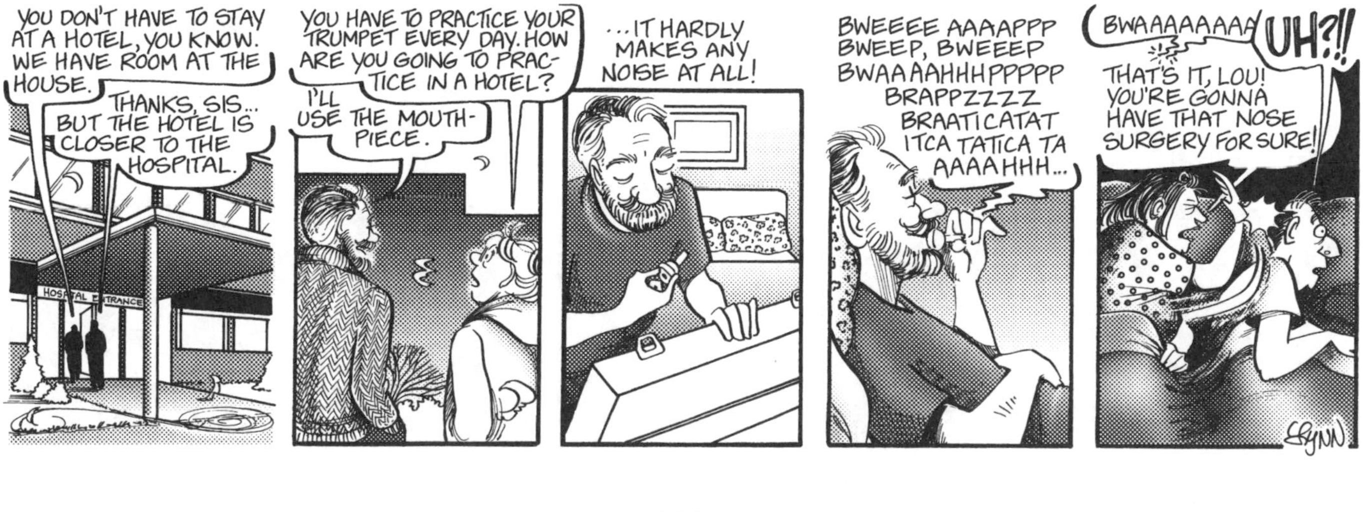
YOU DON'T HAVE TO STAY AT A HOTEL, YOU KNOW. WE HAVE ROOM AT THE HOUSE.
THANKS, SIS... BUT THE HOTEL IS CLOSER TO THE HOSPITAL.
HOSPITAL ENTRANCE
YOU HAVE TO PRACTICE YOUR TRUMPET EVERY DAY. HOW ARE YOU GOING TO PRACTICE IN A HOTEL?
I'LL USE THE MOUTHPIECE.
...IT HARDLY MAKES ANY NOISE AT ALL!
BWEEEE AAAAPPP BWEEP, BWEEEP BWAAAAHHHPPPPP BRAPPZZZZ BRAATICATAT ITCA TATICA TA AAAAHHH...
BWAAAAAAAA
UH?!!
THAT'S IT, LOU! YOU'RE GONNA HAVE THAT NOSE SURGERY FOR SURE!
LYNN

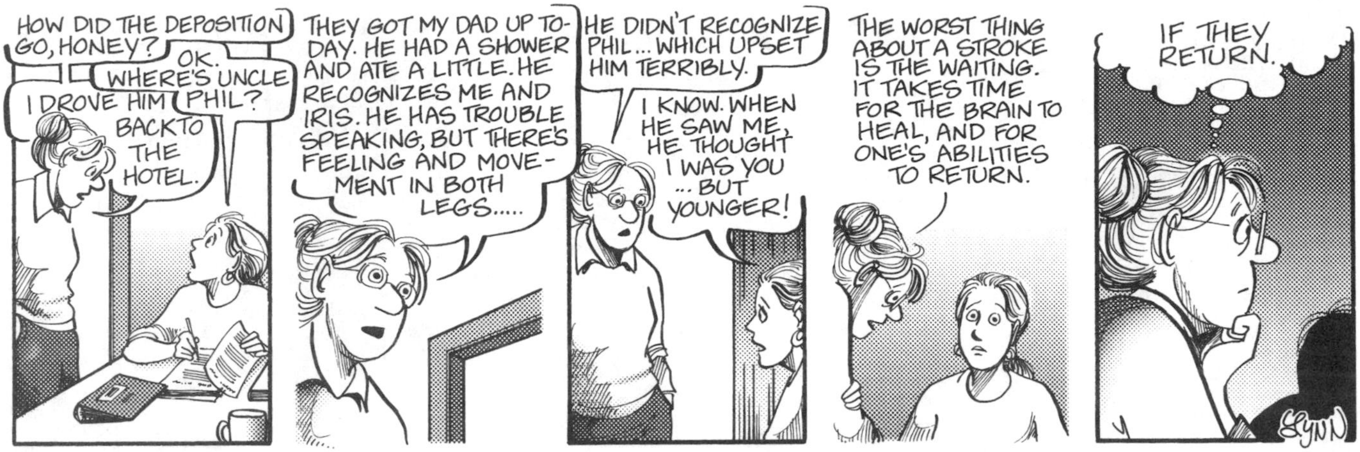
HOW DID THE DEPOSITION GO, HONEY?
OK.
WHERE'S UNCLE PHIL?
I DROVE HIM BACK TO THE HOTEL.
THEY GOT MY DAD UP TO-DAY. HE HAD A SHOWER AND ATE A LITTLE. HE RECOGNIZES ME AND IRIS. HE HAS TROUBLE SPEAKING, BUT THERE'S FEELING AND MOVE-MENT IN BOTH LEGS.....
HE DIDN'T RECOGNIZE PHIL... WHICH UPSET HIM TERRIBLY.
I KNOW. WHEN HE SAW ME, HE THOUGHT I WAS YOU ... BUT YOUNGER!
THE WORST THING ABOUT A STROKE IS THE WAITING. IT TAKES TIME FOR THE BRAIN TO HEAL, AND FOR ONE'S ABILITIES TO RETURN.
IF THEY RETURN.

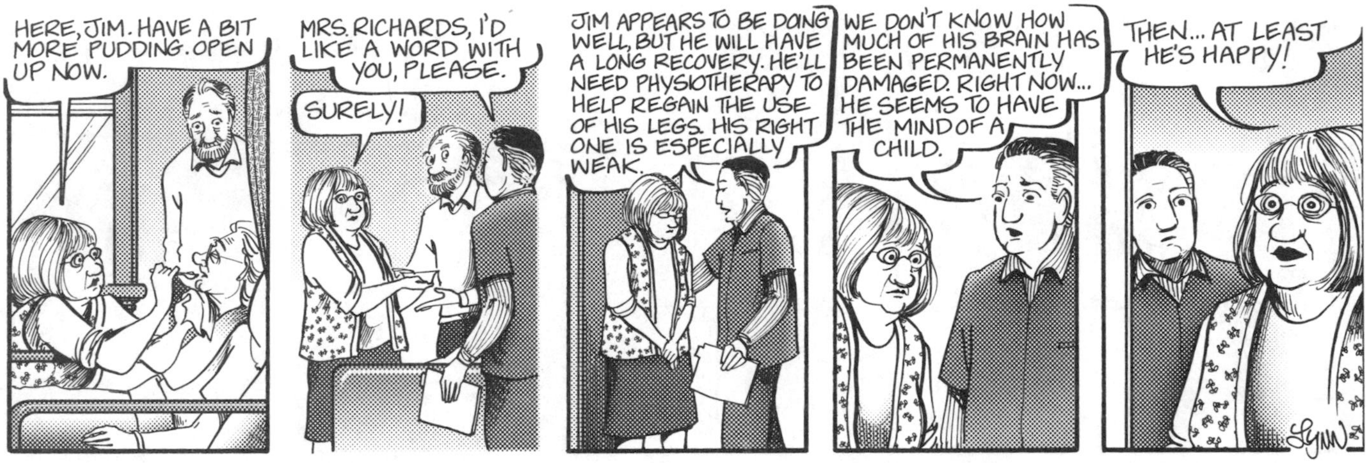
HERE, JIM. HAVE A BIT MORE PUDDING. OPEN UP NOW.
MRS. RICHARDS, I'D LIKE A WORD WITH YOU, PLEASE.
SURELY!
JIM APPEARS TO BE DOING WELL, BUT HE WILL HAVE A LONG RECOVERY. HE'LL NEED PHYSIOTHERAPY TO HELP REGAIN THE USE OF HIS LEGS. HIS RIGHT ONE IS ESPECIALLY WEAK.
WE DON'T KNOW HOW MUCH OF HIS BRAIN HAS BEEN PERMANENTLY DAMAGED. RIGHT NOW... HE SEEMS TO HAVE THE MIND OF A CHILD.
THEN... AT LEAST HE'S HAPPY!

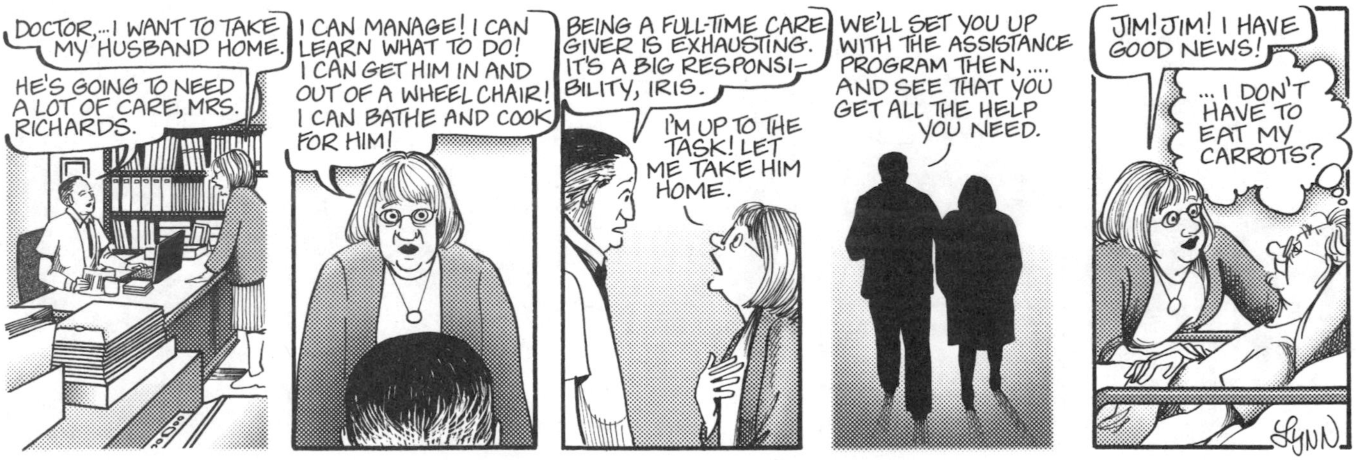
DOCTOR,... I WANT TO TAKE MY HUSBAND HOME.
HE'S GOING TO NEED A LOT OF CARE, MRS. RICHARDS.
I CAN MANAGE! I CAN LEARN WHAT TO DO! I CAN GET HIM IN AND OUT OF A WHEEL CHAIR! I CAN BATHE AND COOK FOR HIM!
BEING A FULL-TIME CARE GIVER IS EXHAUSTING. IT'S A BIG RESPONSI-BILITY, IRIS.
I'M UP TO THE TASK! LET ME TAKE HIM HOME.
WE'LL SET YOU UP WITH THE ASSISTANCE PROGRAM THEN, ... AND SEE THAT YOU GET ALL THE HELP YOU NEED.
JIM! JIM! I HAVE GOOD NEWS!
... I DON'T HAVE TO EAT MY CARROTS?

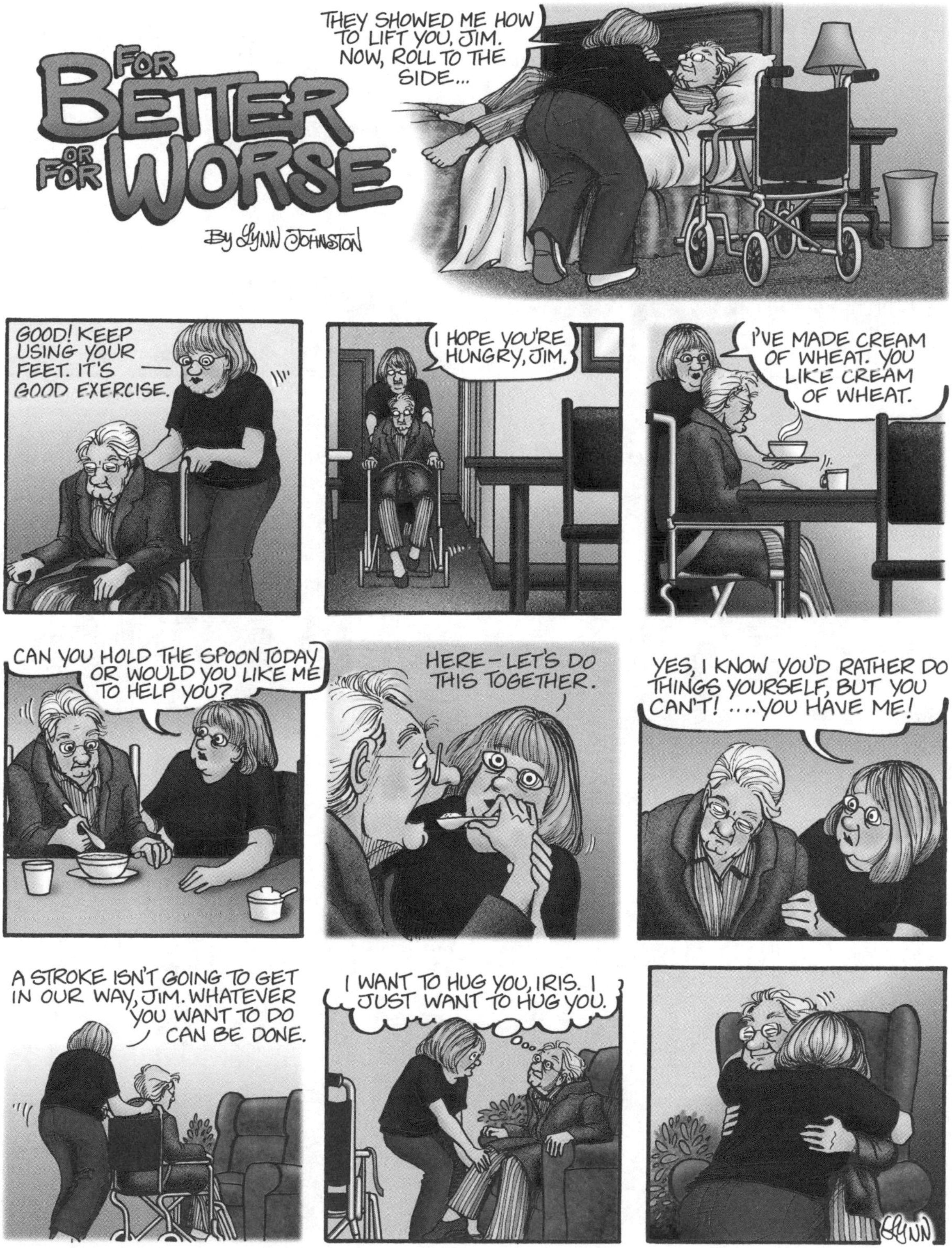
FOR BETTER OR FOR WORSE
By Lynn Johnston
THEY SHOWED ME HOW TO LIFT YOU, JIM. NOW, ROLL TO THE SIDE...
GOOD! KEEP USING YOUR FEET. IT'S GOOD EXERCISE.
I HOPE YOU'RE HUNGRY, JIM.
I'VE MADE CREAM OF WHEAT. YOU LIKE CREAM OF WHEAT.
CAN YOU HOLD THE SPOON TODAY OR WOULD YOU LIKE ME TO HELP YOU?
HERE–LET'S DO THIS TOGETHER.
YES, I KNOW YOU'D RATHER DO THINGS YOURSELF, BUT YOU CAN'T! ....YOU HAVE ME!
A STROKE ISN'T GOING TO GET IN OUR WAY, JIM. WHATEVER YOU WANT TO DO CAN BE DONE.
I WANT TO HUG YOU, IRIS. I JUST WANT TO HUG YOU.
LYNN

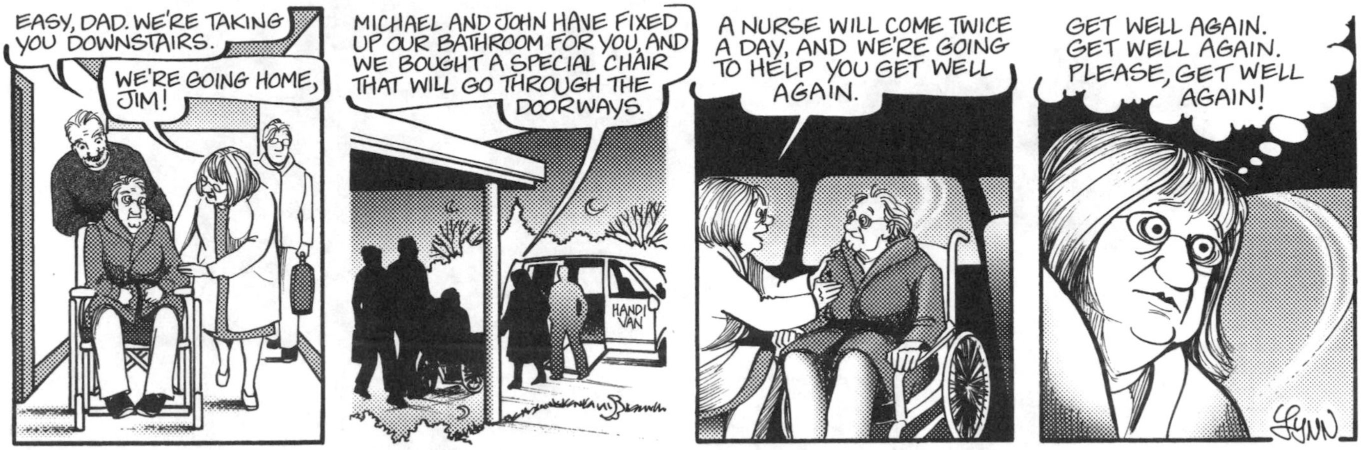
EASY, DAD. WE'RE TAKING YOU DOWNSTAIRS.
WE'RE GOING HOME, JIM!
MICHAEL AND JOHN HAVE FIXED UP OUR BATHROOM FOR YOU, AND WE BOUGHT A SPECIAL CHAIR THAT WILL GO THROUGH THE DOORWAYS.
HANDI VAN
A NURSE WILL COME TWICE A DAY, AND WE'RE GOING TO HELP YOU GET WELL AGAIN.
GET WELL AGAIN. GET WELL AGAIN. PLEASE, GET WELL AGAIN!
LYNN

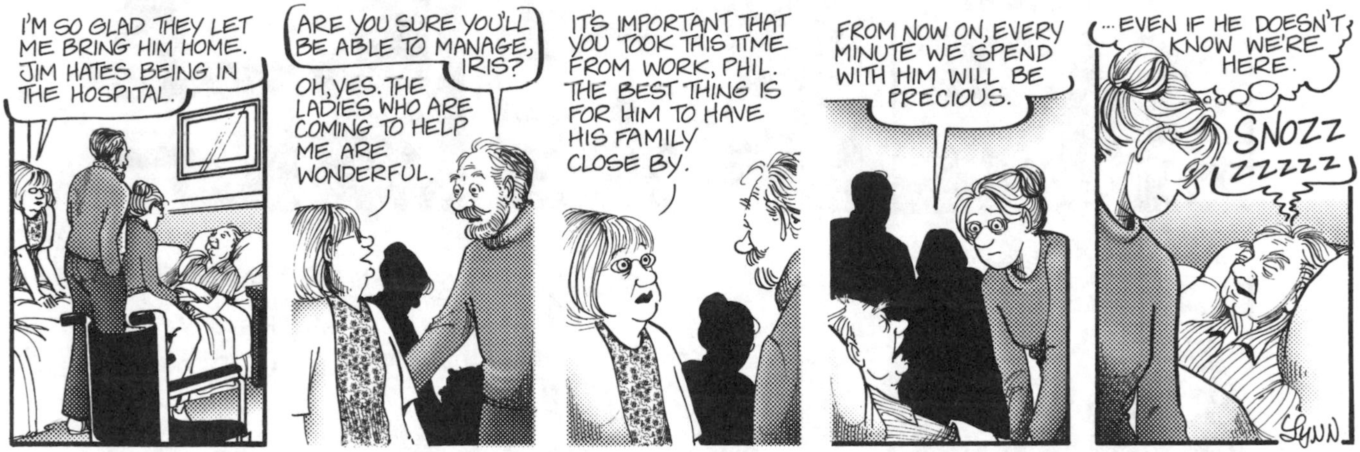
I'M SO GLAD THEY LET ME BRING HIM HOME. JIM HATES BEING IN THE HOSPITAL.
ARE YOU SURE YOU'LL BE ABLE TO MANAGE, IRIS?
OH, YES. THE LADIES WHO ARE COMING TO HELP ME ARE WONDERFUL.
IT'S IMPORTANT THAT YOU TOOK THIS TIME FROM WORK, PHIL. THE BEST THING IS FOR HIM TO HAVE HIS FAMILY CLOSE BY.
FROM NOW ON, EVERY MINUTE WE SPEND WITH HIM WILL BE PRECIOUS.
...EVEN IF HE DOESN'T KNOW WE'RE HERE.
SNOZZ
ZZZZZ
LYNN

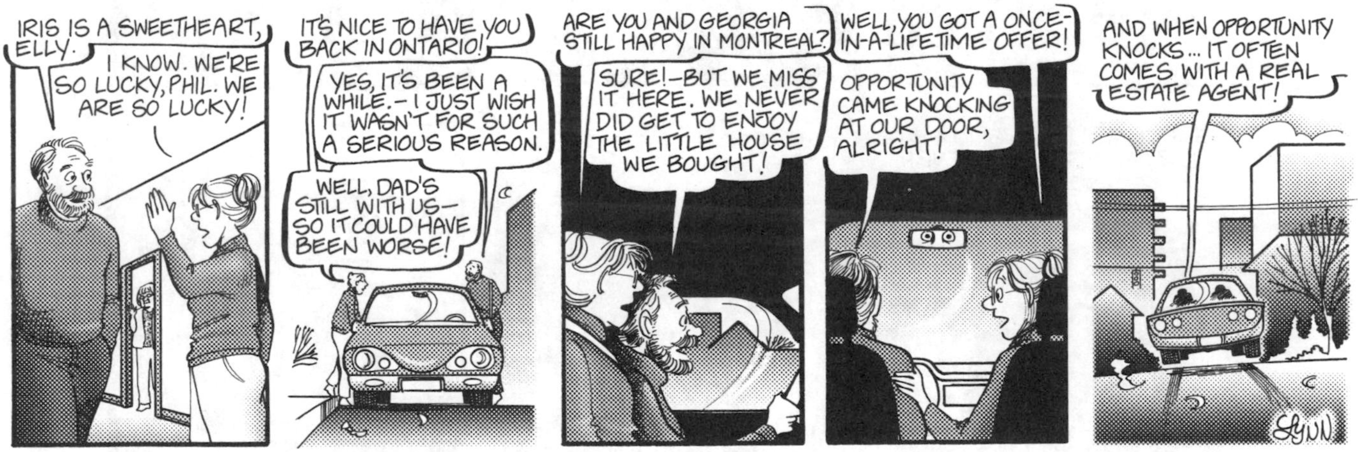
IRIS IS A SWEETHEART, ELLY.
I KNOW. WE'RE SO LUCKY, PHIL. WE ARE SO LUCKY!
IT'S NICE TO HAVE YOU BACK IN ONTARIO!
YES, IT'S BEEN A WHILE.– I JUST WISH IT WASN'T FOR SUCH A SERIOUS REASON.
WELL, DAD'S STILL WITH US– SO IT COULD HAVE BEEN WORSE!
ARE YOU AND GEORGIA STILL HAPPY IN MONTREAL?
SURE!–BUT WE MISS IT HERE. WE NEVER DID GET TO ENJOY THE LITTLE HOUSE WE BOUGHT!
WELL, YOU GOT A ONCE-IN-A-LIFETIME OFFER!
OPPORTUNITY CAME KNOCKING AT OUR DOOR, ALRIGHT!
AND WHEN OPPORTUNITY KNOCKS... IT OFTEN COMES WITH A REAL ESTATE AGENT!
LYNN

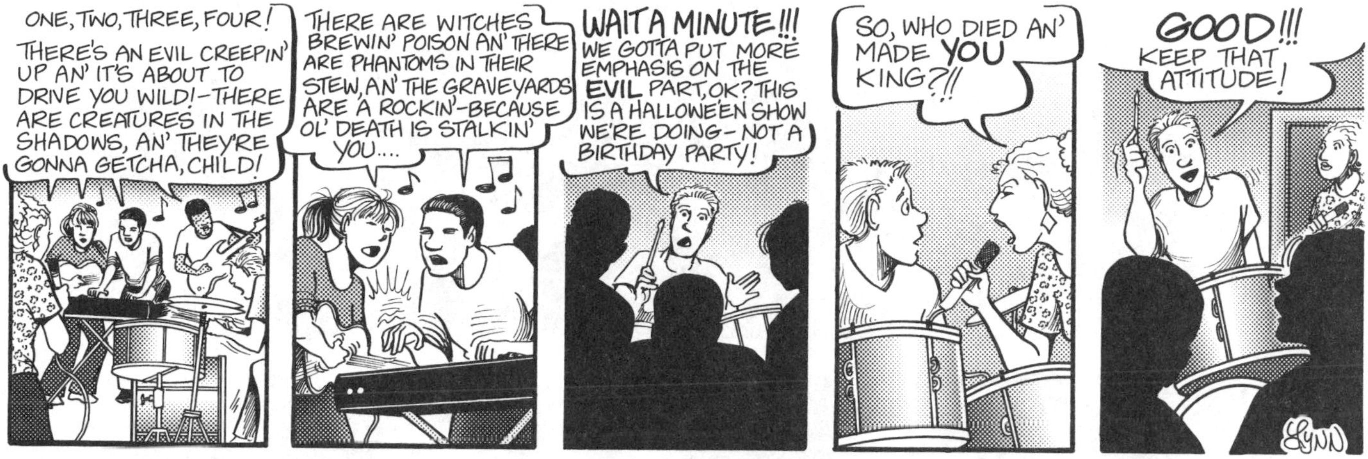
ONE, TWO, THREE, FOUR!
THERE'S AN EVIL CREEPIN' UP AN' IT'S ABOUT TO DRIVE YOU WILD! – THERE ARE CREATURES IN THE SHADOWS, AN' THEY'RE GONNA GETCHA, CHILD!
THERE ARE WITCHES BREWIN' POISON AN' THERE ARE PHANTOMS IN THEIR STEW, AN' THE GRAVEYARDS ARE A ROCKIN' – BECAUSE OL' DEATH IS STALKIN' YOU....
WAIT A MINUTE!!! WE GOTTA PUT MORE EMPHASIS ON THE EVIL PART, OK? THIS IS A HALLOWE'EN SHOW WE'RE DOING – NOT A BIRTHDAY PARTY!
SO, WHO DIED AN' MADE YOU KING?!!
GOOD!!! KEEP THAT ATTITUDE!
LYNN

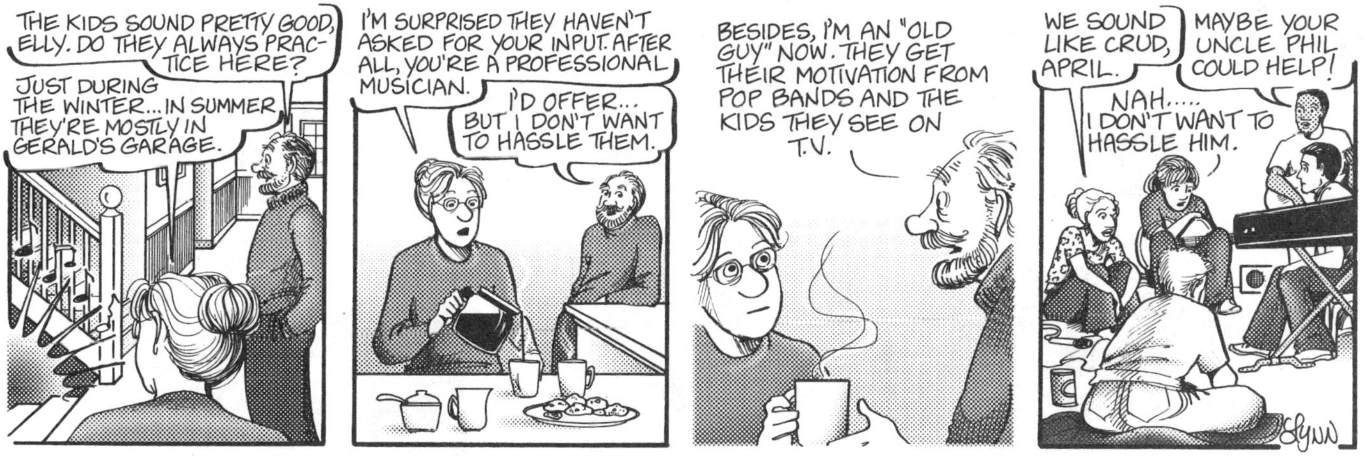
THE KIDS SOUND PRETTY GOOD, ELLY. DO THEY ALWAYS PRACTICE HERE?
JUST DURING THE WINTER... IN SUMMER THEY'RE MOSTLY IN GERALD'S GARAGE.
I'M SURPRISED THEY HAVEN'T ASKED FOR YOUR INPUT. AFTER ALL, YOU'RE A PROFESSIONAL MUSICIAN.
I'D OFFER... BUT I DON'T WANT TO HASSLE THEM.
BESIDES, I'M AN "OLD GUY" NOW. THEY GET THEIR MOTIVATION FROM POP BANDS AND THE KIDS THEY SEE ON T.V.
WE SOUND LIKE CRUD, APRIL.
MAYBE YOUR UNCLE PHIL COULD HELP!
NAH..... I DON'T WANT TO HASSLE HIM.
LYNN

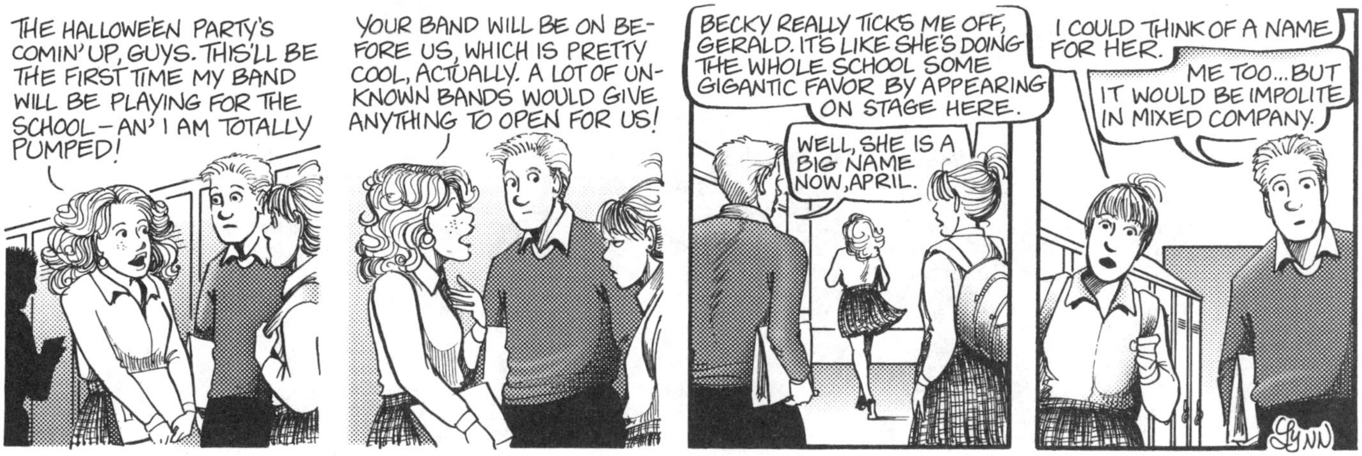
THE HALLOWE'EN PARTY'S COMIN' UP, GUYS. THIS'LL BE THE FIRST TIME MY BAND WILL BE PLAYING FOR THE SCHOOL – AN' I AM TOTALLY PUMPED!
YOUR BAND WILL BE ON BEFORE US, WHICH IS PRETTY COOL, ACTUALLY. A LOT OF UNKNOWN BANDS WOULD GIVE ANYTHING TO OPEN FOR US!
BECKY REALLY TICKS ME OFF, GERALD. IT'S LIKE SHE'S DOING THE WHOLE SCHOOL SOME GIGANTIC FAVOR BY APPEARING ON STAGE HERE.
WELL, SHE IS A BIG NAME NOW, APRIL.
I COULD THINK OF A NAME FOR HER.
ME TOO... BUT IT WOULD BE IMPOLITE IN MIXED COMPANY.
LYNN

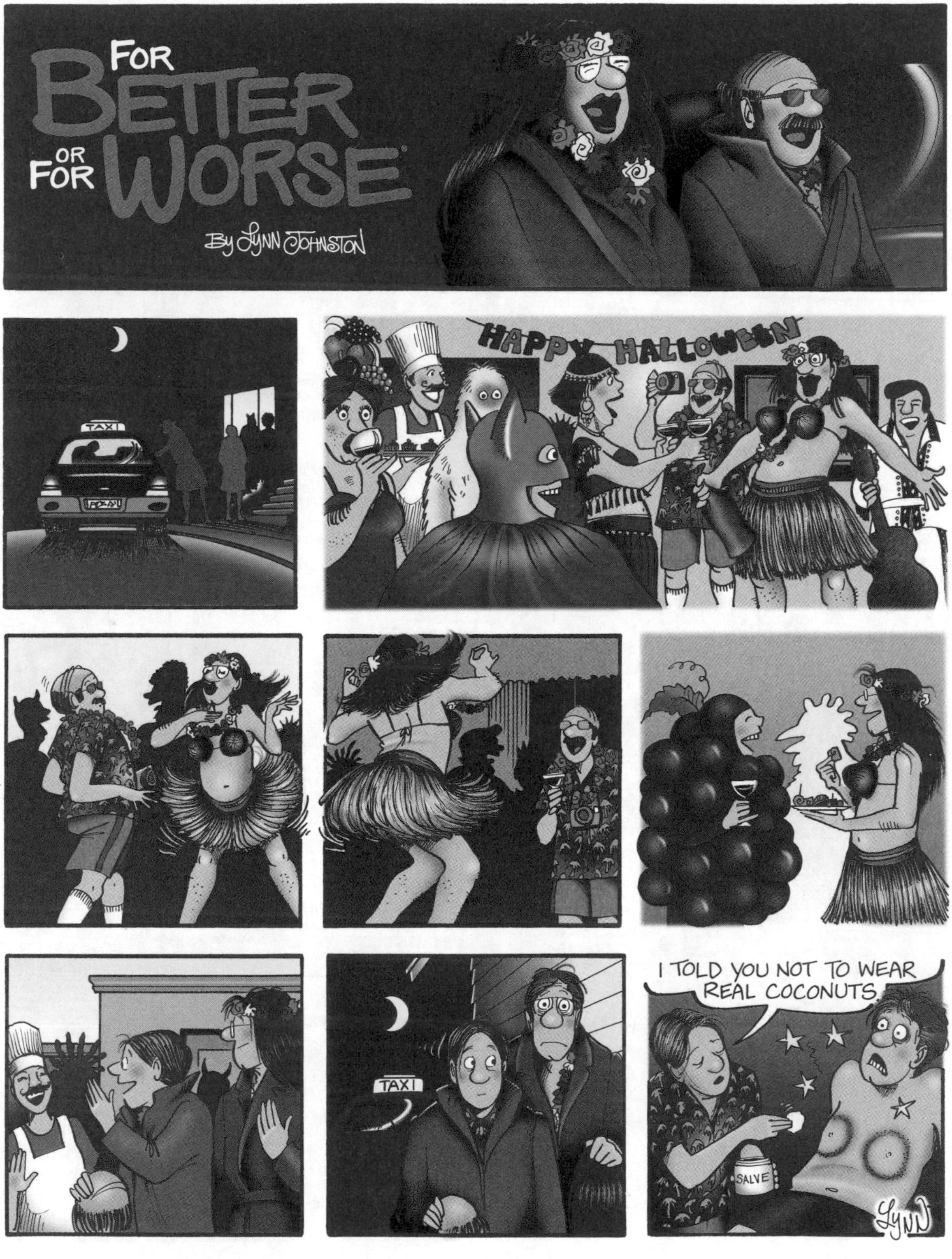
FOR BETTER OR FOR WORSE
BY LYNN JOHNSTON
TAXI
HAPPY HALLOWEEN
TAXI
I TOLD YOU NOT TO WEAR REAL COCONUTS.
SALVE
LYNN

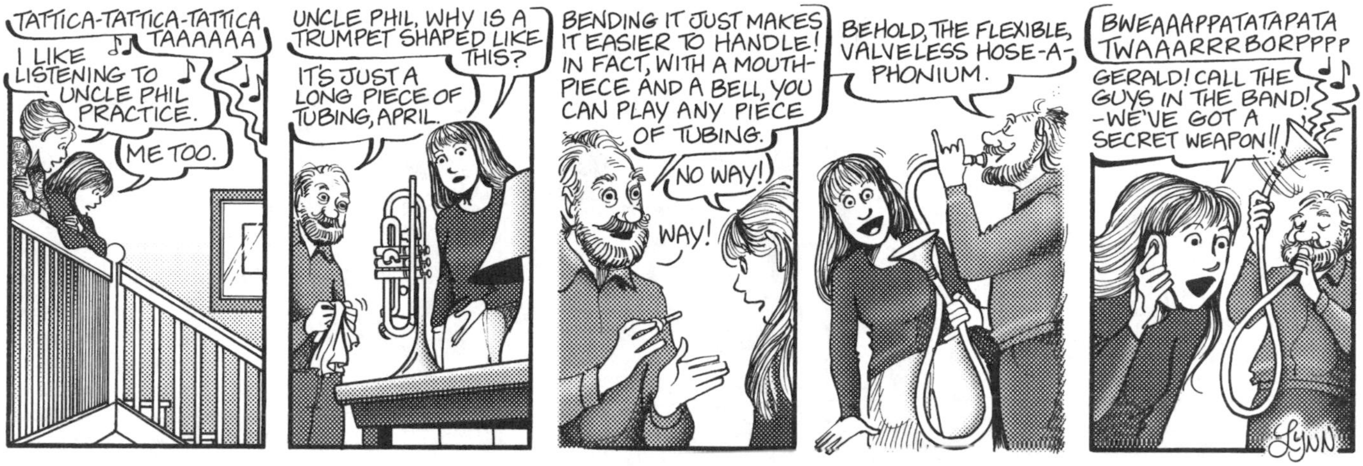
TATTICA-TATTICA-TATTICA TAAAAAA
I LIKE LISTENING TO UNCLE PHIL PRACTICE.
ME TOO.
UNCLE PHIL, WHY IS A TRUMPET SHAPED LIKE THIS?
IT'S JUST A LONG PIECE OF TUBING, APRIL.
BENDING IT JUST MAKES IT EASIER TO HANDLE! IN FACT, WITH A MOUTH-PIECE AND A BELL, YOU CAN PLAY ANY PIECE OF TUBING.
NO WAY!
WAY!
BEHOLD, THE FLEXIBLE, VALVELESS HOSE-A-PHONIUM.
BWEAAAPPATATAPATA TWAAARRRBORPPPP
GERALD! CALL THE GUYS IN THE BAND! -WE'VE GOT A SECRET WEAPON!!
LYNN

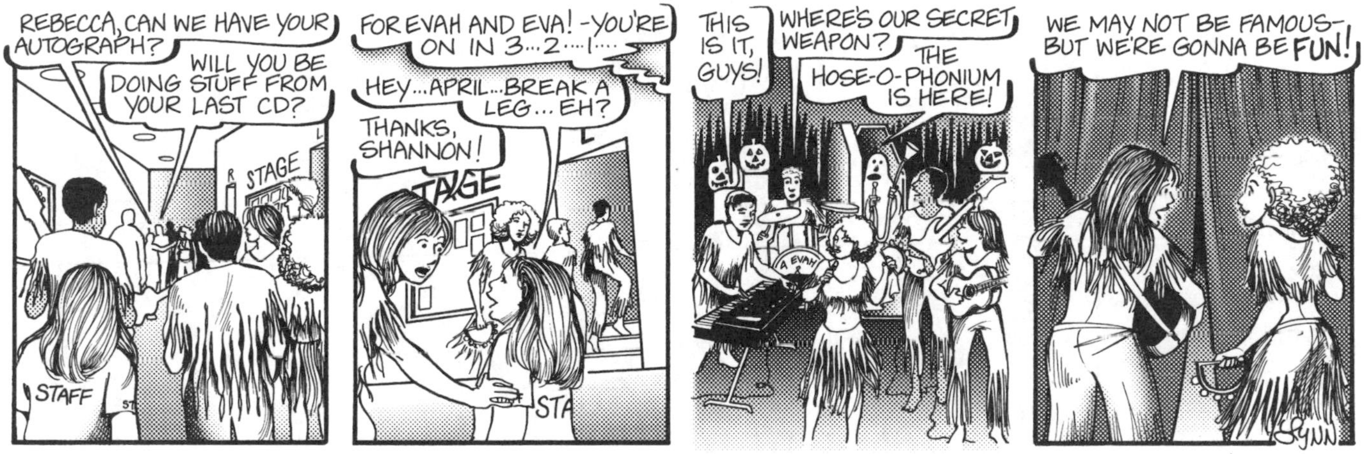
REBECCA, CAN WE HAVE YOUR AUTOGRAPH?
WILL YOU BE DOING STUFF FROM YOUR LAST CD?
STAGE
STAFF
FOR EVAH AND EVA! -YOU'RE ON IN 3...2...1....
HEY...APRIL...BREAK A LEG...EH?
THANKS, SHANNON!
STAGE
THIS IS IT, GUYS!
WHERE'S OUR SECRET WEAPON?
THE HOSE-O-PHONIUM IS HERE!
WE MAY NOT BE FAMOUS- BUT WE'RE GONNA BE FUN!
LYNN

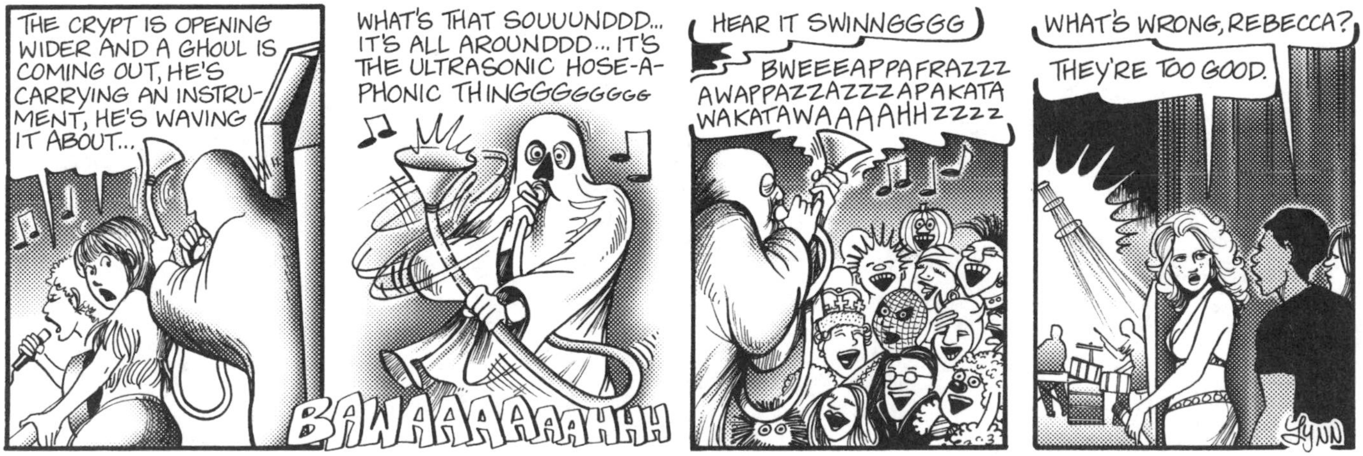
THE CRYPT IS OPENING WIDER AND A GHOUL IS COMING OUT, HE'S CARRYING AN INSTRU-MENT, HE'S WAVING IT ABOUT...
WHAT'S THAT SOUUUNDDD... IT'S ALL AROUNDDD... IT'S THE ULTRASONIC HOSE-A-PHONIC THINGGGGGGGG
BAWAAAAAAAHHH
HEAR IT SWINNGGGG
BWEEEAPPAFRAZZZ AWAPPAZZAZZZAPAKATA WAKATAWAAAAHHZZZZ
WHAT'S WRONG, REBECCA?
THEY'RE TOO GOOD.
LYNN

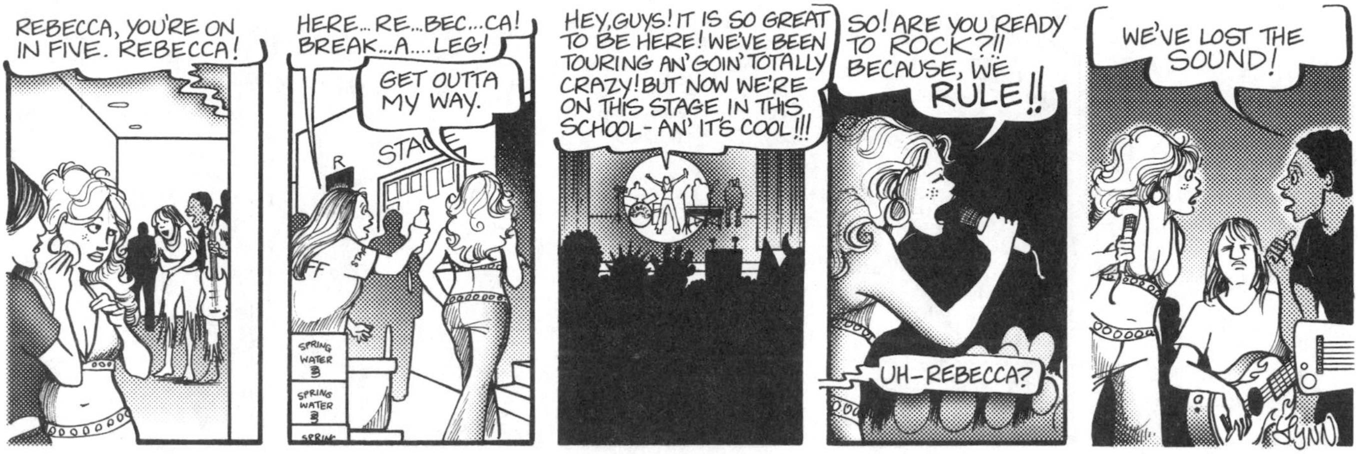
REBECCA, YOU'RE ON IN FIVE. REBECCA!
HERE... RE...BEC...CA! BREAK...A....LEG!
GET OUTTA MY WAY.
HEY, GUYS! IT IS SO GREAT TO BE HERE! WE'VE BEEN TOURING AN' GOIN' TOTALLY CRAZY! BUT NOW WE'RE ON THIS STAGE IN THIS SCHOOL- AN' IT'S COOL!!!
SO! ARE YOU READY TO ROCK?!! BECAUSE, WE RULE!!
UH-REBECCA?
WE'VE LOST THE SOUND!
LYNN

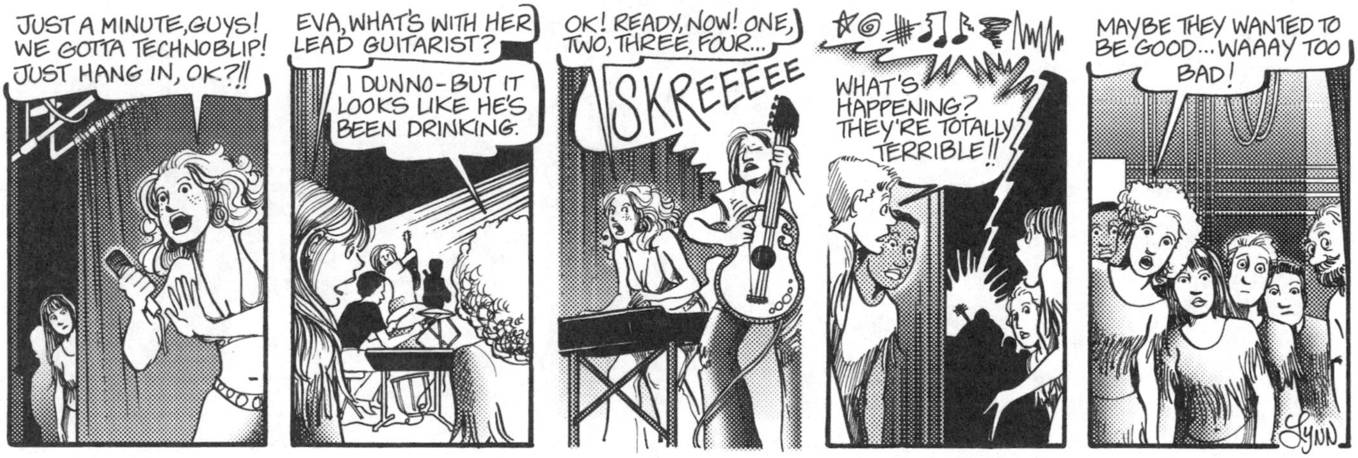
JUST A MINUTE, GUYS! WE GOTTA TECHNOBLIP! JUST HANG IN, OK?!!
EVA, WHAT'S WITH HER LEAD GUITARIST?
I DUNNO- BUT IT LOOKS LIKE HE'S BEEN DRINKING.
OK! READY, NOW! ONE, TWO, THREE, FOUR...
SKREEEEEE
WHAT'S HAPPENING? THEY'RE TOTALLY TERRIBLE!!
MAYBE THEY WANTED TO BE GOOD... WAAAY TOO BAD!
LYNN

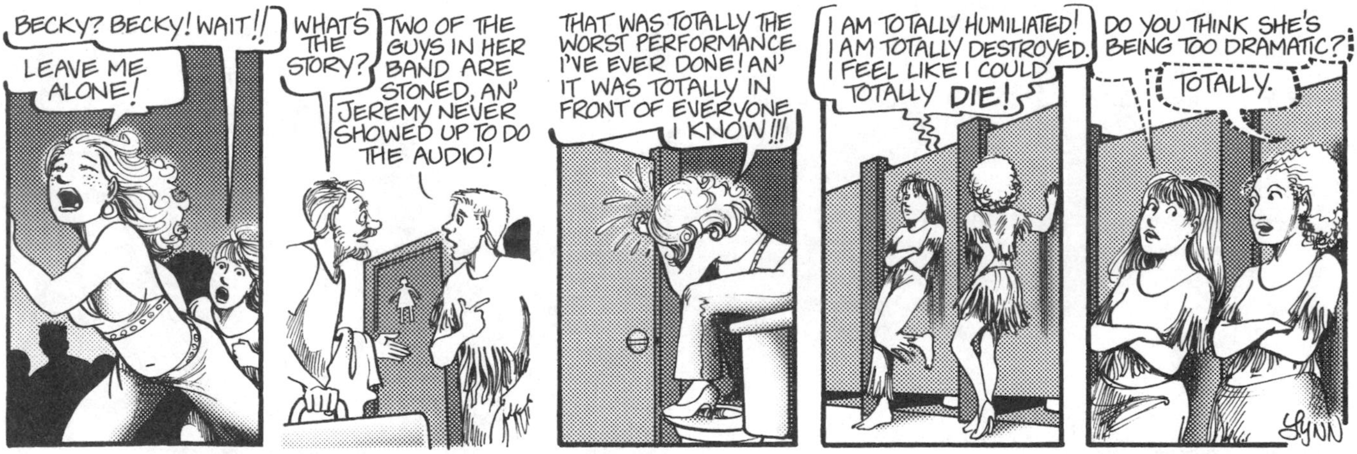
BECKY? BECKY! WAIT!!
LEAVE ME ALONE!
WHAT'S THE STORY?
TWO OF THE GUYS IN HER BAND ARE STONED, AN' JEREMY NEVER SHOWED UP TO DO THE AUDIO!
THAT WAS TOTALLY THE WORST PERFORMANCE I'VE EVER DONE! AN' IT WAS TOTALLY IN FRONT OF EVERYONE I KNOW!!!
I AM TOTALLY HUMILIATED! I AM TOTALLY DESTROYED. I FEEL LIKE I COULD TOTALLY DIE!
DO YOU THINK SHE'S BEING TOO DRAMATIC?!
TOTALLY.
LYNN

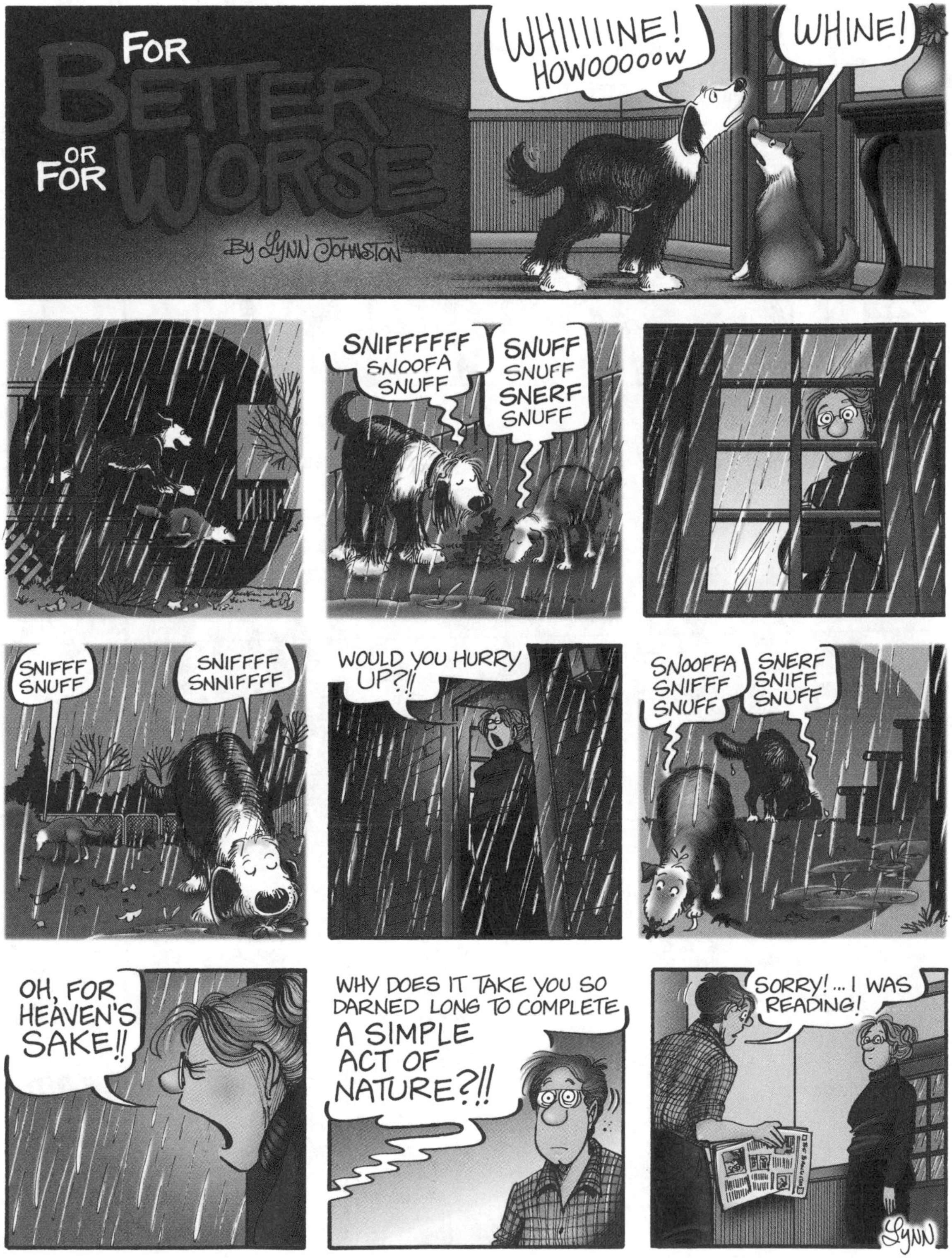
FOR BETTER OR FOR WORSE
BY LYNN JOHNSTON
WHIIIIIINE! HOWOOOOOW
WHINE!
SNIFFFFFF SNOOFA SNUFF
SNUFF SNUFF SNERF SNUFF
SNIFFF SNUFF
SNIFFFF SNNIFFFF
WOULD YOU HURRY UP?!!
SNOOFFA SNIFFF SNUFF
SNERF SNIFF SNUFF
OH, FOR HEAVEN'S SAKE!!
WHY DOES IT TAKE YOU SO DARNED LONG TO COMPLETE A SIMPLE ACT OF NATURE?!!
SORRY! ... I WAS READING!
LYNN

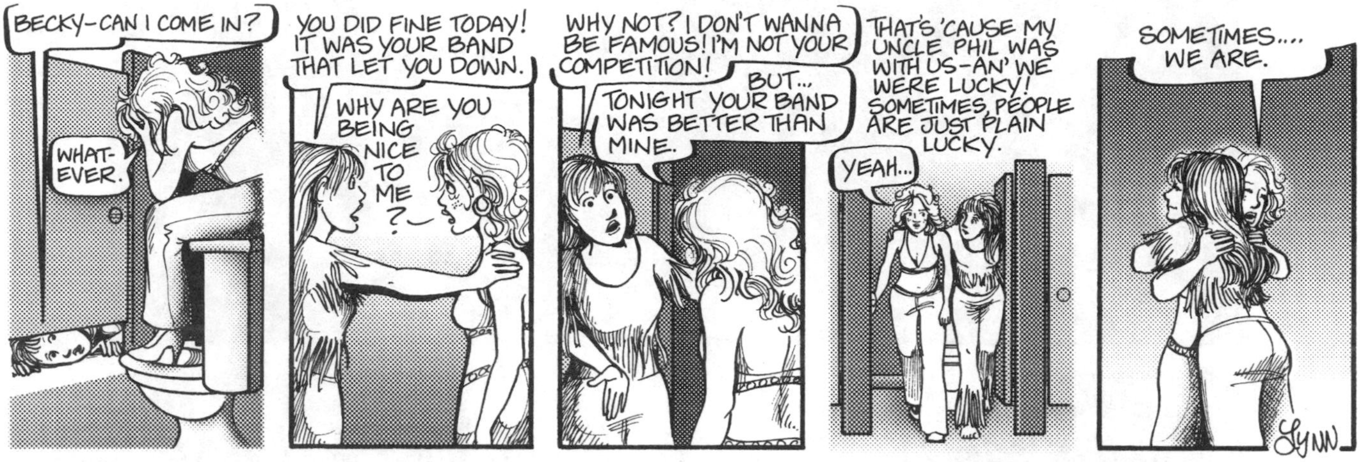
BECKY–CAN I COME IN?
WHAT-EVER.
YOU DID FINE TODAY! IT WAS YOUR BAND THAT LET YOU DOWN.
WHY ARE YOU BEING NICE TO ME?
WHY NOT? I DON'T WANNA BE FAMOUS! I'M NOT YOUR COMPETITION!
BUT... TONIGHT YOUR BAND WAS BETTER THAN MINE.
THAT'S 'CAUSE MY UNCLE PHIL WAS WITH US–AN' WE WERE LUCKY! SOMETIMES, PEOPLE ARE JUST PLAIN LUCKY.
YEAH...
SOMETIMES.... WE ARE.
LYNN

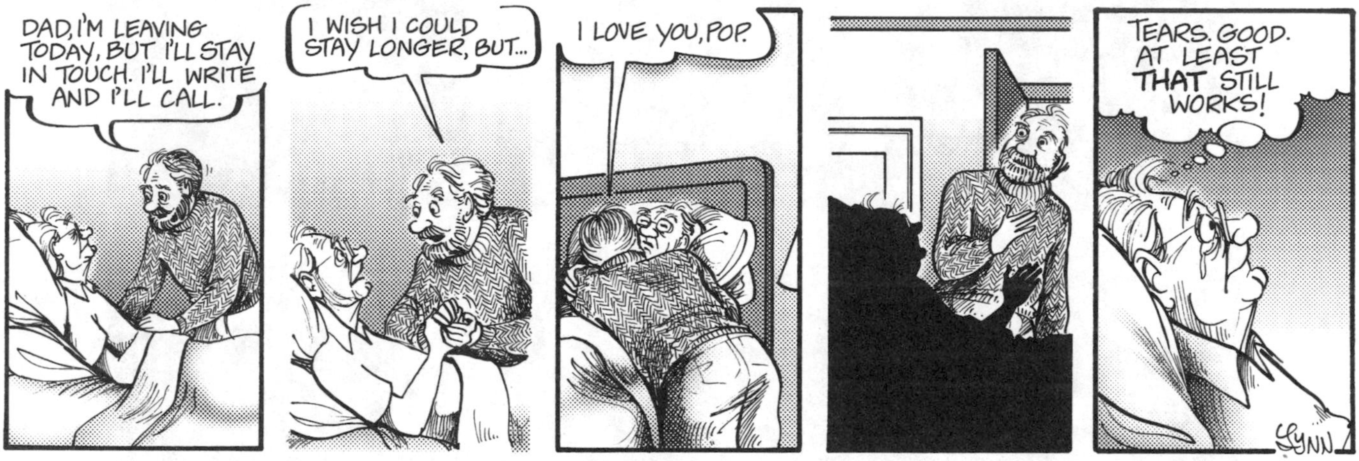
DAD, I'M LEAVING TODAY, BUT I'LL STAY IN TOUCH. I'LL WRITE AND I'LL CALL.
I WISH I COULD STAY LONGER, BUT...
I LOVE YOU, POP.
TEARS. GOOD. AT LEAST THAT STILL WORKS!
LYNN

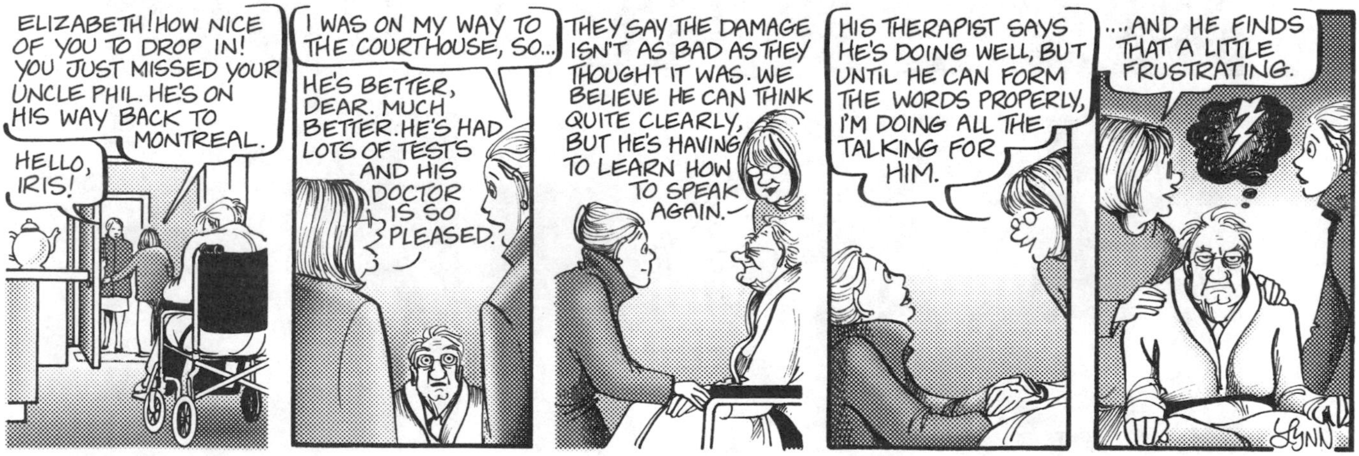
ELIZABETH! HOW NICE OF YOU TO DROP IN! YOU JUST MISSED YOUR UNCLE PHIL. HE'S ON HIS WAY BACK TO MONTREAL.
HELLO, IRIS!
I WAS ON MY WAY TO THE COURTHOUSE, SO...
HE'S BETTER, DEAR. MUCH BETTER. HE'S HAD LOTS OF TESTS AND HIS DOCTOR IS SO PLEASED.
THEY SAY THE DAMAGE ISN'T AS BAD AS THEY THOUGHT IT WAS. WE BELIEVE HE CAN THINK QUITE CLEARLY, BUT HE'S HAVING TO LEARN HOW TO SPEAK AGAIN.
HIS THERAPIST SAYS HE'S DOING WELL, BUT UNTIL HE CAN FORM THE WORDS PROPERLY, I'M DOING ALL THE TALKING FOR HIM.
....AND HE FINDS THAT A LITTLE FRUSTRATING.
LYNN

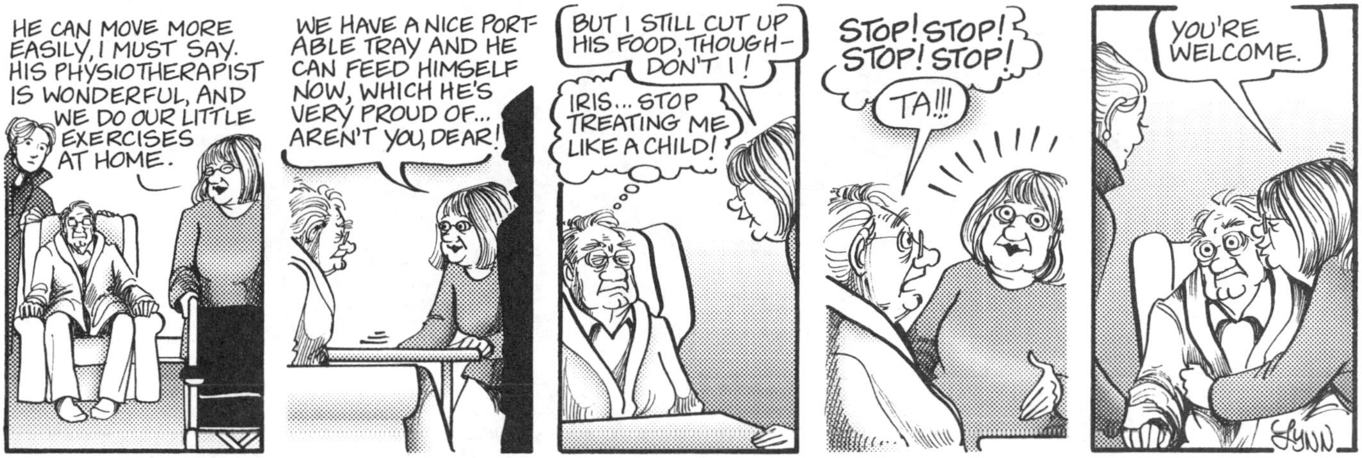
HE CAN MOVE MORE EASILY, I MUST SAY. HIS PHYSIOTHERAPIST IS WONDERFUL, AND WE DO OUR LITTLE EXERCISES AT HOME.
WE HAVE A NICE PORTABLE TRAY AND HE CAN FEED HIMSELF NOW, WHICH HE'S VERY PROUD OF... AREN'T YOU, DEAR!
BUT I STILL CUT UP HIS FOOD, THOUGH - DON'T I!
IRIS... STOP TREATING ME LIKE A CHILD!
STOP! STOP! STOP! STOP!
TA!!!
YOU'RE WELCOME.
LYNN

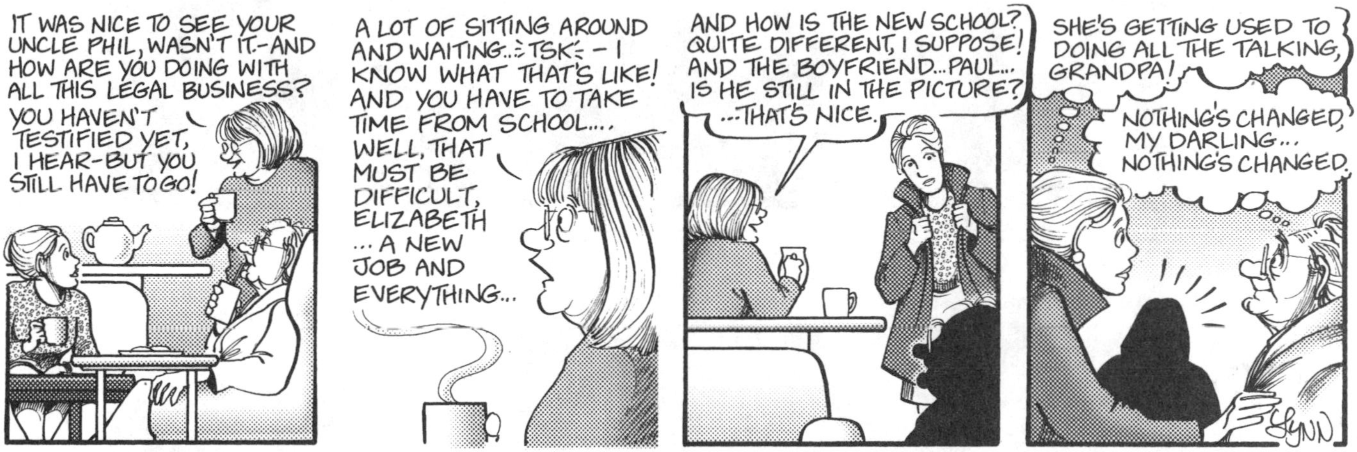
IT WAS NICE TO SEE YOUR UNCLE PHIL, WASN'T IT.- AND HOW ARE YOU DOING WITH ALL THIS LEGAL BUSINESS? YOU HAVEN'T TESTIFIED YET, I HEAR - BUT YOU STILL HAVE TO GO!
A LOT OF SITTING AROUND AND WAITING.. TSK - I KNOW WHAT THAT'S LIKE! AND YOU HAVE TO TAKE TIME FROM SCHOOL.... WELL, THAT MUST BE DIFFICULT, ELIZABETH ... A NEW JOB AND EVERYTHING...
AND HOW IS THE NEW SCHOOL? QUITE DIFFERENT, I SUPPOSE! AND THE BOYFRIEND... PAUL... IS HE STILL IN THE PICTURE? ...THAT'S NICE.
SHE'S GETTING USED TO DOING ALL THE TALKING, GRANDPA!
NOTHING'S CHANGED, MY DARLING... NOTHING'S CHANGED.
LYNN

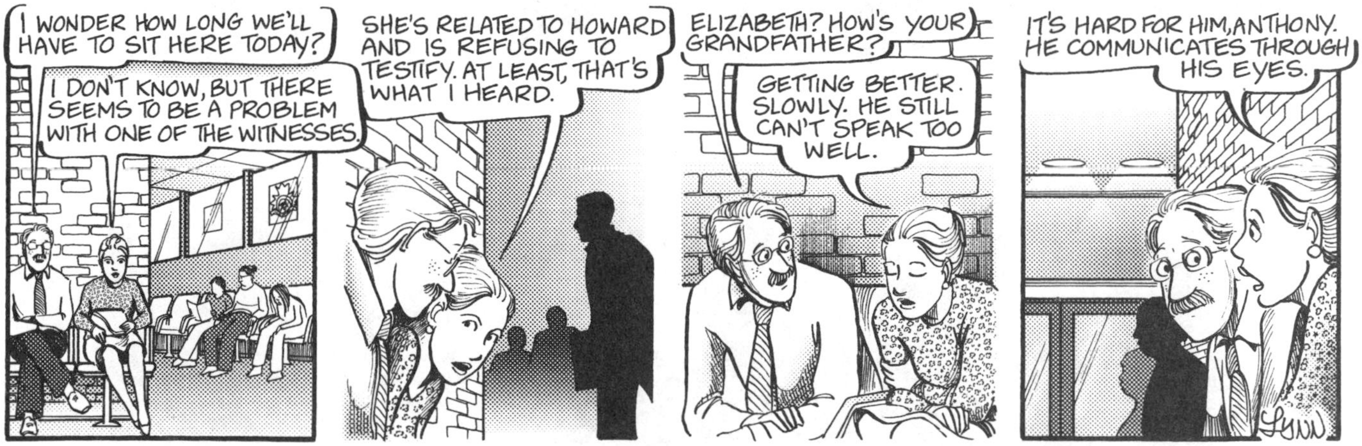
I WONDER HOW LONG WE'LL HAVE TO SIT HERE TODAY?
I DON'T KNOW, BUT THERE SEEMS TO BE A PROBLEM WITH ONE OF THE WITNESSES.
SHE'S RELATED TO HOWARD AND IS REFUSING TO TESTIFY. AT LEAST, THAT'S WHAT I HEARD.
ELIZABETH? HOW'S YOUR GRANDFATHER?
GETTING BETTER. SLOWLY. HE STILL CAN'T SPEAK TOO WELL.
IT'S HARD FOR HIM, ANTHONY. HE COMMUNICATES THROUGH HIS EYES.
LYNN

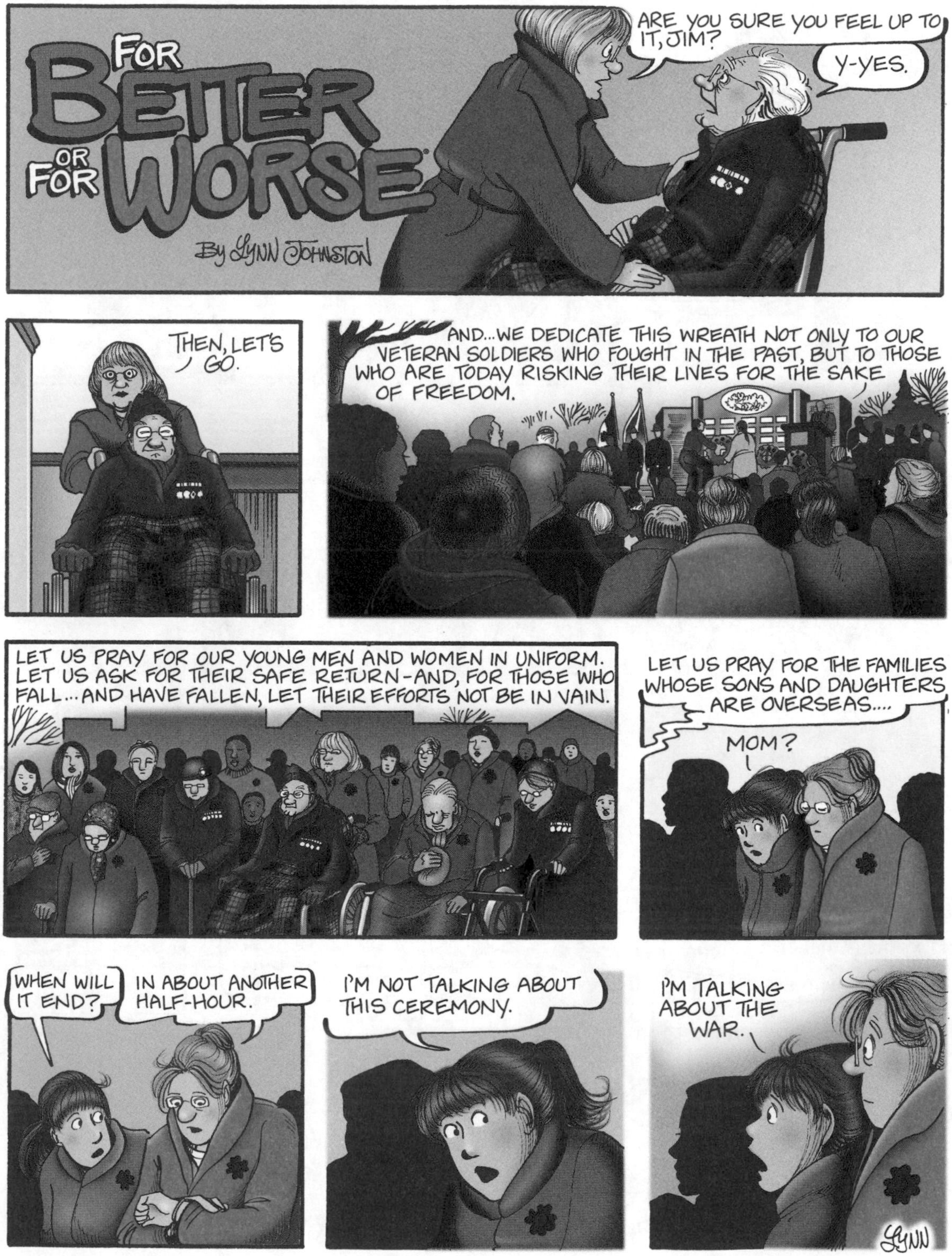
FOR BETTER OR FOR WORSE
BY LYNN JOHNSTON
ARE YOU SURE YOU FEEL UP TO IT, JIM?
Y-YES.
THEN, LET'S GO.
AND...WE DEDICATE THIS WREATH NOT ONLY TO OUR VETERAN SOLDIERS WHO FOUGHT IN THE PAST, BUT TO THOSE WHO ARE TODAY RISKING THEIR LIVES FOR THE SAKE OF FREEDOM.
LET US PRAY FOR OUR YOUNG MEN AND WOMEN IN UNIFORM. LET US ASK FOR THEIR SAFE RETURN-AND, FOR THOSE WHO FALL...AND HAVE FALLEN, LET THEIR EFFORTS NOT BE IN VAIN.
LET US PRAY FOR THE FAMILIES WHOSE SONS AND DAUGHTERS ARE OVERSEAS....
MOM?
WHEN WILL IT END?
IN ABOUT ANOTHER HALF-HOUR.
I'M NOT TALKING ABOUT THIS CEREMONY.
I'M TALKING ABOUT THE WAR.
LYNN

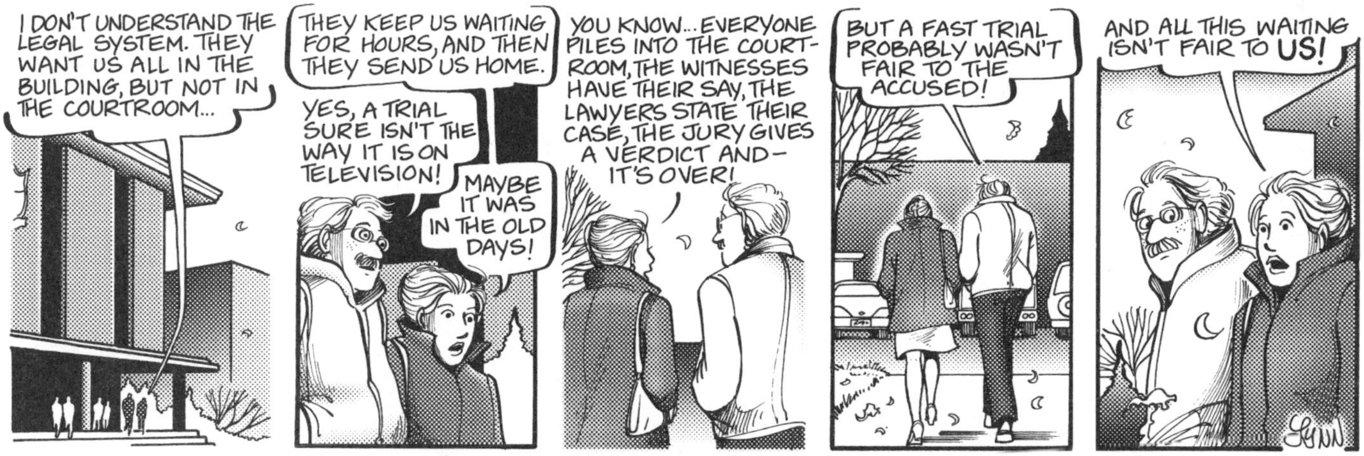
I DON'T UNDERSTAND THE LEGAL SYSTEM. THEY WANT US ALL IN THE BUILDING, BUT NOT IN THE COURTROOM...
THEY KEEP US WAITING FOR HOURS, AND THEN THEY SEND US HOME.
YES, A TRIAL SURE ISN'T THE WAY IT IS ON TELEVISION!
MAYBE IT WAS IN THE OLD DAYS!
YOU KNOW... EVERYONE PILES INTO THE COURTROOM, THE WITNESSES HAVE THEIR SAY, THE LAWYERS STATE THEIR CASE, THE JURY GIVES A VERDICT AND— IT'S OVER!
BUT A FAST TRIAL PROBABLY WASN'T FAIR TO THE ACCUSED!
AND ALL THIS WAITING ISN'T FAIR TO US!
LYNN

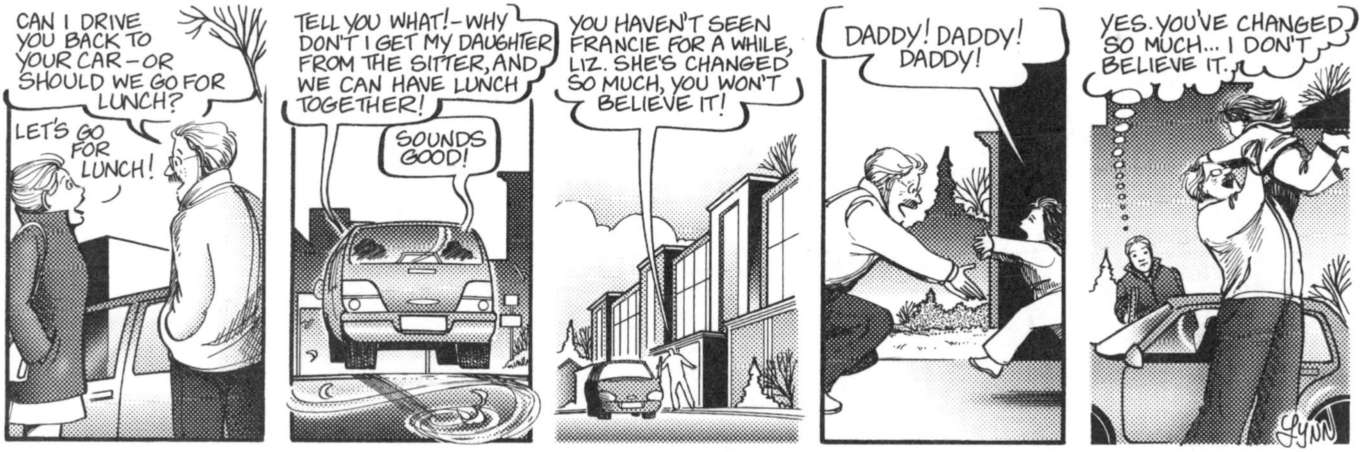
CAN I DRIVE YOU BACK TO YOUR CAR—OR SHOULD WE GO FOR LUNCH?
LET'S GO FOR LUNCH!
TELL YOU WHAT!—WHY DON'T I GET MY DAUGHTER FROM THE SITTER, AND WE CAN HAVE LUNCH TOGETHER!
SOUNDS GOOD!
YOU HAVEN'T SEEN FRANCIE FOR A WHILE, LIZ. SHE'S CHANGED SO MUCH, YOU WON'T BELIEVE IT!
DADDY! DADDY! DADDY!
YES. YOU'VE CHANGED SO MUCH... I DON'T BELIEVE IT.
LYNN

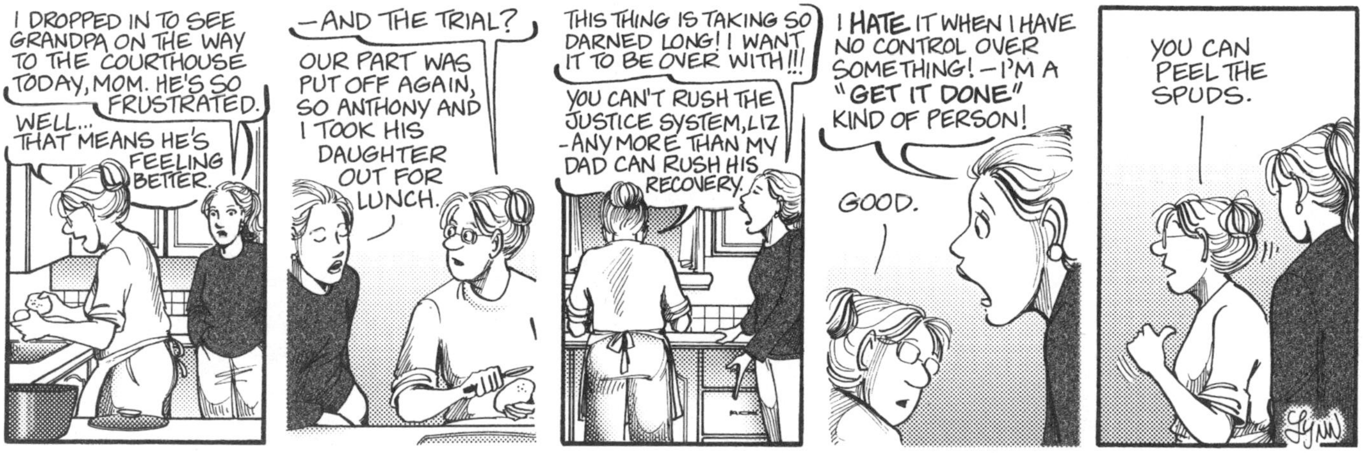
I DROPPED IN TO SEE GRANDPA ON THE WAY TO THE COURTHOUSE TODAY, MOM. HE'S SO FRUSTRATED.
WELL... THAT MEANS HE'S FEELING BETTER.
—AND THE TRIAL?
OUR PART WAS PUT OFF AGAIN, SO ANTHONY AND I TOOK HIS DAUGHTER OUT FOR LUNCH.
THIS THING IS TAKING SO DARNED LONG! I WANT IT TO BE OVER WITH!!!
YOU CAN'T RUSH THE JUSTICE SYSTEM, LIZ —ANY MORE THAN MY DAD CAN RUSH HIS RECOVERY.
I HATE IT WHEN I HAVE NO CONTROL OVER SOMETHING! —I'M A "GET IT DONE" KIND OF PERSON!
GOOD.
YOU CAN PEEL THE SPUDS.
LYNN